THE LAST GREAT ACE

The Life of Major
Thomas B. McGuire, Jr.

CHARLES A. MARTIN

FRUIT COVE PUBLISHING
FRUIT COVE, FLORIDA

THE LAST GREAT ACE
THE LIFE OF MAJOR THOMAS B. MCGUIRE, JR.

Copyright © Charles A. Martin, 1998

Cover design by Carlton Wilder

Library of Congress Cataloging Data

Martin, Charles A.
  The Last Great Ace : The life of Major Thomas B. McGuire, Jr. / Charles A. Martin
  372 p. :ill. ; 22cm
  1. McGuire, Thomas B., 1920-1945. 2. World War, 1939-1945 -- Aerial operations, American. 3. United States. Army Air Forces -- Biography. 4. Fighter Pilots -- United States -- Biography.
  LC Call No. : D790.M3397 1998
  Dewey No. : 940.54/25/092 B 21
  ISBN :   096677910X   98-96647

First printing November, 1998
Second Printing January, 2001
Printed in Florida, United States of America

To Marilynn McGuire Beatty
and
The Americans of World War II

who generously gave their lives,

their loved ones, and precious years

to defeat the enemies of freedom.

Author's Note

This book would never have made it to paper without the help of my wife Antoinette Dean Martin. Known to her fans as "Teaky," she has been a writer all her life. She is one English major who has put her Wellesley schooling to good use. Today she writes newspaper stories in North Florida where we live.

We have spent years on this book and are on our second computer. "Teaky" has suggested, corrected, edited, and encouraged me all through the years. She has helped me do research and has taken notes during some of the interviews. She also allowed me to travel to distant places to visit with many of the fliers and others mentioned in this book. If she was bored with all the visits, or the Hall of Fame and Memorial dedications we have attended over the years, she never told me. For all this I thank her.

INTRODUCTION

I appreciate the sincere honor of writing an introduction for a book about a great fighter pilot, Tommy McGuire.

When I graduated from flying school in April 1941, I was assigned to Wheeler Field, Hawaii to fly fighters. I was elated, as this was my first choice and I arrived there ready to be a gung-ho fighter pilot and to enjoy living it up in Hawaii. Then on 7 December 1941, the Japanese changed my life forever and we were playing a different game. It became a matter of survival ---- kill or be killed.

In August of 1942, I volunteered for the Fifth Air Force in Australia and joined the 7th Fighter Squadron, 49th Fighter Group en route to Port Moresby, New Guinea, flying P-40s. Initially, I was a wingman, then a Flight Leader, and then Operations Officer of the squadron. I hoped that I would become the Squadron Commander of the 7th Squadron, but that was not to be.

In March of 1943, Colonel Hutchison, the Group Commander, told me to pack my bags. I was going to activate a squadron, in a new twin-engined P-38 Fighter Group, being formed in Brisbane, Australia. Starting with experienced cadre from the 49th Group and the balance of the squadron, new personnel from the United States, we were to have the 431st Fighter Squadron combat-ready in three months. I was walking on air. This was a chance to form a squadron using my ideas and my objectives and this is when I first met Tommy McGuire. He had recently been assigned to the 9th Fighter Squadron, of the 49th Group, and was reassigned as one of my combat-ready pilots, and he joined me in Brisbane. McGuire had little combat experience and no victories, but he had been in the Alaskan theater. Though I didn't know it at the time, he was one of the few pilots in the Pacific who had been trained to fly P-38s back in the States, and he was highly-qualified in this type aircraft.

At first I thought he was just another fighter jock and I welcomed him and turned him over to Captain John Hood, my Operations Officer. Two weeks passed before I had my first serious conversation with him. John Hood came to me with a problem of assigning McGuire. He should have been an element leader but none of the Flight Commanders wanted him. They all said that "he talks too much." It was strictly a matter of personality conflicts. I told John to send Mac to see me and I would try to resolve this petty personality problem. Mac didn't know that there was a problem, so I told him I needed an Assistant Engineering Officer who was highly-qualified in the P-38 to test fly all the new aircraft arriving in the squadron. He would okay each plane or   recommend proper maintenance for it. Since I was beginning my flying transition into the P-38, I also told McGuire that I needed an experienced P-38 instructor pilot to check me out and get me combat ready in that aircraft. Mac was delighted with the challenge and he never looked back. From that day on he was a productive member of my squadron. When I organized my special flight, Mac was always my wingman.

We met the three month challenge of achieving combat-ready status and we proceeded to Port Moresby the latter part of August and on the day after our arrival we flew our first combat mission. We were flying out of twelve-mile strip for a month, and waiting for our new strip to be completed across the mountains in the Buna area. In late September we finally got the squadron together as a complete unit. Our combat results had been outstanding. We had been on several successful air-to-air combat missions and our number of confirmed victories was rapidly growing. McGuire's talents as a fighter pilot were soon evident and he was one of the first members of the Group to become an ace, shooting down five enemy aircraft. With long-range P-38s we were able to escort the bombers to new Japanese air bases at Wewak, Rabaul, and Hollandia, and our air-to-air opportunities had increased considerably during the period and Mac become one our leaders in confirmed kills.

On 16 October 1943, I received a call in the evening from Fifth Fighter Command telling me to report to General Wurtsmith the next day. I caught the courier early the next morning and arrived at his office about 10 o'clock. He explained that I had been selected to return to the states for one month's leave and said another month would be approved if I wanted to stay longer. He wanted to award the medals I was due, that day, so I could return that afternoon to make arrangements for change of command of the squadron and take care of details for my departure. I was elated but also sad that I was leaving the best job I ever had with the finest squadron any commander ever had.

Late that afternoon I caught the courier and returned to the squadron. I was met at the airplane with the news that my squadron had been involved in some heavy aerial combat defending American shipping in Oro Bay. The good news was that the 431st Squadron had made a big air-to-air interception of a large bomber and fighter force with great results. The bad news was that McGuire had been shot down after he had destroyed three enemy planes.

Later that evening we learned that McGuire had been picked up by a PT boat twenty miles off shore. He had "borrowed" my airplane, since his was in for repairs, and he had bailed out of the burning craft after being wounded. It was a miracle that he survived as his parachute had become entangled and opened just before he hit the water.

There were standing orders that no one would fly my airplane without my permission. McGuire had taken it anyway, knowing that a maximum effort was important to protect our forces. I was glad McGuire had survived but I was upset that he had taken my plane. The next morning I headed to the hospital where I planned to ream him out real good.

I learned that McGuire had been repeating over and over, "My God, Major Nichols is really going to be mad at me for losing his plane." He was right, but he had broken ribs, shrapnel wounds, severe burns and his eyes were blood shot, and when I saw how badly he was injured I could only console him. I told him how proud I was of him for shooting down the Japanese planes and surviving. I said, "To hell with it, I don't care about the airplane." Of course I was lying about the airplane but it made him feel better.

I was convinced this was his last combat mission and he would not fly combat for a long time, if ever. In fact, when I left in a few days for my trip home to join my wife in San Antonio, I met Tommy's wife, Marilynn, for the first time and I assured her that he would never fly combat again. I told her I was sure he would be coming home after his recovery. How wrong I was and how mistaken I was with his motivation to remain and fight the war to its very end. He would be one in a million and my hero.

I will never forget the last conversation we had when I visited Mac at Hollandia. I was a Lieutenant Colonel with the Fifth Fighter Command and he was now a Major and the Squadron Commander of the 431st Fighter Squadron. He told me, "Colonel Nichols, I remember when we started out in Brisbane last year, you had a goal to make the 431st the best fighter squadron in the Army Air Force. My goal is the same as yours." He gave his life making that goal possible.

Major General Franklin A. Nichols, USAF (Ret)

Preface

On a gray overcast morning in 1945, a small air battle broke out over the remote island of Negros, in the Philippines. It was an unlikely fight. Two Japanese planes, coming from different directions--unaware of each other--tangled with four American P-38 fighters. In a few minutes two Americans died and the rest of the combatants flew from the scene.

Much more happened in a few minutes than you could imagine. One American, Major Jack Rittmayer, was shot down, while his friend Major Thomas McGuire made a dangerous maneuver to save the life of his wingman Ed Weaver. Weaver escaped but the violent maneuver by McGuire, which drove off the Japanese, resulted in McGuire falling to his death. In that moment America lost two of its finest young men.

McGuire's death was noted on the front page of the **New York Times** and in **Time** magazine. Seemingly an ordinary young man, he had risen to be one of America's most decorated heroes and died saving a friend's life. People in Sebring, Florida suffered when one of our boys died in the war. Small towns are like that. When McGuire died it left an empty spot. We knew so little of his exploits or how he died. Years went by and his story was never told. This is his story.

Sebring was started early in this century as a real estate development whose main attractions were land, climate, and a pristine lake a few blocks from the center of town. An early settler, Allen Altvater, said when he first saw Lake Jackson the bottom of the lake was as white as snow and the water was pure enough to drink, straight from the lake.

Sebring prospered and two large hotels were built on Lake Jackson. Citrus groves were planted and agriculture and tourism were the main sources of income. Kenilworth Lodge and Harder Hall were wonderful winter hotels, open only a few months each year. Both buildings still exist today. Besides swimming and boating they had beautiful gardens and golf courses. Musicians, magicians, and speakers came to entertain each evening before the serious card playing started. Kenilworth Lodge was so successful that plans were made to build a "new" Kenilworth at the south end of Lake Jackson--twice as big as the first one. The 1929 crash took care of that, but the plans can still be seen at the Sebring Historical Society.

The environment at these hotels was wonderful, but completely apart from the town and townspeople. A few months each year the parking lots were filled with big black automobiles, often attended by chauffeurs. When the north defrosted, the guests and the hotel employees went home and for the next eight months the hotels were closed. Sebringites and hotel people had almost nothing to do with each other.

Out of this separated existence came the Watson family. They were well-to-do industrialists from Ridgewood, New Jersey, and they had wintered at the Kenilworth for a number of years. They chose to stay in Sebring after the hotel season was over and they became one of the first of the "hotel people" to become citizens of Sebring. They took a cottage near the lake and lived quietly--at least until their daughter Pauline McGuire divorced and moved in with her son, Tommy.

Pauline McGuire, or Polly, as she was called, was a strong-willed woman and she stood out in this sleepy little village. Sebring had more churches than prisoners in the county jail and most of the ministers preached against imbibing alcohol and divorce. Polly was divorced--she drank alcohol--she drove a big car--she had money--she was resented. Polly and her mother, Dora Watson, doted on Polly's son, Tommy, and sent him to school dressed too well. He was resented, too.

This book is about the young boy's life. He grew up without a father and was thought to be a kind of spoiled mama's boy, but when the war came and his country needed leaders--he became a leader. He was one of America's greatest fighter pilots and most decorated soldiers of all time. He was also a leader of men, under the most trying of conditions.

I started out to get information for the Sebring Historical Society. Allen Altvater said, "Tommy McGuire was too important in the war to let his name die. We get requests all the time for information and we don't know anything about his war record." After years of research I knew the story had to be a book--it was too interesting to file away.

I recorded what people told me and I checked it out to see if it really happened. Sometimes I could prove that it did and sometimes I could prove that it didn't. I didn't make up any "facts" for this book. If it is in the book I believe it to be true. What I did do is fill in some conversations as I was told they occurred. I wasn't there to hear the exact words but I know the gist of the conversations and I filled in the blanks to make the story more readable. This book could, for that reason, be called a historical novel, but I think that is going too far. I think of it as a novelized biography. The events occurred--some of the details are filled in to make it easier to read. I have cited my sources.

I've read everything I could find in print about McGuire and the men of the 475th Fighter Group. I've read things in print that were not true. A famous author wrote that McGuire died at Los Negros, and that was repeated over and over in other books. He died at Negros, 1,500 miles from Los Negros. This misinformation originated in the Medal Of Honor citation, signed by President Harry Truman. Even a Memorial Plaque at McGuire Air Force Base, New Jersey, dedicated in 1986, has repeated the error. What chance does an honest historian have?

I tried not to use information published somewhere else, except as a guide. The two exceptions: *GENERAL KENNEY'S REPORT*, and *THE WARTIME JOURNALS OF CHARLES A. LINDBERGH*. Both of these men knew McGuire in the war zone and kept daily notes of what happened. I considered their work to be original source material.

Over the years a few people have said some uncomplimentary things about Tommy McGuire. These statements have been repeated time and time again, in articles in **Air Classics** and other magazines. I have talked to many of the people who made those statements and I feel they were being honest and each of them had their reasons for disliking McGuire. On the other hand I found a number of highly respected people who had a different view of McGuire. General Nichols, Wally Jordan, Fred Champlin, Robert L. Herman and Charles Lindbergh saw a different person. If you want one man's view please go to Appendix A, How This Book Was Written, and read the letter from Danforth Miller. Written 36 years after McGuire's death, it is one of the inspirations for this book. A number of people I contacted wanted to know my motives before they would talk to me. Andy Anderson, unofficial historian of McGuire's fighter group said, "All we need is another writer putting out negative stuff about a guy who isn't here to defend himself."

McGuire was a member of one of America's most effective fighting units of World War II, the 475th Fighter Group. They were remarkable people who organized during the war, and spent more than two years fighting under the most trying circumstances. The Japanese bombed them at night to deprive them of sleep. They were in steamy jungles where fungus and insects were king. The food furnished them was often unpalatable or quickly became moldy and they went hungry much of the time. It was reported Japanese soldiers could live on a handful of rice a day. These Americans proved they could live on meager rations too, and win a war. I'm glad they and Tommy McGuire were on our side.

Charles A. Martin
Fall of 1998

1

"Years later I wondered, if on that wonderful evening, at that moment, a spark of clear, unadulterated patriotism had entered Tommy's heart."
Vera Schneider, Tommy McGuire's cousin

Tom McGuire had raced automobiles through the streets of Ridgewood, New Jersey, before, but never had he done it with his wife, Polly Watson McGuire, and his son, Tommy, in the car. Driving in the town's Labor Day race was a hobby; but speeding along Heights Road early on Fourth of July morning was a chore. Traffic wasn't a problem. It was being late for a family breakfast that was causing the tension. Polly groused that they were always the last ones to arrive.

Tom fumed as he turned his car into the drive which led to the Watson's stately home. As they approached the house they could see the cars parked on the side of the drive and they knew that they were indeed the last to arrive.

Tom McGuire thought it was a hell of a way to start a holiday---eating breakfast at his mother-in-law's house---and he mumbled under his breath. His wife asked him to try to be nice. Polly's mother always bought tickets to all the day's events and the children would have lots of fun. This would be the first year Tommy was old enough to enjoy the day with his older cousins.

Independence Day breakfast at the Watsons---it had been an annual event long before Polly had broken tradition and married an "Irish Mick." Polly's mother, Dora, was sure that Polly had married a Catholic just to prove that she had a mind of her own. Dora had favored Levrick Brett; he was from such a good family. A tiff had developed between Polly and Levrick. Dora tried to patch it up between them. Instead, Polly and Tom McGuire had eloped. It was bad enough that she had picked the only young man in town who wasn't in uniform during the World War---did they have to run off to New York with just a few friends to get married at St. Patrick's Cathedral?[1]

Dora's friends thought that Tom must have paid a bundle for a Catholic boy to marry a Presbyterian girl "in church," especially at St. Patrick's Cathedral. Just like those big cars he drove all the time---they thought it was all for show. Dora had no use for her son-in-law and never missed a chance to tell him so. Even if he was one of Pierce Arrow's top salesmen, he was still a "car salesman," and she thought Pauline could have done a lot better. Spending a holiday at the Watson's

Certificate of Marriage

St. Patrick's Cathedral

- NEW YORK -

This is to Certify

That _Thomas B. McGuire_

and _Pauline H. Watson_

were lawfully **Married**

on the _24th_ day of _November_ 19 _18_

According to the Rite of the Roman Catholic Church

and in conformity with the laws of

the State of New York

Rev. _B. Corcoran_ officiating,

in the presence of _Fred Case_

and _Marjorie H. Pugel_ Witnesses

as appears from the Marriage Register of this Church.

Dated _March 30, 19__

_____

home was usually a very uncomfortable time for Tom. Dora had made it a tradition.

With Tommy, almost five years old, crashing ahead, they entered the house through the portico entrance and were cordially greeted by Polly's

2

ever gracious father, Alfred Watson. As always, he was glad to see them and told them that he didn't think he saw them often enough. He hugged his daughter as he inquired of his son-in-law about the sales of the 1925 Pierce Arrows. As the two men shook hands warmly, Tom allowed that they still seem to have a few customers and he in turn asked how things were going at the family business, Watson Machinery.

The two men drifted into the library while Polly headed toward the back of the house to find her mother. Young Tommy found his cousins and they greeted each other loudly. Polly saw her mother almost every day, but the men never got a chance to see each other. Polly knew her husband would come over more often if her mother would just be more pleasant to Tom.

Soon, the Watson clan was assembled at the banquet-sized dining room table, which was required to seat them all. There was Robert Watson, his wife, and their children Al and Vera, the three McGuires, and Charles Watson, still one of Ridgewood's most eligible bachelors. The Watson's other daughter, Estelle Tolson, her husband Ted, and their children, could never attend this gathering---it was the middle of the season at Lake Hopatcong, and their Bon Aire Hotel was too busy for them to go visiting.

Alfred Watson looked with pride at his children and grandchildren and then bowed his head, "Father in Heaven bless this food and those who partake of thy bounty......" To the rest of the world Alfred Watson was a captain of industry, but when his wife Dora was around he was just part of the crew. He knew that presiding over the breakfast prayer would be the only time today that he would be in charge. When he said "Amen," Dora would take over for the rest of the day. The routine was the same every year, only the details were different. As the maid served breakfast Dora started her instructions. She wanted her son, Charles, to drive the children to town. Tom and Robert would be busy with civic duties and the ladies would travel with Alfred and Dora in their Pierce Arrow. Charles would deliver the children to the Watsons at the reviewing stand before marching with the Veteran's Brigade. Everyone needed tags for the circus and fireworks and Dora passed them out.

Vera was asked to take care of her cousin Tommy for the day. She often took care of her younger cousin, and she loved doing it.

Dora was being indifferent to Tom. A decided improvement, thought Polly. Other years had been difficult. Polly felt embarrassed again as she remembered the year when Tom had first sat at this table and had placed his napkin in his collar as they started to eat. She had almost died trying to get him to remove it from across the table without announcing it to the group.

Ridgewood, New Jersey - July 4, 1925

Dora and Alfred Watson. In the business world he was a powerful and respected captain of industry. Around their home Dora ruled. She made the menu, shopped the markets, and supervised the servants. Alfred appreciated her skills and enjoyed a well-run house.

Her father had noticed Polly's distress and had come to the rescue, placing his own napkin in his collar, too. Only seconds had gone by before Dora had demanded, "Alfred, remove that napkin this minute. Do you think you're a farmer?" Tom had quietly removed his napkin too, undetected, and Polly remembered the sparkle in her father's eyes as she had thanked him with a loving glance.

The next year Tom almost walked out when he and Dora had exchanged cross words---he had gotten as far as the car before Polly had caught him and pleaded with him to stay. She was expecting a blessed event that year, and the glow of their marriage had not yet begun to dim. Tommy had been born a few weeks later on the first day of August, 1920.

Polly was relieved when breakfast was over. They headed to the car where Neil, a large Negro man, neatly dressed in his maroon and beige chauffeur's uniform, had the tan and brown Pierce Arrow shined and waiting for Dora and her entourage. As the car started down the driveway Dora rattled off instructions to Neil: "You'll pick up the children after the parade at 10:30, bring them back home--- they have no use for political speeches. Come back for us just before noon."

"Yes'm," he replied. He'd taken her instructions for many years.

4

Ridgewood, New Jersey - July 4, 1925

Dora and Alfred with son Charles Watson in his World War I uniform.

The children waited in their uncle's red Stutz Bear Cat until he appeared dressed in an Army uniform. He hadn't worn the uniform for six years, but it still fit him well. The youngsters had never seen their uncle in uniform before, and as they drove to town, Uncle Charles patiently answered each question: "The bars show my rank, Lieutenant. The wings show that I am a qualified Aircraft Pilot. These ribbons? They show that I was in the World War, and that I served in France. This tiger patch shows that I trained to fly at Princeton University."

"Uncle Charles, can you still fly an airplane?" ask Vera.

"I could, but your Grandmother won't let me," answered Charles.

Al said, "Boy, if I could fly, nobody would stop me."

"Me either," said Tommy.

"Maybe," said Uncle Charles, "but there would be no peace if you lived with your Mother as I do."

Ridgewood was all decked out with red, white, and blue bunting, and the gathering crowd had balloons and flags. When Uncle Charles and the children arrived in town, Neil was setting up a "throne" for the reign of the grand dame of Ridgewood. He was setting up a camp chair for Dora, in a prized spot across the street from the train station. Fourth of July or not, Dora was wearing a lavender silk dress and a floppy hat adorned with violets. "Let the others wear red, white, and blue. I'll wear what becomes me," she had told her daughter. The parade led off with

5

a marching band followed by the Civil War veterans---fewer than last year---riding in a highly decorated touring car furnished by Thomas B. McGuire. So said the placard on the car door.

Then came the Spanish-American War veterans, a few floats, another band and, marching at a lively pace, the much younger veterans of the World War.

Vera had her hands full with her young cousin, but she held on to the little humdinger until they spotted Uncle Charles marching with the World War veterans.

"That's my Uncle," shouted Tommy, as he pulled his hand free and ran among the troops to his Uncle. Charles joined the crowd in a good laugh, picked up his nephew and hoisted him to his shoulder for a short but gleeful ride, before Cousin Al came forward to escort Tommy back to the crowd on the curb.

Later, back at the Watson's house, Neil lit a punk stick for Al and Vera, so they could light the Chinese firecrackers they had saved several weeks' allowances to buy. Tommy's fireworks were in the form of a small silver cap pistol. His cry was, "Load me, load me!" And before Al or Vera could set off a Roman candle or a three-inch salute, it was, "Load me, load me."

When his caps ran out Tommy begged to throw a torpedo: a round device that was exploded by being thrown against a hard object. Al let Tommy throw several of the torpedoes against the foundation of the house, but he couldn't throw them hard enough to make them explode. Frustrated, he soon took an interest in picking up duds, the firecrackers which hadn't gone off. Vera and Al were relieved when Neil handed them a broom and said, "I'm going to get your Grandma, you'd better clean this mess up before we gets back."

After luncheon, Tom McGuire loaded Tommy, Al and Vera in his car and took them to the circus. The ladies remained at home to take a refreshing nap. When they arrived at the circus grounds Tom said, "Let's get peanuts and cotton candy. It's not a circus without them."

Tom handed out candy and nuts, and kept some for himself. He was a changed man. He no longer had to be on guard. With his red hair, freckles, and the cotton candy, he looked like a big kid. He laughed when the children did and he didn't worry if Tommy dropped peanut shells on his suit.

Near the end of the circus young Tommy climbed into his cousin Vera's lap, snuggled, and fell asleep. He was heavy, but like a little mother, Vera hugged him and let him sleep.

When they arrived back at the Watson's house, Neil's wife, Ellen, rushed the children upstairs to bathe and dress before dinner. Tom also hurried up stairs to freshen up. The rest of the adults were already assembled in the living room where Uncle Charles was mixing and serving cocktails from the brass service cart. Polly was relieved that Tom had gotten the children home at the proper time, but she thought it was just as well that Tom had not arrived there any sooner. The less Tom and Dora saw of each other the better they got along.

She didn't mind that Tom had missed the first round of cocktails, either. After Tom had a few drinks he had a tendency to perform some of his party tricks. The tricks were a lot of fun at the Knights of Columbus hall or at a road house bar, but Polly didn't think her mother had "a broad enough background" to fully appreciate them.

After dinner the family formed a convoy behind the Pierce Arrow, and Neil led them to the Elk's Club grounds where the fireworks show was to be presented after dark. Neil set up camp chairs for the adults, spread a steamer robe on the ground for the children, and then went around the perimeter of the area dispensing from a large bottle of citronella to fend off the mosquitoes which were gathering for a feast of their own. The children discovered these moments before dark were an excellent time to chase fireflies.

Tommy McGuire, about age five, being "mothered" by a neighbor

7

It had been a long day, especially for young Tommy. As the children settled on the blanket for the show, with eyes hardly open, Tommy laid his head in Vera's lap. Polly, seeing this, said, "Vera, put him on the back seat of the car, and cover him with Grandmother's lap robe. You'd better leave the windows open so he can get some air." Vera dutifully followed instructions, and then settled down with her brother Al, to watch the show.

The show was concluding with the famous "Niagara Falls" fireworks display, when someone shouted, "Get him down before he falls!" Everyone turned in the direction of the Pierce Arrow, to see a wide-awake Tommy, dancing on the roof with a small American flag in his hand. Tom and Uncle Charles rushed to grab him, but he only giggled and moved to the other side of the roof.

"Come on Tommy, get down before you get hurt," said his father. Tommy just giggled. The men surrounded the small quarry, and he finally went to his father, who gave him a token swat on the backside as he lowered him to the ground. The band struck up the *Star Spangled Banner* as the final pyrotechnics display, an American flag, was lit.

It had been a great day, and Tommy and Vera smiled at each other as the light from the fireworks placed the reflection of the flag in each of their eyes. This had been the first time Tommy was old enough to enjoy Independence Day. Years later, Vera would have reason to wonder if on that wonderful evening, at that moment, "A spark of clear, unadulterated patriotism had entered Tommy's heart."[2]

[1]Certificate of Marriage, St. Patrick's Cathedral, Nov. 24, 1918, Witnesses Fred Case and Marjorie H. Piaget.
[2]Vera W. Schneider, Tommy McGuire's cousin, contributed this quote and most of the information in Chapter One.

8

2

"Tommy always had a special interest in aviation. His Uncle Charles had been a World War I fighter pilot and they talked about flying at every chance. Tommy always wanted to be a pilot."

----Paul Gustat, Tommy's childhood friend

When their parents traveled, Tommy, Vera and Al often stayed at their grandparents' home. During the summer of 1927, when Charles Lindbergh made his historic flight to Paris, the three cousins were spending several weeks at the Watson's home. Uncle Charles rigged a special radio so they could listen for reports about Lindbergh.[1] He attached an aerial wire to a bed spring under Tommy's mattress so they could pick up radio station WOR in New York, which had regular bulletins about the flight all day long. The children lay in their beds wide-eyed long after bedtime, listening for news of the "Lone Eagle."

Later in the summer, after Lindbergh and his plane had returned from France to the United States aboard a U.S. Navy ship, he announced that he would fly over the Curtiss-Wright factory in Paterson, New Jersey, as a "thank you" to the workmen who had built the Whirlwind engine for "The Spirit of St. Louis." Tommy and Uncle Charles were there as Lindbergh buzzed the factory several times before departing for St. Louis where his financial backers waited to greet the famous pilot and his plane.[2]

Uncle Charles said, "I'll always remember this day, Tommy. All over the world people have read about Mr. Lindbergh's airplane and seen pictures of it in the newspaper, but only a few thousand people in the whole world have seen it in the air. It's lucky for us that Paterson is close to Ridgewood so we could be here."

On a Friday afternoon, in the fall, Robert Watson and his wife drove in from their home in Bound Brook, to attend a benefit ball in Manhattan with Polly and Tom McGuire. The children were again to stay at their grandparents' home overnight and were in the library waiting for their parents to depart. Vera was curled up on a leather sofa with a book. Tommy and Al had an atlas on the floor and were trying to trace the path of Lindbergh's flight.

Tommy's mother danced into the room with a mock fanfare. "Ta, ta, taaaa!" Polly was dazzling as she swished around the room in a gold lame evening gown. She wore large jade earrings with a matching jade bracelet and pendant. She had shopped for days to find a dress to show off the jade which her brother, Robert, had brought her from a recent business trip to China. As she swayed about the room, with her arms around a phantom dance partner, she gave instructions: "Vera, be sure Tommy gets to bed early, and everyone mind Neil and Ellen."

After their parents departed the two boys continued to pour over the maps. They knew Lindbergh had flown from Roosevelt Field, Long Island, but they were having trouble finding Dingle Bay, Ireland, along the route to Paris. Soon an argument ensued and Tommy and Al shouted at each other. Tommy jumped up and said, "I'm going to bed. I'm never going to talk to you again."

Young Tommy McGuire

The next morning, Uncle Charles and his father were out of the house early to play their usual Saturday morning game of golf, and Dora had Neil drive her to the farmer's market on Black Swamp Road so she could select fresh produce for the kitchen. The children were up a little later and all was forgotten about the argument the night before. After breakfast, Tommy, wanting to impress his cousins asked, "Can you keep a secret?"

They followed Tommy upstairs to Uncle Charles' room. He went quickly to the closet and removed a key from a hook and opened a large armoire. Inside was an array of model airplanes. Vera and Al were excited, and Tommy's eyes sparkled as he took out the planes. They were models of World War bi-planes made of fine varnished woods and oiled paper.

"Where did these come from?" asked Al.

"Uncle Charles told me he made them at Princeton when he was learning to fly," said Tommy.

"Does he let you play with them?" asked Vera.

"Not exactly," replied Tommy, "but I come and look at them."

Before long the kids had built runways with shoe box lids and had the planes parked in imaginary hangers, under the bed. They staged dog-fights with all of the sound effects. The morning flew by and they were startled when Uncle Charles returned from his golf game and found them in his bedroom. None of them had ever seen their uncle mad and it scared them when he flew into a rage.

"You have no business being in my room without my permission. It's private, and these are not toys. Tommy, you've let me down---this was our secret."

They trudged out of Uncle Charles' room with their heads hanging. They were sorry that they had angered their uncle and it spoiled the whole day. Late in the afternoon Uncle Charles came into the study where the three culprits were suffering silently, and said, "I've been thinking about the models. I was wrong! They are toys, and I shouldn't have shown them to Tommy if I wasn't going to allow you to play with them. If you promise to put them away when you are through, I will leave the cabinet unlocked and you may play with them whenever you want."

After that, Tommy spent many happy hours playing with the models. Uncle Charles, seeing that Tommy had a great interest in flying, spent hours telling him about his experiences in the World War when he had known Eddie Rickenbacker and other American flying heroes.

Over the years Tommy became the darling of the Watson's house when he stayed over. In the mornings he would remain at the breakfast table with his grandmother, after his Uncle Charles and grandfather had left. Dora would read the newspaper aloud to Tommy, never missing the Will Rogers column. Tommy learned to read the newspaper at an early age and soon read books from the Watson's library. Often he would memorize a poem or a literary passage, and when he was asked, after dinner, he would stand at the end of the table and recite for his grandparents.

Once, Dora gave Vera a little green leather-bound volume of Rudyard Kipling's "If." There was a catch---Vera was expected to recite the poem before Sunday dinner. Vera studied all afternoon with Tommy prompting her. When she stood in front of the fireplace to recite for her grandparents she was nervous and she stumbled through the verse. Then Tommy stood and recited the poem without a hitch---he had learned it while coaching Vera. In later years Tommy would amaze friends by reciting this poem and others as if the words were his own.

Tommy's parents were having a difficult time. Polly had married Tom McGuire partly to prove her independence, but she continued to try to please her mother. She and Tommy were at her mother's home almost every day, and every day Polly heard complaints from her mother about her husband. Dora complained about Tom's manners, his reputation, and his ability to earn what she considered a decent living.

Tom seemed to be living up to his mother-in-law's predictions that he wasn't well suited for Polly and wouldn't be a good provider. Tom never seemed to do anything to please Dora and they could hardly stay in the same room without having words. And Polly would be torn between them.

Polly's marriage was often the subject of conversation when her friends got together: "Tom doesn't come home some nights until after midnight. I don't know how much longer Polly is going to put up with it. She suspects that he has a girl friend."

"What does Tom say?"

"He says he's selling cars, and he may be. They went to Buffalo last year for an award dinner when Tom was one of the top Pierce Arrow salesmen in the country. Trouble is, Pierce Arrows are so expensive that people don't have the money to buy them any more."

Polly and Tom had come from different backgrounds. Polly had always lived a life of luxury and affluence in the prestigious residential Village of Ridgewood. She had gone to the strict Moravian Seminary in Scranton, Pennsylvania.

The Watsons could trace their family back to the Dutch settlers of New York on Dora Hoffman Watson's side, and to Lord Beresford of England on Alfred's side. Alfred's father, James, and his brothers, William and Samuel, had founded the Watson Machine Company which had its plant on Railroad Avenue in Paterson, New Jersey. They had made their money building bridges for the Erie Railroad, Passaic County and New York City. They built the Harlem River Drawbridge, and erected iron work for the Metropolitan Museum of Natural History, Metropolitan Museum of Art, Lenox Library, and the Equitable Building in New York City.

Tom was raised 10 miles from Ridgewood, in the industrialized City of Paterson, where many Irish had settled to work in the textile mills. He said his family had been there since 1817. Tom often told the story: "My great-grandfather helped lay out the streets of Paterson. He had stables on Mechanic Street---22 carts and 70 employees. They'd leave the stable in the mornings single file and people called it McGuire's Parade." Tom's father ran a lumber business and furnished telephone poles to Passaic Bell, Western Union, and the Edison Company. They were hard-working people who had never been part of the country club set.

According to Tom, when the family had a economic setback in 1912, he had to quit Fordham Prep School in New York. He went to work for his father but found the lumber business boring. He had been involved in auto racing locally, and gravitated into the automobile business. He was an aggressive salesman and had landed a job with Pierce Arrow, where he soon became successful.

Tom had the gift of gab. He was naturally friendly and he greeted people on the street, sometimes shaking hands with a total stranger if he got a smile in return for his greeting. He knew every waitress and bank teller by their first name and usually gave them a knowing wink when he greeted them. He knew the politicians, and helped them with their campaigns.

When Tom met and married Polly, after a brief courtship, he found himself in a hostile camp. Dora Watson, his new mother-in-law, was angry that Polly had run off and married without her approval. Further, she was upset that Polly had married a car salesman instead of a banker or a lawyer.

Tom found himself under constant social pressure to be at the right place at the right time. It was driving him to the poor house. Auto sales weren't good, and money was short at times. People said that Alfred Watson had bought a new Pierce Arrow just to help Tom and Polly. Tom and Polly moved several times and lived in Glen Rock, New Jersey, for a year before moving back to 96 Morningside Road in Ridgewood. Polly's friends wondered if they moved because they couldn't pay the rent.

Polly still used her father's department store charge accounts to purchase most of Tommy's and her own clothes. Her father had told her to do it, but Dora said, "I never thought my daughter would marry someone who couldn't support her properly. It's a shame that Tom can't even put clothes on his family's back."

It disturbed Tom, too. "Why do you continue to embarrass me? Your father must not have any respect for me."

"Don't be absurd, my father likes you very much," argued Polly. "He insists that I use his accounts. He knows how hard it is for a young family to get along these days."

"I don't want you to do it anymore," snapped Tom. "Your mother must have a field day, talking about me, every time you charge something on their account."

"Don't be so sensitive. The baby and I have to be properly dressed if we are going to go to the club with my family," concluded Polly.

The Watsons hosted a family dinner once a week at the Country Club. To Tom it felt like a command performance, and he never had much to say when they sat at the table for dinner. Strangely enough, Polly's father and brother Charles didn't have much to say either. Dora and Polly ran the show and did most of the socializing too. They knew everybody at the club, and there was a constant stream of people dropping by the table after dinner to say hello. Tom felt like a stranger there.

Holiday dinners at the club were a festive and special tradition. The Watsons followed the custom of many of the club members and had Thanksgiving and Christmas dinner there to allow their servants those days off.

When Tommy was six, the family gathered in the late afternoon for Thanksgiving dinner at the club. Tommy, feeling his oats, caused an uproar when he picked up a turkey leg and took a bite out of it. Dora Watson was appalled and told her grandson so. Tom got red in the face and choked back an attack on his mother-in-law. Polly, as ever, intervened to smooth things over.

The children were bored by the drawn-out meal and as soon as the plum pudding had been eaten, Polly excused them from the table while the adults stayed for coffee and after-dinner drinks. The children wandered around the club and Tommy led them outside to the swimming pool, where he had taken swimming lessons during the summer. There had been a early snow and the grounds were covered with a few inches of snow. Tommy walked out on the icy diving board as Vera urged him to be careful. He jumped up and down on the board several times and then, without warning, took a head-first dive into a six-foot snow drift in the empty pool.

He was screaming at the top of his voice before Vera and Al could reach him. His face was skinned and bleeding, but he was mainly suffering from wounded pride. His clothes were a mess when they returned to the dining room.

Dora scolded Vera, "Why didn't you watch him more closely, he's only a baby."

Tom stepped in and comforted his niece while Polly hugged her sniffling son. "It's not your fault, Sister. Tommy just doesn't know the word fear. He needs to learn a little common sense."

14

Although Tom wasn't comfortable around the Country Club he was a very active man-around-town. A charmer, he was well known at many of the road houses, like the Meadowbrook in Wayne, and many private clubs of Northern New Jersey. He was the life of any party and always had a new joke or barroom trick.[3]

Among Tom's many activities was his membership in the Pica Club. He started out accommodating them with complimentary automobiles for their activities and ended up becoming a member of the club, although the membership was mainly newspaper writers. Tom was the exception, but he fit right in with the group. They often lunched, played golf or went to the race track together.

One of the club members who befriended Tom was a writer named Terhune, who had turned dog kennel owner. Polly got to know his wife, Anice, and she often visited with her at Sunnybank Kennels in Pompton Lakes, New Jersey. On one visit the women had coffee in the country kitchen and Tommy played with some new-born Collie puppies who were there with their mother. He pleaded with his mother to let him have one of them.

Mrs. Terhune said, "Polly, Tommy loves this dog. Why don't you take it when they are a little older."

"Tommy would love one," said Polly. "I just don't have the strength right now. Maybe we'll consider it later."

At home things weren't going well with the McGuires. Tom was charming the rest of the world, but Polly wasn't amused. She was embarrassed to face her friends with the stories that were going around about Tom. As she and Tom grew angrier with each other, Polly spent more time and money buying Tommy special clothes like a brown velvet Lord Fauntleroy outfit, a blazer and slacks, or an authentic sailor suit. Tom felt that Polly was spoiling his son and the purchases were often the cause of further arguments.

Polly got tired of the arguments and finally told Tom she wanted a divorce. Although he hadn't been very religious since he had married "outside of the church," Tom had strong objections to a divorce on religious grounds. They stayed together, but things were tense.

In the midst of her battle with Tom, Polly sought refuge at her parent's newly acquired cottage in Sebring, Florida. The Watsons had searched for a place in Florida where they could have a social life like they had in Ridgewood and enjoy the milder climate of the "Sunshine State."

Watson Machine Company regularly sold equipment to the Roebling Steel Company. The Watsons and Roeblings had been friends for years. A member of the Roebling family had suggested the Kenilworth Hotel in

Sebring, in central Florida. "It's off the beaten path, but the golf is good and the lake is beautiful. The gardens are wonderful and the evenings are filled with the smell of jasmine and the orange blossoms."

Alfred and Dora tried the Kenilworth and found the winters very enjoyable there. They were rubbing elbows with DuPonts, Fords, and Firestones. They enjoyed the gardens, the fine food, and the late afternoons sitting in a rocker on the front porch and watching the sunset over Lake Jackson. In the evenings there was entertainment like the Redpath Chautauqua Troop, traveling musical groups, or a magician. Later rummy games flourished in the game room. The Watsons developed good friends among the regulars who returned each year.

Now, after trying Green Cove Springs, near Jacksonville, for a few years, they returned to Sebring and acquired a Cape Cod cottage on the edge of the hotel property and near the lake. They named it IDYLOURS, and put the name over the door.

The Watson clan's arrival in Sebring was duly noted in the "Kenilworth Diggings" gossip column in the local newspaper: "A pleasant surprise on Friday evening was to welcome at Kenilworth, after an absence of several seasons, Mr. & Mrs. A.B. Watson, & Charles F. Watson, Mrs. T. B. McGuire & Tommy McGuire.... In the old days Mr. Watson was a charter member of the 'Rummy Club' so naturally a session was held at once."

The Watsons ate only breakfast at the cottage and along with Polly and Tommy, dined each evening at the hotel. Everyone at the hotel dressed for dinner: the men wore dinner jackets and the women had to have a different evening dress for each evening. A small stringed orchestra played dinner music in the lobby, just outside the dining room entrance. It was a lot like dining at the Ridgewood Country Club, just a little fancier. Later in the evenings the Watsons had friends in for drinks and to play cards.

Tommy met children at the hotel and was invited to socials such as the "sub-deb" party for Constance Tuttle. The newspaper reported that they roller skated at the hotel roller rink, fed the exotic birds, and ended with cake and ice cream.

Polly got strong support from her mother concerning her plan to divorce Tom. Her father didn't say much, but he quietly favored giving the marriage a little longer. Polly knew Tom would never change and she had made up her mind to dissolve the marriage.

Polly returned to New Jersey to pursue the divorce, but Tom stood fast. He wouldn't allow it! They were two strong personalities and the fights were loud and bitter. Tommy loved both of his parents and didn't understand what was going on. Polly took Tommy to live with her brother Robert's family in Bound Brook. Uncle Charles and Uncle Robert were in business together in Bound Brook, and Charles stayed at Robert's house. In a last ditch effort to save the marriage Tom showed up one day in Bound Brook with a beautiful young Collie dog.

Tom said, "I got this dog from the Terhunes. They tell me Tommy fell in love with him when you were out there a few months ago. I even got permission to name the dog 'Sunnybank' after the Terhune's kennel."[4] Polly was very angry. "Tom, I told them that I couldn't take care of a dog now. It's unfair of you to bring that dog here and to get Tommy excited about it. You keep the dog. I'll get Tommy a dog later when we get settled."

Thus, Tommy missed a chance to own a Collie from the kennels of Albert Payson Terhune, who wrote warmly about his Collies in a famous book, "Lad a Dog," which many people think was the forerunner to "Lassie."

Polly was eventually granted the divorce and custody of Tommy. She had to make him available for visits with Tom in the summer. When Tommy turned 14 years old his father would have custody. Polly agreed to the special conditions for Tommy's custody because it was the only way to get the divorce from Tom. Polly reasoned that Tommy would be in prep school by age 14 anyway--she'd let Tom take him during the school years and Tommy could spend summers with her. Tom planned to see that his son was exposed to the Catholic Church when the boy was in his custody. Tommy, of course knew nothing of the agreement.

---

[1] Vera W. Schneider contributed most of the information in this chapter about New Jersey.
[2] Bill Dutton, High schoolmate of Tommy McGuire, SHS '37
[3] Joan Mallon, longtime friend of Thomas B. McGuire, Sr.
[4] Ibid.

3

"Polly McGuire was one of the best customers I had. We didn't have that many people getting flowers wired in like she did, but she put a stop to that."   ---Sophie Mitchell, Sebring florist

When the time came for Polly and Tommy to move to Florida, Charles Watson put them on the train in New Jersey for the 24-hour trip, saying he would visit them soon. Dora and Alfred Watson eagerly awaited their daughter and grandson at their new home in Sebring. As part of the divorce settlement Tom McGuire made arrangements for a local car dealer to deliver a new sedan for Polly.[1]

Sebring had been started as a real estate development. On the shore of a large lake, it was founded by the Sebring family of Ohio. Built on virgin land, Sebring was planned before the community developed. The streets were laid out in the shape of a wagon wheel with a round park at the center of the hub. Six streets radiated out like spokes, and other streets circled around like increasingly larger wheel rims. Traffic traveling through town went around the tree-filled park, known as "The Circle." A tall flag pole in the center and multiple-globed light standards around the outer edge made the circle an impressive site.

Most of the buildings in town were Spanish-styled of stucco with terra cotta tiles at the roof line. Some buildings had arcades and many featured an extended roof over the sidewalk. The school Tommy would attend housed 12 grades in a large stucco building with terra cotta tile trim and arched doorways at the main entrance. Across town the City Pier had a band shell where the high school band played a concert each Sunday afternoon. Palm-lined Lakeview Drive, along the lake shore, had large homes which reflected the Spanish style, but the Watson's home was a Cape Code bungalow on the grounds of the Kenilworth Lodge, a Sebring landmark.

A resort hotel, open only three months a year, the Kenilworth was an eye-catcher with its Moorish turrets from which long thin banners flew. The hotel faced the lake and was elevated so its front porch afforded a grand view of terraced gardens and flower-lined walks which led down to a beach. Each evening before dusk, there was a clamor by hotel guests to find their favorite rocking chair so they could watch the sunset over the lake and catch the early fragrance of night-blooming jasmine.

The Watson home, on Kenilworth Boulevard, faced the lower gardens of the hotel and had several apartments on the back of the property. Several hundred feet from the lake, it was a wonderful place for a young boy to grow up.

Sebring, Florida - Late 1920s - Early 1930s

Tommy in front of a Century plant on Kenilworth Lodge grounds

Though Sebring had less than 2,000 residents, it had its own celebrities who loved the lake and the privacy of a small town away from the Florida coasts. Courtney Riley Cooper and Rex Beach, two famous writers of the day, had luxurious homes at the north end of Lake Jackson. To the south of the lake, near the Watson house, a home belonged to a famous actress, Marjorie Rambo. The town ended just beyond the Rambo house though the road continued 14 miles around the lake with just a few homes scattered on the far side. There had been plans drawn up for a second Kenilworth Lodge,[2] twice the size of the first one, to be constructed at the south end of the lake, but real estate development in Sebring fizzled with the 1929 crash.

The only other house on Tommy's street was the home of Clarence Campbell, a boy about Tommy's age. The boys met on Tommy's first day in Sebring and were soon fast friends. Clarence's mother, like Tommy's, was divorced and had moved to Sebring to be near relatives.

The boys spent their days playing in the clear waters of Lake Jackson and toasting in the sun like a couple of coffee beans. The Campbell's home had a beach where the boys seined for minnows which they kept in jars until they were ready to put them on a hook to fish for bass. It didn't matter that most of the minnows died before they could be used--they just seined for more. They rarely caught a bigger fish, but the joy was in the doing, not in the size of the fish. Night time always came before the task was done.

The boys made model boats from scrap wood and when the rains came, sailed them from the top of the hill where the rain water rushed

19

The Watson's home on Kenilworth Blvd.

around the corner of Lakeview Drive and flowed down the paved gutter of Kenilworth Boulevard to the lake. They'd race the small crafts down the "river" until they disappeared into a giant drain at the end of the street and reappeared, moments later, in the lake below. They would jump into the lake, retrieve the boats and return them to the top of the hill for another run.

Kenilworth Beach, across the street from the boys' homes, was not used by hotel guests in the summer and was a perfect spot to swim. The lake had a white sand bottom and clear water and you could see turtles and schools of fish as they went lazily about their business. Every day a group of boys who lived nearby came to Kenilworth Beach to play "Gator." Tommy and Clarence joined in the day-long game of water tag. "The Gator" was "it" until he caught somebody else, who was then "The Gator." At first Tommy spent a lot of time being "The Gator." He didn't know the tricks of the game and rarely caught anybody unless they wanted to be caught. He soon learned to swim under water, tread water, and to hide behind dock posts. This made him competitive and he played the game as an equal.

As the only child in his home, Tommy was spoiled and he tried to use his large collection of toys to get his way with his new friends. If

20

they wanted to play with the toys they would tolerate a certain amount of bossing, but it often wore thin and they would go home. Eventually Tommy used the tactic less. It took him years to abandon it altogether. When the lake got boring the tribe would wander into the orange groves near the hotel golf course. They would look for golf balls and eat a few oranges, and sooner or later they would become involved in an orange fight. It was like a snowball fight--the weapons were just different. A direct hit with an orange could be painful--even dangerous. More than one boy went home with a black eye where an orange had hit him. These fights usually ended when the hotel caretakers chased them out of the groves, threatening to call their parents.

Sometimes they searched for snakes along the lake shore, or harvested a few Cattley guavas from a tree which grew wild there. Other times they would walk to the far side of the hotel and pick mangos or mulberries which grew on unattended trees. There was always a place to get a free snack. They learned to pull the newest frond from the center of a palmetto bush and eat the tender, heart-of-palm tip, and they were forever searching for a coconut that had dropped from a palm tree.

The boys laid in the shade of a moss-covered oak tree and talked about leaving home and "living off the land." None of them were unhappy at home--the idea of living off the land just had a certain fascination.

They experimented with smoking as most boys do. There was no corn silk to try, so the boys searched the fields for a local favorite: Rabbit Tobacco. The silver-gray weed grew wild and was easy to find. It was a simple matter to shuck the small leaves from the stem, wrap them in tissue paper and light up. Several times Tommy or one of his friends turned green from a few puffs on a Rabbit Tobacco cigarette.

For the first time in his life Tommy was playing with friends his own age. He didn't always get along with them but he was learning, and he was becoming independent of the constant and intense "mothering" he got at home.

Meanwhile, about once a week, Polly was receiving flowers from Tom back in New Jersey. He still hoped that he and Polly could get back together. Sophie Mitchell, a local florist, sometimes made several trips from her shop to deliver the flowers, when no one was home.[3] She didn't get many orders for flowers via Western Union, and she didn't want to take a chance that they might wilt in the sun if she left them.

One day while Sophie was delivering a bouquet of flowers, with the usual love note attached, Polly barked, "No more of those damn flowers! Take them away."

21

Sophie was shocked. "Pardon me, Mrs. McGuire. Has there been something wrong with the flowers?"

"No, Mrs. Mitchell," replied Polly. "The flowers have been lovely. It's just that I don't want them. Why can't he give up?"

Mrs. Mitchell stood, holding the flowers--not knowing what to do or say. Polly said, "I'll sign for them, but take them back with you. I don't want them. Tell them back in New Jersey not to send me any more flowers--I won't accept them."

Polly closed the door and left Sophie standing bewildered, with the flowers. She took the flowers back to her shop, and notified the florist in Ridgewood, that the flowers would no longer be accepted by Mrs. McGuire. No more flowers were wired from New Jersey.

A few days later Polly received a letter from Tom asking her to take a cruise with him to the Caribbean. He felt they could resolve their differences if they could get away by themselves and talk things over. The cruise was a business trip and he thought it was a wonderful chance for them to rekindle their romance. Several days later he called to get an answer. It was "no." Many years later, after Polly's death, the letter would be found in her prized possessions, in a safety deposit box[4]---a testimony to her love for the man with whom she couldn't live.

[1] Vera W. Schneider
[2] Plans for the "new" Kenilworth are at the Sebring Historical Society
[3] Sophie Mitchell
[4] Marilynn McGuire Beatty

4

"He was apparently considered 'fair game' for teasing. An only child, with a long face, big nose, and a Northern accent, Tommy looked well-heeled---he was dressed rather impeccably--different from the rest of us Southern kids." ----Patricia Whitmore Carlson, SHS, Class of 1936

As she had promised, Polly got Tommy a dog, but it was as far from a collie as she could get. It was a small black and white Boston Bull, and they named it Jeff. It was ugly and smelly, and slobbered all the time. Children who saw the dog said, "What kind of a dog is that? It's so ugggly." It made no difference. Tommy had a dog and he loved it.

Shortly after the McGuires moved to Sebring, Polly's father started losing his health. He had a bout with Tuberculosis but seemed to get better. Then he found out he also had cancer.[1] He was in great pain and required around-the-clock nursing. At first Dora and Polly tried to take care of him, but soon they had to have a nurse day and night. It was tough on the whole family in the small house with the nurse moving around during the night.

The Watson property had two apartments in back of the main house. One apartment was above the garage behind the house and the other was lower down on the lot near the lake. Tommy and Polly moved into the apartment over the garage where they could sleep undisturbed. Dora moved into Polly's room in the main house and the nurse used Tommy's room to sit and read when the old man slept.

The medical care was expensive and it was long before the advent of health insurance. Polly had been through a lot: withstood the humiliation of a divorce, moved from her lifetime home in New Jersey to a place where she had no friends, and now her father was dying. She took care of everything for the family, and she felt the strain. Often, she'd have a few drinks in the evening to relieve the pain and frustration.

Polly and her mother attended the Presbyterian Church and, except for merchants, it was almost their only contact with the townspeople. It was evident to the people in Sebring, by the way she dressed and by the car she drove, that Mrs. McGuire was rich. There were people in Sebring with money, but they didn't "show it" ---Polly McGuire had the only car in town with white sidewall tires. When people saw the big car it reminded them of the limousines which brought people to the Kenilworth Lodge hotel. Everyone knew that she was divorced, and being rich or divorced was almost tantamount to a crime in a small southern town like Sebring. Polly added the "crimes" of being aggressive and being from New Jersey. None of these things endeared her to the citizens of Sebring.

Almost everyone in Sebring had moved there from Ohio, Indiana, Pennsylvania, Georgia or the Carolinas. They were more slow-paced people than this "New Jersey woman". Polly rubbed most of them the wrong way and was soon known as a caustic person. It was mostly because she was a woman who took care of things for her family, and she would not accept delays or poor workmanship.

The Watsons had hired a Negro woman, named Olive, who was both cook and maid, and a Negro handyman, named Ike, who did extensive gardening and ran errands. The house was heated only by a fireplace and Ike kept the house supplied with firewood. Ike and Olive soon learned that Polly, though demanding, was fair. She wanted things done her way, and at her pace. The two servants knew better than anyone else in town that Polly was also a very generous person. She paid them well over "the going rate" for domestics in Sebring, and if she asked them to do something extra she paid them for it. Word got around Sebring that Polly was over-paying her help and many people were upset that she may cause an increase in the painfully low salaries of domestics.

Polly did get to know her neighbor, Louise Campbell. Louise was friendly and recognized Polly to be an abrupt person with a good heart. She knew the pressure that Polly was under, taking care of her sick father and supervising the household. Being divorced herself, Louise understood some of the feelings Polly was having.

Soon, Louise invited Polly to play poker with her and "a group of sinners." In this group Polly met and befriended newspaperman Hayden Williams and his wife, and recently retired Atlantan, Colley Lewis and his wife.[2] They enjoyed penny-ante poker which was only played in Sebring clandestinely behind closed doors at the Elks Club or upstairs at the firehouse. The group certainly had to be "sinful" if they allowed women to play poker with men. If anyone found out that they drank liquor while they played, it would certainly have been the subject of some prayer meetings on their behalf. Sebring had a church on every corner and every minister preached against the evils of "the devil's brew." Louise made "home brew" to serve the group when they played at her house. Prohibition had made anything better than that too expensive and hard to purchase. Once when Louise's mother was visiting, Louise buried her current batch of "home brew" in the back yard. Her mother was a member of the W.C.T.U. and had a nose like a bird-dog. Louise knew that her mother could have easily detected the smell of the yeast if she had stashed the brew away somewhere in the house. Her mother extended her visit a few days and the home brew, subjected to the outdoor heat, blew up and got Louise a stern temperance lecture.

Louise also raised chickens, and this bothered Polly. Louise kept them on the back side of the house but Polly could hear them and when the wind would shift, she could smell them. One night Polly banged on Louise's door. She was a little tipsy and she said, "Louise, damn it all. You have got to get rid of those goddamned chickens. This place smells like a chicken farm. How am I going to explain that to my friends from New Jersey when they come to visit and we sit out in the garden?" The next day Polly saw Louise and apologized for coming down so late. Nothing else was said about the chickens for a while.

Some months later, late at night, the chickens cackled so loudly that they woke the whole neighborhood. It turned out to be a police matter---not the way you might guess. The sheriff's department had tried to stop a speeding car south of Sebring. The car was occupied by some unsavory characters from Miami who were traveling the back highways at night to avoid the police. They had stopped when the deputy signaled them, but then sped off and left him standing in the highway.

They entered Sebring and missed the right turn of the highway at the corner of Lakeview Drive, and slammed on their brakes just in time to avoid running into Lake Jackson at the foot of Kenilworth Boulevard---in front of Campbell's house. With the sheriff behind them, they were trapped on a dead-end street and fled on foot into the Campbell's back yard where they became entangled in the chicken pens. They were arrested on the spot. The next day, the place was practically a tourist attraction as Clarence and Tommy showed all their friends where the action had taken place.

Tommy found it rough going at school. Sebring had the only school for miles around and children attended from far out in the country. Most of them dressed in clothes which were neat, clean, and plain. Tommy had a grandmother and a mother who didn't have much else to do but dote on him. They dressed him in clothes much too fancy for Sebring and the kids gave him a hard time.[3]

Tommy had grown to a stage in life where his nose was too big for the rest of his face. He had come by the prominent feature honestly---his father and mother were both blessed with rather generous noses. To make it worse, he suffered from sinus trouble and a nose which ran constantly. He was not only kidded about the size of his nose, but also about blowing it all the time.

Tommy wasn't shy. He was encouraged by his family to stick up for himself, and he developed a sharp tongue. When schoolmates kidded him about his fancy clothes, he would answer the barbs with some of his own, often much more cutting than the original remark. It didn't make him any friends. Because of his cutting remarks and his sinus trouble the kids soon had a nickname for Tommy, that they first used behind his back and eventually to his face: "Snotty McGuire." Tommy's feelings were badly hurt by the nickname and it made him even more caustic to his schoolmates.

Some of the kids tried to play tricks on Tommy. He was on to many of the tricks and that angered the tricksters even more.

They did pull a small, daylight version of "snipe hunting" on Tommy during a field trip to Highlands Hammock State Park.[4]   They left Tommy in a small clearing in the woods with a bag to catch the snipe while the other boys went to beat the bushes to drive a snipe his way. Tommy soon caught on to the gag and ran all the way back to the picnic grounds, arriving only minutes after the other boys. He claimed that he knew about snipe hunting all of the time. He was embarrassed but he stuck to his guns.

Tommy was not above pulling a good trick on somebody himself. His best one may have been pulled against one of Polly's friends. One night Tommy was clowning around while Polly's group played poker. After reading aloud the cards someone had in their hand, he was sent to bed. Even though Polly got angry Tommy reappeared several times until Hayden Williams rose from the table and said, "I've got to go home early tonight. Tomorrow is my turn to usher at church, and I don't want to drop the collection plate." The rest of the group left soon after and Tommy went to sleep with an idea for a grand stunt that would have to wait until the morning.

The next morning Tommy sat quietly in church and waited for his big chance. In his pocket he gently fondled a small stack of red, white, and blue poker chips which he had removed from the scene of the previous night's game. He bided his time while Luther Price, the minister, conducted the service. When the time came Hayden Williams and the other ushers were called to the front of the church to get the collection plates. As the choir sang the ushers passed the plates back and forth across the rows working their way to the back of the church. Tommy waited until the plate came to his row. He looked up and smiled at Hayden Williams as he deposited the poker chips in the collection and handed it on.

Tommy watched as the ushers met at the back of the church. He caught Hayden Williams' eye and glanced toward the collection plate. Hayden looked down and saw the poker chips in the plate. Before he could remove them the signal was given and the four ushers started their march back to the front of the church. Hayden was not going to turn his plate in to Luther Price with the poker chips in it. As he walked down the aisle he reached into the plate and dug out the chips while trying to look very casual about the whole thing. He held them in his hand and hoped that the congregation and Reverend Price had not seen him remove them. If they had, he was certain that they would think that he had robbed the collection plate. Tommy giggled out loud but it went unnoticed against the sound of the church organ and the choir.

Polly was concerned about Tommy being raised without a father and she often talked about keeping his upbringing "normal." Nothing seemed more normal to her than summer camp. She had always gone to summer camp when she was a child and her parents had insisted that it broadened her outlook on life. In June, 1932, when Tommy was 11 years old, she and Tommy took a trip to the mountains near Asheville, North Carolina. Tommy attended Camp Sequoyah---proclaimed in its literature: "A REAL CAMP FOR REAL BOYS---In the land of sky."

Instead of going back to Florida, Polly stayed nearby at the Russel Davis house at Beaver Lake. It was a chance for the two of them to get away from the Sebring heat and the sadness of Grandpa's illness.

It was great for Tommy. No one knew him or his family and it was a fresh start for the boy. He was no longer the butt of the damaging barbs, but was just one of the campers, and he enjoyed his status very much. After a few days Tommy wrote to his mother: [5]

Dear Mother

Am feeling fine went to the tree house on Wed. We are going to big poplar 1 1/2 miles away. Somebody caught a blacksnake. Donald caught a rat and we fed it to the snake. We have a cabin supper Mon. at the tree house. Am having a wonderful time. Write soon and send me some papers. I have not read one in a week. We will go to services in a few minutes. Am going to buy a bow and arrows. Be sure to come to camp the 4th of July.

With love Tommy

27

The part about the blacksnake made Polly grimace momentarily, but the request for newspapers from her 11-year-old son didn't surprise her. He had been an avid newspaper reader since he was able to read. She took newspapers with her when she visited the camp on the 4th of July and she was pleased with Tommy's healthy appearance and attitude. Camp certainly agreed with him. A week later Tommy wrote again:[6]

Dear Mother

Went to Bald Knob yesterday got home at 6 o'clock all tird out. Am having a good time and feeling fine, give love to Grandpa and Grandma. Tell Olive I miss her cooking. Bring Jeff when you come up to camp Monday. Got my bow and arrow have $3.42 left. Be awfully glad to see you Monday.

With love Tommy

Polly was concerned that her divorce and the move to Sebring might have had a bad effect on Tommy. The camp had on staff a child psychologist, and Polly made arrangements for Tommy to be quietly examined. She was happy when she received this letter:[7]

ERNEST SEEMAN

Consultant in Personality

personal analysis
the gifted child
vocational adjustment

Durham, N.C.

Tommy McGuire
    This boy is enormously talented and is one of the most interesting young men for his age whom we have ever interviewed. The writer hopes to meet his mother some

28

day as it is evident that her influence and great understanding of childhood has been the powerful developing factor which has brought this boy to such a high state of mental growth. His mind is extremely original but not in the least eccentric. He is alert, persistent, and has a great fertility of ideas. Chemistry seems to be his all absorbing passion, and the study of this with the allied fields of electricity and mechanics appears to undoubtedly be the proper course in which to bend his education.

Socially, he has a fine sense of humor and is extremely sane and well-balanced along with his unusual precocity. Camp is doing a great deal for him, and he should continue such outdoor life all during his adolescence, if possible, as such intense mentalities as his greatly need the relaxation and serenity offered as well as physical building up.

(This is the only example of an only child from a broken home we have ever run across where there was not some morbidity or complex to report, but this boy is so greatly engrossed in his work and has such a finely balanced personality that we do not find the least "kink" anywhere in his make-up.)

Summer of 1932

Ernest Seeman

Polly read the letter over and over again. It was a great comfort to her for she had always felt guilty about the ill-effect her divorce might have on Tommy. Now she had the word of an expert that Tommy was bright and not affected by the whole experience. The writer said Tommy was normal and he said Polly was the reason that he was. Life over the past few years had not been easy--this letter made her feel that she was doing a good job of raising her son without a father.

Back in Sebring, Tommy joined the school band. Sebring High School had an outstanding band. A nice thing about having grades one through twelve in one school building was the band. Children could start band in the lower grades and work their way up from a rookie band, through an intermediate band, to the high school band.

New members of the band got excellent training from the very first day with Mr. P.J. Gustat, whom the students affectionately called "Prof". Not only was he a great music teacher, but he was also a developer of character. He demanded great things of his students, and drove them to excellence. The kids grumbled about the hard work, but the satisfaction of learning to play well, and the recognition they got, made it all worthwhile. The band might well have been the strongest positive influence in the lives of many of the musicians. It was for Tommy.

Tommy was learning to play the clarinet, and it was a shrilling experience. He wasn't an outstanding musician but it gave him great satisfaction because he could play by himself and improve at his own pace. He was luckier than most; he could go to the lower apartment, away from the main house and practice without disturbing anybody. He was very proud when he could play "Mary Had a Little Lamb" for his grandfather.

Polly's brother Charles had always been a special influence on Tommy. When Charles was in Sebring to see his ailing father he sensed that Tommy missed his father and that he was bewildered by his grandfather's illness. To comfort the boy, Charles brought him gifts and on one visit he brought a model airplane kit. Tommy loved building the plane and Charles spent many hours with the boy who was being deprived of the companionship of his father and grandfather.

When Tommy was 12 years old, his grandfather died. He had suffered a long and painful illness which had slowly sapped his strength and robbed him of his quick smile. At the end he had even lost the sparkle that had always been in his eyes. It was hard on Dora and Polly, but they had known for a long time that death was on its way. Tommy was devastated--he had lost another father. He was left to live with two mothers.

[1]Vera W. Schneider
[2]Louise Campbell related the "poker chip story,"the "chicken story" and the "home brew story"
[3]Patricia (Whitmore) Carlson SHS '36
[4]Bill Dutton
[5]Letter in Polly's safety deposit box
[6]Ibid.
[7]Ibid.

5

"It seemed like Tommy always ate onions for lunch just so he could breathe it in my face as we sat next to each other at band practice."

------Joy Satterwhite Eyman, schoolmate, SHS '41

After her father died Polly moved back into the main house, but Tommy stayed in the apartment behind the main house. A pool table and a ping pong table were installed in the lower apartment, near the Campbell's house. The two tables were immediate attractions for Tommy's friends. Ping pong was unheard of in Sebring, and the only pool tables in town were at the Tropical Pool Room and in a few private clubs. Because of the association of the game of pool with pool rooms, where beer was sold, many Sebring citizens considered the game a sin. The pool table equated the lower apartment to a den of iniquity and some parents did not want their children near it.

Mrs. Campbell's patience was tried by the installation of the ping pong table. One night Bill Dutton, one of Tommy's friends, slept over and they played ping pong late into the night. The sound of the ping pong ball hitting the paddles and table top kept Mrs. Campbell awake long after her bed time. At 1:30 a.m. she went to her back porch and called up to the apartment, "Tommy, could you please quit for the night? It's late and I can't sleep with that racket going on."

Tommy replied, "Why don't you mind your own business? Better still, why don't you mind your chickens?"[1]

Remarks like that didn't endear Tommy to Mrs. Campbell. She tolerated him because she didn't want to cause Polly any more grief. She allowed him to make himself at home in her house when he visited Clarence. Tommy showed up every time she served hot dogs or hamburgers to her family. He loved hot dogs and hamburgers but they were never on the menu at Tommy's home.[2]

Polly often invited one of Tommy's friends to stay for dinner. The young man would be furnished with one of Tommy's clean shirts to wear to the table. They sat at a table set with a real linen tablecloth and napkins and more silverware than any of the boys had ever seen before. The food was fancy too: freshly baked rolls, real butter in little square pats, standing rib roasts, roasted duck, or a "peanut ham," served with creamed onions and small green peas known to locals as "English Peas."[3] The food was cooked by Olive, who then served each person so they could help themselves. Being served was a new experience for most of the boys and they were never comfortable at the table. They knew any breach of manners on their part would be pointed out to them.

Tommy's friend, Lamar Hancock, sometimes ate at McGuire's and he invited Tommy to eat at his house. Mrs. Hancock was a good cook, but the food was often plain southern food---ham hocks and black-eyed peas served with rice, and cornbread with oleo margarine, and maybe some collard greens or grits. Tommy loved the food and he invited himself to Hancock's every chance he got. [4]

Polly tried to make the boys feel welcome at her home and encouraged Tommy to be more generous with his toys. She would let the boys play with them even when Tommy wasn't home. She often said, "You are welcome to play with them---just be sure to ask before you borrow them, and return them when you are through."

The boys had heard Polly rant when she was angry and they went to great lengths to stay on her good side. Once, Howard Weems, who lived a short distance from the McGuire's, borrowed Tommy's model sailing boat and took it to the lake. As he played with the boat a gust of wind caught in the miniature sail and took it from his reach. Howard, an excellent swimmer, chased the boat until he was far out in the lake. Every time he thought he was going to recapture it the craft caught a gust of wind and headed in another direction. He started to turn back several times but couldn't bear the thought of facing Mrs. McGuire without the prized model. He was at the point of exhaustion before he recovered and returned the boat. [5]

Every year the Sebring Firemen put on a minstrel show in the school auditorium to raise money. One of the favorite subjects for the program was the local alcohol laws. The following joke is from one of the Sebring Firemen's Minstrels where all of the cast were members of the fire department made up in black face:

"Mr. Bones, I've been told that you are going to name your cow 'Highlands County'."

"Yas sir, Mister Interlocutor, I was goin' to name my cow 'Highlands County,' but the County Agent done told me I shouldn't do dat."

"What possible objection could he have to the name, Mr. Bones?"

"I don't know bout no ob-jection. He jest said he'd be afraid if I name my cow 'Highlands County' it might go dry."

Highlands County was a dry county, meaning that no strong spirits were sold there. Some neighboring counties allowed whisky to be sold and were called wet counties.

Polly knew that many Sebring citizens drank alcohol in the privacy of their homes although they had to go out of the county or to a bootlegger to buy it. Polly was against prohibition and when it was abolished, signed a petition for an election she hoped would change Highlands

County from a dry county to a wet one. She asked others to sign the petition and in so doing offended many of the "blue-nosed" citizens of Sebring. It did not make life any easier for her and Tommy. Many people in Sebring were opposed to drinking on a religious basis, and thought that a "drinker" was surely on his way to hell.

One stormy night Polly was concerned about Tommy being alone in his apartment behind the main house. She was already dressed for bed and was having a night cap. Though it was raining and windy she decided that she should go out to the apartment and see if Tommy was safe. The night was very dark and she lost her way, stumbled, and fell headlong into a large hedge of Brazilian Pepper plants that separated her yard from Mrs. Campbell's. Try as she might, she could not get loose from the hedge. Her dressing gown was entangled in the branches and it held her fast.

It was dark and cold and she was stunned by the fall and didn't know what had happened. The bushes seemed like a monster that had grabbed her and wouldn't let go. She was completely disoriented and cried out at the top of her voice.

Finally the lights came on in the Campbell's house. Louise and her sister-in-law Mary Altvater had heard someone calling out. They found Polly fluttering in the hedge like a moth caught in a spider's web. She was soaked to the skin and bleeding. As they freed her from the hedge Polly tried to explain, but she could hardly speak between the sobs, and she made no sense.

The next day Polly was at Louise Campbell's house to apologize for the night before, explaining that she had just fallen and become excited because she couldn't get loose. Word of the event got around town and everyone assumed that she had been dead drunk. The story was embellished each time it was repeated. Polly's reputation was much worse than she deserved, but she didn't do much to help it. This story, and her outspokenness about prohibition stirred the ire of the teetotalers of Sebring.

Tommy continued to be a bit of an outcast, too. He still dressed better than most of the children in school and he was kidded about it. He fought back, making nasty remarks --- sometimes using words the other kids didn't understand. To get back at Tommy the kids often made slurring remarks about Polly.

On the playground one day the barbs got particularly nasty and one of the boys said, "Your mother is a drunk." Tommy became furious and denied that his mother was a drunk.

"Your mother has liquor on her breath all the time," said one of the kids.

"You're crazy," said Tommy. "She does not."

"Does too," came the reply.

Tommy was outnumbered and couldn't take the harassment so he fled into the boy's bathroom, the only part of the building boys could enter during recess. He could not hold back the tears and he did not want the kids to see him cry. Minutes later Tommy Weaver, a friend, showed up and said, "Tommy, forget those bums. They don't know what they are talking about, and it's none of their business anyway."

Tommy heard the other boys coming in from the yard but he couldn't stop crying. He turned his face to the wall but one of the boys grabbed his shoulder and swung him around so everyone could see the tears.

"Look at the cry baby," said the bully.

"Leave him alone," said Tommy Weaver. "I just beat him up before you guys came in here. That's why he is crying. If you want some of the same, I'll give it to you too."

Tommy was saved a great deal of embarrassment. Only the two boys knew what happened that day. One boy was sympathetic and the other was in need of it, and they became special friends.[6]

Tommy's cousin Vera often visited in Sebring. Once, Vera and Tommy were going to the movies but Tommy was afraid that his friends would see him with Vera and think he was taking a date. He got Tommy Weaver to go to the movies with them. He made sure that Weaver walked between him and his cousin and made him sit next to her in the theater.[7]

Vera and Tommy sometimes fought like brother and sister but they couldn't stay mad at each other for long. Once, Vera came to the breakfast table wearing eye makeup and Tommy kidded her about it until she cried. Later, the same day, when they were shopping at Maas Brothers Department Store in Tampa, Tommy charged a bottle of Chanel No. 5 to his mother's account and gave it to Vera as a good will offering.

Tommy continued to improve his musical skills in the band with encouragement and training from Prof Gustat. One day he rushed to band practice, adjusting the reed on his clarinet as he took his seat in the middle of the band. He wet the reed with saliva and tried a test note. The long black instrument emitted a strange screech that sounded like a wounded animal. The discord sent a shiver up the backs of the other band members who had been quietly harmonizing in their warm-up. As if to assign the screech to someone other than themselves, they moaned as a group ---"M-C-G-U-I-R-E!"

Tommy looked around and to cover his embarrassment let out the same screech again. As the group groaned Patty Whitmore shook her shoulders and said, "Don't do that Tommy, it makes my skin crawl."

The next day when the group sat, heads down, noodling away on their instruments, Tommy placed the clarinet to his mouth and again let out the terrible discord. It evoked a group moan---"M-C-G-U-I-R-E!" It became a daily routine which brought laughter and helped Tommy feel like a member of the band.[8]

The band played for chapel on Friday mornings, pep rallies, football games, parades, and special events. At Halloween and Christmas they played for cakewalks to earn money for band equipment and travel expenses. A lawn area was roped off in a circular pattern. The band sat in the center of the circle with a table displaying home-baked cakes donated by band mothers. Positions around the circle were sold to contestants who would then stand in that spot. When "Prof" started the band playing, contestants marched around the circle like a game of musical chairs until the music stopped. The contestant who stood in a secretly designated spot when the music stopped won the cake. During the evening several winners would donate their cakes to the band and when the cakewalk was over the band members gathered around and ate their reward.

After football season was over the band played a concert every Sunday afternoon at the city pier. The band shell was on a large lawn area which jutted out into the lake. The weather was sometimes brisk but the band always drew a large crowd. It was a regular Sunday event for Sebringites and winter tourists alike. The band dressed in full uniform and played classical music and marches. The best musicians in the band were selected to stand in front of the band and play solo parts.

The Sebring band's blue and white West Point-style uniforms were as distinctive as their music was good. Few other bands dressed as well. The uniform consisted of a blue hat with a white plume, long tailed blue coats with silver buttons and white crisscross webbing with a silver breast plate, white trousers for the boys and white skirts for the girls, and white shoes.

Polly took an interest in the band and with other mothers helped to keep the uniforms in good shape. While others did sewing and repair work Polly was more inclined to quietly donate money for repairs or new uniforms. When her brother Charles was in town he attended band concerts and also became very interested in the band. He regularly made contributions of money to the band, without receiving any public recognition of his gifts. Only Prof Gustat and Mitchell Ferguson, the Principal of Sebring High School, knew how generous Polly and Charles Watson were when it was announced, from time to time, that an anonymous donor had contributed to the band's uniform fund.[9]

Polly and Charles frequently made trips with the band to contests and out of town parades as chaperones. The adults made sure the band members didn't stay out late and that their behavior was proper. Some band parents wondered if Polly was the right person to look after teenagers. Her behavior on the trips was without a blemish, and she and Charles were appreciated by other parents who made the trips.

In the mornings, Polly and Charles stood by the bus door and gave a gift of a dollar bill to each band member. Food and lodging was being provided for the students and the dollar was intended to be spending money. While the gift was considered by many to be very generous, some proud parents considered it an insult. Some families didn't spend that much money to feed the whole family for a day or more. Polly got several phone calls from parents who didn't want their children to have the money.

"Mrs. McGuire, my daughter is in the band. Please don't give her any money. We earn our money and we do not take 'hand-outs.'"

Polly couldn't understand why anyone would object to the gift. Prof Gustat got objections too, and spoke to Polly about it but he didn't insist that they stop giving out the money, and so Charles and Polly continued to hand it out on the trips.

The band was a year-round occupation for the members, when the state and regional band contests were included. Still, Tommy and his buddies found time to try the game of golf. They weren't very good at the game but they attracted the attention of Captain Pringle, a vacationing Great Lakes ship captain. Pringle, a tug boat captain on Lake Michigan, headed for Sebring every winter when the lake froze. He loved to play golf and noticed Tommy, Bill Dutton, and Malcolm Waters struggling to learn the game. He took them under his wing and offered them some instructions. It was an unlikely match-up, but the boys spent many hours with the old captain who sprinkled in his philosophy of life between his golf tips. [10]

Tommy got along with the guys when he was away from home and taking part in activities like band or golf. He was still guilty of reigning over them when it came to his lavish possessions. Once when some of the boys got mad at Tommy they took the balls from the pool table and threw them in the lake. They told Tommy to look around if he wanted them back. A few days later he spotted the colored balls on the white sand lake bottom at the end of the dock. He had no trouble retrieving them undamaged.

Another time when the guys got tired of what they considered Tommy's arrogant attitude they sneaked into the game room at night and messed up the place. They dumped jig saw puzzles on the floor, turned over furniture, smashed ping pong balls, and as a last show of anger, took a couple of pillows outside and slit them and spread the feathers all over the yard. The next morning the lawn looked like snow had fallen. Polly was infuriated when she saw the mess and she called the police.

Chief Stivender asked around and found out who had made the mess. As was the method in those days, the chief picked up the boys and took them to the McGuire's house. [11] Paul Rippberger, Bill Dutton, and Tom Mitchell stood silently with their heads hanging as the chief explained, "These boys say they are very sorry about the mess, Mrs. McGuire. If it meets your approval, they will clean up the whole thing."

"That will be fine, chief. I'm a little shocked that they would make such a mess. We try to keep the game room nice so everyone can have a good time. If people don't appreciate it, maybe we will just close up the place."

The boys went about the job of cleaning the house and soon had it in order. The yard was a different story. The feathers were sticking in the grass. Mrs. McGuire had her handyman, Ike, bring out a vacuum cleaner. The boys ran the vacuum cleaner all over the yard until it was clean, and then knocked on the door and apologized again to Mrs. McGuire.

The boys looked so sad and embarrassed that Mrs. McGuire felt sorry for them. She knew they were good boys and that Tommy could be a pain at times. After talking to Louise Campbell she was sorry that she had called the police. In Sebring, people didn't call the police over such matters---instead they would call the parents of the offenders and the parents would make sure their children didn't participate in such misdeeds again.

A few days later Polly felt that she had to do something to make up for calling the police. She went to the Mitchell's flower shop and spoke to Mrs. Mitchell.

"Mrs. Mitchell, I guess you heard about the boys cleaning my yard the other day," said Polly.

"Yes, Mrs. McGuire. I'm so sorry," replied Mrs. Mitchell.

"I'm the one who should be sorry," said Mrs. McGuire. "They're good boys and they were just cutting up. I wish I hadn't called the police. I've been under a strain, and I just got mad. Would you give your son this boat as a good will offering. I know he has always liked it. Tell him I'm sorry."

She handed Mrs. Mitchell Tommy's scale model of the sailing ship "American Ranger." It was an expensive good will offering, and Mrs. Mitchell didn't want to keep it. Polly insisted.

37

Mrs. Mitchell was relieved that Polly wasn't mad about the whole episode and thought, "I'll never understand that woman." Polly went to the homes of each boy, and much to the surprise of their parents, made similar peace offerings.[12]

At the Sebring Cafe they were saying: "Did you hear that Polly McGuire had them using a vacuum cleaner on her lawn the other day?"

[1]Louise Campbell
[2]Clarence Campbell, SHS '39
[3]Lamar Hancock, SHS '38
[4]Ibid.
[5]Howard V. Weems Jr., SHS '40
[6]Mary Weaver
[7]Vera W. Schneider
[8]Patricia (Whitmore) Carlson, SHS'36
[9]M.M. Ferguson, former principal, SHS
[10]Bill Dutton, SHS '37
[11]Ibid.
[12]Sophie Mitchell, Sr.

6

"If you can make one heap of all your winnings, and risk it on one turn of pitch-and-toss, and lose, and start again at your beginnings, and never breathe a word about your loss."   -----Rudyard Kipling

Over the years Tommy learned to entertain himself. Living in an adult household he often got bored and would retire to his apartment to read. He read the newspaper every day and inspired by his Uncle Charles read about aviators---especially everything he could find about Charles Lindbergh, including his book *We*, which told the story of his flight to Paris. He devoured books about the famous World War flyers of the Lafayette Escadrille, such as Raoul Lufbery, Frank Luke, and Eddie Rickenbacker. Uncle Charles had known "Captain Eddie" at Issoudun, France, and had told Tommy many stories about him. The World War ended years before Tommy was born, but Rickenbacker had been highly publicized as the "Ace of Aces" and had received the Congressional Medal of Honor many years later, when Tommy was 10 years old. Tommy had read about him in the newspapers, and had also read his book, *Fighting the Flying Circus*.

Tommy also continued to build model airplanes. It took many days to construct a model from balsa wood and paper. The parts were printed on sheets of balsa and had to be cut out with a Gem razor blade, then pinned in place on the plans with straight pins and glued together. Finished components were covered with tissue paper. Tommy used one of his mother's old perfume atomizers to spray water on the paper. When it dried the paper was drawn tight to make a smooth surface.

In the beginning the models were crudely built, but the rubber band-powered propellers carried them clear across the yard. Often they crashed with severe damage but Tommy repaired them over and over again until they were beyond repair. Then he would build another. He became more skilled with each model he built, and he took more care to make the new plane look like the picture on the model's box. When he had built each different model available at McRae's Five and Ten Cent Store in Sebring, he bought bigger and fancier models in Tampa. Then, Uncle Charles sent him a gasoline powered model of Eddie Rickenbacker's World War Spad bi-plane. It was an expensive gift that had a special meaning to his Uncle Charles. Tommy had long dreamed of being the pilot of a plane like "The Spirit of St Louis" or "Captain Eddie's" Spad. He was proud to own a flying model of Rickenbacker's plane and found a large piece of corrugated cardboard on which to construct the three-foot-long wings.

The project took months. Tommy's buddies came around to see how the construction was going. The wings covered the whole table top. Most of Tommy's friends thought it was just another expensive toy, and that he would never be able to make it fly. Tommy was completely engrossed in the project--the plane was so real to him that he fantasized that Rickenbacker himself would show up do the test flying when the ship was completed.

The Spad was difficult to build. Due to its weight and size, its parts were made of white pine instead of the soft balsa wood, and they were very difficult to cut out. Besides the engine, the airplane had a gas tank, condenser, and a battery which had to be properly installed so the weight would be balanced for flying. When construction was finished Tommy spent extra hours painting the plane so it looked exactly like Rickenbacker's. The famous 94th Aero Squadron's Hat-in-the-Ring insignia was painted on the side of the fuselage. It was outstanding, and people who weren't even Tommy's friends came to see it.

Getting the engine to run was quite another problem. Tommy had no experience with engines and had to read and re-read the directions. It was frustrating. He could get the engine to sputter loudly a few times but it wouldn't continue to run. After days and nights of trial and error he mastered the engine and could get it to run at will. It made a deafening noise.

On the appointed day a group of Tommy's buddies gathered in the street in front of his house for the Spad's maiden flight. Tommy had decided to fly the plane downhill, toward the lake. The wind was blowing from the lake and he set the controls so the plane would rise from the ground when he turned it loose.

The plane was started, and as the group watched, Tommy released it down Kenilworth Drive. It rose sharply and climbed at a steep angle. The shrill sound of the engine began to fade as the plane cut its way through the wind toward the lake. The spectators cheered at the unexpected success, but quieted as it became apparent that the plane was going straight out over Lake Jackson. Tommy never batted an eye, but watched the plane climb higher and higher, become a speck, and disappear over the lake.

Someone said, "Tommy, I didn't know it was going to go that far. What is going to happen to it?"

"I guess it'll land on the other side of the lake," Tommy said proudly.

"You're crazy. It could never fly that far," said another.

"Yes it can," replied Tommy. "It's only a mile across."

"It could never fly that far," said Clarence Campbell.

"Yes it could," said Tommy. "I read in one of my magazines that a plane with the same type engine flew from Camden, New Jersey, to Wilmington, Delaware, a few years ago and that's 40 miles."

The guys all shook their heads in wonder. If one of them had pulled a trick like this they would be in certain trouble at home for losing such an expensive toy. Instead, it was a triumph for Tommy. He had done something that none of them had ever done--something none of them thought he could do. That afternoon Tommy rode his bike around to the other side of the lake in a futile attempt to recover his prized craft, but it was never to be seen again. His friends said that it went down in the lake. Tommy always maintained that it flew so far that they couldn't find it.

The next day Clarence Campbell dropped by Tommy's house. Tommy had already started another model. He was completely unruffled by the loss of the model which had taken so many months to build. Clarence suddenly thought he understood a Rudyard Kipling poem he had heard Tommy recite. It was the same one Tommy had recited for his mother and grandparents since he was a young child: [1]

> If you can make one heap of all your winnings;
> And risk it on one turn of pitch-and-toss,
> And lose, and start again at your beginnings
> And never breathe a word about your loss;
> If you can force your heart and nerve and sinew
> To serve your turn long after they are gone
> And so hold on when there is nothing in you
> Except the will which says to them: "Hold on!"
> Yours is the Earth and everything that's in it,
> And --- which is more --- you'll be a man, my son!

Tommy had demonstrated that he could take disappointment without being crippled by it. He went about his life with determination although he'd gone through the trauma of his parents' divorce and the loss of his grandfather. He'd developed a thick skin when children around him subjected him to unmerciful kidding, and he had gained a sense of his own self-worth which allowed him to be happy with his own company, yet enjoy the company of friends when they were about. He was developing into a tough minded young man who could accomplish almost anything he set his mind to do.

* * *

In spite of the objections of some parents Tommy's pool room remained a favorite place for the boys to wile away the hours. Polly stayed clear of the group although they sometimes got a little rowdy. Tommy had all-night ping pong contests and dart games when several of the guys spent the night. At one time the boys took up knife throwing and almost destroyed the door which supported the bull's-eye target. Tommy ruled the roost. Anybody who challenged him was in for a hard time. He was highly competitive and often won at ping pong, pool, and darts. The boys discussed anything and everything, and frequently had fierce arguments. Tommy would argue religion with anyone. It didn't matter which part he took, pro or con, he argued aggressively, and usually won the argument.

One night in the heat of an argument Tommy picked up his Remington .22 rifle and ordered Jack Ingle, his only guest, to get out if he couldn't see the value of a superior argument.

Jack refused and said, "Tommy, you are crazy. Don't point that gun at me."

Jack made a quick move, grabbed the rifle barrel and pointed it at the ceiling. The boys tussled and the gun fired with a loud report that echoed off the walls and rang in their ears. Both boys stared at the hole in the ceiling with disbelief.

"God, Jack. I'll swear that gun wasn't loaded. I never keep bullets in it," said Tommy, as he turned pale with the thought that he might have shot his friend.

"It's always the empty gun that kills. You shouldn't point a gun at anybody unless you intend to shoot them," said Jack.

The next day Tommy showed up at Jack's house and asked him to come out in the yard.

"Jack, I'm sorry about last night. I know I'm an ass hole at times, but I'd never point a loaded gun at anybody on purpose."

"I know you wouldn't, Tommy. All the same, it scared the hell out of me," replied Jack.

"It turns out that my mother let somebody borrow my gun, and they returned it with a shell in the chamber. I never checked it. I didn't even know that she had loaned it out. Believe me, I've learned my lesson," said Tommy.

The boys remained friends and on a rainy fall evening at Kenilworth beach, Tommy and Jack Ingle were shivering with cold while they and several other chums tried to start a fire with some wood they had gathered on the beach. Tommy said, "Save your matches--this wet wood is never going to burn. I'm going up to the house to get some alcohol. That will make it burn."

Tommy returned a few minutes later with a pint bottle of rubbing alcohol. He opened it and poured it on the wet wood. He intended to light it with a match, but there was just enough fire to ignite the rising alcohol vapors into a giant swooosh! Jack, who was crouched near the fire, was caught up in the flames. He bounded for the lake a few feet away, and emerged unhurt but shivering and smelling of burned hair. Luckily, his eyebrows, hair, and his wool trousers had just been singed.

Life around Tommy McGuire was usually fun, but it could also be dangerous. Jack Ingle had more than his share of close calls with Tommy but he was never seriously injured. Jack's parents worried even more when they heard that Tommy was driving a car.

Tommy learned to drive when he was just 14. Farm boys in Florida often drove in their early teens, but few were allowed to drive on the highways. Tommy was the first boy of his age to drive the family car around Sebring, and in a short time had a reputation as a wild driver, although it may have been partly sour grapes. It was easy to resent a 14-year old who drove one of the finest automobiles in town.

Polly wanted Tommy to drive. He could run errands and share the driving when they traveled. When Tommy's cousin Vera visited, Polly allowed the two of them to take trips to Tampa with Tommy doing all of the driving. When a barn-storming Ford Tri-motor plane flew into the Sebring airport Tommy gathered a carload of his friends and drove them out to see the high-winged monster.

Aviation had come to Sebring back in the twenties when an American Airlines executive was staying at the Kenilworth Hotel,[2] and one of the company's experimental seaplanes had landed in Lake Jackson as a demonstration of how accessible airline travel might be in the future. This time the airplane was on solid ground and the public swarmed all over it.

Tommy was there every day and he befriended the crew. They knew him by name because he paid a dollar to go up every time they got a load of paying customers. The crew had never had anyone spend so much money riding on their plane, and they allowed Tommy to sit in the co-pilot's seat and get a feel for the controls. In turn he drove the crew into town at the end of the day and took them back to the airport the next morning.

Driving made Tommy more popular with the girls. Tommy could get the car almost anytime he wanted it and he was very generous about giving people rides. It caused great resentment among the boys in town. Most of them weren't allowed to drive and some came from families that didn't even own an automobile.

On a Friday or Saturday night when there wasn't anything to do, Tommy would stop by at the Circle, where the boys hung out under the large clock on the Title Guaranty Building. They would pile into the car for a challenge of the Sebring to Avon Park speed record. Avon Park was 10 narrow and winding miles away and every driver in town wanted to drive the distance in 10 minutes or less. Tommy got close to the eight-minute mark for the 10-mile trip. He was driving a very powerful and heavy car which sat on the road well, particularly on the railroad crossing at Lakemont. While other drivers slowed down for the rough crossing Tommy took it at top speed. When he approached the crossing with a carload of boys the excitement mounted. They knew the car was going to leap into the air as it went over the tracks. When the bump came they all shouted like riders of a roller coaster do when they go over a crest of track. It was generally conceded that Tommy held the speed record to Avon Park.

Another favorite drive was the road to DeSoto City, south of Sebring. The terrain was hilly, like the ripples on a washboard, and the road builders had followed the terrain. A fast ride on this road was such a violent series of ups and downs that it often resulted in nausea for some of the passengers. Tommy loved to drive a carload of kids down that hectic stretch of road.

Tommy's driving was often the subject of conversations around Sebring. Tommy had another prized possession, given to him by his Uncle Charles, and it was no less famous than his driving. His uncle sent him a sailing canoe for his birthday and it came into town by Railway Express. The Railway Express delivery man was talking about the canoe at the soda fountain of the City Drug Store before Tommy had a chance to get it into the water. "Damnedest thing I've ever seen, it's like a regular canoe except for a sail and a stabilizer to keep it from tipping over."

Tommy's cousin Vera had taught him how to handle a canoe, and he had sailed at Lake Hopatcong, New Jersey, in the summer. He was far from an expert but he had enough experience to get started. He and Paul Gustat struggled for days and finally got to be very good with the canoe. Tommy took a ribbing from everybody about the unusual looking craft. By now he expected to be kidded. It seemed that everything he and his family did was different and Tommy had reached a point where it didn't bother him so much.

The canoe turned over easily and soon had a reputation around town for being dangerous. Once Tommy and Paul Thomas found themselves hanging on for dear life to the inverted craft in the middle of Lake Jackson. They lost the paddles and their rod and reels when the boat went over, but that was the least of their worries. The lake was so rough and the canoe so heavy that they couldn't right it. They had moments when they thought that they wouldn't make it, but they hung on and pushed it to shore by flutter-kicking their feet. It took over an hour.[3]

44

The event everybody remembered was when the Hancock boys took the canoe for an afternoon of sailing. Herman and his cousin Lamar got bored after an hour or so of relatively normal sailing and decided that it might be fun to sail without the out-riggers in place. Near shore, they were fine, with the out-riggers out of the water, so they headed out in the direction of Harder Hall, the large hotel across the lake. When they got to the middle of the lake the winds were stronger and the boys leaned over the windward side of the boat to fight the tipping effects of the wind. Before long they were at the complete mercy of the wind. Going back toward the shore was out of the question. Staying afloat was their top priority. They could always walk home if they ended up on the other side of the lake. About two-thirds of the way across the lake they made a decision to take the sail down. While they tried to lower the sail, the canoe tipped over.

The boys struggled to hang on, but the mast struck Herman on the head and he slipped below the surface of the choppy water. Lamar panicked when his cousin disappeared, and made a couple of quick surface dives to see if he could find him. On his return to the surface, he saw his cousin floundering toward the boat. Quickly he helped Herman to the overturned canoe. They held on as the waves carried them to shore near the Harder Hall bridge.[4]

Luckily for the boys Lamar's father had gone to McGuire's looking for his son. Mrs. McGuire had told him that the boys were out sailing. When he had surveyed the lake from the Kenilworth beach he couldn't see them. He decided to drive around the lake and look for the canoe from the other side. Instead he met the boys walking toward town. Herman had a huge gash in the top of his head and was bleeding profusely. He had to have stitches to close the wound. The word buzzed around Sebring, "Did you hear about that damn canoe of Tommy McGuire's? It almost killed the Hancock boys!"

Tommy sailed the canoe when the world seemed to be against him. He had conquered the canoe and though it was a small victory, it made him feel better when he was in the dumps. Late on summer afternoons Tommy would sail past the backyards of Sebring's top citizens. All of the homes on Lakeview Drive had a backyard on the lake. These beaches were the perfect late afternoon cooling-off spot for their owners. Tommy sailed past the homes and each family in turn waved, and some shouted greetings. He returned the greetings knowing that they were probably saying, "There goes Tommy in that crazy canoe. It's no wonder he sails all the time. They say Polly was at Beaver's Grocery store in the middle of the afternoon with liquor on her breath."

Even if they weren't talking about him and his mother, Tommy thought they were. He knew they had to admire his skill and courage for sailing the "dangerous canoe." Tommy thought, "Someday I'll show them around here. I'll do something that nobody has ever done--I'll show everybody." He would sail to the end of the lake, to Caravacious Point. Then he'd sail back past empty beaches--everyone was in having dinner. Somehow the lonely trip back gave Tommy a feeling of triumph.

Sometimes, on a hot night, Tommy and some friends would sail the canoe to cool off. They never gave a thought to the added danger of taking the "killer canoe" out in the dark. One night was a little different. Jack Ingle was spending the night, and the two boys went rabbit hunting along the lake shore. While one boy aimed the flashlight in the rabbit's eyes, the other would take a shot with the .22 rifle. After shooting at several cats by mistake, Tommy said, "It's hot. Let's go sailing."

As they shined the flashlight into the boathouse a pole cat ran to the far end of the building. Tommy aimed the rifle. Jack said, "Let's get the boat and get out of here. If you shoot that skunk he's just going to smell up the place."

"It's too late," said Tommy, "He already smells. Besides it's the only wild animal we have seen all night."

He fired a few shots into the dark boathouse as the skunk scurried to get away. Later, they got the canoe out of the boat-house, rigged the sail, and started paddling away from shore. After a few minutes Tommy said. "Grab that can and start bailing. There's water in the boat."

Jack grabbed a can laying in the bottom of the canoe and started bailing. He dipped can after can of water out of the boat, but the water got higher. Finally it dawned on him, "Tommy, you idiot! You shot a hole in the boat! We're sinking."

The water was shallow and the boys beached the canoe. Jack said, "Tommy, are you trying to kill me? Last year you set me on fire and tried to shoot me. Now you're trying to drown me."[5]

While each incident with Tommy's canoe added to the McGuire lore which circulated among Sebring citizens, there were things the McGuire's did which went unnoticed. Reverend Price at the Presbyterian church learned how generous Polly and her mother were when they gave money for much needed repairs to the church building. Later, Mr. Price happened to mention to Polly that certain members of the church who had once been generous contributors were now in a state of poverty as a result of the stock market crash. Polly wasted no time in providing food and money to the families, through Mr. Price, insisting that he not reveal the source.[6]

Polly's doctor and Prof Gustat sometimes mentioned needy people to Polly and she quickly became their unknown benefactor. Polly's next door neighbor, Louise Campbell, often delivered the anonymous donations. Polly said, "Please don't tell them where this came from. I know they are proud people."[7] The irony of these secret donations was that several people who had been severely critical of Polly benefited from her generosity--a trait none of them would have attributed to her.

[1] Clarence Campbell
[2] Highlands County News
[3] Paul Thomas
[4] Lamar Hancock
[5] Jack Ingle furnished the stories in this chapter which involve him and Tommy
[6] Rev. Luther Price
[7] Louise Campbell

7

"I entered Latin classes later than most. Tommy must have been advanced in Latin because of the great declension which he originated, 'Rex, regis, rectum.' Perhaps that should be included as his contribution to richer speech." --Neil Campbell Tappen, McGuire's friend from SHS

Latin was a problem in Highlands County. It wasn't being taught in any of the high schools and graduates wanting to attend a college where Latin was an entrance requirement were behind the eight ball. They had to study the language elsewhere--some in a prep school after graduating. Sebring High did start Latin classes and they were open to students from all over the county. Patty Whitmore transferred from Lake Placid and Charlie Sheppard from Avon Park to take the language. It was taught in a cycle and Tommy had to start in his freshman year or miss it.

Tommy's mother had mastered Latin in boarding school and she helped him with his homework. Tommy, Patty and Charlie had a feel for the language and were the best students in Mrs. Nina McIntosh's Latin class. Tommy and the two upperclassmen recited with comfort while other members of the class stumbled through the lesson or used ponies. In class a student might hem and haw until someone sneaked a translation to him or her so they could read aloud from it. Tommy, Patty and Charlie were the exception. Mrs. McIntosh knew this and rarely called on them to recite.

One Monday morning after the band had been on a weekend trip Mrs. McIntosh called on Tommy, Patty and Charlie. They had neglected their lessons and they struggled with the recitation. Mrs. McIntosh said, "Well, I know I have at least three students who aren't using ponies." It was a message to the others in the class to study and quit using the ponies.

Some teachers in Sebring thought the band took too much of the students' time. In the small school the same students who participated in band were frequently on a sports team and the coaches for boys' sports were forever complaining that their athletes had conflicts with band activities. Prof Gustat had developed the band into a state-wide champion. Although Sebring was a small town, they won competitions against the largest schools from Jacksonville, Orlando, Miami, and Tampa.

When Gustat first came to Sebring he also taught band in Avon Park, 10 miles to the north, and Lake Placid, 20 miles to the south. After a few years, his doctor advised him to restrict his work to Sebring. Students in the other towns could continue their training only by attending school in Sebring. Campbell Tappen, from Lake Placid, came to Sebring for the 10th grade to take Latin and play in the band. He rented a room from Mrs. Pierce on Rose Avenue. His family was better off financially than most, and he was considered to be an outsider, much like Tommy. He sat a chair ahead of Tommy in the clarinet section of the band and they became pals. Sometimes he spent the weekend at Tommy's to play in the Sunday band concert. Campbell, a year older than Tommy, was small of stature and took up weight lifting to develop his physique. Tommy took up the activity too. It's not recorded that either of them became muscle-bound but Tommy eventually got his own set of weights.

A group of parents in Avon Park converted an old grove truck into a crude bus and Billy Martin drove 17 mischievous boys to Sebring each day to attend high school and play in the band. Martin eventually attended the University of Tampa on a music scholarship, one of the first of many students who used their musical ability to gain a college education they might not have been able to otherwise afford.

This association of Avon Park and Sebring students encouraged the time honored "trip to Avon Park." Anytime somebody had the family car and things got boring, they would drive to Avon Park. Avon Park had a National Guard armory and it was frequently the site of dances. Sebring boys always thought there were more girls in Avon Park, and would frequently go over to check out the dances. Needless to say, they weren't all that popular with the Avon Park boys and sometimes a good fist fight would break out.

Tommy often drove to Avon Park, where he met and was smitten with a beautiful young Avon Park girl named Frances Brown. Her folks were very particular about whom she dated but Tommy won them over with his manners and invited her home for dinner. Polly and her mother served a perfect dinner and they were impressed with Frances. Unfortunately Frances frequently called Tommy "Mickey" and it upset Dora. When Tommy got back from taking Frances home he got a lecture from his grandmother.

"Tommy, that young lady called you Mickey all night."

"So what?" answered Tommy. "I don't care."

"Well, you should care," said his grandmother. "That's a slur on your character."

"How can a nickname be a slur on my character?" asked Tommy.

"Haven't you ever heard of an Irish Mick?" she asked.

"Yes, I have," answered Tommy. "I don't know what it means, and I don't see what all of this has to do with Frances anyway."

49

"'Mick' is what they called those Irishmen who came over from Ireland after the potato famine. So many of them had 'Mc' in their names and they were a rowdy lot, most without jobs, and they stayed drunk all the time. Is that what you want people to think of you?"

"Grandmother, Frances doesn't know anything about people from Ireland. People in the South don't know anything about the Irish and besides Frances doesn't know I'm part Irish," grumbled Tommy.

"With the name McGuire, she knows you're Irish," assured Dora.

"Well, I'm proud to be Irish, but if it will make you happy, I'll ask Frances not to call me Mickey around you."

Uncle Charles Watson, Grandmother Dora Watson and Tommy

He never spoke to Frances about the nickname. Instead, he made a date with Frances the following week to go dancing at the Hammock Tavern. Frances didn't want to go there because her guardians did not think highly of places like the Blue Anchor or the Hammock Tavern. Friday night Tommy picked up Frances and headed for the Hammock Tavern. Frances still had her doubts.

"Lets go to a movie," she pleaded. "My folks will find out."

Tommy replied, "George Lilly runs the Tavern and it doesn't get wild like it was before. Your folks won't find out. Do you think your name will be in the paper because you went there?"

Tommy prevailed and they went to the Hammock Tavern. Frances still had her doubts. When they entered the cypress paneled rustic inn they were greeted from across the room, "Tommy, you and your friend stay right there," shouted George Lilly. "I want to talk to you."

Frances felt like slipping through a crack in the floor as everyone turned to see who was at the door. "You see," she said. "We're too young. We shouldn't have come here."

"Don't worry," said Tommy. "He just wants to meet you."

George Lilly came over, carrying a small box and said, "Tommy, your guest has won the door prize."

"George, this is Frances Brown from Avon Park. Frances, this is George Lilly. He runs this place."

"Frances, it's my pleasure to meet you. I have a corsage here for you. You are the one-thousandth customer since we took over the place," said George, as he led them to a table.

Everyone applauded Tommy and Frances as they sat down. It took several dances before Frances could get her heart out of her throat but they had a nice evening. In the **Highlands County News** the following Thursday there was a small article with a headline:

"FRANCES BROWN OF AVON PARK WINS PRIZE".

Frances' guardians saw the article and the budding romance ended. [1]

[1] Frances Brown

51

8

"I had just moved to Sebring and I didn't know Tommy very well. He was the only kid in town who had his own car and he didn't like it at all when I beat him to Ft. Meade."

---Ike Hart, Jr., SHS Classmate of Tommy's

Howard McDonald was a classmate of Tommy's and his lab partner in chemistry class. They worked across the table from Suette Blanding and Capitola Kelly. Fred Wild taught the class and he usually graded papers while the students worked on their experiments. One day Tommy and Howard finished their assignment early, and to impress the girls, started an experiment of their own. They mixed a concoction that blew up in Howard's face. It didn't hurt anybody but Fred Wild threatened to break up the partnership if they didn't behave.

The next time Tommy was through with his work early, he looked around for something else to do. He pestered Paul Thomas, who was still working on his experiment. Paul got upset and pushed Tommy away from his table. Tommy pushed back. Mr. Wild thundered from the front of the room, "If you two boys want to fight, go outside." He opened the door and ushered them out.

When the boys got out of earshot Paul asked, "Do you really want to fight, Tommy?"

"No," replied Tommy. "I figured we could stand a little break."

The boys stayed out of the room about ten minutes, then pulled their shirt tails out, mussed their hair and returned to the lab for generous applause from their classmates.

A year later, Paul and Tommy double dated for a school dance and had to have their dates home by midnight. Tommy drove 30 miles to Avon Park and DeSoto City in 30 minutes. Paul remembers:

"We drove down Lakeview Drive so fast that those Royal Palms looked like fence posts, but we got them home on time."[1]

Tommy's car was a source of fun for the boys when they'd take a drive around Lake Jackson. The road followed the lake shore for 14 miles, and there was no civilization on the far side of the lake. The area was a favorite lover's lane where the occupants of a parked car could enjoy hours of privacy. Tommy would drive around the lake after dark until they came upon a parked car. He would pull alongside and one of the boys would shout into the parked car, "Pa said to bring sis home."

Tommy would speed away hoping that the surprised couple would be so startled that they wouldn't recognize his car. Often the parked car would give chase. Tommy loved the chase because he was sure he could out-drive anybody. On the way back to town there was a hazard which he enjoyed more than his passengers did. It was the "S" curve near Caravacious Point. Tommy would see how fast he could take the dangerous curve. Legend was that he could take the curve at 60-miles-an-hour but had to put the car on two wheels to do it. Over the years a number of people have died on that curve, which is the same today as it was then except the road is wider and the surface is smoother.

Another favorite night-time trip was a ride through the local cemetery. Tommy often took this drive when he had girls in his car. They always screamed as he followed the unpaved road among the tombstones. Once, when a murder had been committed near the cemetery, the police took tire castings from the cemetery road. After worrying for a few days, Tommy went to the sheriff's office and told them he had taken a carload of kids through the cemetery on the same night.[2] They had his tire prints and were looking for his car. Having a car full of witnesses made it clear to the police that the tire tracks were useless. The trips through the cemetery were curtailed, but on Halloween, Tommy drove when they took the sign from Stephenson's funeral home and placed it in front of the high school--a yearly tradition.

There were times when Tommy's driving made his passengers wonder if they would get home safely. Once on the way to Ft. Meade for a football game, Tommy got caught behind a stopped car on Ridgewood Drive. Ike Hart Jr., who had just moved to Sebring, pulled his car out and passed Tommy as one of his passengers shouted, "Catch us if you can!" That was all Tommy needed. Ike didn't really know Tommy or his reputation as a fast driver, and he drove to Ft. Meade making no special effort to win a race. He did take every opportunity to pass a slow car when he got behind one. As luck would have it Tommy would get behind a slow car that he could not pass because of oncoming traffic. Ike and his friends arrived at the football field in Ft. Meade just moments before a frustrated Tommy McGuire. Tommy did not ignore the defeat. Instead he accused Ike of having a special engine in his car. Ike had to raise the hood and show Tommy the car's standard 65-horsepower Ford engine. Tommy said, "No one has ever beat me and my straight eight before. You're a hell of a driver."[3]

On the way home it was no contest. Tommy got out front and Ike didn't challenge. Ike knew if his father found out he was racing his car it would be the last time he'd be allowed to have it. Along the road Tommy got behind a slow moving log truck which he couldn't pass. Long tree trunks stuck 10 feet beyond the back of the truck bed and Tommy drove closer until the hood of his car was underneath the protruding logs. His passengers were staring at the ends of the logs which were just a few feet in front of the car's windshield. They pleaded with Tommy to back-off lest the truck stop and ram the logs through the car, beheading them all. Tommy laughed and kept the hood under the logs a few seconds before dropping back. It wasn't the smartest thing Tommy ever did and his passengers swore they would never ride in his car again.

Dora Watson was not well and Polly spent most of her time taking care of her mother. Polly was glad Tommy was able to drive and run errands for her. She worried about the large medical bills, but did not trouble Tommy with the details of their financial situation. Tommy would be going to college in a few years, but Polly wasn't worried about that. Dora had known that Tommy would need money for school and she wasn't sure his father would be willing or able to furnish those funds. She had set up a trust fund for Tommy's college expenses. She didn't do this for any of her other grandchildren because she felt that their fathers would be able to take care of their college expenses.

In May of 1936, Dora Watson died. Polly and Tommy traveled to New Jersey on the train with her body. She was buried in the family plot at Cedar Lawn Cemetery near Ridgewood. Tommy's father came to the funeral and Tommy heard someone say, "Poor Dora, she must be turning before she is in her grave."

Dora's death left Polly with a terrible loneliness. Dora had been a constant influence on Polly and that was missed. Dora's will distributed her estate between her children but it would act to separate Polly from her brothers and sister. There wasn't much of an estate left to be divided, and her siblings wondered where everything had gone. Polly was incensed. She had taken care of her mother and father through their illnesses and had done her best to manage their resources. Eventually, she went to court and had the will set aside. She was awarded the house, which was about all that was left. Polly was upset that she had to go to court to battle her own brothers and sister for the meager remains of her parent's estate, but she had no place else to go. It left her and her family on the "outs" when she needed them more than ever.

Tommy's cousin Vera and her family moved from New Jersey to North Florida. Vera visited in Sebring often. Polly needed someone to talk with and Vera was like her own daughter. They wore the same dress size and this benefited Vera in an unusual way. Polly couldn't make up her mind whether to let her hair go gray or to have a periodic henna rinse to keep it reddish brown. She tried both ways and changed her wardrobe to complement her hair color. When her hair was brown she bought green dresses. When it was gray she bought red dresses. Every time Vera visited she would go home with a selection of beautiful

54

dresses which had hardly been worn. The color of the dresses was either red or green, whichever didn't fit in with Polly's current hair color.

Polly gave Vera another gift which had special meaning to them both. Vera was packing to go back home when Polly came into the room and presented her with a small jewelry case. In it were a Jade necklace and earrings which Vera's father had given to Polly, his sister, after a trip to China. Polly said, "I don't have any place to wear it around here. If I had a daughter I would want her to have the Jade, but I don't, and so I want you to have it. I can't take a chance of something happening to me and someone else getting it." Years later, Vera passed the Jade to her own daughter in the same fashion.[4]

[1]Paul Thomas
[2]Broward Coker
[3]Ike Hart, Jr.
[4]Vera W. Schnieder

9

"Police Chief Jim Hancock told the city council he plans a crack-down on speeders in Sebring. He said, 'It's not out-of-towners traveling through town who are doing the speeding. It's local people, some of them prominent citizens, who should know better.'"

----**HighlandsCounty News**

On Sebring's main street, Ridgewood Drive, two blocks from the circle, there was a single parallel parking spot marked "POLICE CAR ONLY." Next to the parking spot, on a pole, right in front of the Ford dealership was a call box with a phone inside, and a large bell on the side. After dark you could find Sebring's only police car sitting in that parking spot. Phone calls to the police during the night rang the big bell, which was loud enough to be heard several blocks away.

Early in the evening the town's only on-duty policeman went door to door in the business district, checking doors, to see if they were locked. Later he could be found drinking coffee across the street from his car at the Sebring Cafe, where he could reach the phone on the third or fourth ring. The cafe was open all night, and the red and blue neon sign in the window was a welcome sight for weary nighttime travelers, who might have to travel 60 miles or more to find the next cup of coffee.

After the Tropical Pool Room closed at midnight, Sebring's night people, such as Slim Brown, a gentle six-foot-nine-inch tall handyman, or house painter Tom Mayo, still dressed in his paint spattered clothes and shoes, could often be found drinking coffee and eating a piece of pie at the cafe's spotless counter. Almost always, you would find a night fireman from the firehouse a block away, and maybe a deputy sheriff sitting there, too.

One of the owners of the Sebring Cafe was a distinguished graying Cuban gentleman named Raymond Canto. Mr. Canto took the night shift and except for the time he spent at the coffee urn, brewing the coffee, he stayed at the cash register next to the front window. During slow periods, he would put a foot on the eighteen-inch-high window ledge, rest an elbow on his raised knee and while the palm of his hand supported his chin he would peer out at the street through his gold-rimmed glasses. Often while observing the scene Mr. Canto saw Tommy McGuire whiz past the parked police car across the street at such a rate of speed that he would vanish into the night before the policeman could put down his coffee and come to the window to see for himself.

Broward Coker, a young deputy sheriff, was in the cafe often, and he told Mr. Canto, "Sheriff Shoemaker gets complaints from all over the county about Tommy's driving. They'd love to catch him in Avon Park---he's over there all the time and he crosses the railroad tracks at Lakemont, doing 75 miles an hour."

Mr. Canto shook his head and replied, "Uncle Jimmy tells me he's always going around the circle in the wrong direction, but they can't catch him. I understand you have talked to him several times about speeding."

"Yeah, I did, last Christmas when he got the new Pontiac. I asked him to take it easy, and he did for a while. We'd talk to Mrs. McGuire about it, but nobody wants to tangle with her."

One night Tommy and three or four of his schoolmates were sitting at a table in the Sebring Cafe discussing an upcoming band trip. Ruby, everybody's favorite waitress, was keeping their coffee cups warm, with refills. They were laughing and making a lot of noise. Raymond Canto was observing from behind his cash register and happened to catch Tommy's eye from across the room. Tommy knew Mr. Canto had something on his mind, and wasn't surprised when he removed the toothpick from the corner of his mouth and motioned with it for Tommy to come over.

Tommy rose and walked over to Mr. Canto, expecting a stern request to keep the group quiet. "Yes, Sir?" asked Tommy.

Mr. Canto smiled, showing his gold teeth and said, "Tommy, don't get angry about what I'm going to say, I'm only trying to help you. You don't have no daddy here to talk to you, so take what I'm saying like I was your daddy. You've got everybody in Highlands County upset with your wild driving. I see you going by here at 70 miles an hour myself." He reached under the counter and pulled out a folded copy of the **Highlands County News** and pointed to a small article which quoted Police Chief Jim Hancock, known to everyone in Sebring as "Uncle Jimmy." "Do you see what Uncle Jimmy says here? He says he's going to stop the speeding in Sebring, if he has to arrest everybody. Son, he didn't mention your name, but you are one of the people he has in mind. Uncle Jimmy and Broward Coker would have talked to your Mother, but they know she just lost her mother, and that she has been sick lately. They don't want to cause her more grief."

Tommy listened, and though he was angry, he knew Mr. Canto was right, his mother didn't need any more grief. Tommy's head lowered as Mr. Canto talked on for a few minutes. Tommy heard little of what he said, as his anger turned into embarrassment. Mr. Canto sensed that he had said enough, patted Tommy on the shoulder and said, "Go on son, join your friends, but think about what I said." Tommy nodded and rejoined his friends.

When Tommy paid the check a half hour later, he told Mr. Canto, "I've thought about what you said. I'll slow it down. Thank you, sir." They smiled at each other as Tommy left with his friends. Tommy did slow down his driving--until he got another new car the following Christmas. [1]

Most students at Sebring High School had been instructed by their parents to stay out of Tommy's car. Still, when Tommy would offer a group of walkers a ride most of them would pile into the car. When Tommy saw Howard Weems walking he would look the other way and drive on. He and Howard didn't care much for each other.

Howard was from a good family. His parents were pillars of the community. Mrs. Weems was an outgoing woman who was always involved in church and civic affairs, while Dr. Weems was a quiet man who mostly took care of his medical practice. Every Sunday they were in their pew at the Methodist Church. Howard had been one of the smaller boys in his class when he was younger and his father had encouraged him to defend himself. He had become a tough guy, with muscles, who loved the contact of the football field and never backed away from a confrontation even if it led to a fist fight. He wasn't looking for trouble but he never backed away from it either. He was willing to fight to prove that he was the toughest kid in the school, and he had most everybody convinced.

Tommy and his friends had each been intimidated by Howard even though he was a year or more younger than any of them. The group which included Artie Lewis and Clarence Campbell made an informal agreement to protect its members from a fight with Howard. Tommy was reading Robert Louis Stevenson and quoted him to his friends: "'You cannot run away from weakness; you must some time fight it out or perish; and if that be so, why not now, and where you stand?' Why don't we talk to Howard and set him right?" They never got around to the "talking to Howard part" but agreed to help each other if trouble brewed with Howard.

Meanwhile a new fad was sweeping over the Sebring High School campus. Someone discovered that strips of rubber cut from an automobile innertube could be mounted on a pistol shaped grip carved from wood, to produce a formidable slingshot. At first the boys shot wads of paper or pieces of pencil erasers. Then they discovered acorns from the oak trees on the school grounds and the nature of the toy began to change. It was now a dangerous weapon which could break a window or put out an eye. A bird sitting on an electric wire near the school yard was surely a daredevil.

Then someone made the toy weapon more dangerous, experimenting with a fencing staple as the projectile. It was a natural. The staple was made of heavy-gauge galvanized wire which was bent into a "U"-shaped device, an inch-and-a-half long, with both prongs sharpened so they could be driven into a fence post. They were the proper weight for the slingshots and could be shot 50 feet. Many of the boys became so skilled with this new missile that they hunted squirrels on the school grounds. It seemed inevitable that someone would eventually be injured with this new weapon. Tommy and Howard, like most boys on campus, carried a slingshot in their hip pocket, and they were destined to use them in a way which would bring the fad to an end.

One day Tommy and Howard met alone on the school grounds. Tommy made a remark which offended Howard and after a brief discussion Tommy produced his slingshot with a staple loaded and ready to shoot. He aimed it at Howard and said, "You take one step toward me and I'll let you have it."

Howard said, "You're too chicken to shoot!"

Howard paid no attention to the drawn slingshot and glared at Tommy. Tommy fired the missile and it hit Howard on the thigh. The staple bounced off Howard's leg with a sting. He was so surprised that he stood motionless for a few moments.

Tommy was speechless, too. He did the only thing he could to avoid a beating---he ran. Howard produced his own slingshot, loaded a staple, and with blood in his eyes took aim at McGuire. He released the rubber band just before Tommy made it to the corner of the school building. The shot was at least 50 feet and was made in anger with little thought that it would hit home. Tommy let out a howl of pain as he rounded the corner. Howard knew that his desperation shot had hit its target and he worried that he may have done some serious damage.

When Howard rounded the corner he found Tommy, pale, and on his knees, clutching a bloody hand. Both prongs of the staple were deeply embedded into the back of Tommy's hand.

"Damn, Tommy, I didn't think I could hit you from that distance."

"Just pull the damn thing out, Howard, before I pass out," said Tommy.

Howard tried to pull the staple out as Tommy screamed with pain. The staple was too deeply embedded and it wouldn't come out. Someone found the school custodian who brought a pair of pliers and pulled the staple from Tommy's hand. Blood spurted from the hand, and Tommy had to leave school for treatment of the wound and a tetanus shot. Dr. Weems was upset to learn that his son had inflicted the wound and he vowed to speak to Howard.

Howard went into the school office and sat down in one of the chairs outside the principal's door. Miss Pierce, the school secretary, looked up and asked, "What do you want, Howard?"

Howard said, "I think Mr. Ferguson will want to see me."[2]

Tommy's hand was stiff for a month or more and he worried that it may effect his clarinet playing. His skills had improved each year he was in the band and he had moved up in the clarinet section. Prof Gustat suggested that a summer music camp would benefit Tommy and in the summer before his junior year he went to Interlochen National Music Camp, at Traverse City, Michigan.

Interlochen attracted top musicians from all over the nation, but Tommy did not feel out of place. They trained in small groups and in orchestras, and each week ended with concerts by the various groups.

Tommy played everyday and heard a lot of good music. He could play with the best of them, and he went home confident of his musical talent.

Back in Sebring, he had many stories about his trip to Interlochen, including great details about a love affair he enjoyed with a beautiful young lady. He gave the boys all the details about her seduction. According to Tommy, the days were filled with music, and the nights with repeated passion. Tommy had plenty of listeners for a few days as he told them about each of his encounters with the young lady. After a few days Tommy said, "My conscience is starting to bother me. I did meet a girl, but the stories about me seducing her are all lies. I did try, but I only got to kiss her a few times. I got bored on the long train trip home and made up the stories."[3]

The guys had believed the stories and were disappointed with Tommy's confession. Several of them thought the stories were true anyway. Bill Dutton said, "I think Tommy was telling the truth in the first place. He told us he was lying to soothe his conscience." They never knew which of Tommy's stories were true.

One thing was evident after Tommy's trip to Michigan: he had shifted gears, and his clarinet playing and his attitude were greatly improved. Prof knew it, and made Tommy first chair in the clarinet section for his senior year.

[1]Broward Coker, Deputy Sheriff
[2]Howard Weems, SHS '40
[3]Bill Dutton, SHS '37

10

"Sebring citizens were as proud of the Newark Bears as they were of their high school band."

---Hy Goldberg, **Newark News**

One of Sebring's big events was the yearly visit of the Newark (New Jersey) Bears baseball team. Major league baseball teams and their minor league farm teams came to Florida each year for spring training. The Bears were the number one farm team for the New York Yankees and players on the Newark roster were one step away from the Yankee club.

Since baseball was America's only national professional sport, and the Yankees were the dominant team in the sport, it was exciting to see future stars of the game and try to guess which ones would become famous.

Polly had friends from New Jersey who came to Sebring to see the Bears play and she welcomed them to her home and entertained them in the tropical garden she had cultivated next to the house. She also escorted them on visits to two local attractions, Highlands Hammock State Park and Bok Tower in Lake Wales. In turn her friends asked Polly to accompany them to the Bears' games at Firemen's Field and she became a baseball fan.

Fireman's Field was a custom-built baseball field with the same dimensions as Yankee Stadium in New York City. It was so large that local ballplayers playing there had little chance of hitting a ball over the outfield fences. There were five white "Xs" painted on the right field fence, just in fair territory. Each "X" was a spot where a major leaguer like Lou Gehrig had knocked a home run over that fence. Big league teams played the Bears in Sebring each year and major leaguers were the only players who had ever hit a ball out of the mammoth park.

Polly became a fixture at the Bears' home games and sometimes made trips to Lakeland or Tampa to see their out-of-town games. When she heard that George Weiss, the General Manager of the Bears, wanted to rent a house in Sebring, she offered her home. It was just what Weiss was looking for and he rented it for the spring training season.[1]

Polly and Tommy moved into the Sebring Hotel where the Bears players were also staying. The players practiced every morning and played a baseball game each afternoon. Once they had seen the movie at the Circle Theater there wasn't anything to do for several nights, until the movie changed. There was a game room off the hotel lobby where the players gathered each evening to play gin rummy and poker. Tommy watched for a few evenings before accepting an invitation to sit in. He had watched his mother play poker and he wasn't afraid to take a chance.

Polly and Tommy were soon favorites of the team and were greeted at the hotel like members of the Bear's official family. It was a common site on a spring afternoon to see Tommy's car speed into the parking lot at Fireman's Field, and skid to a halt that sent a cloud of dust floating out over the diamond where the Bears were playing. The car doors would open and Tommy and his friends would pop out. Tommy stood out from the rest when he wore white flannel trousers, a polo shirt and saddle shoes. The boys would go over to the Bear's dugout and Tommy would introduce his friends to members of the baseball team.

After the Bears returned to New Jersey, Polly and Tommy missed the near-celebrity status they had enjoyed with the team. The Sebring Fire Department had a baseball team in the Orange Belt League, and Tommy and Polly attended the games regularly. Many of Sebring's prominent citizens played for the Firemen, or attended the games regularly. A young man who edited one of the local newspapers played on the team and later wrote about the experience in a book, called *Life in a Putty Knife Factory*. H. Allen Smith was a better writer than he was a baseball player. He recounted in the book a Sunday afternoon when he was, at the last minute, asked to fill in for the star pitcher who couldn't make it to the game. After Smith had allowed a number of runs he heard the team manager pacing up and down the dugout shouting "pain--pain--pain." In fact the manager was shouting "Payne--Payne--Payne" as he lamented the absence of his regular pitcher Payne Sebring.

Tommy was always welcome at the Gustat's home. Paul's father, the band director, saw Tommy often at school, but was also a big influence on his personal life. Prof was the closest thing to a father Tommy had, and Paul and Tommy were almost like brothers.

Paul and Tommy made a summer trip to New Jersey. Tom McGuire welcomed his son and his friend and planned activities for them. He had a driver take them into Manhattan to see the sights.

The chauffeur-driven limousine had seats covered with light tan doe-skin leather, and a glass window separated the driver from the passengers. The boys were agog as they spent the day seeing the city. They were driven through Times Square and Central Park, and went to the top of the Empire State Building, the tallest building in the world. They rode on the Staten Island Ferry, and got a good look at the Statue of Liberty.

Late in the afternoon they met Tommy's father and were driven over the Brooklyn Bridge to Lundy Brothers, a picturesque seafood restaurant overlooking the waters of Sheepshead Bay. Tom insisted that the boys have a lobster dinner, something neither boy had ever had. They were equipped with bibs and claw crackers, and Tom instructed them carefully on the proper way to crack the lobster's shell, remove the tender morsels and dip them in the drawn butter. All the while Tom entertained the boys with jokes and sleight of hand tricks. It was a great day for a couple of kids from Sebring.

The boys next traveled to Lake Hopatcong, New Jersey, where Tommy's aunt and uncle, Stella and Ted Tolson, ran a hotel. The Tolson kids, Al, Ted, and Elizabeth took great pleasure in showing them around Hillcrest, their home and they ended up at the lake which was deep and cold. Tommy and Paul were accustomed to the warm waters of Lake Jackson in Sebring, and this ice-cold water was a refreshing treat to them. There was a raft in the middle of the lake but they were told not to try and swim to it because it was too far out.

Tommy questioned that and insisted that he could easily swim to the raft and back without any problem. "Remember," said Tommy, "we live at the lake all year. That raft is just a trifle to us."

With that Tommy dove from the dock and swam to the raft. The cold water took his breath and he gasped for air all the way out to the raft. When he started the return to shore he could hardly breathe, but his pride wouldn't let him return to the raft for a rest. Halfway back to shore he gasped for air and inhaled a large amount of water. He went under water and thought he was a goner. He was scared. He thrashed to keep his head above the surface. No one on shore understood how much trouble he was having, and they made no move to help him. Through shear determination he kept his head up long enough to get a good breath. He turned on his back and floated for a minute and then paddled to shore.

Tommy confided to Paul, "I thought I was a goner."

Paul said, "With your Irish, I never doubted you'd make it."

Back in Sebring, Polly gave a party for Tommy, Jacob Dunn, and Lamar Hancock. The boys' birthdays were close together and they wanted to celebrate with one big party. There wasn't enough room at anyone's home to accommodate the party, so Polly arranged for the ballroom at the Sebring Hotel. The guest list included over 50 people from Sebring, Avon Park, and Lake Placid.

A record player filled the room with dance music and there were large quantities of food and punch. The boys spiked one punch bowl with gin and spent the rest of the evening keeping the chaperones away from that bowl. The chaperones were pleased when the boys were so polite, and kept their punch cups filled. They were bringing the chaperones punch to be sure that none of them got close to the "loaded" punch bowl.

Polly had the music turned off and the boys and girls paired up for a scavenger hunt. Each couple was given a list of items to collect and bring back. Jean Wagner and Herman Hancock were the first to return with all of the items on the list.[2] The evening was topped off when a giant birthday cake with candles was brought into the darkened room to the singing of "Happy Birthday." All three boys gathered and blew out the candles together.

Over the remainder of the summer Tommy and his friends made frequent trips to Bradenton Beach. Bill Dutton, Malcolm Waters, Herman Hancock, Lamar Hancock, Tommy Weaver, Paul Gustat, Jacob Dunn, Campbell Tappen, Artie Lewis, Chubby Fulton, and Tommy took dates to the beach[3] early in the morning and spent the day swimming, sunning and picnicking. A record player played Artie Shaw, Tommy Dorsey, and Glenn Miller music and they danced barefoot in the sand. Late in the afternoon they returned to Sebring, changed and met at the Hammock Tavern for dinner and dancing until closing time. It was their last summer as high school students, and a summer they'd all remember when times weren't so pleasant.

[1] Newark News, Newark, NJ
[2] Highlands County News
[3] Ibid.

11

They out-talked thee, hissed thee, tore thee
Better men fared thus before thee:
Fired their ringing shot and passed,
Hotly charged---and broke at last.
Charge once more, then, and be dumb!
Let the victors, when they come,
When the forts of folly fall,
Find thy body by the wall.

----"The Last Word" by Matthew Arnold

In the summer of 1937, the Sebring High School Band went to the National School Music Competition Festival for the Southeastern Region, at Winthrop College, in Rock Hill, South Carolina. Although Sebring High School's enrollment dictated that the band compete in the Class "C" competition, they chose to compete in Class "A," the large school category. They were rated "Superior Plus" in all phases of judging: concert, sight reading, marching, and solo performances.[1] School band officials of the Southeastern United States confirmed something Floridians had known for sometime, Sebring's band was one of the finest in America.

At the Sebring firehouse, after Sebring High School had lost a football game they were expected to win, you might hear this statement: "As a football town, Sebring has a damn good band!"

The firehouse in Sebring was more than a place to park fire trucks. It was the home of the Sebring Firemen, a volunteer fire department, and the town's most active civic and, some said, social organization. With a small paid staff, which lived in, the firehouse was always open. It wasn't considered a waste of time, day or night, to lean back in a captain's chair in front of the firehouse. It was shady in the afternoon and with the station doors open, there was always a breeze that passed through the high ceilinged bays. It was the most comfortable spot in town.

Sitting in front of the firehouse was like being a part of a living bulletin board. Everything that went on in town was repeated at the firehouse. Merchants, grovemen, politicians, and the unemployed would drop by during the day to visit a while, and it wasn't unusual for an insurance policy or a used tractor to be sold during a casual visit.

The fact that it was an outstanding fire department in no way prevented it from being a gossip center that would put most women to shame. If anybody in town was "running around," it would probably be discussed at the fire house before there was another call to put out a fire. One popular subject discussed were the activities at the school, which was just a block away. Athletic teams and Sebring's championship band were the most popular subjects.

One evening, a group sat in front of the firehouse discussing world problems. The air was heavy with the smoke of a second round of Tampa Nugget cigars when the subject changed. One of the men asked, "Is the football team going to be any good this year, or are we going to have another championship band?"

"Maybe we'll have a good band and a good football team," suggested one of the optimistic firemen.

"With just a few hundred kids in high school, how could you expect them to have enough people for a good football team and a band? A few years ago some boys would play football in the first half then go in and change clothes and march in the band at the half-time. Coach Melton put a stop to that."

"Prof Gustat works the kids in the band so hard that they don't have time to be in the band and play football, too," said another.

"Prof Gustat has got the likes of Tommy McGuire who will never go out for sports. Let them and the girls play music, and let Herman Hancock and Howard Weems and those guys play football."

"That's where you are wrong," said the first fireman. "Tommy McGuire is going out for football this fall."

A third fireman spoke, "You're crazy. That kid only weighs about 125 pounds. He's a senior and never played a lick of ball. He'll stay in the band and leave the football to the big boys."

"You'd think so," said the first fireman. "But Jim Melton says Tommy is going out. He's telling his regulars to take it easy on him for a few weeks so the boy has a chance to learn something about the game."

"Hell, it isn't his weight or lack of experience I'd worry about. They'll need a separate dressing room for him. I wouldn't be surprised if he squats to take a leak."

"I think you guys are being unfair to the boy. He's never had a father around. He's lived with two women all of his life. I don't think there's anything wrong with him, except maybe he just has a silver spoon in his mouth and dresses a little too fancy."

"Wait till the Freeland boys and some of the others knock him on his ass a few times. Tommy won't last the first week."

Football practice started in August, the hottest and most humid month of the year. Practices were twice a day, 7:00 a.m. and 5:30 p.m. After the first practice the pads never had a chance to dry out from one practice to another. It was no fun at 7:00 in the morning, with sleep still in your eyes, to strap on smelly, mildewed shoulder and hip pads, still

66

wet with the perspiration from the previous afternoon's practice. After a few days the dressing room was really ripe and not too pleasant for someone with "a silver spoon in his mouth."[2]

Practice started with four or five laps around the field, and Tommy was able to handle that part. When they started blocking and tackling exercises, Tommy was at a loss. Jim Melton, the head coach, and Fred Wild, the assistant coach, used terms that the rest of the team understood, but Tommy didn't. Tommy would get near Clarence Campbell and ask, "What does submarine mean?"

Tommy had always had sinus trouble and after a few days of rolling around in the dust his nose ran like a faucet and he was constantly blowing it. The veteran players heeded Coach Melton's request and took it easy on Tommy, but they made jokes about him right to his face and before the week was over, they were calling him "Snotty McGuire." The kids had forgotten about that name in recent years. Now, because he was constantly blowing his nose and was giving them some pretty nasty replies to their barbs, they thought the name was fitting, again.

Tommy wondered why he hadn't listened to his Mother when she had said, "Tommy, you aren't cut out for football. You are too small and you don't have any experience."

Tommy had replied, "Size isn't everything. Besides, Prof told me I could do anything I set my mind to do."

"But son, he meant in the band," argued Polly.

"Mom, that's not what he said. He said, 'anything'."

Maybe she was right, but he couldn't stop now. People called him a coward last year when he had dodged Howard Weems, but the fear of being called a coward wasn't his reason for sticking it out. Tommy had always done what his Mother wanted him to do, and it was time to make decisions for himself. As bad as this was going, he would stick it out, because he'd made the decision.

School started and so did the scrimmages at football practice. The "first few weeks" were over, and Tommy's learning period was unofficially ended. He found out how rough football could be. Now, along with the barbs, the guys expressed their displeasure with Tommy by knocking him flat, play after play.

Tommy would stare back with tears of pain in his eyes. Then he'd line up and take another crushing block on the next play. They took turns blocking him, "I'll get him this time--he won't be back tomorrow."

Coach Melton saw what was going on, but knew that Tommy had to "want it" enough to stick it out. Tommy asked Lamar Hancock, "Do the fellows think I'm yellow?"

Lamar replied, "No, Tommy, they give any new guy a hard time until he proves he can take it. That's just the way it is. The guys are mad about your wise cracks, but they'll get over that."

"Well, you can tell them I'm no quitter," said Tommy. "I'm out there to stay. No matter what!"

The next few days were tough. Tommy was so sore he could hardly walk, but he wouldn't let on even to his Mother. At school, when he saw a football player, he would straighten up and try to look normal. At practice, the battering continued but the conversation in the huddles changed: "That panty-waist little son-of-bitch is tougher than he looks. He can't even stand up, but he crawls back to the line for the next play."

The fun was over, the regulars knew that Tommy was going to "take it." Johnny Freeland said, "I'm taking it easy on him, we've hurt him enough."[3]

By the end of the week Tommy was considered "one of the guys," and was giving some of the fellows a ride home after practice. They knew he wouldn't contribute to the team's winning record, but he had "guts," and they admired him for that.

Prof Gustat was upset with Tommy for risking his new position as first chair of the clarinet section with the possibility of a football injury which might leave him unable to play the clarinet and thus deprive the band of one of its best solo artists. Tommy didn't get to play in the games and so was allowed to go to the dressing room late in the second quarter to change to his band uniform for the half-time show. As it turned out Tommy's biggest moment on the football team would come off the field.

On the Saturday afternoon before Thanksgiving, Tommy was driving past Page's Standard Oil station when somebody yelled, "Hey McGuire, get over here."

Tommy saw Herman Hancock and Johnny Freeland from the football team, did a U-turn, and whipped into the station. "How is your car running?" Hancock asked.

"Pretty good," replied Tommy, "You guys need a ride somewhere?"

Tommy lifted the lid on the red and white Coke box, plunged his hand to the bottom of the icy water, fished out a bottle of Coke and said, "Who wants a Coke, I'm buying."

Tommy stuck the bottle into the opener on the side of the box, snapped the cap off and handed it to Herman Hancock as Johnny Freeland explained, "Tommy, it's time to paint the Red Devil at Avon Park High School. We always do it before the Thanksgiving game, and the game is next Thursday afternoon."

"Damn," said Tommy, "I always wanted to do that."

"Well, this is your chance," said Herman. "What are you doing Tuesday night about ten-thirty?"

"I just happen to be planning a trip to Avon Park," said Tommy.

During the weekend Tommy drove to Avon Park to see where he could park the car near the school without being too obvious. He found a spot a few blocks away near the Coca Cola bottling plant. Tommy wondered why they were just taking one carload of guys to Avon Park but he soon found out that the rest of the team would be protecting Sebring's school from the Avon Park team. The year before they had painted the school's front door red. Then it dawned on him that the Avon Park football team would probably be expecting them at their school. The thought was a little scary.

Clarence comforted him, "The guys wouldn't have asked you if you hadn't shown how tough you are at football practice. You all will probably just waltz in and paint that red devil without any problems. They won't let anything happen to you, you're driving."

Tuesday night Tommy drove downtown and brazenly turned left and drove around the circle in the wrong direction. Herman Hancock and Johnny Freeland and a couple of other guys were waiting under the clock at the Abstract Building. They piled in the car with cans of paint and paint brushes. Tommy screeched off down Ridgewood Drive. Herman said, "Save the fancy driving for the trip home, we don't want to attract any attention now."

On the way out of town, they discussed a plan. They'd enter town by the truck route and quietly cruise past the school. If things looked right they would discreetly park the car, walk to the school and casually paint the red devil--- BLUE.

At the blinker light in Avon Park, Tommy took the truck route. During the day grove trucks, loaded with field crates of oranges, crowded the truck route, but at night they had it to themselves. Just like Sebring, Avon Park was so quiet at night that a car entering the south side of town could be heard on the north side. Tommy slowed down so the straight-eight Pontiac engine purred. He drove beyond Avon Park High School, giving it a wide berth. Then he turned to approach the school from a northerly direction--a move designed to fool any observers. Everyone but Tommy ducked down as they drove past the school. The full moon illuminated the front of the school, and it was apparent that its hated "Red Devil," a four-foot-high figure mounted on the front of the building, was expecting only a quiet night of rest.

Several blocks past the school Tommy turned off the car lights and quietly coasted the car to a stop near the Coca Cola bottling plant. The "coke" plant was easily distinguished even at night because of a giant coke bottle, reportedly the largest coke bottle in the world, which stood towering beside the building.

As the daring band of raiders approached the school an advanced scout was sent out. After peering around the corner for some long minutes, he returned with the expected report--"all clear." The moon was so bright that the trees cast shadows in its light. The raiders scurried from the safety of one black patch of shadow to the safety of the next. It was quiet except for the sound of an occasional night traveler passing through the center of town four or five blocks away. In the shadow of one of the trees the cans of bright blue paint were opened and divided into empty cans which had been brought for that purpose. The target was selected, and they moved out, paint and brushes at the ready. Tommy's heart was beating so loud that he was sure everyone heard it. As they approached the front of the building it seemed too easy. Their feelings were well founded. Dark figures moved from the bushes near the building, and a voice shouted, "Get the Bastards!" It looked like the whole Avon Park football team! Herman Hancock shouted, "Let's get-the-Hell-out-of-here!"

It wasn't going to be easy, fists were flying and they were being pelted with oranges. Tommy had been instructed to flee, in case of trouble. He was to get to the car and get it started! What was he to do with the half gallon of paint he was holding? Only one thing---as a figure approached, ready to land a blow, Tommy pitched the bucket forward. Its contents flashed out in the moon light like a flame from a blowtorch, and amid the screams Tommy knew he had painted "one of the devils."

One by one the boys weaved their way through the yelping and swinging crowd. After this, the game Thursday would be easy, the odds would be even. Tonight the Red Devils had a three-to-one advantage. The Sebring boys left the grounds in all directions, and each with his own pursuers, and each intending to reach the car by his own route-- Tommy heard the cry, "Go get the car!"

After weaving around trees and bushes, Tommy got away and left the campus. He arrived at the car unfollowed. He started the car and circled the school blowing the horn. People were running everywhere, but somehow Tommy slowed down for the right ones and sped up for the wrong ones. After two trips around the school, everyone was accounted for--even though two were still on the running board. Everyone chattered with excitement. The two guys on the running board scrambled through the windows. Tommy noticed in the rear view mirror that a car was following them at a high rate of speed. It could be the Red Devils in a car, or it could be a policeman. They had made quite a disturbance in the quiet of the night, and somebody could have called the police.

Tommy said, "Hold on guys. I'm not waiting to see who that is!"

They whizzed past the blinker light, the beginning of a mile-long straight-away out of town. The white stones of State Road 8 glistened in the bright moonlight and as they rounded a curve, Tommy switched off the car's headlights. There was enough light to find a dirt road which led into an orange grove and Tommy quickly turned off the highway and jammed on the brakes. A few seconds later the other car flashed past and sped toward Sebring.

Everyone hooped and hollered. They had met the challenge, and although they had not painted the famous Avon Park Red Devil, they had looked danger in the eye and they had escaped to laugh about it. No one was hurt, and they surely got blue paint all over the sidewalk. When daybreak came, it would be apparent to all of Avon Park High School that the "Blue Streaks" had struck![4]

After a brief wait, Tommy backed out of the grove, wheeled out onto the highway and treated the "raiders" to a eight minute trip to Sebring, including a 70 mile-an-hour trip over the railroad crossing at Lakemont. When they arrived at the high school the home team rushed out to tell them that they had just fended off the "whole Avon Park football team." The result had been about the same in Sebring as in Avon Park, they had a battle that resulted in a few blows being struck, and the only damage was red paint on the sidewalk.

Thanksgiving afternoon at Firemen's Field the annual Avon Park-Sebring football classic took place. It had the air of an Army-Navy Game. One of the Avon Park football players had a tuft of blue hair that hung from his helmet. The Sebring boys knew he had to be one of the guys they had painted at Avon Park High School two nights before. The Sebring players called him "Blue Boy" across the line of scrimmage to get his goat. After the game, the name stuck, and in Avon Park the poor kid was called "Blue Boy" until he went off to war and returned as a high ranking Army officer and thereafter was known as "Colonel."[5] Down at the firehouse the "Blue Boy" incident brought a lot of discussion. Nobody could be completely sure who painted "Blue Boy," but they were willing to give Tommy part of the credit.

"Who would have guessed, a few months ago, that Tommy McGuire would go out for football, much less go to Avon Park to paint the Red Devil? He has more guts than I thought."

"You remember a few months ago when they painted the sign on Mitchell Ferguson's house? Well, I wouldn't be surprised if Tommy was in the crew that did the painting."

"What they painted was pretty funny: 'Fertile Myrtle'."

"They might have needed Tommy to do the spelling."

After that, Tommy's name was, rightly or wrongly, associated with a two-foot high sign which had been painted on the side of school principal Ferguson's house, after he and Myrtle welcomed the birth of their third child in about as many years.

Before the season ended, Coach Melton found non-critical spots to put Tommy in the line up for a few plays--it was only fair, he had worked hard. Tommy didn't win the friendship of everyone on the team--some of the guys still couldn't stand him. They did have a new degree of appreciation for "the plucky little guy" and they gave him two new nicknames: "Honker" and "Snoz." Tommy thought either of them was better than "Snotty."

On a late fall afternoon members of the band were surprised as they were called to the stage during a chapel exercise at school. Payne Sebring, President of the Sebring Band Association, awarded each of them a gold medal attached to a red, white, and blue ribbon. It was recognition for their top ranking at Rock Hill.

L to R Gene Sebring, Clair Farr, Leon Kahn, Kathryn Emmitt , and Tommy

Jacob Dunn, Betty Tripp, and Tommy McGuire

In West Palm Beach and Tampa, Tommy played solos in state band contests and received top ratings. Betty Tripp, who had graduated two years before, played piano accompaniment for Tommy and other soloists. She spent many hours rehearsing for these performances. Tommy's mother appreciated the hours Betty donated to the band's success and wanted to show her appreciation. Polly arranged for Betty to visit the Polly Prim Beauty Shop to get her hair done before each band trip. Polly paid for the visits.[6]

73

Championship Sebring High School Band. Tommy McGuire first chair clarinet

Later Prof Gustat took Tommy, Gene Sebring, Mark Robinson, Chubby Fulton and Arthur Lewis to Deland for the Florida High School Band Clinic. Because of the Sebring Band's high standing each of the Sebring boys played a solo part in the concert given by the 127-piece band. It was a very proud moment for Prof Gustat and his musicians.

Christmas night the band played a concert of Christmas music in the school auditorium. The auditorium was filled as the citizens of Sebring came out to hear their nationally acclaimed band.

On January 9, 1938, when the band opened its winter concert season at the city pier, Tommy stood at the front of the stage alone, and played the clarinet solo part of "Desolation" by Boccalori Heldreth.[7] He drew warm applause from the crowd. His dream of playing a solo at the Sunday concert had come true. Although Tommy didn't become a football hero in one year, his years of hard work in the band had paid off. It was not the last time that Tommy would make a dream come true through hard work.

The Sebring High School Band's hard work was rewarded, too. In following years they represented Florida in the Mardi Gras Parade in New Orleans, and the Macy's Thanksgiving Parade in New York.

[1]Highlands County News
[2]See Appendix A, How this book was written
[3]Johnny Freeland SHS '38
[4]Lamar Hancock, SHS '38
[5]Leoma Maxwell, Avon Park Historian thought that
"Blue Boy" might have been Bud or Cleland Belin. It
has never been confirmed.
[6]Betty Tripp Burton SHS '36
[7]Highlands County News

12

"As I grew older, and we attended the services at Cedar Lawn
Cemetery, the Watsons always said, 'What a family, the only time we get
together is at funerals.' Somehow, it never seemed a sad time, one we
dreaded to attend, nor did we have a morbid fear of death."

----- Vera Watson Schneider, Tommy's cousin

After graduation from high school Tommy made his annual trek to
New Jersey to visit with his father. When he returned to Florida Tommy
and Polly spent a month at Vero Beach. The cottage was filled with
Tommy's buddies from Sebring. They came in twos or threes, and they
stayed a few days or a week. Polly welcomed them all. She knew some
of them were not really Tommy's friends, but were just taking advantage of a free stay at the beach. "I don't care why they come," she had
once said to Mrs. Campbell. "If they are nice to Tommy, that's all that
matters."

Polly got a severe sunburn and did a disappearing act, retiring to her
room for a couple of days. Everyone thought she was drinking, but they
never talked about it. They had kidded Tommy about it in years past,
but now they just overlooked Polly's behavior--just as Tommy had done
for years. After three days Polly reappeared, and they all acted like
nothing had happened.

Near the end of their stay at Vero Beach Polly took Tommy on several trips to Palm Beach, in search of a proper wardrobe for college. She
said, "It's important that you dress well. You'll be meeting people from
all over, and you don't want them to think you are a hayseed."

Flannel trousers, tweed sports coats, cashmere sweaters, cordovan
and saddle shoes, were all purchased. No Ivy-Leaguer would be dressed
better.

When they returned to Sebring, they make several trips to Wolf
Brothers in Tampa to complete the wardrobe. On one trip she asked
Clarence Campbell to go with them, and she bought him a suit at Wolf
Brothers, too. Clarence was sure that the suit was intended to make
amends for some transgression Polly thought she had committed against
him in the past. It left Clarence puzzled.

Wolf Brothers custom tailored all of the clothes, and there was
never a more demanding customer than Polly. Tommy had always worn
nice clothes and he now had everything a student could ever need, even
formal wear complete with white gloves.

Campbell Tappen spent time with the McGuires and noticed Polly
seemed to say mean things to Tommy without any reason. In later years

he came to think that Polly felt she was being abandoned with Tommy leaving for college and the anger was her way of expressing her feeling of the impending loss.

When time came to leave for Georgia Tech they loaded the car to the roof with tennis rackets, golf clubs, new luggage and a new record player. Tommy couldn't take his special collection of broadcast transcriptions of classical music on 16-inch records or the turntable required to play them. He had new records and a new player.

The first day they traveled to Robert Watson's home in north Florida and spent the night. The following afternoon they checked into one of Atlanta's finest hotels, the Henry Grady. It was a gracious hotel, with outstanding furnishings, and courteous service. The extra water faucet in the bathroom was ice cold drinking water. How fancy could it get?

Polly loved being in a city. Atlanta was quite a cosmopolitan city with fine restaurants, theaters, and music. The people dressed well, and the city bustled. It was exciting. It had a spark of life that was missing in Central Florida. The **Atlanta Journal** was more like the **New York Times** than the **Tampa Tribune**.

The next few days were spent shopping and testing Atlanta's finest restaurants. Polly was so happy to be alone with her son for a few days, away from the ever watchful eyes of Sebring. They took cabs everywhere and both of them enjoyed the excitement of the city. It was a chance to wear fancy clothes, eat fancy food, and spend money without raising a single eyebrow.

When the day came for Tommy to check into the dorm at Georgia Tech, they were both sorry. Tommy couldn't remember seeing his mother as happy as she was for those few days and as she prepared to leave he asked her to come back and visit soon. Polly said she'd love to come back sometime and go to the Atlanta Symphony. They made a date.

Tommy was soon into school activities and he loved it. Nobody knew anything about him or his family. It was a chance for him to make new friends based on who he was, and not for what he had. They would like him or dislike him just for himself, and not for his boats, pool tables, or his automobile, which had been sold.

He took advantage of fraternity rushing to visit various houses. Along the way he ran into Tommy Weaver who had graduated from Sebring High School a year earlier, and had spent a year at Bolles Academy in Jacksonville, and was now a freshman at Tech. They went through rush week together and both of them wanted to pledge Beta Theta Pi Fraternity. When the pledge invitations were sent out Tommy

Weaver received a bid to pledge Beta Theta Pi. Tommy McGuire did not.

Tommy Weaver said, "Maybe it's a mistake. I'm sure they meant to pledge you, too."

"No, it isn't a mistake," said McGuire. "I asked them. They said I was black-balled."

"So, are you going to join another fraternity?" asked Weaver.

"I don't know," replied McGuire. "I had other bids, but I'm not interested. I guess I'll be an independent."

McGuire's name came up at the next chapter meeting of Beta Theta Pi when one of the brothers stood and said, "I'd like to ask for another vote on Tommy McGuire."

A second brother said, "Doesn't McGuire know he isn't wanted? He's hanging around the house like he lives here."

The first brother said, "He knows he has been black-balled. His friend Tommy Weaver says he had other bids but isn't interested in any other fraternity."

A third brother said, "He's so dammed pushy, too aggressive, and he wears expensive clothes. Let's tell him to get lost."

Another brother who had been silent stood and spoke, "Are you guys so sure that he should get lost? How many of you would hang around after you had been black-balled? That says something special to me. Maybe he isn't perfect. Who among us is? Weaver says he is a good guy---just comes on a little strong."

The first brother said, "The aim of our fraternity is to help each other for the betterment of all. Let's pledge him and help him change for the better. If we do, he'll be an asset to the fraternity. He wants to be a Beta and I think he'll be a damn good Beta. I say let's vote again!"

On the next secret vote the two black marbles required for a black--ball disqualification never dropped into the balloting box. McGuire was pledged and Jeff Hooker became his pledge father. He did not have to be forced to take part in fraternity activities. Many pledges had to be told to show up for events. McGuire did not. It made no difference if it were a house party or a clean-up party, he showed up and took part.

Tommy McGuire and Tommy Weaver tried out for the Georgia Tech marching band and were both accepted at once. The band uniforms were rather drab and dour compared to Sebring's sparkling outfits but McGuire was proud to be in the band, and he had a portrait taken in the uniform, and sent a copy to his mother and father.

Most of Prof Gustat's "kids" played in college bands wherever they went to school. Campbell Tappen was in the University of Florida band and came to Atlanta with the Gator football team for a game with

Georgia Tech. Tech had a powerful team with a national reputation and the Florida band had came along to play and cheer at a sure slaughter of the "Fighting Gators."

Tommy McGuire in his Georgia Tech band uniform

The game was played in a driving rain storm. The Florida and Georgia Tech bands were dismissed after marching at half-time, so they could get out of the rain. McGuire took Campbell to his dorm room which overlooked Grant Field where the game was being played. They opened the windows and took turns cheering their teams. Tommy had a few Tech band members with him and they overwhelmed "Tap" with school yells and their own rendition of "Rambling Wreck from Georgia Tech." Campbell could only answer with Florida's favorite cheer--- "Gator Bait, Gator Bait." The underdog Gators played over their heads and tied nationally ranked Georgia Tech, 0-0. Campbell Tappen and the Florida fans were happy. McGuire and his Tech friends were not.

By the second semester McGuire had Georgia Tech and Atlanta under control. Coley Lewis, a friend of his mother's back in Sebring, was a former resident of Atlanta, and had made arrangements for Tommy to have privileges at the Atlanta Athletic Club. McGuire had arranged his classes so that he was free most afternoons. He would go by the Beta house and find a brother, Andy Speed, and the two of them would walk down to the Atlanta Athletic Club. Tommy usually had a bowl of French onion soup and a Swiss cheese on rye for lunch. Not exactly items you might find on the menu at the Sebring Cafe, or many other southern restaurants of the day. Then, the two of them would spend most of the afternoon shooting pool. Tommy won most of the pool matches.[1]

Beta Theta Pi Fraternity, Georgia Tech. Tommy is second from right -back row

At the fraternity house ping pong was a popular pastime and Tommy soon got a reputation as a killer ping pong player. His reflexes were so quick and his desire to win was so apparent that he was soon conceded the ping pong championship of the chapter.

Tommy acquired a nickname. Because his initials were T. B., for Thomas Buchanan, many of the guys called him "T.B." Not so much because of the initials, but because someone had pointed out that Tommy was so skinny that he looked like he had Tuberculosis. Tommy didn't care. His father was often called "T.B." and Tommy liked it a lot better than his old high school nicknames: "Snotty McGuire," "The Snoz," or "Honker."

On Sunday evenings when the fraternity did not serve meals, Tommy would get a friend, George Kehr, and another brother or two and they would go to Herron's, a restaurant on Marietta Street, and have supper. Tommy seemed to have more money than the other guys, and like his mother, enjoyed spending it on others. He always picked up the check.[2]

Social life at Tech was good. There were many activities, but participation was sometimes difficult because Georgia Tech was a boy's school and there was a shortage of girls to date. Social life was an important feature of belonging to a fraternity because the brothers knew local girls and could fix-up pledges with dates--often a friend of a friend. Sometimes the girl had "a terrific personality" and might not be much in the "looks" department. Tommy surprised everyone by showing up with beautiful girls which nobody had ever met. Before long brothers and pledges alike were asking, "Does that girl you were out with last Friday have a sister?"

For years, Tommy had secretly nursed a crush on Carol Russell, a beautiful young lady in Sebring. In March, Tommy asked Polly to call Mrs. Russell, in Sebring, and see if she would allow her daughter to attend a house party at Georgia Tech. Mrs. Russell was pleased that Tommy would ask her permission before asking Carol.

Carol was surprised by the invitation. She had graduated from school two years before Tommy, and remembered dancing with him a few times at the Hammock Tavern, and had attended a party or two at the McGuire's home. She was intrigued with the idea of a big weekend in Atlanta, but hoped Tommy's dancing had improved in the last few years. She remembered how polite Tommy was, but dreaded a whole evening of dancing with him.

Tommy sent Carol a round-trip train ticket to Atlanta, and at her request, made reservations for her so she could stop overnight in Jacksonville, to visit her sister, Betty. When she arrived in Atlanta, Tommy met her with a car he had rented for the weekend. He took her claim checks and picked up her luggage and loaded it into the car. When they arrived at the fraternity house, where the boys had moved out for the weekend, he took her to the housemother for an introduction. Carol was very impressed with Tommy's manners and thoughtfulness.

Tommy and Carol were very popular the whole weekend. With one of the only automobiles available, they made several trips to every event, circling back to the fraternity house to pick up a second or third load of people.

The Saturday night dance featured Hal Kemp's Band with singer Skinny Ennis. It was thrilling to dance while Ennis sang "Got a Date with an Angel" and his other hit songs. Carol didn't think Tommy's dancing had improved much. It was the custom for others to "cut-in, "and she danced with almost all of Tommy's fraternity brothers. By the end of the evening she had new respect for Tommy's dancing ability. Tommy took Carol's dance program to the bandstand and got Kemp, Ennis and other band members to autograph it as a keepsake for her scrapbook. Carol boarded the train Sunday to return home after a wonderful weekend which she and Tommy would remember for a long time, but they never dated again.[3]

Tommy enrolled in the ROTC program to earn a reserve Army commission while one attended college. Most of the guys in the program viewed it as insurance against being a foot-slogging infantryman if a war ever started. ROTC cadets were issued uniforms which they wore for the weekly parade. Tommy had always worn uniforms well, and had looked natty in them since the day Polly had dressed him in a sailor suit at age five. He made a good impression on his ROTC instructors and its student leaders, and they encouraged him to volunteer for extra duties.

His fellow students thought he was an "eager-beaver," but Tommy didn't care. When they discussed it, he explained, "If I can be a leader, why should I be a follower? Don't worry, guys, when I'm running the Corps of Cadets I'll lookout for you 'troops'."

When the school year ended Tommy had a great sense of accomplishment. He had made a new life for himself, full of exciting new experiences. He was part of a great social group, Beta Theta Pi. They were like a new family. He was excelling in ROTC and he had a good chance for advancement in the Corps. He had at last been on his own without his mother's control or reputation. He had a new life and he enjoyed it.

With school out for the summer Tommy went alone to Ridgewood, New Jersey. He stayed with his father and renewed acquaintances with the men at his father's Packard automobile agency at 51 Chestnut Street. Since he had been a small child Tommy had always wandered through the garage and the lot inspecting every car he saw. He followed his tradition of many years and spent hours roaming the car lots. When he spotted a special one Tommy would climb in and sit, adjust the seats to fit his economical frame and try the gadgets. Often, when the keys were in the car, he would start the engine.[4] He felt closer to his father, when he was around cars. Besides his father's "Irish," Tommy had also inherited his father's love of automobiles, and the sound of a big engine running. There was no sound like that of a well-tuned Packard engine.

On one occasion, Tommy borrowed a car and took a ride along the Hackensack River, where his mother, years ago, had driven him and his

T. B. McGuire Motors, Packard Dealership, Ridgewood, New Jersey

cousins in her open touring car. Tommy remembered sitting in the back seat while Polly drove at the break-neck speed of 35 or 40 miles an hour. The kids had thought they were flying. Tommy held his hand out the window and let it fly up and down in the wind as he had done when he was a child. He had never understood the effect of the wind forcing his hand up or down, depending on which direction he pointed it. Now that he was studying engineering he understood, but now it seemed very important, instead of a childhood pastime.

He wandered toward Paterson and along the way he recognized Cedar Lawn Cemetery as the place his grandparents were buried. He remembered coming there for his grandmother's funeral and now as he entered the grounds he remembered coming there as a child. He drove around until he found the Watson's plot. It had a large Weeping Willow in the center and he wondered if that could be the tree they planted when he was a small child.

He remembered, many years before, they had met one Sunday afternoon, at the Watson's big house for a "surprise." The Watson's Pierce Arrow had led a caravan of family cars. They had come to this exact spot, and his grandmother had announced to everyone's surprise, including her husband's, "I have purchased this large family plot and there is room here for all of us." Before anyone could say a thing, Neil, her chauffeur, had removed a shovel from the trunk of the car and started digging a hole. A Weeping Willow had been delivered, and awaited planting. Dora made a small dedication speech, the tree was planted,

82

and the burial plot was officially the Watson's. The grounds looked more like a park than a cemetery.

Uncle Charles, following orders, produced a basket of hors' d'oeuvres, and a large thermos of cocktails for the adults, and sandwiches and lemonade for the children. As the children ate and played, the adults surveyed the land, marked off plots, using broken tree limbs for the boundaries. The children had taken an interest, and Tommy remembered saying, "This is where I want my room."

Uncle Charles claimed a spot, and stretched out on the ground and crossed his arms on his chest. Tommy, Vera, and Al joined in, laying on either side of their uncle and crossing their arms over their chests. Laughter rang out over the usually quiet grounds of Cedar Lawn as the youngsters kept changing their "rooms."

Over the years, they had visited here, to see how the tree had grown, and it had never been a place to be sad. It didn't seem so now either, even with his Grandparents "in their rooms." Tommy remembered when his Grandfather had been the first buried here, his grandmother and mother had dressed in beautiful white afternoon dresses instead of the traditional somber black.[5]

Tommy couldn't help but think how his grandmother had run everyone's life, as much as they would let her, and she had even planned for them after death. Tommy's thoughts shifted to his Uncle Charles, and the way he had never flown after the war because his mother objected.

Tommy left the cemetery and drove to Paterson, to visit with his Uncle Charles. They discussed flying as always, but now the young college student asked his childhood hero what he thought about the possibilities of war.

Uncle Charles told Tommy he didn't think things looked too good. Tommy said he was fearful that his Coastal Artillery training at college would sentence him to a gun emplacement if a war came. He told his uncle he was going to join up to fly at the first sign of war.

"What does your mother say about that?" asked Charles.

Tommy replied, "I don't discuss it with her. She'd give me a hard time, just like your mother did when you wanted to join up. She is easily upset these days. Now that Grandmother Watson isn't there, it doesn't take much to make her a little crazy. She misses her mother and now that Vera is married, she never sees any of the family. I wish you two would make up. She misses you."

Charles consoled Tommy, "I know she has been through a lot. I've tried to talk to her on the phone, but she is still mad about that mix-up when your grandmother died. I'll give her a call one of these days."

A few days later Tommy was joined in Ridgewood by Bob Stephens, a friend from Sebring, who was spending the summer in Washington, D.C.. Bob had moved to Sebring, after graduating from high school in Knoxville. Tommy had met him at the City Drug Store where Tommy was a frequent customer and Bob was a soda jerk.

Tommy and Bob spent three days at the New York World's Fair. Then, with a Packard borrowed from Tommy's father, they set out with one of Tommy's Ridgewood friends to visit Maine. The friend's family had a beautiful mansion on Penobscot Bay. Tommy was a demon at the wheel of the Packard. They whizzed up to Maine, and only by luck avoided being arrested for high speed driving. They had a great couple of days, boating and eating lobster, before they returned to Ridgewood, where they parted. Bob returning to Washington, and Tommy eventually to Sebring.[6]

Back in Sebring, Tommy and Paul Gustat lifted weights in Tommy's garage every day. Paul, being a larger person than Tommy, was able to lift the barbell easier than Tommy, and one day pressed 140 pounds. Tommy vowed that he, too, would lift the 140 pounds. He struggled, but couldn't do it. Paul saw a glare of "Irish determination" in his eyes. He had seen the look before. He knew that Tommy would do it if it killed him. Paul remembered the near fatal swim to the raft, in New Jersey, a few summers before. This was no different--Tommy would do it because he said he would.

"You better forget it, Tommy, at least until you've worked up to it," said Paul.

"The hell you say," said Tommy. "If you can lift it, so can I."

Tommy tried once again, with a loud grunt, and he swung the weights up into a press, and then dropped them loudly to the floor. "Damn, I busted a gut."[7]

Tommy was gripping his abdomen. Indeed, he had "busted a gut". He had a hernia from the lift, which would eventually require surgery, but he bragged about the lift the rest of the summer

[1]Andy Speed, Beta Theta Pi, Ga. Tech '42
[2]George Kehr, Beta Theta Pi, Ga. Tech '42
[3]Carol Russell Gentile, SHS '36
[4]Joan Mallon, friend of Thomas B. McGuire, Sr.
[5]Vera W. Schneider, McGuire's cousin
[6]Bob Stephens
[7]Paul Gustat, SHS '40

13

Chem-ur-gy (kem'ur je), n. chemistry concerned with the industrial use of organic substances, esp. from farm produce.

Tommy entered his second year at Georgia Tech with enthusiasm. He loved being with his friends at the Beta house, and he loved being in Atlanta. He continued to be the ping pong champ of the fraternity and took up contract bridge with a passion. He worked hard at ROTC where his talents were appreciated. He had done well in the Reserve Officers Training Corps his freshman year, and he had been thinking about it all summer. His hard work paid off and he got promotions in the cadet corps.

Football season opened with Georgia Tech playing at the University of Florida. Tech was still smarting over the previous year's 0 - 0 tie game, which had been played in a rain storm. It had thrown them off, and they had been tied again 0 - 0 later in the season by their arch rival, Georgia. They blamed the Florida Gators for both losses and they arrived in Gainesville, determined to make them pay for the year before. Tommy was determined to witness the slaughter and to rub it in. He showed up in Gainesville, with a car and a date. Campbell Tappen was shocked---cars were rare at Florida, but dates were even more unusual. Gainesville was a small town, and the school was all male. Dates were usually imported from Florida State College for Women in Tallahassee, 150 miles away. Tap never found out where Tommy got the car or the date.

The game was played in bright sunlight, and Florida's only chance against the powerhouse from Atlanta was the hope that the heat would tire the "Rambling Wrecks". A stadium full of Florida fans interlocked arms and swayed to and fro as they sang "We Are The Boys From Old Florida," but the effort went unrewarded as Tech beat Florida 21-7.

Later in the year Tommy had a visit from Claude Hamrick, who was a senior at the University of Florida. He had caught a ride to Atlanta with one of his professors. Claude graduated from Sebring High School in 1936, two years before Tommy, and had also been a clarinetist in the band. He and Tommy had played a lot of music together, and he had often visited Tommy's apartment in Sebring, to play pool and ping pong. He was looking for a job and wanted to talk to some CPA firms in Atlanta. Then he wanted to visit his fiancee, Laura Green, a Georgia girl, whom he had met when she was visiting the Stephens, in Sebring. She lived in Smyrna, about 15 miles outside of Atlanta. Tommy said, "No problem. We will rent a car and I'll drive you ."

Claude went from firm to firm but didn't find anybody hiring. Then they drove to Smyrna. At the Green's house on Love Street, Tommy made himself right at home. While Claude and Laura sat on the front porch, Tommy sat and talked to Claude's future mother-in-law, Mrs. Green. She was interested in his course of study at Georgia Tech. When she learned that he was taking chemistry, she asked if it involved "chemurgy."

Without batting an eye Tommy said, "No, while I am studying chemistry, I won't be studying any of its application to agriculture. I'm studying Aeronautical Engineering."

"I'm surprised that you know what chemurgy is," said Mrs. Green. "I haven't known many people who knew it involved chemistry. You may study it later, as it does involve industrial use of organic materials."

"I don't mean to disagree with you," said Tommy. "It's my understanding that it involves only farm produce."

"You are partly right," stated Mrs. Green, who was a school teacher, and was sure of this funny word's meaning. "Farm produce is organic, but chemurgy isn't limited to it. Organic materials also come from other sources."

The words got sharper, and Mrs. Green and Tommy were soon in an argument loud enough to bring the love birds in from the front porch. Tommy was sure of the word's meaning but he apologized. So did Mrs. Green, who knew she was right. She was impressed that a college sophomore even knew the word.[1]

On their way back to Atlanta, Claude said, "We've driven a lot of miles today. We'll owe a lot for mileage."

Tommy said, "Don't worry, I have a way of reducing it."

"What are you going to do, disconnect the speedometer cable and turn it back?" asked Claude.

"No, we can't do anything that crude--besides they have a seal on the cable," said Tommy. "Remember, you are at one of the world's greatest engineering schools. We don't want to take a chance of breaking the seal. We will execute the famous 'auto reversal mileage minimizer maneuver.'"

"It sounds like chemurgy to me," said Claude.

Tommy went to the car, removed the jack from the trunk, and jacked up the rear wheels of the car so that they were off the ground. Then he started the car and put it into reverse. They watched the speedometer for a few minutes and sure enough it was turning backward.

Tommy said, "We mustn't take off too much."

Tommy found a pledge and had him watch the car while he and Claude went to wash up before supper. When they turned the car in to the rental agency there was a minimum mileage charge due. Much less than it might have been without Tommy's engineering maneuver.[2]

Later in the year Polly visited Atlanta and she and Tommy planned to attend the opera although it was the weekend of a big school dance. When Tommy's date couldn't make it to the opera, he invited one of his fraternity brothers, a music lover, to go instead.

Tommy and his friend called at the hotel and surprised Polly by presenting her with an orchid corsage. Polly, in her mink stole, and the two young men dressed in tuxedos made a handsome trio. When they arrived at the concert hall Tommy's friend noticed that all the men, including Tommy, where wearing white gloves and he said, "I'm embarrassed, Tommy, I forgot my gloves."

Tommy thought a minute and said, "Don't worry, take my right hand glove and put it on. Put your left hand in your pocket. I'll wear the other glove and keep my bare hand in my pocket too. Nobody will notice."

After the concert the two young men escorted Polly back to her hotel. They hung around for a while and Polly thought Tommy had something on his mind. She thought, "Maybe he needs money."

Finally Tommy said, "Mother, I guess the orchid will go bad just sitting here in the hotel room."

Polly replied, "I guess you are right, it should be kept in a refrigerator to keep it fresh. What do you have in mind?"

Tommy stammered, "Well, I was thinking, since it's going to go bad anyway, maybe it would be better if I gave it to my date for the dance tomorrow night. I'm a little short of funds."

Polly was amused. "Tommy must be growing up," she thought. "It's the first time he has ever done anything to save money."

At year's end Tommy survived a marathon bridge game which was played at the fraternity day and night during final exams and, before he left school, got some good news. His hard work in ROTC had paid off. He had been selected to be the Sergeant Major of the Corps. There was only one Sergeant Major, and Tommy was going to be it for his junior year. It also foretold a command position for him in his senior year. He undoubtedly would be one of the handful of student officers who would run the Corps. He might even find himself the Commander of the Corps.

When Tommy got to Sebring he was uncomfortable. Polly had found it impractical to live alone in her home, which required two servants to take care of the house and grounds. She had moved into the Sebring Hotel as a permanent resident and Tommy didn't enjoy living there for the summer. He missed being in the house near the lake and he spent most of the summer traveling. They rented a cottage at Daytona Beach, but it wasn't the same without friends about. In the late summer,

Tommy packed up to leave Sebring early. He wasn't due in Atlanta for a week, but he had an invitation from his Uncle Bob to stop in Melrose, Florida, and do a little fishing and hunting.

Tommy got out his Fox Sterlingworth double barrel shotgun and cleaned it. Uncle Charles had given him the gun on his 15th birthday, but he hadn't used it for several years. Tommy always remembered his uncle saying when he gave him the gun: "Take good care of this gun and it'll last a lifetime. Teddy Roosevelt always used a Fox Sterlingworth shotgun just like this."[3]

Tommy and his uncle were out in a boat "drowning some worms" when Tommy told him about his appointment as Sergeant Major of the cadet corps. Then he confided, "I'm going to take flying lessons as soon as I get back to school."

"Does your Mother know that?" asked Uncle Bob.

"No sir, she doesn't. I'm afraid she'd keep me from flying like my grandmother kept Uncle Charles from flying."

"Mother did keep Charles from flying," said Uncle Bob. "Polly protested about mother controlling her life, but she controlled everybody, too. Neither of them realized they were doing it. They were just looking out for the people they loved. I know you took the brunt of it."

"Well, I didn't mind it when I was young, but I'm old enough now to make up my own mind," said Tommy.[4]

Before Tommy left Melrose, he borrowed some "flying" money from his Uncle and promised, "I'll pay you back when my next trust fund payment comes in."

At school Tommy went about his duties as Sergeant Major of the Cadet Corps, and looked for a place to take flying lessons. Tommy borrowed a car and he and his fraternity brothers drove to one of their favorite haunts, the Varsity Drive-in, on North Street, near the Georgia Tech campus. As they entered there were four or five Negro men standing by the driveway. Tommy slowed the car and one of the men, wearing a white coat and a turban, jumped onto the car's running board and rode with them until Tommy pulled into a parking spot.

Swami was the star of the drive-in and picked Tommy's car because he was sure he would get a big tip. The young man hopped off of the running board, bowed, and said, "Good evening Mr. McGuire. What may I serve you this fine night?"

"Evening Swami. What do you have?" asked Tommy.

These were the magic words and the young man bowed again, and started reciting the menu in a sing-song, rapid-fire and non-stop delivery. It took but a minute for him to cover everything from chili dog, to steak, to peach pie to frosted orange drink.

When the recitation was over they ordered a tray full of food and sat back to enjoy the world's largest drive-in. This was a right of passage for Georgia Tech students. When they finished eating, Tommy flashed his lights and Swami came and took away the tray and a large tip.

Across town, Howard Weems, Tommy's old nemesis from Sebring, started as a freshman at Emory College. Tommy Weaver was busy playing trombone with the much heralded Emory Jazz band, although he was still a student at Tech. In Gainesville, Florida, Paul Gustat started his freshman year at the University of Florida.

When the University of Florida football team came to Atlanta, to play Georgia Tech, Paul Gustat was with the Gator Band. Tommy went down and met the Gator bus late in the evening. Tommy escorted Paul to a battered old jalopy he was driving and said, "I'm going to take you out on the town."

Paul asked. "Where did you get the Rambling Wreck?"

"I borrowed it from the handyman who works over at the fraternity house," answered Tommy. "Thank God it doesn't have doors. I discovered on the way over here that the brakes are shot. We may have to drag our feet to stop it."[5]

They drove the hilly streets of Atlanta as Tommy gave Paul a tour. He was constantly shifting gears to slow the car, and they did have to jump out of the open doors several times to stop it. They stayed out most of the night.

The next afternoon at Grant Field, Florida upset Georgia Tech by a 16 to 7 score. It didn't seem as important to Tommy this time. He had other things on his mind.

The following week Tommy went to an airport, south of Atlanta, and made arrangements to take flying lessons. It was a strange field located between two large hills, and the center of the runway dipped at least a hundred feet lower than either end. It looked like the back of a sway-back horse. It made no difference to Tommy, he had made up his mind that he was going to fly, and this would be the place he'd start.

By the time he and Tommy Weaver traveled home for Christmas, McGuire had taken a few flying lessons and told his friend about it, "Tommy, you've got to try it. Ever since I took those plane rides on the Ford Tri-motor down in Sebring, I've known I had to fly. I feel it even more now. I'm thinking about enlisting in the Army at the end of the year, if I can get into Air Cadets."

"Aren't you rushing things a little?" asked Weaver.

"I can't keep my mind on school any more. The news is so bad. I think we are going to be at war soon and I'm afraid that I might not get a choice if I wait," said Tommy,

89

Tommy McGuire's 1940 Photo Christmas card, with his dog

In Sebring, Tommy and his friends got together one night, as had been the custom, on Kenilworth Beach. A bonfire roared as they drank a few beers and chatted about school. Tommy's eyes sparkled as he told them about his flying lessons. Like most young American men in 1940, they were interested in flying, and they wanted to hear about it.

Tommy sat on the pier and started talking, "Guys, it's everything I dreamed it would be. Someday I'm going to be a fighter pilot in the Air Corps. My instructor tells me I'm a natural---I'll solo soon." Nobody

90

said anything. They stared into the black sky as Tommy told about his dreams. Someday, each of them might also be flying an airplane!

Christmas night the Weavers invited Polly and Tommy to come to their house for eggnog. Mary Weaver, knowing that they were living at the Sebring Hotel, wanted them to come for a family Christmas dinner, but Polly wouldn't hear of it.

When the McGuires came into the house, Mr. Weaver asked, "Have you had a nice Christmas?"

"Yes sir," replied Tommy, "Only one bad thing about living in a hotel, there's no turkey to nibble on after dinner."

Mrs. Weaver said, "Go in the kitchen, turn left and open the refrigerator, and let your conscience be your guide."

Polly was horrified and said, "Tommy, don't you dare!"

"Come on Polly," said Mrs. Weaver, "these boys don't ever get to raid the ice box at school. Eating leftover turkey is half the fun of being home for Christmas."[6]

The two Toms vanished into the kitchen and gave the Christmas turkey a working over while the adults sat in the living room and chatted over homemade eggnog dusted with freshly ground nutmeg.

In February 1941, Tommy read an article in an Atlanta paper which said the Royal Air Force was welcoming Americans into their ranks to help defend England from German bombings. He went to a Western Union office and sent a wire to the British Consulate in Jacksonville, Florida, asking how he could volunteer. Two days later he received a letter thanking him. Enclosed was an RAF application form. Tommy quickly filled it out and returned.

On February 26 an Eastern Airlines plane approaching the Atlanta Airport, in a late-night rainstorm, crashed near the small village of Morrow, Georgia. By the next morning it was known that the President of the airline, and America's World War Ace of Aces, Eddie Rickenbacker, had been aboard the airplane.

Eight of the 16 people aboard the plane died in the first passenger plane crash in the history of Eastern Airlines. Rickenbacker survived although he was severely injured. He was credited with saving the lives of those who survived when he talked the other passengers out of lighting a match near the gasoline soaked wreckage.

Tommy bought a copy of a special midday issue of the **Atlanta Constitution** which recounted the details of the accident. He wrote his uncle and enclosed the news clippings which listed Captain Eddie's injuries as: a broken hip, many broken ribs, a broken elbow, a one-inch-deep dent in his forehead, and an eye that was liberated from its socket.

As fate would have it, Rickenbacker was a patient in the same hospital as an old friend, Ernest Norris, president of the Southern Railroad. Ironically, Mr. Norris was in the hospital as the result of a train wreck on his own railroad.

Not once did Tommy relate the airline tragedy to his own flying lessons. He thought several times about going to the hospital to see Mr. Rickenbacker, but he could never work up the courage to do it.

Weeks later Tommy got a letter from the RAF. They appreciated his application but needed experienced pilots who could go into action against the German Air Force with a minimum of training, in what Winston Churchill eventually called "The Battle of Britain."

Tommy resolved to take a different course, and when school ended, he bade his friends farewell and told them he was joining the Army Air Corps. He never considered the possibility that he might not be accepted by the Army.

While America's Ace of Aces still lay recuperating in Atlanta's Piedmont Hospital, a few miles away, a quiet, unheralded Georgia Tech student, who had taken a few hours of flight instructions, decided to forfeit a position of rank he had earned in ROTC, and delay his senior year of college to venture forth and make his own mark in aviation history. Who could have guessed that his adventures would exceed in many ways those of a man he greatly admired--Eddie Rickenbacker?

[1] Claude Hamrick, SHS '36

[2] Ibid.
[3] Paul Gustat, SHS '40
[4] Vera W. Schneider
[5] Paul Gustat, SHS '40
[6] Mary Weaver

14

"We all knew we were going to be in the Army one way or another. I was working as a school band director and I had tried to get a commission as a band director but I didn't have any luck. Tommy talked me into going to Hendricks Field for the air cadet exam--we both passed."

------Albert "Chubby" Fulton, SHS classmate

Polly was upset. She and Tommy argued loudly in her room at the Sebring Hotel. It had been done. Just like Polly had defied her own mother, when she had married, Tommy had joined the Army Air Corps and hadn't asked his mother. The Army had lowered the age requirements for entry into cadets, and Tommy had been able to sign up for flight training without his mother's consent.

Tommy and Chubby Fulton, a classmate from high school, had talked about it. With selective service going full steam they both thought they might be drafted sooner or later. Chubby was directing a school band in Ft. Myers, and didn't have the possibility of a deferment. He had tried to use his directorship position to get a commission in the Army as a band director. He told Tommy, "All of the big band leaders are getting those jobs. I'm going to end up carrying a rifle, and I know it."

"Don't be too sure, Chubby. Come with me to Hendricks Field and take the air cadet exam," said Tommy.

Hendricks Field was still under construction south of Sebring, near the shore of Lake Istokpoga, on mostly undeveloped land. This new Army air field was part of America's massive military build-up anticipating another world war. Sebring and county officials had traveled to Washington to lure the Army to this site so the area might enjoy some of the economic advantages of a prewar boom. The county was so crowded with construction workers that every available hotel room and every rentable room in private homes had been taken. Tommy and Chubby had to fight construction traffic out DeSoto City road and beyond on the first trip either of them had ever made to the air field.

Chubby said, "I'm still not sure what I'm doing taking this exam. I don't know anything about flying."

"Don't worry, you'll pass it, and you'll learn to fly. It beats the devil out of being drafted," said Tommy.

The exam was grueling, but they both passed, and Tommy accepted a July entry date. Chubby would go later.

Now, Tommy was trying to explain it to his mother. "You're just like your mother, you want to run everybody's life. You fought your mother because she always thought she knew what was best for you. I'm doing the same thing you did--I'm sticking up for myself. I've been flying in Atlanta anyway. I might as well go in the Army and let them pay for my flight training. I don't want to be a civilian when everyone else is in the Army. Your mother never let us forget that Uncle Charles had been in the service and my Dad never was."

There was a long silence. Polly knew she had lost. First her father had died a long painful death, and then her mother had gone suddenly, causing alienation and a falling-out among her family. Now she was losing the only one she had left. Tommy was literally flying from the nest. At least she'd lose with style. She said, "Tommy, I know you're right. I used to feel like my mother was smothering me, and I swore I'd never do that to you. Your Uncle Charles used the war to get out of my mother's grasp, and then came right back home, and let her do it to him all over again. He didn't fly, just to please her, and he never married either because he couldn't find a girl she liked. I don't mind your going in the army as much as I mind your flying."

Tommy argued, "We're going to be in a war soon. Wouldn't you rather have me fly than be in an artillery battery somewhere?"

"Your Uncle Charles knows people in the military," said Polly. "If he spoke to someone he might be able to get you a good job in Washington, or maybe even right here at Hendricks Field."

"Mother, don't you dare." said Tommy. "I want to fly, and I can't do that sitting behind a desk. I'm going to New Jersey to visit Dad, and I'm going to tell Uncle Charles to stay out of this, even if you ask him behind my back."

"I'll leave things as they are," said Polly. "I am going to open the house for your last few weeks at home. When you get back from New Jersey I'll be living there. If you want to invite some friends from college we will have a place for them to stay, and we'll have some fun."

In Ridgewood, New Jersey, Tom McGuire seemed happy when his son told him that he was going into the Army. Although he had never been in the Army himself, Tom thought that the military would be good for his son.

"So, I guess your mother had a fit about your joining the Army," mused Tommy's father. "Did you tell her I've been giving you money for flying lessons?"

"No, Dad, I didn't tell her anything about the money. She was upset enough about the Army. She's known for several years that I wanted to take flying lessons, but I guess she never thought that I'd join the Army to do it. I had to have a hernia operation and she always thought that would keep me out of the service."

A few days later Tommy approached his father on another subject, "Dad, I noticed you've got a good looking brown and tan Packard convertible out on the lot. They tell me the Krafts just traded it in. I was wondering if I could borrow it while I'm in the Air Corps?"[1]

There was a long silence. Tommy continued, "It's been terrible at Tech for three years without transportation. I'd sure like to have a car while I'm in the Army and this one would be great."

"Son, that's a Packard Victoria. I could sell it tomorrow. If you want that car you and your mother will have to buy it. The Watsons always had money to buy whatever they wanted. Your Mother has all the money now with her parents gone. She can afford it."

"She doesn't have much money now," said Tommy. "They took a beating in the market and her Dad was sick so long, it took almost everything that was left. Maybe I can get a job."

Tom's father leaned back in his chair and said, "Your mother always did spend money like a drunken sailor. I'll bet she is running low on funds, living in the hotel and all."

Tommy remained quiet, he knew there was some truth to what his dad had said, but he also knew his mother had spent most of the money on others. He remembered the band uniforms, the gifts of food she had secretly sent to people in Sebring, even the dollars she used to hand to the members of the band each day when they were on a trip--probably enough over the years to buy this car.

"Dad, do you know anybody in Ridgewood who would give a job to a three-quarters engineer?" asked Tommy.

"If he was willing to sell cars, I think we could find him a position," said his dad.

Tommy had never considered being a car salesman, but he knew his father was offering him a way to earn the car. "When do I start?" he said.

When Tommy visited Charles Watson, his uncle said, "I'm delighted that you're going to be a pilot. Thanks for the Rickenbacker clippings. I just read in the paper that he left the hospital yesterday."

Tommy said, "He was in the hospital just a few miles from the Tech campus for all those months--probably bored to tears. I wished I could have gotten in there somehow, just to meet him."

"I wish you could have too," said Uncle Charles. "He probably is the finest fighter pilot that ever lived."

"Well, maybe I'll be a fighter pilot soon," said Tommy.

"That's just wonderful, Tommy. Where will you go for training?"

"It looks like Texas, maybe Randolph Field or Kelly Field," answered Tommy. "Did you ever get down there?"

"No, I never did," reminisced Uncle Charles. "I took my training at Princeton, and went overseas green as a pea. We got more training at Issoudun, France. People like Rickenbacker and Raoul Lufbery took all of their training in France and they were stationed right there while I was getting the finishing touches. I know I've told you a lot about it. It was very exciting."

"Who was Lufbery?" asked Tommy. "I've heard his name, but why was he so famous?"

"At one time Lufbery was our leading Ace and the newspaper men followed him around because he was a good interview. He came up with a maneuver called the Lufbery Circle which was designed to ensnare an enemy plane when we had him outnumbered. Raoul was teaching his tactics and he always had something quotable to say.

"Nobody had ever heard of Rickenbacker. Then one day, at a field where they weren't expecting any enemy action, Lufbery jumped into somebody else's plane to chase off a surprise German attack. His own Nieuport was out of service. Something went wrong, and his plane burst into flames. He crashed and died right in front of his comrades. It was a shocking thing to see."

"Was that when Rickenbacker became the top man?" asked Tommy.

"Not quite. For a few weeks Frank Luke was the leading American pilot--he shot down a number of stationary observation balloons. He didn't last very long, and we never understood what happened. He went down in German territory--landed safely and had nothing to fear. Flyers were special people and the Germans would have treated him like royalty. He would have returned home a hero. Instead, he took out his pistol and refused to surrender--killed six or seven Germans before they killed him.

"Then, in the last few months of the war, Rickenbacker shot down a number of balloons and aircraft to became our top Ace. He had been a race car driver before joining the Army and he went overseas as General Pershing's driver. He talked his way into flight training and ended up a pilot, and a Squadron Commander.

"That's why he has done so well as President of Eastern Airlines. He runs it just like he ran his fighter squadron. They said that he commanded his men 'by being a good example.' He runs Eastern the same way--they say he's down in the hangers at seven in the morning checking with the maintenance people.

"Things have changed since I flew. We had more people killed in training than we did in combat. Most Army fields are named for people who were killed in training and never even learned to fly. The Jenny, for all it's reputation as a trainer, was not a forgiving airplane."

"Uncle Charles, do you remember the time you and I saw Charles Lindbergh?" asked Tommy.

"Yes, I do," replied Charles. "We went to the Curtis-Wright factory, in Paterson. Lindbergh buzzed the factory to thank them for building the engine for his plane, 'The Spirit of St. Louis'."

Tommy said, "You reminded me when you mentioned flying a Jenny. I've read Lindbergh's book, *We*, and he and I have something in common."

"I'll bet I know," said Uncle Charles. "I'll bet it's the fact that both of you once lived in New Jersey."

"That, too," said Tommy, "but what I was thinking about was that we both learned to fly in the state of Georgia."

"Are you sure of that, Tommy? I thought he was from the midwest."

"I'm sure," said Tommy. "He went down to Americus, Georgia, to buy a war surplus Jenny. He had never soloed, although he had been barnstorming with a flying circus. He got somebody to go around the field with him a couple of times, and then he soloed."

"I never knew that," said Uncle Charles. "He must have been a natural. To me, the Jenny was a tricky plane to fly, especially for your first solo. Having some flying experience before entering the service as you do should make it easier for you."[2]

For a few weeks Tommy tried to sell cars, with little success. His dad didn't seem to care. He was proud to have his son around and he arranged to have a couple of sales go Tommy's way. He even allowed himself the thought that Tommy may one day join him in the business.

For the first time, Tommy saw his father in his element. When they went to lunch, or stopped for a drink after work, people always came by to speak to "Tom" the car salesman, or "Mac" the lodge member, or "T. B.," the back-room politician. Tommy had often wondered why his mother married this man, whom his grandparents had disliked so much. Now he was beginning to understand his father. He was a charmer and a salesman. He sold himself and he did a good job of it.

On several occasions, Tommy had dinner with his dad and his friend, Joan Mallon. His dad and Miss Mallon had dated for years, since Tommy's parents had divorced. Tommy could see that she was in love with his father. His dad said that if it weren't for his being Catholic, and divorced, they probably would have married.

Miss Mallon was a very independent woman. She owned a corset shop in neighboring Summit, New Jersey. She was an attractive woman and she wore beautiful, expensive clothes. There was a soft hint of her South Carolina heritage in her speech. She was nice to Tommy, and he was polite to her, but he wasn't comfortable around her. He never knew what to say.

One night at dinner, when the subject of the Packard convertible came up, Tommy had an ally. Joan Mallon repeated what she had already said to Tommy's father in private, "Why don't you give the boy the car. That is the least you can do. You haven't done all that much for your son over the years."

"And whose fault was that," barked Tom. "The boy lived in Florida all these years. What could I do?"

"Now is your chance, he's here now," she urged.

"Mind your own business," snapped Tom. "Let's dance."

Joan Mallon smiled at Tommy, and shook her head, as she and Tom stepped on to the dance floor. Tommy had heard that his dad was an outstanding dancer, but he had never seen him in action. After a few minutes, it was apparent that his Dad and Miss Mallon cut a mean figure on the dance floor. Like a scene from a movie, the other couples worked their way to the edge of the floor where they half danced, half stood, and watched as the pair performed. Tommy was beginning to understand a lot about his dad.

Tommy appreciated Miss Mallon's efforts to have his dad give him the car, but he enjoyed working for it. Tommy had been around the shop since he was a child and he knew everyone. It was no trouble getting the convertible in first class shape. It was already in fine condition, but every time one of the men had some free time he would turn his attention to "the kid's car."

When it came time to go, the car was perfect, and Tommy went around the shop and thanked each man. They gave him advice, like he was their own son:

"Change the oil every 2000 miles."

"You better hope you get an airplane that runs as good as this Packard."

"Write and let us know how the car is running."

[1]Joan Mallon, a friend of Tommy's father, related most of the events in this chapter. At the publishing date, late in 1998, she is alive and very bright in her late 90s, and she and the author talk often, as they have for 20 years.

[2]See Appendix A, How this book was written

15

"I'd been in bed for some time, but I couldn't sleep. I guess the letter I'd written for Tommy had started me thinking. It made the war seem near at hand when a boy I'd watched grow up was on his way into the Army. Then I heard Tommy's car coming from halfway across town."

----Luther Price, Tommy's minister

Back in Sebring, Polly had the house open for the first time in several years.[1] The lake was grand, and for the first time in a long time, Tommy felt at home. He even walked up the hill to the Kenilworth Lodge, and for old times' sake, he strolled into the hotel garden and picked a rose for his mother. She loved it, and for the next two weeks she did everything she could to make Tommy's stay a happy one.

Georgia Tech roommate Walter Weissenberger visits Tommy in Sebring

Polly knew that she couldn't keep the house. She couldn't afford it anymore. She would have to have help with the yard and someone to keep firewood in the house. Leasing it had helped pay her expenses, but the house needed maintenance. She had made up her mind to wait until Tommy was gone and then sell it.

Walter Weissenberger, Tommy's roommate from Tech, came to visit and Polly entertained the boys royally.[2] They visited with some of Tommy's old friends like Clarence Campbell and Paul Gustat and they played a round of golf with Bill Dutton, who, along with Howard McDonald, was also headed for the Army. Walter had a movie camera and some of the recently introduced Kodachrome color film. One afternoon before dinner he got Tommy and his mother to clown around in the back yard, while he shot movies.[3] Tommy saw his mother laughing and having fun for the first time in years.

Another friend from Ga. Tech, Robert Higgins,[4] came and visited. "Hig" was disappointed that Tommy wasn't going back to school, but showed great interest in the Air Cadets. "Tell me about it, Tommy. I don't want to end up in the Coastal Artillery either."

Just as it was when Walter had visited, they spent most of their time dating girls Tommy knew from high school. There were days at Bradenton Beach, swimming and sunning, and nights at the Hammock Tavern, or the Blue Anchor, in Avon Park.

Robert Higgins, Polly McGuire and Tommy, Summer of 1941

They stayed up late each night and slept late the next day. By mid-morning they were on the beach, and in the afternoons they were cruising the town and visiting with people like Hayden Williams, Tommy Weaver's mother, or Prof Gustat. Along the way Tommy gathered letters of recommendation he needed for the Army.

On the Fourth of July they had a big party on Kenilworth Beach, and before the day was over, it seemed that everybody Tommy knew came by for a while. The Maxcy boys showed up with a power boat, and everybody took a try at riding the surfboard. It was a large board that was attached to the boat by a long rope and the rider stood and held on to a rope from the board. Hardly anyone could stay on around the corners.

Late in the afternoon there were events at the City Pier and later they went to the Firehouse for a picnic dinner, featuring Bar-B-Que that had been cooked over a charcoal pit all day, and Chicken Perloo (chicken and rice with cracked black pepper corns) served from a large black iron pot. Polly, as her Mother had done years before, bought tickets for everyone. The day was a big farewell party for Tommy. He knew that in about a week he would enter into a new phase of his life, and it would take him away from his friends and his mother for a long time.

Hig and Walter were gone, and time was running out. Tommy had put off some very important business. Since he was going into an Army program which would result in his being a Commissioned Officer, he needed three letters of recommendation. He had one from Prof Gustat and Uncle Jimmy, Sebring's police chief.

On the last day before he was to report in, he tracked down Luther Price, the Presbyterian minister.

Reverend Price had known Tommy for a long time and he inquired, "How is your mother doing ?"

Tommy said, "We are back in the house now, and she is doing well. I came to ask you to write a letter of recommendation to the Army. I'm going into the Air Cadets."

"How does your mother feel about that?" asked Mr. Price.

"She isn't too happy about it but I think she will eventually feel that I did the right thing. We are all going to be in the service soon. This is just a chance for me to get into the branch I want."

"I'd be glad to give you a letter. When do you need it?"

"I'm leaving early in the morning," replied Tommy.

"That's a problem," said Reverend Price. "I have a meeting in the church in a few minutes. Could you come by later?"

"Yes sir, I could," replied Tommy.

"I'll be done in an hour and a half. If you like, I'll write it and place it here in the mail box. You can come by and get it when it's convenient."

"Thank you, sir," said Tommy. "I'd appreciate it if you would keep an eye on my mother while I'm gone. She's been lonely these last few years with me away at school. I guess this isn't going to help either."

"I will, Tommy," replied Reverend Price. "We'll pray for you, too."

Later, Luther Price sat down and wrote a letter for Tommy. He mentioned his outstanding character, and his devotion to his mother. He placed the letter in an envelope and left it in the mail box on the front porch, as he had promised.[5]

The letter started a stream of thoughts which disturbed the minister. The world had been troubled for sometime. He had hoped things would be worked out before the United States got involved. Now one of his congregation was being touched by the threat of war. He had seen Tommy grow from a young boy into manhood, and now he would soon be a soldier.

These thoughts repeated in his mind as he lay in bed trying to sleep. If he could just make some sense of it all, then he could fall asleep. The warm July night was quiet. With the windows open, the only sounds he heard were the crickets, and the frogs, and of course the ticks of the alarm clock that seemed so loud.

Sometime after midnight, the Reverend was in a fretful half-sleep, when he heard the sound of a car engine in the distance. As he listened, it became apparent that it was Tommy. He could hear the sound of tires as the car turned corners, accelerated, slowed down, screeched around another corner, getting louder and louder, as it got closer to the house. He had an urge to get up and meet Tommy at the door, and speak to him once again--to wish him Godspeed but, before he could arise, the car skidded to a stop in front of the house.

He heard the car door open, the engine still running. He heard Tommy come up the walk, open the screen door, cross the wooden porch, remove the letter from the mail box, cross back across the porch and out of the door, which he let slam gently. It took only a few seconds and the car raced off into the night. Luther Price's last thought before he slept was: "That's the last time anyone in Sebring will hear Tommy McGuire screech around a corner, for a long time."

Tommy sped from Sebring, dreaming of a triumphant day when he would return to town in an Army fighter plane. A year before Bob Satterwhite had flown home from Montgomery, Alabama, in an Army plane.[6] The whole town had been excited when Bob buzzed his parents' home, in the Woodlawn Terrace section of town. It was a signal for his family to drive to the Avon Park airport, where he was going to land. If people in Sebring thought Tommy was a wild driver, he would soon give them reason to wonder about his flying style.

An hour and a half later Tommy parked his car on Bradenton Beach. He set his Big Ben. The salt air and the sound of the waves reminded him of the good times he had experienced here over the years. Tomorrow would be the start of a new life, more exciting than anything he had ever done. He stretched out in the seat and fell asleep at once.

Tommy woke before the alarm sounded. In spite of the shortness of the night he was wide awake and excited. As the sun rose in the east the western sky, over the Gulf of Mexico, was filled with clouds which changed color from purple, to lavender, to peach. He thought again of the good times he'd had at this beach and was glad he had come here to see it one last time.

He opened the Packard's rumble seat and withdrew a record player. Winding it up, he placed it on the hood of the car, and played a record. The saxophone and trombone music of the Glenn Miller band lilted out over the deserted beach. Tommy listened for the clarinet parts as he took his shaving mug to the water, dipped it in, worked up a lather with the brush, returned to the car and shaved, using the car's outside mirror.

An hour's drive north took Tommy through Ybor City, and other parts of Tampa that were so familiar. At 9:OO a.m. he arrived at McDill Field, the place where he was to enter the Army Air Corps.

It was July 12, one of the hottest days of the year. Not the worst day of the year to take a physical exam military style. No place for modesty though, most of the day was spent in the buff, or wearing only shorts. These future fighting men walked from room to room with nothing to protect them from a breeze but a file of paper work each of them carried. It is doubtful that the sight of these pilots-to-be would have thrown fear into Adolph Hitler, had he happened on the scene.

Complete educational, health, and employment history had to be given. Tommy was a little embarrassed when he was questioned about his ROTC training, but the sergeant seemed to be impressed and wrote everything down.

He was proud that he could fill in a space where it said "Employment." He wrote in "Auto salesman" and thought how his mother would be embarrassed, and his father pleased at this. The eye exams were particularly difficult. One eye was covered and a chart across the room had to be successfully read. Then a book was produced that had colored dots covering each page. This test for color blindness was tough. The colors were pale, and it was difficult to read the numbers hidden away among the dots.

The test for depth perception was toughest, reflecting the importance of this ability for a pilot. The candidate sat in a chair with a string in each hand which led across the room to a box. Inside the box, and in view through a square opening, were two vertical sticks. The object was to pull on the strings until the two sticks were beside each other. It wasn't easy to do from that distance, but that was the point. Failure on any part of the eye exam was cause for immediate disqualification.

When the day was over, it seemed that there wasn't any place that they hadn't looked, probed, or listened. His hernia repair was inspected and he was relieved when he learned he had passed the physical.

He wasn't even disappointed when he learned that he would be going to Corsicana, Texas, for training instead of Randolph or Kelly Field. He was to start his training the next week at a contract school, but nobody seemed to know where Corsicana was. Tommy was relieved to find out that he was headed southeast of Dallas, and not to west Texas.

Along with other cadets, he reported in late Friday, July 18. They drew only bedding. Saturday morning they were up early and stood in line to get shots, get a hair cut, and draw clothing. Supply didn't have low cut shoes in his size and he was told that he would have to wear his wing tip shoes until his size came in.

Sunday was a badly needed day of rest. Everybody had a sore arm from the shots, and some were sick and feverish. They slept between meals, hoping to feel better by Monday morning, when they would embark on the greatest adventure of their lives, learning to fly.

[1] Highlands County News, June 12, 1941
[2] Walter Weissenberger, McGuire's Ga. Tech roommate
[3] The McGuire Museum at McGuire AFB, NJ has copies of these movies
[4] Martha Durrance Howett, SHS '40
[5] Reverend Luther Price
[6] Highlands County News, July 25, 1940

16

"Wait but for wings, and in their season---fly."

------Alexander Pope

On Monday, July 21, the cadets were roused at 5:30 a.m., and hustled into a mess hall. Bewildered, they wandered about like zombies. They all looked the same with their short hair cuts, and their brand new, dark green, twill one-piece fatigues. After breakfast they were assembled for greetings and indoctrination.

The Detachment Commander, Capt. Oliver E. Ford, Jr., rose and spoke, " Welcome to Corsicana Field. As members of the cadet class 42B, you are among America's finest young men. You have passed rigorous mental and physical exams to get here. Your biggest tests are yet ahead. Look at the man on either side of you--chances are good, that they might not be with you if you complete cadet training and become a Army pilot. That's right, gentlemen, if this group is typical, up to sixty percent of you may not be able to complete this training.

" If you give your best, and don't make it, there's nothing to be ashamed of. Some of you won't be able to fly an airplane, some may become air sick, and some may not pass ground school.

"If you are not able to qualify as pilots, you may go on to win your wings as a navigator or bombardier. Some of you may end up in Officer Candidate School to earn a commission in other branches of the Army. A few might be discharged from the Army.

"I hope that we will not lose any of you for disciplinary reasons. If you complete your training, you will be an Officer in the United States Army, and you must start acting like one now. Never do anything to disgrace your uniform. Good Luck!"

Next, Lt. Robert Ensminger, Commandant of Cadets, spoke: "Gentlemen, President Roosevelt has said that we need to produce 30,000 trained pilots a year, to protect the shores of the United States. Pilots are needed faster than the Army can train them.

"This is one of fifty contract schools which are presently or will soon be training pilots for the Army. It means that this post and its training group are manned by civilians.

"Your instructors are eminently qualified, and are entitled to the same respect as an Army Officer. If you are smart you will also give your instructors your full attention--they will have more to do with your success here than anyone else. All check rides will be with military personnel, and every effort will be made to give each cadet a fair chance to complete his training.

Air Cadets - Corsicana, Texas - July 1941

Tommy McGuire, a few days after flight training began at Corsicana, Texas. McGuire is wearing his ever-present onyx ring and his civilian wingtip shoes. His foot was narrow and his size military shoe had to be special ordered.

"If you are successful, you will leave here with sixty hours of flying time, about half of it solo. You will also have ground school training in mathematics, navigation, engine and aircraft, radio, weather, small arms, and military customs and drill.

"The designation 42B means that you are scheduled to graduate in February, of 1942. Aviation Cadets in the past have had 10 weeks of pre-flight before their flight training. Instead of a 40-week course, you will train in 30 weeks. Your training will be much more intense, with ground school subjects being studied when you are not flying. Primary flight training here at Corsicana will take 10 weeks, starting today."

There was no mistake, this was the Army. Even though it was run by civilians, they had one thing about the Army down pat: "Hurry up and wait." The old adage was as true here as anywhere in the Army. Cadets stood in long lines to draw equipment, to get a locker assignment, and to get their training schedule. They drew flying gear, a seatpack parachute, and a cloth flying helmet with goggles, and waited in the ready room until their name was called. While they waited they were shown how to adjust the helmet, goggles, and parachute. Then they were instructed on bail-out procedures.

That afternoon Tommy and four other cadets were introduced to their instructor who told them, "If you are to become a pilot you must listen to me at all times. Speech in flight is in one direction. I will be able to talk to you through a tube that hooks up to your flying helmet. There is no way for you to talk to me. Pay attention at all times, I don't like to repeat myself.

"I can give you hand signals and save my voice. When I hold both hands above my shoulders I am signaling you to take the controls. When I want to take control I will pat myself on the head with one hand, or I will give the stick a violent wiggle. If I give either of these signals relinquish the controls to me at once.

"Before we fly an airplane we do a pre-flight inspection. We start at 12 o'clock--that's the nose, and we go 360 degrees around the plane."

After a check of the propeller they moved under the fuselage where they were shown how nuts and bolts were safety wired, to keep them from vibrating loose. Then they learned how to drain the sediment bowl in the gas line, to rid it of debris or water. They worked their way around the plane checking tires, control surfaces, cable connections, and cowling Dzus fasteners. They checked for oil or hydraulic fluid on the exterior of the plane which might indicate a leak somewhere inside of the airframe. The Fairchild PT-19A was an open cockpit, low-winged craft. It was trim, with its inverted six-cylinder in-line engine, and wide landing gear. Its wings were constructed of thin plywood veneer with metal and fabric covering the fuselage. The fuselage was painted blue and the wings were bright yellow. The tail had bright red and white horizontal stripes. This startling color combination made the planes highly visible in the air and helped avoid mid-air collisions in crowded training areas.

When it was Tommy's turn to take his first flight he was shown how to strap himself in and to adjust the seat for proper vision. The instructor asked, "Have you ever done any flying?" Tommy answered, "Yes, sir. I've had a few hours of dual."

"OK, when we get airborne I'll let you take the controls for a few turns to see what you can do."

Upon take-off, Tommy got his first look at Texas from the air. Compared to Florida or Georgia it looked barren. The air was clear, lacking the haze that was always present in the hills around Atlanta, and often seen in the peninsula of Florida. The sky seemed much higher, and the horizon much more sharply defined.

Ten days before, Tommy had been a college student on vacation. Now he was high above Texas, in the Air Corps, and the sight of the red, white and blue star insignia on the wing of the plane was a thrill. He had dreamed of this moment for years, and he wasn't disappointed.

The instructor had Tommy take the controls and try some turns.

"Your nose is dropping." He instructed, "Don't ride the rudder! Start the turn, then let off. Try it again."

Tommy tried again and did better.

Back on the ground there was a chance for the instructor and student to talk.

"You didn't do too badly," said the instructor. "What type of aircraft did you fly?"

"I flew a 40-horse power Piper Cub. I've never flown anything this large," replied Tommy.

"How did this plane feel to you?" asked the instructor.

"It felt heavy, sir," replied Tommy.

"Did you understand about the rudder?"

"Yes sir, I did. I was giving it a little lower rudder."

"That's right," said the instructor. "You'll do OK."

That seemed like high praise to the other cadets who had heard the conversation. Now Tommy sat on the bench with three of the group, while the last cadet took his flight.

One of the guys looked at the name plate over Tommy's breast pocket and said, "McGuire, are you a pilot?"

"Not exactly," answered Tommy. "I just took a few lessons while I was going to Georgia Tech.".

"How many lessons did you have?"

"Just enough to be dangerous," replied Tommy.

"At least you know how the controls work!"

"Yeah, but it is a little different."

One by one they asked Tommy questions, and before he knew it, he was sitting forward on the bench, with his feet extended. He was demonstrating how the stick and rudder pedal had to be coordinated to make a turn. From that day on, Tommy conducted ground school for his pals, while the instructor had one of the group in the air.

The first few evenings were spent in the barracks trying on uniforms and sewing. They had until Saturday morning's inspection to struggle with needles and thread and to affix a Training Command patch to the left shoulder of their class A uniforms, and an Air Cadet patch to their garrison caps.

Some of the guys had already learned to remove the grommets from their flat-top service caps. They hadn't learned to fly yet, but they were already modeling their hats in the famous "fifty mission" crushed style. Pilots often removed the grommet from their hats so earphones could be worn over the hat. Removing the grommet was a violation of the Cadet Dress Code so they had to be carefully replaced. At the Post Exchange, Tommy ordered Air Cadet stationary with his name imprinted on it. He sat on his cot in his underwear and wrote notes to his mother, father, and Uncle Charles. It was a thrill to write on this stationary with his name beneath the Air Cadet's propeller and wings insignia. Most of the cadets spent their spare time reading. There were aircraft manuals, math books, navigation guides, and a lightly written cadet's manual entitled "Air Cadet Tips," which passed on tips such as these:

"If you have ever been troubled with an undeveloped right arm, your worries are now at an end. You salute all officers, colors and standards twenty-four hours a day. You salute on the stoops, going to formations, in the mess halls, at the end of a conversation with an officer, and every time that a salute is required. Just remember the old Army saying, 'When in doubt, salute,' and a gig will never raise it's ugly head on that count."

Forgetting to salute wasn't the only way to get a gig. Having an unbuttoned shirt pocket, unshined shoes or brass, failing to initial by your name when it was posted on the bulletin board, or not knowing Squadron regulations, could all result in demerits.

Saturday morning inspection was held in the barracks with each cadet standing at attention at the foot of his bunk. Beds had to be made-up to military standards, with hospital folds on the corners. The blanket had to be drawn so tight that it would bounce a half dollar when one was dropped from shoulder height.

Every piece of clothing had to be properly folded and placed in the locker according to a diagram. It was explained that flying was a precise business, and a cadet who couldn't keep his bunk area in order was considered "suspect" when it came to flying.

Cadets were placed on duty rosters to clean the latrine and other public areas of the barracks. A dripping faucet which left a drop of water in a sink could get the assigned cadets a gig. They learned that a wad of toilet paper stuffed in the faucet spouts would absorb a potential drip until inspection was over.

Often a cadet who had failed to fold his clothing properly would stuff it into the bottom of the public phone booth near the barracks door. This saved many a gig until an officer opened the door during one Saturday's inspection. The culprits had to step forward--the laundry marks on the clothing were incriminating.

After a cadet exceeded a given number of gigs he was ordered to walk "tours" while his buddies were going to town Saturday afternoon or Sunday. "Tours" consisted of walking-off demerits at 120 steps per minute, with a bulky parachute hanging low from the cadet's back so that it rubbed against his legs with each step. It was hot, irritating, and embarrassing. McGuire made up his mind that he would avoid this wasteful activity. He had been neat all of his life and his R.O.T.C. training helped. He did not let his mind stray from the day to day requirements of being a cadet, and he got few gigs.

As the days passed, it became apparent that McGuire had done a good job of preparing himself for pilot's training: he knew math and military routine from college, and the few hours of dual in Atlanta had given him an edge on the flying lessons. His confidence grew everyday as he scored well on ground school courses, and his flying as well.

The upperclassmen of the class 42A called the newer men of class 42B, "dodos". The flying maneuvers that a dodo most dreaded were the stall and the spin. A pilot must recognize a stall to avoid it, or a spin would follow. A stall or spin at low altitude was almost always fatal. Stall and spin training separated many a cadet from the Air Corps.

With the engine cut back to idle, the plane's nose was pulled up at a sharp angle far above the horizon. As the propeller swished in the wind and the engine backfired, the instructor's voice in the student's ear phones coached him to keep the wings level and the nose up, until the plane lost flying speed and shuddered into a stall.

Then came a sudden and sickening drop of the nose that lifted the student out of his seat and forced him against his seat belt. Torque from the turning propeller caused the plane to drop with one wing low---resulting in a spin. No amount of schooling could prepare a dodo for the sheer violence of this maneuver.

Most cadets felt a pang in their stomach when the nose of the plane suddenly whipped past the horizon and pointed straight down, and the earth spun before their eyes. Many were overcome by nausea and became air sick. Early in training the instructors had said, "If you puke in an airplane you will clean it."

Many a cadet could be seen after a flight, with a bucket of water, cleaning the interior and exterior of a plane, even before the nausea impulse had died down. It took great fortitude to clean up the mess without getting sick again. Pity the next cadet to use the plane. The smell was impossible to remove, and he might feel sick before the plane ever left the ground.

As others struggled to avoid nausea and what the cadets called the "washing machine," McGuire excelled. On August fifth, after 52 minutes of dual training, his instructor got out of the plane, secured the seatbelt and shoulder straps in the front cockpit and said, "OK Mac, you are ready! Take her up. Just remember one thing. I'm going to be holding my left nut for luck. Don't make me hurt myself!"

McGuire taxied the open-cockpit airplane to the end of the runway, checked for incoming aircraft, turned the plane down the runway and made a take-off run. Minus the instructor's weight the plane rose quickly from the sod. At 800 feet he kicked the plane into a left turn with an authority he had never exerted before. This was the most exciting thing he'd ever done and he let out a screech of joy. He followed the prescribed course around the field and made a slightly bumpy three-point landing. After nine hours and eight minutes of dual instruction, he was one of the first members of 42B to make a solo flight.[1]

The field at Corsicana was all grass. Even the flight line and the ramps in front of the hangers were unpaved and the grass never seemed to be able to catch hold in these high traffic areas. Every time an engine started or a wind blew, a cloud of dust was created. Cadets struggled to keep their shoes polished and the barracks clean, but the dust was everywhere. When it rained the dusty soil became mud, and it stuck to shoes and clothing like glue. A common complaint was: "Corsicana is the only place in the world where you can walk in mud up to your ass and have dust blow in your face"

The dust aggravated McGuire's sinuses and his nose ran constantly. He worried that it could cost him his flying career if he had trouble breathing. As he stood at attention in formations, he sniffed gently, to prevent his nose from dripping. He feared that one loud snort might call the problem to the attention of his superiors. He stood at Saturday morning inspections almost gagging--wanting to cough up the phlegm from his throat. Sometimes he felt like he would choke--even felt faint, but he was determined to fly, and he didn't cough.

He worried even more when they started training with high altitude oxygen equipment, which consisted of a bulky mask and a balloon-like bladder that strapped over the mouth and nose. He was concerned that

111

he wouldn't be able to breathe, the mask was so confining. Somehow he survived the ordeal.

Cadet class 42B, Corsicana, Texas. McGuire is fifth from right, standing.
Only 47 of 80 cadets remained. The lack of a crease in the cadets' trousers is indicative
of the inadequate laundry services available to the cadets. Sept. 18, 1941

As training went on, so did the high rate of wash-outs. By the end of the fifth week of training the 80-man class of 42B was down to only 50 men. In the sixth week of training they became the upperclassmen as the Class 42A moved on to basic training, and a new group of 80 dodos started training as Class 42C.

McGuire was assigned to instructor D. F. Sheppard, who would give him his next five weeks of primary flight training. Flying became a more important part of each day's activities. There were Air Corps flying schools all over the southwest and it seemed that every day there was a new story about a cadet death or serious accident somewhere in Texas or Oklahoma. There were accidents at Corsicana, but they usually involved a ground-loop with only a wingtip or propeller damaged.

At any time, a scan of the sky would reveal 20 to 30 aircraft in the sky. Several near mid-air collisions were reported each day, and at least one plane a day landed somewhere other than the home base. Fortunately there were auxiliary fields and ranch land nearby where a plane could be landed safely.

One afternoon after his dual instructions, McGuire took off solo, and flew to a training area to practice on his own. The sky was stormy to the west, but McGuire felt that it would hold off until he finished his training course. He became absorbed in his flying exercises and didn't give the weather another thought.

Back at the field other planes were returning one by one, as the storm approached rapidly. Blue-black clouds swept over the field, and cadets scurried from their parked airplanes to the operations office. The ground crews hurried about the flight line tying down the planes and putting canvas covers over the open cockpits as a heavy rain set in.

The cadets milled around, peering out at the storm, and someone started a nose count--who had gone out--and who had checked in? McGuire was the only one still out, and they began to wonder if he was in trouble.

The storm raged on, like a small tornado. Debris was lifted in a whirlwind and blown across the field, and the planes rocked and tugged at their tie-down ropes in the violent wind.

After 15 minutes of looking out the windows, everyone agreed that McGuire had to be in trouble. Somebody even suggested that he may have "bought the farm." The storm swept to the east and the sky began to clear. The rain lessened to a drizzle and two by two, like animals leaving the ark, the cadets wandered outside to scan the brightening sky.

Someone said, "What is that across the field where the rainbow is touching the ground?"

Everyone strained to see what looked like an airplane. As they watched, it started to move across the field and they could see the propeller flashing in the late afternoon light. With the class of 42B watching, McGuire taxied his PT-19 to the flight line and with some flair, swung the plane into its parking spot.[2]

McGuire had not been able to get back to the landing area because of violent winds. Instead of fleeing in front of the storm to God knows where, he had made a quick decision to sneak in on the far edge of the field which wasn't yet involved in the storm. He had waited out the storm and gotten wet, but had not damaged the airplane. When he climbed out of the cockpit, the whole cadet corps cheered. He bowed and gave them a big victory smile. Later in the barracks he explained, "Any port in a storm."

[1]McGuire's Log book

[2]Most of the information in this chapter furnished by
George Lawson, a member of McGuire's Cadet class at
Corsicana, Texas

17

"Go get the biscuit gun. This washing machine driver is never going to make it down."
"Here's the biscuit gun, Sir. We await your order."
"Shoot that cadet a biscuit. There is no reason for him to starve just because he can't land his plane."

> -------A Cadet folk tale. A cadet who can't land his
> plane is prime candidate to wash out of training.

The days at Corsicana rushed by and the class size dropped to 47 cadets as the "washing machine" took its toll. The surviving cadets learned to stall, spin, crab, slip, identify cloud types, read rising smoke and ripples on water to determine wind direction, and to dead reckon using a Mark VII plotter. They figured magnetic variations, crosswinds and complicated navigation problems on a E6B computer, and if a cadet failed to "clear himself" before making a turn (look over his shoulders for traffic) he was in trouble. There was so much to learn and not much time to learn it.

Five-and-a-half days a week were filled with being a cadet. After morning inspection, Saturday afternoon was errand time, and Saturday night everyone attended a dance hosted by the young ladies of Corsicana. Sunday mornings were prized as the only day cadets could sleep-in. Corsicana was closed on Sunday, but the citizens of the town welcomed the servicemen to their churches and often invited groups of cadets to Sunday dinner in their homes. McGuire found himself very popular because of his Packard convertible. The guys all wanted to go with him so they wouldn't have to wait for the bus into town.

When the 10 weeks of primary training came to an end everyone watched the bulletin board to see where they would be stationed for the next phase of their training. No matter where the men were reassigned they were scheduled to get the same training. Most of the men hoped they would draw Randolph Field outside San Antonio. It was the Air Corps' permanent training facility and it had been featured in Hollywood movies and in **LIFE** magazine.

With the great number of men now in training most of those advancing would find themselves in one of the contract schools spread across the Southern United States from California to Florida. McGuire was at the top of his class and when his notice was posted it read: Air Corps Basic Flight Training School, Randolph Field, Texas.

When one of his friends asked, "How did you swing that?" McGuire kidded, "Nothing to it when you have friends in high places."

In reality he had no idea how he had been lucky enough to get Randolph Field while most of his friends were being sent to West Texas, Oklahoma, and Mississippi. He felt that his high ranking in the class may have earned him his new assignment. He told his pals, "It doesn't matter where we are going as long as we all get our wings."

Thus on September 30, McGuire and a few friends arrived at Randolph Field. Known as "The West Point of the Air," the 2,300-acre installation had been carefully designed for the training of Air Cadets, and was the pride of the Air Corps. It was planned for flight training from the front gate to the back fence, before ground was broken in 1929. Originally Randolph Field had primary, basic, and advanced flying and a civilian entering cadets would expect to graduate and be commissioned at the one location. In the accelerated plan only the second phase, basic, was being taught at Randolph and cadets would be transferred elsewhere for the last phase of flight training.

After an 18-mile drive from San Antonio through the dusty, tan, mesquite-covered countryside, Randolph Field was an oasis. A long drive, with a grassy mall down the center, led from the front gate to a large circle where the Air Corps insignia was outlined in neatly trimmed hedges. There stood the Base Headquarters, a pink sandstone building nicknamed "The Taj Mahal." It had an ornate 170-foot sandstone covered tower which concealed the base's 500,000-gallon water tank and was visible for miles around. On the roof was a beacon which proclaimed the base's location to any airplane in South Texas after dark.

The base spread symmetrically behind the "Taj" and consisted of terra cotta roofed stucco buildings in a Spanish mission style. The three-storied cadet barracks were distinguished by rounded arches, wrought iron railings, and mosaic red, white, and blue Air Corps insignias embedded in the stucco walls.

The cadet dining hall seated the entire Cadet Corps at linen-covered tables. A 30-foot-high map of the United States covered one wall from floor to ceiling. When the Cadet Adjutant stood in front of the map and read the orders of the day his echoing voice sent a shiver of pride up the spine of cadets like McGuire--Randolph Field was the real Air Corps, the way they had envisioned it

Beyond the academic buildings were hundreds of training planes, parked in neat rows in front of identical hangers which faced the flight lines on either side of the base. The 16 hanger roofs were painted with a large checkerboard pattern, making them an easy landmark from the air, and a welcome sight for a disoriented cadet trying to find his way home.

McGuire's training began on October 8, in a North American BT-9, a large, high-powered, low-wing plane.[1] His instructor, 2nd Lt. B. P.

Doyle, gave the group a quick run down: "Primary training taught you the fundamentals of flying. Basic training will increase your flying skills and make you a military pilot. The BT-9 has a two-position variable pitch propeller and a two-way radio, neither of which you have used before. The instrument panel is equipped for instrument flying. She's a heavy bird, and not as forgiving as your primary trainers. This one requires your full attention."

The first few days were devoted to learning about the new airplanes. Then the cadets learned to fly at night, on instruments, in formation, and cross country.

Randolph Field reflected the military customs and practices of the regular Army and observed many of the traditions found at West Point. It had been designed to train cadets from civilian life to officer, with advanced cadets sharing in the discipline. In normal times a cadet who had completed primary training became an upperclassmen and was encouraged to haze the young "dodos." Training priorities changed because of the war, and only basic training was now taught at Randolph. Now, McGuire and his buddies were subjected to hazing until they completed half of their training; then they became upperclassmen.

For McGuire it was like his days at Georgia Tech. He had been the subject of scorn as a freshman, but had risen to be the Sergeant Major of the Corps and had been in a position to dish it out for a change. McGuire, because of his ROTC training, took to the hazing more easily than some of the others. They learned a rule McGuire knew from ROTC. It was simple: "Don't be a quibbler. Remember that as an aviation cadet you have only three answers--'Yes, sir,' 'No, sir,' and 'No excuse, sir.'"

One day McGuire left the flight line area and walked through a hanger to exit the building on the other side. In the hanger he encountered a cadet lower classman--a "dodo bird." Exerting his rights and authority as an upperclassman he called the cadet to attention.

"What is your name, Mister?" asked McGuire.

"Cadet Edwin Weaver," replied the cadet.

"Are you aware that this area is off limits to dodos?" asked McGuire.

"Yes sir, I am," replied the flustered lower classman.

"Why are you in this restricted area?" asked McGuire.

"No excuse, Sir," replied the cadet.

"Mister, do I detect a smile on your face?"

"No, Sir. You do not!" replied the cadet.

"All the same, I want you to wipe the smile from your face and throw it on the ground," said McGuire.

116

The cadet complied, wiping a hand across his face and making a motion toward the ground.

"Now Mister. I want you to step on it," said McGuire.

The cadet followed instructions and made a motion with his foot, as if stepping on something on the ground.

"I am recording your name and company number. You will receive demerits for being here. If I see you here again they will be doubled."

Weaver had just been cutting through the hanger to make a formation on time. Not only did he get gigs for cutting through the hanger, he also got them for being late to formation. He ended up walking a tour to erase the gigs. He swore he would never forget the name Thomas B. McGuire, the upperclassman who had single handedly caused him to walk a tour while his friends were enjoying Saturday afternoon in San Antonio.[2]

San Antonio was a city of Army bases. Most servicemen liked the city and the people of San Antonio loved the Army. Somebody once said, "San Antonio seems to remember the days when the Army protected them from invaders."

Air Cadets were odd balls. They were neither officers nor enlisted men. They could not go to the Officer's Club or to Enlisted Men's Clubs for social affairs. Nor did they associate with either group. They were all interested in female companionship and attended special cadet dances or visited the Cadet Club at the Gunter Hotel in San Antonio.

McGuire and his friends tried the club and the dances but McGuire felt uncomfortable with the whole thing. He felt funny crowding into a club when there were cadets standing in line to ask a girl for a dance. Instead of going to town with the guys he would sometimes hang around the barracks "hanger flying" with anybody who would take the time to swap stories with him.

On December 7 military police entered a club where McGuire and his buddies were having a few drinks and had the juke box turned off. They announced: "This is an emergency! All military personnel are ordered to report to their post at once!" The silence of the room broke into a hum as the MPs left giving no further explanation. Before McGuire and his friends left for Randolph Field they heard that Pearl Harbor had been bombed by the Japanese. No one knew where Pearl Harbor was located.

The following day President Roosevelt spoke to a joint session of Congress asking for a Declaration of War. He called December 7, "A day that will live in infamy." The long expected war had come and Tommy McGuire and his fellow cadets would soon be asked to help the United States turn the tide against the Axis Powers.

The tempo of military life was increased and the cadets took on a new attitude. They were no longer just learning to fly. They were now getting ready to go to war. McGuire studied and wrote letters to his family and when he didn't feel like going out, let Charles Haltom and other cadets use his car. Having a car they scouted around San Antonio and found night spots which weren't so crowded with cadets. They felt guilty taking McGuire's car and leaving him at the base. One of the guys met a young lady named Sidney Bowers, and he described Tommy to her and asked her to bring along a girl for him.

December 11, 1941, McGuire agreed to go to a club called The Tower with his friends to meet a young college girl named Marilynn Giesler. When Sidney Bowers introduced Tommy to Marilynn she said, "We call her 'Pudgy'." Marilynn was a shapely young lady with auburn hair and blue eyes, and she was anything but pudgy. She blushed and explained to Tommy that she had been given the nickname as a joke when she had once complained that she needed to lose some weight.

Marilynn was a student at Incarnate Word College. She had graduated from Jefferson High School in San Antonio, and lived with her mother on Ridgewood Street, near the college. She often played bridge afternoons after school at Earl Abel's restaurant near the college. She and a group of friends would take a table in the back and play until it was time to go home, never buying anything but a cup of coffee.

Once on a dare Marilynn and a friend had shimmied up a tree at the college to peek into the windows of the indoor swimming pool. Everyone wondered what the nuns at school wore when they went swimming. Some thought that they might go nude during the hour that the pool was closed to the public for their use. When Marilynn and her friend saw the strange black outfits they wore, they laughed so hard they almost fell out of the tree.

Tommy and Marilynn danced, and talked and soon found that they liked each other, as their friends had predicted. McGuire saw an attractive young lady who laughed easily and loved to dance. Marilynn saw a well-mannered young man who loved good music and enjoyed her company.

When he transferred across town to Kelly Field it was another dream come true for McGuire. Kelly Field was one of the Army's oldest air fields and had been an important training base since World War I. Charles Lindbergh received his wings and Army commission at Kelly Field and later wrote in his book *We*: "....when he (a cadet) receives the wings at Kelly ....he has the satisfaction of knowing that he has graduated from one of the world's finest flying schools." McGuire and every other cadet who made it to Kelly Field could expect to follow Lindbergh and get their wings and Army commission.

Instead of slowing down for Christmas, the training schedule was accelerated because of Pearl Harbor, and the Declaration of War. Even so, the upperclassmen were happy because they had survived the rigors of primary, basic and advanced training, with the testing, inspections, and hazing, and now were just six weeks from graduation. They ordered their officer's uniforms so they would have them for an early graduation.

McGuire had developed a swaggering manner. It wasn't just the way he walked. There was a confidence that showed in everything he did, but mostly in the way he flew an airplane. Lieutenant John Kline, his instructor, recognized him as an able pilot who was eager to fly. Kline had graduated in Class 41-F only six months before, and knew McGuire could fly as well as he could.

McGuire's social life was better than ever before. He no longer stayed around the field on weekends. He knew Marilynn, and liked her. He called her for Sunday afternoon dates and they enjoyed dining out or dancing at the Anacacho Room or the Kit Kat Club.[3]

San Antonio was full of soldiers looking for girls. It wasn't unusual for a college girl in wartime San Antonio to have lunch with one young man, dinner with another, and then go dancing with a third. Marilynn was a typical college girl and she had lots of dates. She had been surprised when she met Tommy. Sidney Bowers had told her that he hadn't liked any of the girls he had met, and she thought he might be a "drip."

Instead, Marilynn liked Tommy. She had never known anyone his age with such good manners. They seemed to like the same things, and she felt very comfortable with him. He was busy with extra training, but she was glad when they were able to get together. It was no time to get serious, with a war on, but it was a great time to have fun. Tommy and Marilynn told themselves that they were "just having fun," but something special was happening--they were becoming very fond of each other.

The flying was exciting for McGuire, all AT-6s now. This was a real airplane. It was big and sleek, with retractable landing gear and a powerful 550-horse-power engine. It was named the "Texan," but the cadets knew it as "the pilot maker." It was said, "If you can fly an AT-6, you are ready for anything." It was a high performance airplane which could snap roll and do other maneuvers these advanced cadets were eager to try.

Advanced training included taking off and landing in formation. Kelly Field had a large grass area suitable for formation take-offs and landings, no matter what direction the wind was blowing.

On one flight, Lieutenant Kline led a formation of six AT-6s in two V elements. The tower gave them a green light to land on a compass heading of 330 degrees. It was a test of precision, and each pilot had to take his directions from Lieutenant Kline, to avoid a disaster. Everything went well as the planes turned into the wind and approached the field. The signal was given to cut power, and the six planes settled toward the turf. McGuire was flying to the right rear of Lieutenant Kline, in the first element. He eased the stick back, holding the large trainer off the ground until just the right moment.

As his plane settled to the sod McGuire felt his right wheel hit a low spot, and the plane veered to the right. He added pressure to the left rudder pedal to straighten the plane's path. He felt the plane swerve violently to the left--he had added too much left rudder. He remembered D.F. Sheppard, his primary instructor, saying "Don't pussy-foot--kick it!" as he kicked in full right rudder. The plane continued turning to the left. He felt sick as his plane spun in a violent ground loop--into the path of the three planes which followed in the rear element.

The formation was fairly loose, but McGuire gritted his teeth, as he was sure that he would hit at least one of the planes of the second element. Much to his surprise, he saw the planes of the second Vee flash past before he swung into their path. He held back on the stick to keep the plane's tail down. He feared the plane would still tip over, and he waited for the crush of his wing tip hitting the turf--it never came.

For the first time as a cadet, McGuire was embarrassed by something he had done in an airplane. All cadets feared a ground-loop--it usually resulted in damage to a plane's wingtip, or propeller. If he had hit a plane in the second element it could have destroyed two aircraft and resulted in injury or death and might have washed him out of cadets.

He was shaken, and the thought went through his mind that he had become a little cocky. When he taxied his AT-6 into its parking place on the flight line, Lieutenant Kline was already out of his plane and waiting. McGuire climbed down the wing of his plane prepared for a good ass chewing. Instead he got a smile from his instructor.[4]

"I guess any landing you can walk away from is a good one. What happened?" asked Lieutenant Kline.

"Yes sir," agreed McGuire, "My right gear hit in a hole. Guess I got a little excited and over-corrected."

"You did a good job, that could have been a mess. My knees are a little weak after that," said Kline.

"I thought I was the only one," said McGuire.

Flight training took place every weekday in December except Christmas Day. McGuire got two hours in the air each day. When he wasn't flying he was in a class or training in a Link trainer.

On New Year's Day, Tommy and Marilynn were able to spend the day together. He gave her a miniature figurine, and they dined at the Louisiana Purchase.[5] The next night they went to the Carnival Club and the Tower, where they had met. As they danced to "Red Sails in the Sunset," they were falling in love, but they didn't talk about it.

Saturday noon in downtown San Antonio. Tommy called Marilynn, she changed quickly from riding clothes and they lunched. This is a rare photo of the two of them clicked by a street photographer and reproduced from Marilynn's scrapbook

In January, McGuire flew 70 hours in just 21 flying days. He now had 206 hours of flying time and he was completely confident and comfortable in the air. He could do about any maneuver the plane was capable of, and he could fly at night or on instruments in bad weather.

Official Air Cadet photo taken at Kelly Field (USAF Photo)

McGuire had demonstrated the skill and "that something extra" that separated fighter pilots from all the rest. He had never thought of himself flying anything but a fighter, and was elated when he was informed that he had been selected for fighter training when he left Kelly Field.

At the end of the month training tapered off and McGuire concentrated on seeing Marilynn. They had seen each other only once in the last few weeks. Marilynn went horseback riding early in the morning and met Tommy in mid-morning in downtown San Antonio. As they walked to a restaurant a street photographer took their picture and handed them a claim slip. Film for civilian use was in short supply. Marilynn sent for the picture. It wasn't a very good picture of either of them, but it was her only picture of them together.

On February 6, 1942, McGuire graduated from training, received his wings, and his commission as a Second Lieutenant. There were 228 cadets receiving their wings, and embarking on flying careers in the Air Corps. That same day an Air Cadet named Herman Hancock arrived at Kelly Field to start his advanced training.[6] He was McGuire's friend from Sebring and one of those who had almost fallen victim to the infamous sailing canoe.

Lieutenant McGuire and Marilynn Giesler celebrated that night at the Anacacho Room and the Tower. It was the end of a bittersweet day for them as they danced the last dance to "Good Night Sweetheart." They were proud of his wings and commission, but unhappy that they wouldn't be seeing each other for a while. He was on his way to Key Field, Meridian, Mississippi, the next day.

---

[1]McGuire's Log book
[2]Edwin Weaver in an interview. Ironically they would meet again.
[3]Marilynn McGuire Beatty's diary
[4]McGuire's instructor, Lt. John W. Kline, though he never knew it, was McGuire's fraternity brother. He remarked years later that he never learned how to get upset about events like McGuire's ground loop. His even temperament served him well--he rose to Major General in the Air Force and Vice Commander of the 2nd Air Force.
[5]Marilynn McGuire Beatty's diary
[6]Highlands County News

18

"The shock came when his letter arrived telling of his flight training in the Air Corps. Not too much later he arrived in all his glory at the Beta house on leave, wearing that sharp uniform, hat at a rakish angle, 2nd looie bars and the pilot's wings, together with the pronouncement he'd been selected for fighter training. Invariably, when he came back to Tech he had an Army buddy or two with him. Nice regular guys."

---Jack Bruda, Beta Theta Pi, Ga.Tech. Class of '43

When McGuire got settled at Key Field, he phoned Marilynn to tell her how much he had enjoyed their last few days together. She was thrilled two days later when a dozen roses arrived.

McGuire was assigned to the 50th Pursuit Group. A fighter pilot from the group took him for an hour-long check-ride in a BT-14 training plane to verify his flying ability. They had to be sure he could fly before he piloted one of the high performance combat planes, which were single-seaters and had no space for an instructor to go on a check ride. McGuire flew the indoctrination flight with better than average technique and was checked out for his first solo flight in a fighter plane --a P-40E.

The P-40 was a wonderful plane to fly. The 1150-horsepower engine created tremendous torque on the take-off run, and the plane lifted effortlessly off the runway and climbed at a steep angle. McGuire quickly took the plane to high altitude, and flew for a while on oxygen. Then he returned to a lower altitude and went through a series of throttle back maneuvers to get a feeling for the plane's landing characteristics. When he returned to Key Field he made a perfect three-point-landing.

Key Field was in turmoil. The war had changed everything and Key had a temporary glut of people passing though. Pilots were standing in line to get their hands on an airplane so they could qualify for flight pay. McGuire stayed at the flight line and took every minute of flying time that wasn't spoken for. They had a strange collection of planes in service and McGuire flew every one of them.

Several times over the next month McGuire and friends caught a Friday afternoon military flight from Key Field to Atlanta. The Betas put them up and listened to their "war stories." Other Betas had left Tech for the war and a few had returned to visit, but none of them made it look as glamorous as McGuire and his friends.

They looked stunning in their forest green blouses and contrasting desert pink trousers. The gold bars on their shoulders and the silver wings on their chests made them the envy of every ROTC cadet at Ga. Tech. They also had money to spend.

McGuire's little black book still had some good numbers in it and he and his friends wowed the girls of Atlanta too. Dating a fighter pilot was much more glamorous than dating a college boy. When McGuire dated he couldn't help but think about Marilynn, back in San Antonio. He couldn't get her out of his mind, and he wrote to tell her that he would be leaving Mississippi soon.

McGuire's new station was Orlando Air Base. Fair weather and flat terrain made Florida a perfect place for the all-out, day and night, training of pilots. Orlando Air Base was headquarters for a new fighter command school whose motto was: "We progress unhindered by custom." This was where many fighter pilots would get their final training for combat before going overseas.

As the war progressed, new tactics and techniques were developed in each war zone and these were passed back to Orlando to update the new pilots. Tactical training was carried on in the form of a mock war which was constantly going on in an area across central Florida and out into the Gulf of Mexico. Fighter planes came from twelve air fields, some quickly bulldozed out of the Florida wilderness, to take part in the aerial battles.

The war wasn't going well in the Pacific. American forces were still reeling from the Japanese surprise attack at Pearl Harbor. The Japanese were forcing American troops off islands all over the Southwestern Pacific and were heading toward Australia. New pilots were needed if the Japanese were to be stopped.

The new pilots gathered in the ready room to hear about the program. The Director of Training stepped to the stage and the men stopped talking and came to attention.

"At ease gentlemen. Welcome to Orlando. Your time here will be very busy. As you know, pilots are in great demand. We have been asked to speed up your training. You will be flying every day and many nights---that includes Saturdays and Sundays."

The room full of pilots groaned as one. "We know your training has been accelerated already and you'd like to lay on the beach awhile. This war came sooner than anticipated, and you are desperately needed in combat areas.

"Besides flying, you will have survival training. You will be instructed in techniques to save your lives if you get forced down in hostile territory. The enemy isn't always the biggest danger in one of these situations. Often the elements could be more deadly. Since we don't know where you might be stationed, every pilot has to know how to survive if he goes down in the water, in the Arctic, in the desert, or in the jungle. You will be taught how to forage for food and fish with a string. You will be taught how to catch rain water, purify jungle water, or refine sea water for drinking purposes.

"Every day there will be a different mission to be carried out, enemy aircraft to intercept, an air field to be bombed, or a convoy to be strafed. You will fly the Curtis P-40E. This is the latest version of the Kittyhawk fighter which has proven so effective with the Flying Tigers in China."

Thus began an exhausting training period which had McGuire in the air every day for 21 straight days. Once in a three-day period he flew 17 hours.[1] McGuire was tired, but glad to be back in Florida, and to be involved in the final phase of his training. Training had gone so well that he had no doubt about his flying ability. In fact, he was supremely confident of his ability--a feeling well known to most fighter pilots.

Feeling he needed something to make himself look more mature, McGuire decided to add to the glamour of being a military aviator by growing a mustache. Movie stars of the era, like Clark Gable, looked distinguished with a mustache and McGuire hoped he would too.

Polly loved having Tommy stationed near Sebring, and she drove to Orlando to have dinner with him and spend the night. She couldn't believe how handsome he was in his uniform. As they ate dinner in the Officer's Club Polly said, "I'll have to admit it, son. The Army must agree with you. I've never seen you look more handsome or healthy."

"I love flying, Mother," said Tommy. "I'm flying every day and that makes me very happy."

McGuire spent the night in Sebring a few times and the hotel staff always found him a room near his mother's. He had to leave early the next morning to be back in Orlando in time to fly. During one visit to Sebring he told his mother, "I met a girl in San Antonio and I miss her very much. Her name is Marilynn Giesler. I'm thinking of asking her to marry me."

Polly said, "Watch out for those wartime romances--your Uncle Charles was in love with the actress Peggy Wood. There was a story after he came home from the war that he had a romance going with her in London. I don't know if it was true, but nothing ever came of it."

Tommy said, "He would have been a lot better off if something had come of it--even if it didn't last. Maybe he wouldn't be a bachelor after all these years."

The next day he wired Marilynn a dozen and a half red roses. He hadn't been in touch with her since he left Mississippi, and he hoped he hadn't waited too long.[2]

Meanwhile, Polly appointed herself entertainment committee of one for the military brass at Hendricks Field, in Sebring. The field was bubbling with B-17 bomber training, and was glutted with pilots, navigators, and bombardiers learning to function with enlisted men as a crew. Polly thought someone should look out for the base commander and his staff on a social level.

Since Polly didn't have a home in which to entertain these new dignitaries she hosted the Colonel and his staff at a spaghetti dinner at the Hammock Tavern. Col. & Mrs. McDaniel welcomed the opportunity to socialize with local citizens and they brought along Col. Savage, Maj. & Mrs. Passell, Maj. & Mrs. R. J. French, and Maj. & Mrs. Lightbody. From Sebring, Polly asked Mr. & Mrs. Vernon Higgins, Mr. & Mrs. Mitchell Ferguson, and Mr. & Mrs. Hayden Williams to attend.[3]

Of course Polly told them all about her son, and arranged another party to coincide with one of Tommy's overnight visits to Sebring. Tommy was embarrassed to be with this group of senior officers, and of all things, bomber pilots. They had wives and he didn't even have a date. When his mother had a few drinks and started talking a blue streak he was mortified. Before he left for Orlando he told his mother, "Don't invite me to another one of these parties. I'm uncomfortable with those people."

Polly replied, "You're just as important as any of them. Besides, it's my party and I'll invite whomever I like. If you tried, you could make some good connections."

"Leave me out next time," barked Tommy, as he left.

As training proceeded, daily combat missions were the rule. A pilot and his aircraft were sent out to meet the challenge. In the afternoon they met fighters from other groups over Tampa Bay for aerial combat. Dog fights occurred at every altitude with dozens of fighter planes in the sky at once. Nearby McDill Field, where McGuire had entered the Air Corps, and Drew Field added bombers to the crowded skies. It was a full-time job just avoiding a collision with one of the many planes in the sky.

McGuire and his fellow 313th Pursuit Squadron pilots from Orlando soon realized how lucky they were to be flying the P-40s. The "enemy" over Tampa Bay was often P-39 aircraft from elsewhere in Florida. It was clear after a few days that the P-40 was a superior airplane and almost always seemed to have the upper hand against the P-39.

McGuire remarked to a friend, "The P-39 has got the same engine as the P-40, but it sits behind the pilot. The propeller is turned by a long drive shaft which runs through the floor of the cockpit. That allows a

37MM cannon to be mounted where the engine should be--in front of the pilot. The cannon fires straight through the propeller spinner."

His friend replied, "I hear that having the engine in back of the pilot causes the plane to be out of balance--tail heavy. They tell me those cannon jockeys won't even try a loop for fear that the plane will fall out of it at the top."

"That's not true," said McGuire. "Yesterday I saw a P-39 do a loop. It went around just like any other plane that had the speed to do the maneuver."

"I don't care. I'm glad we have P-40s!" replied his friend.

One afternoon, after engaging in a combat exercise, McGuire made a break from the area and flew across Tampa Bay to St. Petersburg Beach. He searched for his Aunt Stella's house on 77th Ave. and buzzed it. He didn't see anyone so he returned to Orlando. A few days later he phoned his aunt and told her to be on the lookout.

"Aunt Stella, I'm over Tampa almost every afternoon. I flew over your house the other afternoon, but I didn't see anybody. When I get a chance, I'll come over again and wiggle my wings."

Thereafter, McGuire often flew low over his aunt's house. Reportedly, there had been enemy submarines spotted near the mouth of Tampa Bay, and Stella's neighbors were sensitive to the flight of military aircraft in the area. They noticed a fighter plane was flying extremely low over the area almost every day, and threatened to report the pilot if they could get his number.

One afternoon Stella's daughter, Elizabeth, who had been McGuire's childhood playmate back in New Jersey, was visiting with her mother in St. Petersburg. A plane flew over the house so low that it rattled dishes on the shelf.

Elizabeth said, "Hit the deck mother, he's coming back."

Much to Elizabeth's surprise her mother grabbed a dish towel and ran to the back yard. When the plane came back she waved the towel over her head. The plane dipped its wings and sped out over the Gulf and disappeared.

Stella Tolson turned to her daughter sheepishly and said, "That's Tommy, but don't tell anybody around here--they are all trying to get his number so they can turn him in."[4]

On other days McGuire flew north to Melrose, Florida, where he buzzed the home of his uncle, Robert Watson. He started thinking about giving Sebring a good buzz, too.

On April 30, McGuire was on a special navigation exercise which required him to land at two other air bases. He picked Hendricks Field, in Sebring, as his first stop. When he took off from Orlando he circled and picked out Bok Tower, at Lake Wales, on the southern horizon. Iron Mountain, where the tower stood, was the highest elevation on the Florida peninsula, and could be seen clearly from all over central Florida as a bump on the horizon. Sebring was about 40 miles beyond the Tower and he would be there in minutes.

McGuire got a thrill as he called the Hendricks Field control tower to get landing instructions. He had taken his air cadet exam there, but never dreamed he would fly a P-40 into the base and dodge B-17 bombers for a spot in the landing pattern.[5]

He had a special reason for landing at Hendricks Field. He had heard that his old high school chum, Campbell Tappen, was there. "Tap" had qualified for cadets, and had been in training at Dorr Field in Arcadia, Florida, but found that he was one of the unfortunate ones who couldn't stand the rigors of flying. He was temporarily at Hendricks Field awaiting reassignment. McGuire couldn't think of anything that would be more fun than to find him and "jack him up"--make him stand at attention and answer a bunch of crazy questions, before they had a brief reunion.

After McGuire parked his fighter plane at the visitor's ramp he asked the driver of the flight line Jeep to drive him to the squadron area where he knew Tappen was assigned.

Unfortunately Campbell was out of the area on a work detail. McGuire's flying mission had a time frame which had to be met, so he could not wait for his good friend to return. He left a note and returned to the flight line.

McGuire noticed that his P-40 was attracting a lot of attention, and didn't pass up the opportunity to show off a little at a bomber base. On takeoff he held his plane close to the ground and built up speed, then pulled its nose high and disappeared into some white clouds at 2500 feet. The rapid climb to altitude was exciting to everyone at Hendricks Field. They were used to the lumbering B-17s.

After takeoff McGuire flew north for a few minutes and came to Lake Jackson. He looked down at the home where he was raised, and flew along the shoreline exactly where he used to sail his canoe. He wondered what those same people would think if they knew who was flying the fighter past their backyards.

Near the other end of the lake he dipped his wings, and waved from the cockpit to a group of children who were swimming at Varena's beach. When he reached Caravacious Point at the end of the lake he thought, "What the Hell, I've got a few extra minutes. It wouldn't be right to fly off without saying a proper hello to everybody in Sebring."

He turned the plane and circled around the lake to approach again from the south. When he passed his home again he started a descent, and when he arrived at the intersection of Lakeview and Ridgewood Drives he turned and followed Ridgewood toward the center of town. He passed over the flagpole in the circle at 500 feet. He pulled the ship up and did a couple of barrel rolls. At the other end of town, he pulled the plane up and did a wingover, circled Dinner Lake and headed back down Ridgewood Drive.

Merchants and their customers crowded into the streets to see the low-flying plane. They were accustomed to the drone of B-17 bombers flying over town day and night, but they never had a fighter plane fly over town at low altitude. McGuire had the plane going at top speed as he again passed over the circle at low altitude and pulled up into a series of barrel rolls. When he reached Lake Jackson he turned north and buzzed the kids on the beach again. Then he turned toward Tampa wondering if anybody in Sebring could guess who was flying the fighter.

At the sheriff's office in the courthouse someone said, "Call Broward Coker, Tommy McGuire is back in town."

McGuire's mustache had grown well since he stopped shaving his upper lip and Polly thought he looked quite handsome. She urged him to have a portrait made. He went to Alan Anderson Studios on North Orange Street in Orlando, and sat for a formal portrait. The picture was the best one he'd had taken since he was a child in a sailor suit. His cadet picture had looked dopey, but this one looked like an Army pilot should look. He sent 11 x 14 sepia tone prints to his mother, father, and his aunts and uncles.[6]

In early May McGuire finished his course in Orlando. He would be going to the 56th Fighter Group in Baton Rouge, for reassignment somewhere else, possibly overseas. He flew up to five hours a day. He wanted all the flying time he could get before he left Florida.

Polly invited him to another party. He complained, but decided to go just to make his mother happy. After all, he would be gone for a long time and his mother would be alone again. He flew three hours Saturday morning, showered, and headed to Sebring to spend the night. One of the Sebring Hotel staff greeted him, "Tommy, we're ready for your big going- away party tonight."

"Damn!" said McGuire. "Is that what she's calling it?"

"She sure is. She told us it has to be special because it's your going-away party."

McGuire was upset, but said nothing to his mother. He did notice that his mother had already started the party and he warned her.

"Mother, take it easy. You'll be smashed by tonight."

McGuire in early 1942, taken in Orlando

Party time arrived and McGuire found himself greeting the guests alone. He sent one of the hotel employees to his mother's room with the message that the guests were arriving and her presence was needed. An hour went by and she still hadn't shown up. He was embarrassed, and didn't know what to tell the guests.

131

After another hour Polly showed up. It was apparent, at least to Tommy, that his mother had been drinking. She was loud and very gay as she went around the room greeting her guests. It was more than McGuire could take. He quietly left the party; went to his room, and in a rage threw his clothes into his B-4 bag. He stormed down the stairs and told the people at the desk, "When my mother sobers up, tell her I got called back to Orlando."

Sunday morning McGuire took his last flight at Orlando. For three hours he roamed over central Florida taking one last look at the places he had been the happiest while growing up in Sebring. He circled Bok Tower at Lake Wales, where he and his mother had always taken out-of-town guests, buzzed the giant coke bottle and high school in Avon Park, where he had tried to paint the red devil, and then he followed the railroad track past Lakemont crossing, where he had frightened many of his classmates with his high-speed driving.

Over Sebring he kept his altitude to conceal his identity. He just wanted to see the lake and beach where he had been so happy, and the high school where he had enjoyed his music, and had suffered the barbs of schoolmates.

He couldn't help but feel the humiliation of the night before when he saw the Hotel Sebring where he was sure his mother was still in her bed. He was above all of that now as he triumphantly soared above Sebring. There was no one to call him names, no one to tell him how to drive his car, no one to chide him about his mother. He was alone and free. Free to make his way in the world depending only on his ability as a flier.

As a final adieu he pointed his speedy plane to the west and in 15 minutes was over Bradenton Beach where he and his friends had enjoyed so many fun filled days. From there he flew north to St. Petersburg where he buzzed his Aunt Stella's home one last time. The next day he left for Harding Field, Baton Rouge, Louisiana.

[1] McGuire's Log book
[2] Marilynn Giesler McGuire Beatty's diary
[3] Highlands County News
[4] Elizabeth Tolson
[5] McGuire's Log book 4-30-42
[6] The picture is on the cover of this book

19

"I couldn't believe it myself. I said, 'yes'."

----Marilynn Giesler McGuire

In mid-May, 1942, the United States was still stunned by the Japanese attack on Pearl Harbor, six months before. There were rumors that Japanese submarines had been seen off the coast of California and the Army Air Corps ordered East Coast pursuit units transferred to the West Coast to help protect it from possible assault.

The 54th Fighter Group at Harding Field, Louisiana, transferred its three squadrons at once. No sooner did the 42nd, 55th, and 56th Fighter Squadrons and their new P-39 fighters arrive in California, than they were ordered to Alaska. On May 15 McGuire arrived at Harding Field, where the 54th Group Headquarters was still located. His squadron, the 56th, was on their way to Alaska, and he was put on restriction so he could follow on short notice.

McGuire got three hours of P-40 flying time the next day. The units in Alaska were flying P-39s, and everybody had to check out in that type of aircraft. McGuire wasn't looking forward to the P-39. He had heard so many things about the plane and just didn't feel good about it.

He called Marilynn in Texas and said, "I just transferred to Baton Rouge, but I am restricted to the area."

Marilynn said, "You aren't too far away. Can't you jump on a plane and come to San Antonio for the weekend?"

"I can't leave this area. We are confined to a 50-mile radius," Tommy replied. "For now it's a real snafu."

In a few days McGuire flew a P-39 fighter for the first time. The P-39, designed to intercept bombers, climbed to altitude rapidly, carried a heavy cannon, but had a short operational range. It was equipped with an Allison engine like the P-40, but that was the only thing the two planes had in common. A revolutionary airplane, the P-39 had tricycle landing gears and its engine was mounted in mid-plane, behind the pilot. The landing gear gave the pilot superior vision on the ground, because the plane sat in a level position, instead of the nose-high position of the P-40. These pilots, P-40 devotees, joked about the design, "Do you think they saw an airplane before they drew the plans for the P-39?"

The two cockpit doors opened like car doors, and the 37mm cannon in the nose fired a shell large enough to pierce the armor plate on an army tank. To bail out, the pilot had to jettison a door and climb out. It was thought to be more difficult to exit this plane in a hurry.

"We better learn to like it. It's the only plane we are going to be flying from now on," said McGuire.

McGuire asked if his off-duty travel restriction could be lifted and was told to stay within 50 miles of the base because he would be leaving soon. He called Marilynn with the bad news, "It looks like I'm stuck here. We will be moving soon. Why don't you come up here and visit?"

"I can't come now. Maybe I can come over there in a few weeks," replied Marilynn.

McGuire pleaded, "We may not be here that long."

The next week was busy. Tommy and Marilynn didn't get a chance to get together before he left Harding Field at daybreak on May 27, flying a P-39. It would be an all-day trip to California. His first fuel stop was Kelly Field in San Antonio, where he had ground looped an AT-6 just a few months before. His instructors would no doubt be surprised if they saw him flying into Kelly Field in a P-39 fighter.

He stayed with his plane until the fuel truck arrived and then got a ride to the operations office where he phoned Marilynn to tell her he was on his way to California and to tell her he was sorry they couldn't get together.[1]

Marilynn asked him to write and let her know where he ended up. She promised to write, too.

He left Kelly Field at 9:30 a.m. and flew west with the sun. All day long he navigated over parts of the United States he had never seen. He refueled at Biggs Field, in El Paso, and at Tucson, and arrived at March Field, California, in late evening. He had logged 10 hours flying time.

The word on the West Coast was simple--things looked bad in Alaska and he would be on his way as soon as transportation was available. The next morning McGuire resumed training in the P-39. On June 2, knowing he would not be able to make long distance phone calls from Alaska, Tommy made up his mind that he had to call Marilynn and have a serious talk. He was afraid he would lose her if he waited any longer.

He got to a phone and waited for hours for the operator to call back with Marilynn on the line. He spent the time rehearsing his speech over and over: "Will you marry me when I get home from Alaska?" Finally the phone rang and Marilynn was on the line. They talked small talk for a while and then he popped the question. Marilynn was surprised. She was even more surprised when she heard herself answer, "Yes, I will!"

Due to wartime conditions long distance phone calls were limited to three minutes, but they talked wildly for the allotted time, making plans, and then the conversation ended. Early the next morning he got his mother on the phone in Sebring, and told her of his plans. Much to his surprise she sounded pleased.

That night Marilynn's phone rang. It was Tommy's mother, "I just called to say hello. Tommy tells me that you two are getting married. I'm so happy!"

"Yes ma'am, I'm so glad to have a chance to talk to you. Tommy has told me so much about you," replied Marilynn, although Tommy had told her very little about his mother.

"Was Tommy at a race track?" asked Polly.

"I'm not sure I know what you mean," said Marilynn.

"He called me this morning and said he was at Santa Anita. That's a race track, isn't it?" said Polly.

Marilynn said, "Maybe you had a poor connection on the phone. He's at Santa Ana Air Base, not Santa Anita."

The United States had been separated from other wars by the oceans that boarded its shores. This time it was different. German submarines had been spotted in the shipping lanes off the Eastern seaboard and armed Coast Guardsmen patrolled beaches from New England to Florida, around the clock, lest spies might be put ashore. On the West Coast wreckage of devices had been found in the Pacific Ocean indicating that the Japanese had tried to send bombs, attached to gas-filled balloons, possibly launched from submarines, to land on American shores .

Newspaper headlines proclaimed, "JAPANESE ATTACK DUTCH HARBOR ALASKA WITH CARRIER BASED AIRCRAFT." This was the attack that had been dreaded--it was on this side of the Pacific Ocean and it scared officials out of their wits.

On June 7, Federal Marshals started rounding up and moving 99,770 Japanese-Americans from California to inland internment camps. Although most were American citizens they were moved because of their ancestry. There had been stories that Japanese laborers who lived near Pearl Harbor spied on and sabotaged the Navy bases and Army air fields, before and after the attack by the Japanese air armada. It was expedient to gather up everyone of Japanese descent rather than try and sort things out.

In Washington DC, Senator Claude Pepper of Florida told a Congressional Committee: "We should hang or guillotine Hitler and his gang when the war is over."

By June 12, the Japanese landed troops at Attu near the American base at Kiska, on the Aleutian chain. Thus far the war had taken place on distant islands in the Pacific. Now Japanese were landing on our continent. The 54th Pursuit Group had been sent to Adak, Nome, and Kodiak, Alaska, to deny an enemy foothold on U. S. soil, but the Japanese had landed anyway and announced that they were changing the name of Kiska to Narukami.

On June 14, McGuire boarded a C-53 transport plane at Lindbergh Field, San Diego, for a six day trip to Alaska. During a Burbank refueling stop, he wired Marilynn: *"Heading North, will write soon. Love, Tom."* They arrived at Boise, Idaho, at 5:30 a.m., after flying all day and night. They slept and at 3:00 p.m. flew to Felts Field, in Spokane, where they waited 36 hours for the weather to clear. On June 17 they flew all day over desolate forested territory and saw no sign of civilization from the air. At midnight they landed at Edmonton, Alberta, Canada. Again they held over a day for bad weather, and proceeded to Watson Lake, Yukon Territory. After spending the night they flew out at 6:00 a.m. the next morning for Nome, The Territory of Alaska.

All day they flew past snow-capped mountains which rose thousands of feet above their cruising altitude--some as high as 19,000 feet above sea level. Mt. McKinley, North America's tallest peak, was visible in the distance as they landed to refuel at Fairbanks. The sun was still high in the sky at 7:00 p.m. local time, when they landed at Nome,[2] only 37 feet above sea level. It looked like they had stopped just a few miles short of the end of the earth. That day they flew 17 hours, crossed four time zones, and ended up 160 miles from Russia, across the Bering Strait.

Nome was on the south shore of Seward Peninsula, which jutted into the Bering Sea near where it narrowed to become the Bering Strait. It was 1,000 miles northeast of Kiska, where the Japanese had landed. The intentions of the Japanese were not known. Some thought they took Kiska to keep it from being used as a stepping stone to Japan's northernmost island of Paramushir, 1,000 miles to the west. Others thought it was a diversion to keep America's forces out of the war in the Western Pacific.

Perhaps the Japanese took Kiska to locate a new base from which to capture all of Alaska, and eventually invade the rest of the North American continent. If Nome was the next target, McGuire's 56th Fighter Squadron would be the first line of defense.

Important as Nome might be, it wasn't an impressive place to see. Only 100 miles south of the Arctic Circle, the place was devoid of trees, and the air base consisted only of a windswept landing strip with tents to house the enlisted men and officers.

McGuire was assigned quarters in a pyramidal tent with five other officers who watched in awe as he unpacked and hung his uniforms. They had seen uniforms like his before, but not since they left the states. "How did you get here with those uniforms?" asked one of the men.

"I just brought them on the plane," replied McGuire.

"What kind of plane did you fly, that had room for a B-4 bag, a duffel bag, and a musette bag?" asked another.

"I didn't fly a plane up here, I rode up in a C-53 transport plane. How did you guys get here?" asked McGuire.

"We flew up here in P-39s," answered Converse Kelly. "Have you ever seen the baggage compartment in a P-39 ?"

"What baggage compartment?" asked McGuire.

"You catch on quick. We all flew up here with a razor, a tooth brush, and a change of underwear," answered Kelly. "Our baggage has never found its way up here. You'd better hide everything you own or you may be the victim of a midnight requisition. People around here would do anything to get a change of clothes."

The next day McGuire wired Marilynn: "*Arrived safely. Am well. Can't wait. Love, Tom.*" Later he wrote: "*This is some place, it hasn't gotten slightly dark since I have been here. The damn sun just goes around in a big circle above the horizon...the really bad thing is there are no Japs.*"

The sun never set and it never got dark, so patrols were flown around the clock. McGuire was assigned three hours' patrol duty every day. He was a Johnny-come-lately to the men who had been in Alaska for a month or more, and they ignored him, or worse, tried to brush him off. "Who is this guy with all the uniforms and the mustache? He looks like Errol Flynn in the RAF."

They were bored with Alaska. There wasn't any action. Just fly your three hours, play poker, and sleep. One diversion was the town of Nome. Nome had been the site of a gold rush many years before and had declined since. The main street ran parallel to the Bering Sea and consisted mainly of several weather-beaten saloons built on pilings over the beach. Much like an old western town it had boardwalks in front of the buildings so patrons could walk above the muddy ground. The bars never ran out of liquor, but everything else was scarce. A few served moose steaks but not much else. McGuire and the troops liked a watering hole known as the Polar Bar. It later became notorious when Bob Hope, Jerry Colonna, and Frances Langford visited there after performing at the air base.

The men would arrive there in parkas or flying suits, the only clothes they had. All except McGuire. He would show up wearing a blouse, a tie, a silk scarf and a tailored top coat and this attracted the attention of the other patrons. Occasionally he bought a round of drinks for the house. It made him a celebrity.

Saturday nights were pretty wild, the parties at the Polar Bar never seemed to end. It was still daylight at midnight and the bars stayed open.

The party went on continuously up and down the strip, and at breakfast time everyone went home to sleep it off. Once one of the pilots left alone to go home and in his state, stepped off of the boardwalk. Hours later they found him face down in the icy mud. He had apparently passed out and was lucky he hadn't suffocated or gotten frost bite.

There was always a poker game going on in the alert shack, which in fact was the CAA radio station. McGuire demonstrated his skill as a poker player and won often. The years of watching Polly's poker group and playing with the Newark Bears and later at Ga. Tech had turned him into an effective gambler. McGuire sat at the card table wearing his flying jacket, a silk scarf, and a crushed hat at a rakish angle. He always had a pile of money on the table and it bothered the guys.

It rubbed them the wrong way, too, when he made some outlandish claims about his flying abilities. One member of the group shook his head in disbelief and said, "This guy can't be for real. He believes he is in the movies!"

One day, during a game, the subject of the P-39's flying limitations came up. One of the guys said, "When I fly a P-39, I feel like I have a weight on the tail of the plane."

"You haven't got it trimmed-up," volunteered McGuire.

"I've trimmed it up. The plane just feels tail heavy. The engine has no business being behind the pilot. It should be in the nose like a normal airplane," replied the complainer.

"Yeah," chided another pilot. "Why else would the plane tumble like they say it does after a high speed stall? There is only one reason. The plane isn't properly balanced."

"Hell, that tumble isn't as bad as they say it is," chimed in McGuire. "I saw one tumble over Tampa Bay--it must have fallen 10,000 feet. The pilot kicked out the door and stepped out like he was getting out of a taxi cab. I thought I could have pulled it out if I had been flying it. A week later I saw one tumble and this time the pilot straightened it up."

"Well then, McGuire, you must be doing loops all the time when you are out on patrol," said Jack Rittmayer.

"I've done a loop or two," answered McGuire.

"You're talking through your hat," said Con Kelly.

"Hey, McGuire!" said another. "Why don't you put your money where your mouth is? Bet you won't do a loop the next time you're up?"

"You've got a bet," said McGuire, pushing his poker winnings into the middle of the poker table. "Who wants to cover this?"

"Where are you going to do it, out over the Bering Strait where nobody can see it?" asked Rittmayer.

"I'll do it over the field," suggested McGuire.

"I've got another 10 bucks that says you won't do it over the field," said Rittmayer.

So it was that on August 10, McGuire took his P-39 to 4,000 feet over the runway, put it into a dive, and pulled it up and over into a complete loop.[3] It was a maneuver the men below had never had the courage to do in a P-39. McGuire had never done one before, either. He just knew that page 16 of the P-39 pilot's manual said: "Normal loops, slow rolls and Immelmans are done with ease."

When McGuire landed, the ground crew instructed him to report to the Squadron Commander, Major Bill Litton. Litton gave him a good chewing, and restricted him to his tent for a few days, except for flying duties. McGuire didn't mind, he had earned the respect of his fellow pilots, not to mention a lot of their money. He noted in his log book: Aerobatics - Looped runway (confined).

The boredom of patrol was broken a few days later when McGuire and his wingman spotted a submarine in the Bering Sea. It crash-dived before they could identify it as Japanese, but they had something to report to intelligence when they landed.

54th Fighter Group, Nome, Alaska. McGuire is ninth from right, front row

Meanwhile, far to the South at Kiska, the Navy and the two squadrons of the 54th Group were taking a heavy toll on the enemy, sinking their 24th Japanese ship. McGuire's Squadron begged for a chance to join the other P-39 pilots from their group in the fight but they were out of operational range of the action. Their Commanding Officer told them: "What you're doing here is just as important--what's the sense of guarding the front door if the Japanese could just walk in the back door?"

Several times in September, McGuire was involved in scrambles. When the alarm sounded the pilots ran from the alert shack to their P-39s, and raced into the air. They never saw any Japanese but the exercise got their blood flowing.

There were Russian pilots attached to the base for on-the-job training. Russia was going to receive P-39 fighters as lend-lease from the United States and these pilots were learning everything they could about the airplane and its operation. They seemed to have a much higher opinion of the plane than did the Americans. They loved the 37mm canon---thought it would be effective against German tanks. Tommy wrote to Marilynn: *"These guys don't mind the cold. Somehow we don't trust them. We never know what they are thinking, but they can put away the booze."*

On the first of October, McGuire and his wingman flew in heavy snows, the first of winter. B-24 heavy bombers were driving the Japanese from Kiska and there were no enemy assaults anywhere in Alaska. A popular rumor had the 54th Group home by year's end.

McGuire hoped the rumors were true as he flew at 15,000 feet and read the outside temperature as 55 degrees below zero. The P-39 was the worst airplane ever built for cold weather. With the engine behind the pilot, the designers never found a good way to transfer engine heat to the cockpit for the pilot's comfort. The ground crew added weather stripping to the P-39s doors, but it was little help. After 30 minutes in the air their hands got so cold that they couldn't feel them, even though they were wearing three layers of gloves.

Living in a tent in winter weather was no picnic either. The Sibley stove in the center of each tent had to be stoked 24 hours a day. Even so it was miserably cold, and the men slept in their winter flying clothes. McGuire suffered continuously from sinus congestion and headaches as a result of the constant cold.

The cold tents made the 24-hour-a-day "Red Dog" poker game in the alert shack even more inviting. McGuire continued to win and soon turned into a banker of sorts. Near the end of the month he was often the only person who still had money left. He made small loans to fellow officers[4] so they could stay in the game or go to the Polar Bar for a few drinks. They repaid the net amount each payday. Charging any sort of interest on the loans would have been considered poor taste.

On October 15, McGuire got a letter from Marilynn and she said Paul Gustat from Sebring had called her, wanting to meet his friend Tommy's girl friend. She invited him and his cadet friends to her house over the weekend and she and her mother had a cookout for them. McGuire wrote back: *"Have you seen a Zoot suit? Do they actually look as horrible as they do in pictures? You should hear the remarks made when they show the pictures in Life Magazine."* He also told Marilynn about a diamond he intended to give her as an engagement ring. He needed her ring size so he could have the family heirloom made into a ring.

The next day McGuire, Major Litton, Lt. Alexander Nicholson, Lt. Carter, and one other pilot took off from Nome to fly to Fairbanks. It was the first leg on the way back to the states. The flight was to be a long one. Even with each plane equipped with a 75-gallon external fuel tank the distance would leave little fuel to spare, and the weather didn't look good.

After an hour it was apparent that the flight was in jeopardy. Head winds were strong and they were flying into snow. The margin of safety was vanishing and they knew their fuel tanks would be dry when and if they reached Fairbanks. Visibility was poor and they were nearing the rugged 5,000-foot Kuskokwim Mountains.

After two hours they were getting near Fairbanks, and Major Litton called for help from the Fairbanks control tower. Radar on the ground could give them a compass heading which would lead them to the base. Fairbanks control asked the Major to identify his group by giving the daily identification code. The code was a secret password which changed each day. Every pilot had access to the code so he could identify himself as an American. In this manner, people on the ground were protected from mistakenly directing the enemy to their location.

Nobody in the McGuire's flight knew the day's code word. They tried to convince Fairbanks they were American, but their arguments fell on deaf ears. Major Litton spoke, "Men, the radio signal is coming in five by five, we are near Fairbanks but they won't help us. We have one chance. We'll turn south and try to find the CAA auxiliary field at McGrath."

They turned south and searched for an opening in the overcast. They were flying in a full-blown blizzard and were having trouble just seeing each other. Their eyes ached from staring into the snow surrounding them, which might obscure a mountain. They checked their turn-and-

141

bank indicators and artificial horizons often to be sure they were flying level. In these conditions there was a danger of becoming disoriented.

A hole finally opened in the clouds and they slipped below the overcast to search the terrain for any landmarks which might lead them to McGrath. Major Litton spoke on the radio, "I'd rather take my chances landing in that frozen swamp below, than flying in circles until we run out of gas or hit a mountain. Drop your belly tanks, leave your landing gear up, and follow me."

The P-39s circled the frozen swamp and one by one took their turn, until they were all down safely. Four of the planes landed near each other. The fifth one strayed some distance away and nobody saw it land. They were sure it had come down safely--they hadn't heard an explosion or seen a fire.

The four men set up a camp. They followed survival procedures and strung a parachute from a wing tip to form a tent, and then lit a fire. Snow covered the make-shift tent and the heat from the fire melted it, dropping water on the men huddled below. The fifth man finally showed up with a sprained ankle. He swore that an animal had been following him. They decided that each man would retreat to his own P-39 and sleep in the cockpit. It was cold but offered more protection than the parachute tent. They were wet, cold and hungry, but lucky to be alive.

In the morning they could see that they were surrounded by mountains and had landed in the only suitable site for miles around. They also discovered that the fifth pilot had been followed by a bear the night before. The bear's foot prints were twice the size of a boot print, and they followed the same path the pilot had walked. Search parties from Fairbanks found them by mid-morning and by late afternoon they were safely at the base. McGuire felt a cold coming on, but thought it wasn't too bad considering the possible outcome of their adventure.

A few days later McGuire and the other pilots were flown to Elmendorf Field, at Anchorage. Elmendorf had a number of new P-38 fighter planes and the pilots of the 56th Fighter Squadron were checked out in the twin-engined planes. They found the new airplane far superior to the P-39 they had been flying.

After a day of P-38 flying they were taught skip-bombing. A bomb was dropped at low altitude and allowed to skip across the ground until it collided with the target, ideally destroying it. McGuire's tentmate, Converse Kelly, had a hairy experience on a bombing run--one bomb hung in the rack. He had to land with a live bomb still attached to the wing of his P-38. It probably was the smoothest landing he ever made, and he couldn't have picked a better time to demonstrate his flying skill.

McGuire heard the news that 52-year-old Eddie Rickenbacker had gone into the sea with a B-17 crew somewhere in the Southwest Pacific. McGuire knew Rickenbacker had survived the Eastern Airline crash in Atlanta, and was sure he would also survive this challenge. The old guy seemed to have nine lives. Maybe there were still a few left.

McGuire wrote Marilynn to tell her about the forced landing--he knew that the newspapers would carry the story in the states and he didn't want her to read about it in the paper. He also told her he was on his way home and looking forward to marrying her. One of the other pilots was heading home and agreed to mail the letter stateside, getting it to Marilynn several weeks quicker than the normal Alaskan mail.

[1]McGuire's Log book and Marilynn's diary agree on the date
[2]McGuire's 201 file--Itemized Schedule of Travel Expenses
[3]McGuire's Log book, 4-10-42
[4]McGuire's 201 file contained notations with names and amounts owed

20

"The following named O's, orgns as indicated, are granted a leave of absence of fifteen (15) days, eff the day after arrival in the United States. MIL-AIR auth, if available. CML-AIR at O's exp." 2ND LT THOMAS B. MCGUIRE 0437031 56th Fi Sq November 28/42
----McGuire's orders granting him leave

Civilization was never more appreciated than it was by McGuire and his fellow escapees from the desolate Alaskan winter. As they circled to land at Mitchell Field, Long Island, they could see the skyline of Manhattan. From the traffic pattern they could also see Roosevelt Field, the famous old field where Charles Lindbergh had started his historic flight to Paris. Lindbergh had wanted to use Mitchell Field, but it was tied up by competitors readying for their own trans-Atlantic attempt.

When they landed McGuire called Marilynn to tell her he was in New York. "I have to stay here until I get my orders. I'll visit my dad for a few days. I can't wait to see you." They planned to marry as soon as he got to Texas.

He wired his mother: "In New York. Waiting orders. See you soon." He would go to Sebring, then on to Texas. His new assignment would be overseas and he wouldn't be back for a long time. He wanted to see his mother.

A few days later he wrote Marilynn: *"I have no priority on travel and can't get reservations by air...also must cross the Canadian border on the 29th according to orders. I've got two weeks from the time I crossed the border until I recross it. I was told when I left, I would get an extension, and be told when to report to Baton Rouge..I know I won't have to go back, but until I receive definite orders, my old ones hold..Mother has stone so your engagement ring may be a little late."*

McGuire was caught up in a red-tape trap. He couldn't move until his orders came through. He took advantage of the time to visit his father and other relatives in New Jersey. His dad was beaming with pride as he took his smartly uniformed son through the shop at McGuire Motors. Tommy remembered each man and told them how much he had enjoyed the Packard convertible they had fixed up for him a few summers before.

Uncle Charles was tickled to see Tommy in his Air Corps uniform and he took him around the New Era Company and introduced him to everyone. New Era was manufacturing aircraft instrument panels as their contribution to the war effort. Afterwards, they sat in Charles' office for a long conversation about flying. Uncle Charles had kept up with the new airplanes and had lots of questions. He wanted to know all about the forced landing in Alaska.

Uncle Charles had the latest news about Eddie Rickenbacker. "The papers say he is OK since his rescue. He's remarkable to survive that Atlanta crash and now 23 days on a life raft in the ocean. He'd appreciate that forced landing of yours. You must meet him some day."

Tommy urged his uncle to go to Sebring and see Polly. He told him that she had sounded very lonely when he talked to her the day before.

"Our defense contracts keep me busy here," said Uncle Charles. "I'll get down there one of these days."

That evening Tommy and his father had dinner with Joan Mallon and the subject of marriage came up. His father was against it. "It looks like you are rushing into this thing. Most wartime romances don't work out."

"Dad, I've heard all the arguments. This isn't what you think. If you could meet Marilynn you would understand."

Joan Mallon kept quiet, but Tommy could tell by the gleam in her eye that she favored the romance.

Tommy was dying to see his cousin Vera, who still lived in New Jersey. He called and asked her to meet him and his dad in Manhattan for dinner. "It'll give us a chance to talk. I want to tell you about Marilynn."

Vera said she would love to do it, but had two very sick kids. "They have scarlet fever and I've been up with them for two nights and I'm not feeling too well myself. Fred is down south building an air base."[1]

Tommy was disappointed that she couldn't make it. They had spent so many happy hours together in Ridgewood, and in Sebring. Tommy had been there when Fred and Vera were courting. If anyone would understand how he felt about Marilynn, it would be Vera.

The orders came: Report to Harding Field, Baton Rouge, Louisiana, for reassignment. There was a two-week delay en route, time enough to see his mother and a few friends in Florida, then fly to Texas and get married. The trip to Baton Rouge would be a short one and Marilynn could go with him.

There were no flights from Mitchell Field directly to Sebring, but McGuire was able to catch a military flight to Tampa, and then another to Hendricks Field, in Sebring.

After a jeep ride to the Sebring Hotel and greetings from the hotel staff, Tommy went to his mother's room and knocked on the door. A hotel maid said, "Sir, she won't answer today. Maybe you could slip a note under the door."

He knocked some more, then gave up. He went down to the desk and spoke to Gatchel Burton, who said, "She's up there, Tommy.

Sometimes she won't answer the door for days. Go back up and make sure she knows it's you---she talks about you all the time."

He returned to the third floor and knocked on the door again, "Mother, it's Tommy; I'm home from Alaska. I want to see you." There was no answer. He checked-in to the hotel and walked the several blocks to the circle. He saw a lot of people, but he didn't know anybody. The war had turned Sebring into a thriving town. He thought he'd get a hamburger at the Sebring Cafe and he walked on down Ridgewood Drive. He saw several people he knew, but they walked past him with no sign of recognition. "Must be the uniform, or may be it's the mustache," he thought.

"Tommy, is that you?" It was Tommy Weaver's mother.

"Yes, ma'am, it is," he replied.

"I hardly recognized you, with the mustache," said Mrs. Weaver. "You're very handsome. But, you look lost. What are you doing wandering around Sebring by yourself?"

Tommy said. "My Mother isn't feeling well and she can't see me. I am lost. I don't know a soul in this town."

"I'm sorry to hear about your mother. Nothing serious, I hope?" asked Mrs. Weaver.

"No, I'm sure she'll be all right," replied Tommy.

"Have you had lunch?" asked Mrs. Weaver.

"As a matter of fact, I haven't," answered Tommy.

"Come on home with me and have lunch and I'll bring you up to date on my Tommy and everybody. We can call the hotel and see how your mother is feeling."

"OK, but don't go to a lot of trouble," said Tommy.

"Don't worry, we'll raid the icebox. We don't have a turkey in there this time, but we'll find something."

McGuire sat on the front porch of the Weaver's home and watched the traffic bustle past on Lakeview Drive. "Do you take the Correct Craft out much these days, Mr. Weaver?" he asked.

"Not much, Tommy. Can't get gas for a boat these days," answered Mr. Weaver. "I keep the tank full in case a plane goes down in the lake. The boys at Hendricks Field asked me, Mitch Ferguson, and the Maxcys to do that."

They sat and talked and Mrs. Weaver set up a card table and fed Tommy right where he sat. He ate like a horse and Mrs. Weaver was very happy. They laughed about old times and she told Tommy about all of the excitement that Hendricks Field had brought to Sebring. She knew where his old gang was and brought him up to date. Tommy Weaver had also gotten his wings and was in B-26 bomber training.

146

McGuire had some advice: "Tell my old fraternity brother to keep his air speed up, that plane has mighty short wings. When I was stationed in Orlando they used to say 'One a day in Tampa Bay,' and the B-26 was what they were talking about."

Mrs. Weaver told a funny story which caught Tommy with a mouth full of baked beans---he laughed out loud and spewed baked beans all over the porch. It startled Mr. Weaver, but Mrs. Weaver never skipped a beat. She went right on talking as she cleaned up the mess. After the meal, Tommy stretched out on a sofa in the living room and took a long nap. He was relaxed. He felt at home.[2]

The next day Polly was up and about and apologetic about being sick the day before. She did not look well and Tommy told her she should take better care of herself.

"I do the best I can, Tommy. I miss you and my mother so much, and nobody ever comes to see me since she died. I wish we'd never had the fight over the house."

Tommy knew it was true but he changed the subject and told his mother that he planned to marry Marilynn next week. "I love her, and I don't want to wait. I'll be going overseas again, and I want to marry her now."

Polly knew his plans and said, "I'm so happy for you. Marilynn and I have talked on the phone many times. I feel like I know her. She is a sweet girl, and she loves you."

"I'm sorry you won't be able to be in San Antonio for the wedding," said Tommy.

"I am sorry too, but I understand," said Polly. "Your father and I ran off and got married, without telling our parents. I've never been sorry we did. If we'd waited somebody may have talked us out of it, and then there wouldn't have been a Tommy McGuire."

Tommy gave his mother a hug. "At least, you told me about it," said Polly. "Just get Marilynn to come visit me real soon. I want everybody to meet her."

Except for the staff at the hotel, and a few people like Prof. Gustat, Uncle Jimmy, and Mr. Canto, Tommy couldn't find anybody he knew. George Lilly, Rev. Price, and Broward Coker were all in the service, as were all of his old buddies; Paul Gustat, Chubby Fulton, Bill Dutton, Herman Hancock, and Malcolm Watters. He made a trip to Arcadia to see a Ga. Tech buddy, Air Cadet Robert Higgins, who was in flight training at Carlstrom Field. When he found Higgins he shouted at the top of his voice, "Cadet Higgins, you miserable dodo, snap to attention when you're in the presence of a superior officer."

"Yes, Sir." Cadet Higgins snapped to attention and threw a mock salute. "You superior son-of-bitch. You look like a million bucks with that mustache. What are you doing here? I thought you were in Alaska."

"We cleaned up the Japs, so here I am," said McGuire.

"Why are you at Carlstrom Field?" asked Higgins.

"Just came here to see you," said McGuire.

"I'll be off tomorrow. Can you stay a few days?" asked Higgins.

"No chance my good man, I'm going over to Ft. Myers this afternoon to look up a buddy, another 'superior officer,' and then I'm off to Texas to get married," said McGuire.

"You're kidding me. Who do you know in Texas?" asked Higgins.

"Hig, she's terrific. Her name is Marilynn. I met her while I was stationed in San Antonio. Here's her picture."

"You dog, she is a real beauty. Let me have her address, I'm going to write and give her the real low-down on you."

At Ft. Myers, McGuire went to Page Field but Malcolm Watters was off the base. Malcolm was a fighter pilot, too, and had just returned from the Panama Canal Zone. Like McGuire, Watters had rushed out of the country to fly patrols in a non-combat area, and Tommy had wanted to compare notes with him.

Back in Sebring, McGuire's disappointment was eased when two of his good friends showed up. Lamar and Herman Hancock were home for a few days. Herman had arrived at Kelly Field the very day McGuire had gotten his wings. He had since earned his wings and his commission and was on his way to Europe as a P-38 pilot. Lamar was not in the service and he was upset about it. His employer had declared his forest management job "vital to the war effort" and he was frozen in his job for the duration.[3]

The three pals got together for an evening at the Hammock Tavern. Tommy and Herman had a lot to talk about but they knew that conversations about the Air Corps and flying were tough on Lamar. He had said, "I feel left out of things because I'm a civilian and everybody I know is in the service." They tried to talk about something else but they could not stay away from the subject of flying. They lapsed into it unconsciously, and one story led to another. Lamar could only grit his teeth and listen.

McGuire told how he had returned to the scene of his driving crimes, so to speak, buzzing Sebring, in a P-40. "I guess my driving wouldn't seem too wild, compared to the buzz job I gave them. Afterwards I circled the lake at tree top level and people along the shore waved to me. It reminded me of the times I sailed up and down the lake in my canoe.

You remember the 'killer canoe' don't you?" The Hancock boys remembered the canoe as no one else would.

McGuire contacted Base Operations at Hendricks Field, and, when the time cane, it was no problem getting a military flight to San Antonio. At 5:30 in the morning he stood in the dark in front of the Sebring Hotel waiting for Belcher's Taxi to pick him up. Wayne Taylor, Charles Martin and several other paper boys were folding their **Tampa Tribunes** in a store front newspaper office and he bought a copy of the paper from one of the boys to read while he waited. He was on his way to Texas to get married. What lay beyond that? Only time would tell. Before Tommy arrived in Texas, Marilynn received a letter[4] from someone she had never met:

A/C Robert Higgins
Riddle Aviation Inst.
Carlstrom Field
Arcadia, Florida
Dec. 1, 1942

Dear Marilynn,

Tommy was over to see me last weekend and I tried to get him to stay a few days but he said, "Hig", I've met the most gorgeous creature and she has consented to marry me next week. He showed me your picture—it's a good thing he saw you first or he would have had to defeat me first to get you. My sincere best wishes to you both.

Robert A. Higgins

When Tommy arrived in San Antonio, he surprised Marilynn with the family heirloom diamond in a new setting, in her size. Polly had made sure that her daughter-in-law would have a proper ring.[5]

On December 4, at 4:30 in the afternoon, Tommy and Marilynn were married at the Base Chapel at Ft. Sam Houston, in San Antonio. It was only one week short of a year since Sidney Bowers, Marilynn's friend and maid of honor, had insisted, "I know you two will get along," when she had talked Marilynn into a blind date with Tommy. Tommy knew no one in San Antonio, so Lt. Albert "Ned" Gates, who was married to one of Marilynn's friends, was kind enough to serve as his best man.

They hadn't had time to arrange for photographs to be taken and there wasn't time to travel on a honeymoon. Instead they checked into the St. Anthony Hotel, in San Antonio, for the few days they had before leaving for Harding Field. During one of their first dinners as Lt. and Mrs. McGuire, in the hotel dining room, Tommy insisted on ordering the meal. He introduced Marilynn to two foods she had never eaten; artichokes and Hollandaise sauce.

Lt. and Mrs. Thomas B. McGuire, Jr. Taken by a street photographer

They strolled downtown San Antonio to shop and lunch at one of their old haunts. Again, as a year before, a street photographer stepped in front of them and snapped their picture. It was to be their only wedding photograph, and it pictured a handsome young pilot and a radiant bride--a happy couple, walking arm in arm and facing an uncertain future without any trepidation.

The Alamo Plaza Hotel Court was no palace, but during wartime in Baton Rouge, they were lucky to get a place at all. That's how the honeymooners felt when they observed the time-honored tradition of the groom carrying the bride over the threshold.

"Welcome to the Alamo," said Tommy, as he put Marilynn down.

"Isn't it a scream, moving all the way to Louisiana to live in the Alamo? Nobody in San Antonio will believe it!" said Marilynn.

The Alamo Plaza, constructed of stucco, had an entrance to the interior court through an arch which resembled the real Alamo. The green and white striped awnings worked against the illusion of the famous old landmark. It was a place to "hang your hat," and as it turned out, a place to hang Marilynn's wardrobe. Marilynn's mother had insisted that her daughter be prepared for the social obligations of an Army Officer's wife. Her clothes were proof of this, as her formal dresses filled the closet.

"Why did your mother want you to bring so many dresses? You can't wear but one at a time," said Tommy.

"A lady can't wear the same dress twice. Women notice things like that, and I wouldn't want anyone to think that I only had one dress." Marilynn could attend many Officer's Club dances without having to wear the same dress.

The Alamo Plaza was full of pilots and their wives and in a few days Tommy and Marilynn were among friends. They were all in the same boat. Tommy and the other men were up early each day to report to Harding Field, the Headquarters of the 54th Fighter Group. The wives had each other to visit with during the day.

Tommy and several of the guys met each morning and headed to the base together. It was back in the air after several months layoff, and Tommy flew everything he could get his hands on. He'd fly a P-39 one day and his old favorite, the P-40, the next.

Harding Field offered a wide variety of aircraft and Tommy flew a twin engine DB-7B dive bomber and its cousin the A-20 Havoc bomber.[6] He even flew an L-4, a military version of a high wing civilian plane. It was like the plane he'd flown at Ga. Tech.

These were very romantic times for Marilynn and Tommy. They had been rushed into marriage by the circumstances of war. They hadn't known each other very long before they were separated, and then, after 10 months apart, they had married the day after his return. Now that they were together for a few weeks, as husband and wife, they knew that they had done the right thing. They were very much in love with each other.

When Tommy arrived home in late afternoon there was usually a impromptu cocktail party in somebody's room. The rooms weren't big and three or four couples made a crowd. They'd have a few drinks and then crowd into a taxi and move on to a restaurant for dinner. Everybody was from another part of the country, and they talked a lot about "back home." It was fun, lots of joking and laughing, and later they'd find a place with music, and dance.

It was the McGuire's turn to host the evening cocktail hour in their room, and they had crackers and cheese to go with the drinks. Tommy was assigned the task of chopping up some anchovies to go on the crackers. Finding no other suitable place in the cramped quarters, he sat in the bathroom, on the edge of the tub, placed the plate on the closed toilet lid, and cut them.

Marilynn cleared the dresser top to make room for a makeshift buffet and bar. She placed all of their personal things in the dresser drawers. Halfway through the party, a loud ringing noise came from one of the drawers. Their alarm clock was set for 6:00, and had gone off. This was Tommy's usually morning waking time. The alarm brought laughter and a search to find which drawer it was in. Then a round of jokes about the newlyweds, "They set that alarm to get rid of us, so they could be alone." Marilynn was embarrassed, and blushed to prove it.

"Let's get going or we will miss our reservations," Tommy advised.

As the ladies rushed to freshen up and check their makeup, one of the men, Captain Kenneth George, gave Marilynn a playful bump that caused her to spill a large amount of perfume on her silk dress. The dress absorbed every bit of the perfume. When they all crowded into a cab, Ken, who had gone to Alaska with Tommy, said, "Somebody in here smells like a Singapore whore house."

For all of her association with military people in San Antonio, Marilynn had never heard such language, and she was shocked, and embarrassed. She was glad it was dark in the cab, and no one could see her blush again.

Having been raised in a city with over a century of military tradition, Marilynn was well schooled in military etiquette. She mentioned to Tommy that it was traditional for a new officer and his wife to make a social call on the Base Commander at his home.

Tommy said, "I've heard of the courtesy call, but I think it's an out-dated custom."

"I don't think so," said Marilynn. "Any man who has risen to Base Commander is bound to be an old Army man, and I'm sure he would honor the tradition. All you have to do is ask."

"Who do I ask?" asked Tommy.

"You ask the Colonel's aide if they are 'Receiving.' If they are, he will set up an appointment for us to call."

The next day, Tommy stopped at the base headquarters and asked the Colonel's aide, "Are the Colonel and his wife receiving?"

"Yes, they are," replied the aide. "The Colonel has been very disap-pointed. None of the young officers seem to be acquainted with the tradition. He and his wife would be pleased to have you call."

Tommy set up an appointment for several nights later. Marilynn knew how to dress. She wore her best "early evening" dress, and she had her hair done that afternoon. Tommy wore his green blouse and "pink" desert tan trousers, a very attractive uniform, and he remarked to Marilynn, "We look fit enough to meet a General."

They arrived at the Colonel's house five minutes early, and at seven o'clock Tommy rang the door bell. They were shown in by a servant, and quite formally ushered into the living room and introduced to the waiting Commanding Officer and his wife. Marilynn had been correct in every aspect of the visit. They were dressed just as the host and host-ess, and they were warmly greeted.

The Colonel observed, "Not many of the young officers and their wives are bothering to call. I guess it's the war. My wife and I have al-ways enjoyed meeting the new couples as they arrived."

The McGuires were offered a drink. Marilynn knew this was a good sign. They might have gone through a few minutes of small talk and been dismissed, or they might have been offered coffee. Tommy could tell by the gleam in Marilynn's eye that they had made a good impres-sion. The Colonel asked Tommy, "What was your last station, Lieuten-ant?"

"Alaska, sir," answered Tommy.

"I thought this might be your first station. How long where you there?"

"Only about six months, sir," answered McGuire.

The ladies had their own conversation. The Colonel's wife asked, "Have you been to an Officer's Club dance yet?"

"Yes, we have," answered Marilynn.

"I don't like the way the young wives are dressing to attend dances," said the Colonel's wife. "I can see that you know how to dress, but some of the young woman are wearing short dresses to the club and it doesn't look right."

She seemed to know that Marilynn would understand that a long dress was the proper attire for the dance and told Marilynn, "You should pass the word along to the young wives. The Colonel and I would be happier if they would wear long dresses to the dance."

"Yes ma'am, I will mention it," said Marilynn.

The Colonel and his wife were enjoying their visitors and a second drink was offered and accepted. The men and women had their separate conversation until the Commanding Officer's wife interrupted her husband to tell him that the young wives would soon be wearing long dresses to the club dances. The Colonel was angry that his wife interrupted him and an argument ensued.

Tommy and Marilynn were embarrassed as it developed into a loud fight with both the Colonel and his wife shouting at each other. Finally, red faced, the Colonel turned to the McGuires and said, "I guess you two need to run along. I know the Lieutenant has an early start in the morning, and he needs to be wide awake to fly." Tommy and Marilynn were glad they had been dismissed. They had not known what to do when the Colonel and his wife fought.

The next day Marilynn passed the word that wives should wear long dresses to the dance on Saturday. The following day Tommy got static from the other young officers: "My wife doesn't have a long dress and I can't buy her one. It takes everything I make to pay for the motor court."

"What are you and your wife doing calling on the Colonel and his wife, anyway? It makes the rest of us look bad because we didn't do it, and now our wives need long dresses by Saturday's dance."

Tommy thought a moment and said, "Marilynn has a closet full of long dresses. Your wives can borrow one."

That evening a group of wives showed up at the McGuire's room, each to select a dress from Marilynn's collection. Marilynn was taken by surprise and she complained to Tommy.

"You can only wear one at a time," said Tommy.

It was like a department store sale. The girls handed dresses back and forth. They passed through the crowd with a dress held over head, into the bathroom to try it on, then back out to see if the rest of the girls thought it looked OK. Marilynn grabbed one and put it away for herself.

Saturday night arrived and there was a new feeling of formality at the dance. The young wives were wearing their newly found formals, some even sporting flowers. Couples danced near the McGuires and said, "Isn't this great? Everyone looks so nice."

The Colonel and his wife came by the table and thanked Marilynn for passing the word to the other women. "Doesn't everybody look so nice?" said the Colonel's wife. "This is the way it should be."

Marilynn agreed, but as she looked around the room, she said to Tommy, "I wonder if I got the right dress? Seeing my dresses all over the room is almost like seeing my life flash before me."

In the weeks that followed, the girls worked out an elaborate scheme to switch dresses after each dance. As one of the girls said, "Marilynn, I love this dress, but I'd just die if I had to wear it to two dances in a row."

Saturday nights at the Officer's Club dance you could hear this joke: "Pardon me miss, haven't we met before? I'm sure I remember your dress."

The 54th Fighter Group received a warrant for pilots who had P-38 flying time and McGuire was first in line to sign up. Many of the fellows had put in a few hours of P-38 time in Alaska and that was enough to qualify. One pilot, Wally Jordan, had been stationed at Elmendorf, but hadn't gotten a chance to fly a P-38. By the time his records were reviewed for the new assignment, he made sure they showed some P-38 time.[7] McGuire was among the eight pilots selected to report to Orange County Airport in Los Angeles for a few weeks of P-38 training and reassignment.

[1] Vera W. Schneider
[2] Mary Weaver
[3] Lamar Hancock, SHS '38
[4] Marilynn Beatty still has the letter.
[5] Marilynn McGuire Beatty furnished most of the information in this chapter
[6] McGuire's Log book
[7] Wally Jordan

21

On February 7, McGuire took his last flight at Harding Field in a P-39. Alas, the honeymoon was over and it was time to move on to California for an overseas assignment. Sadly, Marilynn would be going back to San Antonio. They discussed the possibility of her making the trip, but they had orders: "Wives are forbidden to accompany their husbands to California, there is no housing available." Some wives were going anyway, but Tommy insisted that Marilynn return to San Antonio. Trains were crowded with troops and travel would be difficult for her.

McGuire accompanied Marilynn back to San Antonio. The newlyweds had not been apart since their wedding but now they were down to their last few days together. They had known all along that this time would come, but it came too soon. Early in the morning Marilynn accompanied her husband to Kelly Field. After checking in at the operations, he hugged and kissed his wife for the last time and vanished into a C-54.

The next day McGuire was at the Orange County Airport, Santa Ana, California, where he would be stationed while undertaking P-38 transition training. A few days later he was flying with the Operational Training Unit, at Muroc Army Air Base, on the edge of the Mojave Desert, northeast of Los Angeles.

In the year since earning his wings, McGuire had accumulated 500 hours of flying time and was a skilled pilot. Now there would be a month in which to become proficient in this new twin-engined fighter plane. McGuire soon felt that the P-38 was the finest plane he had ever flown.

At Muroc, later to be known as Edwards Air Force Base, they flew RP-38s, a stripped-down version of the P-38. The planes had no guns, armor plate, superchargers, or oxygen equipment. It also lacked the weight of a P-38 and flew like a "bat out of hell" up to 14,000 feet, where its super-chargerless engines ran out of oxygen. Most of the pilots in the group had little or no twin-engine flying time and the first week allowed them a chance to get comfortable with the duplicate engine and propeller controls.

McGuire recognized some familiar faces among the pilots in training. Gerald Johnson had traveled to Alaska with McGuire but had been stationed near Kiska. Jack Rittmayer had come home from Alaska with McGuire. Wally Jordan had been with him at Harding Field a year before, and he had also gone to Alaska with McGuire, although they had not been at the same base. Jordan and McGuire were the only pilots in the group with mustaches, and they took some ribbing about it. Jordan had grown a mustache for years and showed McGuire how to trim his.[1]

After a week at the desert they moved back to Santa Ana. McGuire and Jordan and several other pilots hit Los Angeles' best night spots. They knew where they were headed. Good food and Tommy Dorsey Band music, like they enjoyed at the Palladium, would be lacking.

At Santa Ana, they flew P-38Fs and it was a popular plane with the pilots. Designed by Lockheed as a high altitude interceptor, it had two supercharged Allison engines to lift a devastating cluster of guns, which could knock down incoming enemy bombers. The design had yielded a large airplane that was surprisingly agile, and also suitable for combat against fighter planes.

The unique design placed the pilot, four 50-Caliber machines, and one 20mm cannon in a short fuselage, called the gondola, in the center of the wing. The engines were mounted in the front of twin booms, one on either side of the pilot. The booms housed the superchargers, engine coolant radiators, oil coolers, batteries, and the retracted main landing gear. They extended back beyond the wings, where each had a vertical stabilizer. The horizontal stabilizer connected the booms between the rudders.

The pilots wondered, "What happens if you bail out of this one? That horizontal stabilizer is sitting back there like a big knife blade, just waiting to slice a pilot in half."

The instructor answered, "Don't worry. The elevator is further back on the P-38 than it is on other fighters. This gives you a better chance to miss it. On other fighter planes you've got to avoid a tall rudder that is directly behind the cockpit. On the P-38 the rudders are shorter and are off to the sides, making them less of an hazard than a standard rudder. Just roll her over and drop out. You've got less to worry about with the tail planes of a P-38 than with other fighter planes."

The pilot of a P-38 had excellent visibility. The nose of the gondola was relatively short and housed neither an engine nor a propeller to turn in front of the pilot. The engines did cause a blind spot at two o'clock and ten o'clock, but a slight tipping of a wing opened up that view momentarily.

Other fighter planes had wing-mounted guns. Each of those guns being outside the arc of the propeller, had to be aimed slightly inward, so that the projectiles formed a cluster at some distance in front of the plane. If a target was at the proper distance in front of a P-40, or a P-51 where the bullets converged, it would be hit by a very damaging cluster of fire. If the target was closer, or further away, the pattern of hits was less effective.

The fire power of the P-38 was remarkable. This rare bird had all of its guns mounted in the nose of the center fuselage. The five guns were aimed in parallel to fire a cluster pattern from the moment the projectiles left the guns. The devastating stream of lead from these guns could easily saw the wing or tail off an enemy airplane. When the guns were fired the strong smell of cordite filled the cockpit and many of the pilots found the gunpowder smell intoxicating.

Above 15,000 feet the air was thin, but the superchargers allowed the engines to run like they were at sea level. The superchargers used exhaust gases from the engines to propel compressors which pumped air into the carburetors. In other fighter planes the exhaust stacks on the engines were short and emitted the sound of each cylinder separately. On the P-38 the engine exhaust was collected in the exhaust shroud and directed through the supercharger before being expelled aft of the cockpit. This gave the P-38 a wonderful purr.

McGuire tried everything in the P-38. He knew his life could depend on his ability to fly the plane under every condition. He flew it on one engine, he looped it, barrel-rolled it, and forced it into violent maneuvers to find it's weaknesses. In dog fights he pushed the plane into high-speed stalls and found that it retained remarkable aileron control although the inner wing was losing lift and causing the plane to buffet violently. There were none of the problems associated with propeller torque since the two propellers were counter-rotating.

They took gunnery practice, flew over the Pacific Ocean, flew high altitude missions, and put in a few hours of night flying. At the end of the four weeks the group was ready for combat. McGuire, Jordan, Johnson and several other pilots were processed for overseas and while other pilots boarded ships for a long trip to Hawaii, and additional training, these veteran pilots boarded a transport plane to fly all the way to Brisbane, Australia.

For five long days McGuire and the other pilots rode the hard metal "bucket seats" of various C-54 military transport planes. They played cards, read, drank coffee from giant thermos bottles, and slept. To break the monotony, McGuire wrangled his way into the co-pilot's seat in the cockpit as often as possible. The transport pilots appreciated a chance to take a break on the long flights.

They also enjoyed the chance to needle a fighter pilot, "How does it feel to fly a real airplane instead of a pea-shooter?"

"I'd rather fly a pea-shooter than be a bus driver," replied McGuire.

They kidded McGuire about fighter pilots wearing such large wristwatches. Self-consciously McGuire covered his own wristwatch with his sleeve. He had been using the chronometer to time each of the island-hopping flights since they had left California. When they landed in Brisbane, he recorded the 37 hours and 30 minutes of flying time in his log book as passenger time. They had crossed the International Date Line and the Equator in their travels.

From Brisbane they caught a flight 600 miles north and reported to the 370th Service Squadron of the 5th Fighter Command at Charters Towers Air Base, near Townsville. McGuire was beat after traveling so far but he contacted a florist and wired a dozen red roses to his bride back in San Antonio. He figured, "Marilynn will know I arrived safely --you can't wire roses from the middle of the ocean."

On March 23, McGuire got back in the air as a pilot. He got an hour in a P-39F and 45 minutes in a P-38G. Flying a P-38 and a P-39 in the same day left no doubt that the P-38 was the aircraft he wanted to fly. As a new pilot he knew his chances of flying a P-38 might be slight, since they were still rare in this theater. He had signed on as a P-38 pilot and had taken the P-38 training. He could hope. As boring as it might have been, that stint in Alaska looked good on paper. Not many pilots reporting to the Southwest Pacific theater had flown in a combat zone. He hoped it would give him an edge when his assignment was made.

He wrote to Marilynn: *"The four of us are building a platform to raise our tent off the ground. As carpenters we would make good bartenders, but as long as it works who cares what it looks like....by the way, are you playing any bridge? I hope you keep in practice and a little improvement wouldn't hurt."*

For the next few weeks McGuire got in as much flying time as he could. There was a shortage of aircraft for unassigned officers. He hung around the flight line and took every 30 or 45 minutes of "unspoken for" flight time. When his assignment came, he wanted to be ready.

McGuire, Wally Jordan and Gerald Johnson went to Camp Muckly near Brisbane and discussed their assignment with General Wurtsmith of Fifth Fighter Command. To their surprise they were given a choice of assignments. They all chose the 9th Fighter Squadron, the only P-38 squadron in the 49th Fighter Group.

Back at their quarters, Wally Jordan produced an unopened bottle of Yellowstone sour mash bourbon he had brought all the way from San Francisco, and the three of them sat down and toasted the good fortune on their new assignment, until the bottle was empty.

[1]Col. Wally Jordan, USAF Ret., furnished most of the information in this chapter

22

"You should see this church. I've never seen so many lilies. It's like a wedding. The church smells like perfume."

--- Marilynn: in a letter to her mother from Sebring.

Marilynn was relieved when she got the roses from Tommy and told her mother, "He must be somewhere fairly civilized, or he wouldn't be able to wire roses." There was no time to feel blue as she arranged to travel to Sebring to meet Tommy's mother. Polly and Marilynn had become good friends over the telephone and she wanted to make the trip before she got tied down with a new job at the phone company.

The trip from Texas to central Florida was very tiring and Marilynn was nervous as the train pulled into Sebring. She tried to remember all the things Tommy had told her about his mother. Her own mother's advice was still ringing in her ears, "Just be yourself, you already have something in common with her--you both love Tommy."

When Marilynn stepped from the train she was met by one of Polly's friends who explained: "Polly isn't feeling well. Nothing serious, but she asked me to get you settled in the hotel, and she will be able to see you tomorrow." Marilynn was disappointed, but in a way she was relieved. After the two-day trip on the train she felt like she reeked of coal smoke, and was dying for a bath. She'd get a good night's sleep in a real bed, fix her hair, and be at her best when she did meet Polly.

Polly was "well" by the next day and she and Marilynn hit it off at once. Polly spent several hours showing Marilynn around. It was apparent that she was the grande dame of the hotel. She got immediate attention wherever she went. When she appeared in the doorway of the dining room someone came forward at once to escort her to her table. If she moved toward the elevator, one of the bell hops would come forth to operate it for her. The hotel was crowded with wartime guests but everyone knew Polly.

They moved around the hotel on a schedule which one of the bell hops told Marilynn was designed to avoid the Lewises, who also lived in the hotel. Apparently Polly and Mrs. Lewis had argued when Polly felt that Mrs. Lewis was getting too involved in Marilynn's visit. Polly, jealously, wanted to handle everything and had told Mrs. Lewis to mind her own business.

Sebring was not the sleepy village it had been. Sebring and Avon Park, 10 miles to the north, were now heavily involved in military aviation. Hendricks Field, south of Sebring, was going full blast training bomber crews and Avon Park had the Lodwick contract flight school, much like the one Tommy had been through at Corsicana. In addition the Avon Park Bombing Range drew bomber and fighter training missions from bases all over the South. Air traffic from the three bases filled the skies, day and night. A glance into the sky often revealed 40 to 50 aircraft. The drone of the four-engined B-17 bombers never ceased and mammoth double-trailer tanker trucks roared through Sebring in an endless 24-hour stream, delivering aviation fuel for the bombers.

Sebring also hummed with social activities for Polly and Marilynn. There were morning coffees and afternoon teas, and guests for dinner at the Hotel. As the two women moved about town, Marilynn was given a running tour. After a few days she knew where most of Sebring's prominent citizens lived.

Marilynn met the Gustats. Tommy had spoken of them so often, and she had met Paul while he was in Air Cadet training in San Antonio. She also met Mrs. Rex Beach, wife of the famous writer, who sent a bouquet of tropical flowers to her hotel room the next day. She also met Dot Rudasill, a classmate of Tommy's from high school.

Dot issued an unusual invitation: "Marilynn, come join me for breakfast in the morning. There will be over a hundred handsome men there." Marilynn looked bewildered.

"I'm not kidding," assured Dot. "We will have breakfast with 100 British pilots. At least they'll be pilots soon. They're English Air Cadets coming to this country for flying lessons. They get off of the train here and go by bus to Carlstrom Field, at Arcadia. We feed them at the hotel before they board buses and we need volunteers to serve food and make them feel at home."

Six forty-five the next morning Marilynn, Dot, and the other women greeted the cadets as they came in from the train station. The blue-uniformed young men had arrived in New York the day before, and had been hustled onto a train, for the trip to Sebring. Now they were in Florida smelling orange blossoms and being served breakfast by a group of beautiful young ladies with southern accents--"This must be heaven!" one of them said.

The hotel dining room buzzed with conversation.

"Pardon me, miss. What is this called?" asked a cadet.

"Those are grits. Put butter on them," answered Dot.

"What are grits?" asked the cadet. "It looks like mush."

"It's like mush, but it's ground corn," replied Dot.

They ate the grits and seemed to enjoy them. They also drank as much orange juice as they could get. One cadet explained, "We haven't had oranges at home in years."

Marilynn had met many cadets in San Antonio and except for the British accent and blue RAF uniforms, these guys weren't much different than American cadets. As the cadets loaded onto their buses one of them said, "I liked the orange juice, but I really loved the 'Hot Ones'." It took a while to figure out that the Englishman liked the hot biscuits that had been served. The girls had moved from table to table offering more hot biscuits saying, "Have a hot one."

A few days later Marilynn and Polly made a trip to Winter Haven where they met L.B. Anderson, the trust officer of Tommy's trust account in the Exchange National Bank. Polly explained: "We have always been private people. My mother set up the trust here instead of in Sebring, because she figured it wasn't anybody's business. She wanted to be sure that Tommy's education was taken care of--she knew we couldn't depend on his father to do it."

After the banking business was done they lunched at a tea room and then went shopping for liquor. Marilynn was surprised. They had been served drinks by Polly's "inner circle of friends" in Sebring, but why was she buying so much liquor? Polly explained, "Sebring is a dry town. Some of us are not Southern Baptist, and we like a drink occasionally. With gas rationed, we replenish our friends' supplies when one of us goes out of town."

The next day Polly and Marilynn made the rounds in Sebring delivering the liquor. Polly had a large purse which held the "delivery" until she was into the house. Nobody advertised the fact that they had whiskey in their home, and when Polly handed over the liquor it was quickly stashed in a hidden liquor cabinet.

Polly had a "C" gas stamp on the windshield of her car, but there seemed to be an endless supply of gas for trips around central Florida, and another day they visited Bok Tower in Lake Wales. Edward Bok's tribute to the opportunity America offered to emigrants featured a carillon which could be heard for miles around. Standing on the highest spot in Florida, the pink marble tower rose 500 feet above large, lush gardens and a reflecting pool in which foot-long goldfish swam. The McGuires always took visitors to see Bok Tower and Marilynn recognized it from family pictures Tommy had shown her.

They lunched at Chalet Suzanne, one of the finest restaurants in Florida. After a dessert of crepes, the ladies proceeded to a lingerie shop in Lake Wales. Polly explained, "This is the finest shop this side of Palm Beach. I want you to have something nice for your trousseau when Tommy comes home and you go on a real honeymoon."

Polly was known in the shop and she said to the owner, "This is Tommy's wife. I want her to have the prettiest nightgown in the shop."

The ladies were seated in the back of the shop and the owner and a clerk proceeded to show the most elegant night gowns Marilynn had ever seen. One beautiful champagne colored silk and lace gown pleased them both and Polly insisted that Marilynn try it on. "Your daughter has excellent taste," said the owner, "this is one of the finest items in the store."

In the dressing room Marilynn was shocked to find out that the gown and matching peignoir cost $350.00. She loved it, but knew she couldn't accept it. In the few days she had been in Sebring she had never seen a more generous person, but she sensed that Polly was spending more than she should. Tommy had said, "Mother spends like a drunken sailor, even if she doesn't have it." She modeled the gown and Polly was telling the clerk that they would take it when Marilynn said, "Polly, may I speak with you?"

The clerk excused herself.

"I've never seen anything this lovely, but I can't let you buy it for me," said Marilynn.

"Why not," asked Polly, tersely.

"You are a very generous person, but this is too expensive," replied Marilynn.

"But I want you to have something nice," said Polly.

"It would be a shame to spend so much and pack it away until Tommy gets home. Maybe just before Tommy gets home you could buy something for me," said Marilynn.

"Perhaps you are right, but I want you to have something today," said Polly.

Marilynn agreed and Polly bought her some very elegant intimate apparel at a fraction of the cost. Polly had been a little miffed, but she truly appreciated what Marilynn had done. She knew that Marilynn was a thoughtful young lady and she loved her for it. She was starting to understand why Tommy had fallen in love with this pretty young lady.

In the evenings before dinner Polly invited Marilynn into her room for cocktails. She explained, "It's nice to have someone I can invite in for a cocktail. This town is somewhat Puritan. I think most of them drink, but they wouldn't admit it under oath. I used to have the Lewises in once and awhile, but we aren't speaking. The people from Hendricks Field aren't shy and I entertain a group of them occasionally."

Polly's room was a large corner room over-furnished with a combination of hotel furniture and treasured items from her home. She had her oriental rugs on the floor and crystal lamps on the tables. Over the days Polly paraded out her treasures to show Marilynn. She had pictures of her family and their New Jersey home, and of course pictures of Tommy from infancy to his college days. Marilynn got the story behind each picture and she was delighted. Tommy had talked so much about his relatives, particularly his Uncle Charles, she enjoyed learning about them.

Polly's closets were filled with expensive and classic dresses, shoes, purses and furs. It was easy to understand Polly's reputation as a spender, she was accustomed to fine things. She had many fine pieces of jewelry, each with a story, and she told Marilynn that her expensive pieces were in the hotel safe.

Polly shared her room with Toni, her beloved Boston Bulldog. The ugly little dog was showing its age and hardly did anything but sleep. Polly's maid, a hotel employee who had worked for Polly before she sold the house, walked the dog several times a day.

Each day Marilynn felt more and more at home. They had time to drive down to Polly's old house on Kenilworth Drive. Polly had mist in her eyes as she told Marilynn of her parents, and the good times they had before they both became ill and died. Polly said, "Tommy and his friends lived in the lake. It's a wonder they didn't drown the way they clowned in the water all day long."

Marilynn understood how lonely Polly had become. Everybody was gone, even Tommy. She was separated from her home and all of it's memories. All she had now were the treasures in her hotel room and a few friends.

Polly surprised Marilynn one day when she said, "We are taking the Girl Scout troop for a tour of Hendricks Field. Sophia Mae Mitchell runs the troop and I've been helping her." They loaded the girls in cars and drove to the air base. They toured a giant B-17 bomber, ate lunch in a mess hall and swam in the service club pool. Marilynn was amazed how involved Polly was with the Scouts. Polly explained, "It's wartime and they had trouble finding leaders. I've been helping with the Cub Scouts too."

Marilynn stayed in Sebring for five weeks and Polly wanted to honor her before she departed for Texas. She asked Vernon Higgins, who ran the Hotel Sebring, to cater a party at the Pinecrest Hotel near Avon Park. The old Spanish hotel had a spacious ballroom with a patio that overlooked a lake. It was a beautiful place for a party. Polly invited a distinguished group of people to the party including: the Commanding Officer of Hendricks Field, Col. and Mrs. James Daniel, Sebring's Mayor and Mrs. M.F. McGee,[1] and just about everybody Marilynn had met.

Marilynn spent much of the time talking with Herman Hancock, Tommy's school friend, who was home on leave before heading to England to fly fighter escort for the Eighth Air Force. He told her every story he remembered about Tommy's boyhood.

The day came for Marilynn to leave. She and Polly had become more than in-laws. They were friends. Polly had told Marilynn things she couldn't tell anybody else. She hadn't had anybody like that since her mother died. When they said goodbye at the train there was a genuine affection between them, and Polly said, "Marilynn, you are so sweet. I'm going to miss you." Polly stood alone on the platform and waved as the train pulled out of the station.

[1] Highlands County News

23

"Tommy McGuire walked right up to me at Dobodura, and asked if I knew where Dutton was. He didn't know it was me. I was wearing a heavy beard. I thought I knew the voice, but I didn't know who he was for a moment---you know how it is when you see somebody you know, in a place they aren't supposed to be---and he had that mustache, too, and I'd never seen him wear one before."

---- Bill Dutton, McGuire's high school friend

On April 16, 1943, McGuire, Johnson, and Jordan boarded a C-47[1] for the long flight from Australia to Dobodura on the eastern coast of New Guinea, where they would be assigned to the 9th Fighter Squadron of the 49th Fighter Group.

The 49th Group had been in battle since early 1942, and was loaded with seasoned combat pilots. They had been stationed in West Palm Beach, Florida, when the war broke out, and were the first fighter group to leave the United States for a combat zone, after the bombing of Pearl Harbor. The 49th Group proudly boasted that it was the home of the top aces in the Pacific war zone.

On April 22, McGuire went on his first combat training mission.[2] It was a local patrol which lasted for one-and-a-half hours. Similar flights followed for a week. McGuire was getting itchy for combat. He had trained for it for 18 months--had been cheated out of it in Alaska by bad weather and a poor fighting machine. Now he had to learn the 9th Fighter Squadron's combat techniques. Team work was vital, and these combat pilots had learned things that were not "in the book." The 49th Group had been highly successful and McGuire knew he had a lot to learn, but he couldn't help resenting this return to training.

One morning McGuire and two other pilots were learning to fly in combat formation with an experienced flight leader in the lead position. The leader was rough on the new pilots over the radio--extolling the virtues of tight formation flying and the importance of sticking with your wingman in combat. The flight was making a turn to the left. McGuire was flying off the right wing and to the rear of the leader when the radio cracked in his ear, "Come on, McGuire, close in. You're an experienced combat pilot. Didn't you guys fly formation in Alaska?"

That did it! That got his "Irish" up. McGuire had expected to be treated with some respect, because of his six months of flying in a combat zone. He didn't appreciate being chewed out like an air cadet. He rammed the throttles forward, pushed the left rudder pedal, and turned the wheel to the left to close in tighter--maybe just a little too aggressively. As the leader looked to his left, McGuire's left wingtip touched the lead plane's right rudder ever so gently.

"What the hell is going on, McGuire?" inquired the leader. "Did you hit me?"

"I don't think so, Sir, it must have been turbulence," answered McGuire.

"McGuire, you son-of-a-bitch, you're too close. Don't be a wise-ass. Back off!" replied the leader.

"Just trying to fly a tight formation, Sir," said McGuire.

It was not unlike the retorts he had made a few years ago on a football field in Sebring.

"You do that one more time and you will find yourself grounded," shouted the leader.

"Yes, Sir," said McGuire.

McGuire stuck to the leader. Back in high school he terrorized his schoolmates by driving the hood of his car up under the overhanging logs on a slow moving logging truck. This wasn't that much different. Now he knew what the lead pilot was going to do, and he wasn't endangering the lives of his friends just to show off. If they could see him now!

The flight leader landed first and was waiting for McGuire when he taxied his P-38 into the revetment area, and shut down his engines.

"Either you are a lousy pilot, or a wise guy. Either way, I don't want you flying with me until you get on the stick. There are too many Japs up there trying to knock me off--I don't need one of my own people trying to do it."

McGuire stood at attention and replied, "Yes, sir!"

The flight leader turned and stormed away. The word soon got around that McGuire was a good pilot, but he was considered to be a bit of a wise guy by some of the older pilots. Combat missions followed every day or so. They weren't very exciting, just escort or patrol missions, but at least it wasn't training. They saw a few Japanese but never got a chance to tangle with them.

McGuire wrote Marilynn: *"This place isn't bad---of course, it is hot but you can stand it. We are living in tents, but are fixed up nice and have a stream nearby where we can bathe."*

McGuire had time on his hands and he picked up some V-Mail forms and wrote to let some friends know his new address. V-Mail had to be written on a form with dark ink. To avoid shipping bulky bags of mail back home, letters were photographed on 16mm microfilm which was developed and sent back to a V-Mail center, stateside, where it was reconstituted to a small letter reproduced on photographic paper. In 1983

Malcolm Watters was able to produce such a letter he had saved for 40 years which is reproduced here:

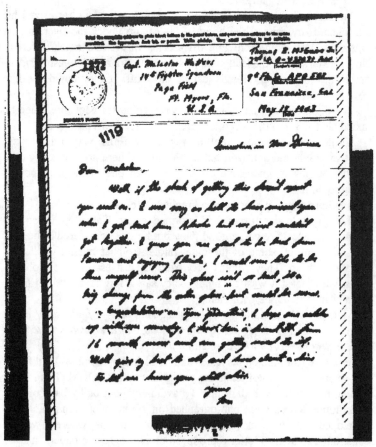

For clarity this V-mail letter is type written at the end of this chapter.[3]

In a few weeks McGuire got word that he was to be transferred to a new fighter group being formed in Australia. He was angry to be leaving a combat area without a chance to tangle with the enemy and wondered why he had been selected for the new group. He even thought that he was being transferred because of the collision incident, but changed his mind when he found out that the new group was looking for trained P-38 pilots. The new group would be the first all P-38 fighter groups anywhere in the world.

McGuire remained "attached to the 9th fighter squadron for flying" for the next six weeks, accumulating 50 hours of combat time. He was like an outsider already, and didn't even have an aircraft assignment. He flew whatever aircraft was assigned for that day's mission. He flew wing to someone else, never getting the opportunity to be the lead pilot. It was standard operating procedure for new pilots to draw the less glamorous assignments.

He got to know the 49th's hottest pilot, Richard Bong, who was also a member of the 9th Squadron. Bong already had a dozen enemy aircraft to his credit. He had been in combat for six months and had become an ace by shooting down his fifth Japanese plane just 12 days after he had shot down his first one.

There was a story often told about Bong: When he was stationed near San Francisco, he had flown under the five-year-old Golden Gate bridge and down Market Street so low that he could wave to the secretaries in the buildings. General Kenney, then the Commander of the 14th Air Force, had summoned Bong, a 2nd Lieutenant, to his office and personally dressed him down and assigned him to go to Oakland, and help a housewife rewash laundry he had blown off of her clothes line, when he buzzed her backyard. When Kenney became the Commanding General of the Air Corps in the Southwest Pacific, he had requested Bong be stationed there because he liked the young man's spirit.

McGuire picked up whatever tips he could get from Bong and the other pilots, figuring he would get his chance sooner or later. The proposed 475th group, which was waiting for new planes, was beginning to sound like a good deal.

General Kenney had gone to Washington to beg for fighter planes and had agreed to accept whatever models could be spared from the more glamorous European theater. The P-51 seemed to match up best against the German ME-109. The P-38s had developed a reputation for engine trouble over Europe. They escorted bombers at 30,000 feet over Germany, where air temperature was minus-55 degrees F. The oil cooler apparently worked too well under those conditions, and the engine oil congealed, leaving the engine unlubricated, and a candidate for disaster over enemy territory.

Thus the P-38 was the plane most available for the Southwest Pacific. Kenney had heard about some of the problems but he knew that his "kids" were having good luck with the P-38 and he felt that the long-range ability of the plane outweighed any prospective problems. He accepted all the planes they could spare and said, "keep them coming." While the 49th Group was equipped with single-engined P-40s and twin-engined P-38s, Kenney decided that the new 475th Fighter Group would be the first group totally equipped with P-38s. Maintenance would be simpler with only one type of aircraft to work on and stock parts for.

It all sounded exciting to McGuire. He liked the P-38, and he would be a veteran pilot in a new organization. He'd get the respect he had always wanted. On his present assignment and in Alaska, McGuire had been a "Johnny come lately," when he joined units already operating in a combat area. This time he would be the established veteran and anybody else who came in would be the outsider who had to prove himself. Maybe if he did well he could get a promotion, or even work his way into a command position.

Meanwhile, McGuire heard that John Bates from Sebring had been assigned to the 49th Fighter Group in West Palm Beach when they moved out of the states, just a few days after Pearl Harbor. He checked Group Headquarters and found that Bates was still in the group. He wondered what the odds were of two guys who graduated from high school together in a class of 48 (24 boys) ending up in the same fighter group, on the other side of the world.

Their reunion was a happy one. They were thrilled to see each other 10,000 miles from home. Bates was an enlisted man but that made no difference. They threw their arms around each other and hugged. As kids, they had often flown kites together, and several times Polly had taken the two boys to the Florida State Fair in Tampa. They had not seen each other since high school.[4]

"Tommy, what ever happened to your Sunday-go-to-meeting kite?" asked John.

McGuire had forgotten all about his special kite--the one he and John flew, only when all the conditions were just right. That one question brought back a flood of memories about Sebring and they spent hours trading news of their old buddies from home.

"Tommy, my brother Junior is out here, Amos Freeland is stationed in Perth, and Bill Dutton and Howard McDonald are stationed with a bomber group right here at Dobodura."

McGuire reported, "Ike Hart is in the China-Burma-India theater flying B-25s. Herman Hancock is flying P-38s over Germany, and Clarence was in Panama but is back at Ft. Myers and says he can't get out of the states. Paul Gustat was in Cadets in San Antonio, but nobody knows were he is now. Chubby is a B-24 instructor, and the last I heard Broward Coker was at Camp Blanding."

A few days later McGuire went to the area across the base, where Bill Dutton's 8th Bomber Squadron, 3rd Bomb Group, was located, and wandered around asking for Bill. Several GIs pointed a direction where they thought Bill could be found, and McGuire went to those areas only to be directed somewhere else. He wandered into an area where two men sat under a tree, on vine swings, playing chess on a board that sat on a tree stump between them. McGuire said, "Do you guys know where I can find Bill Dutton?"

One of the men, heavily bearded and bare chested, stood up slowly and looked McGuire in the eyes for a moment and then asked, in a familiar voice, "Tommy, is that you?"

"Bill? I can't believe it. Is that you under all of that hair?" said McGuire.

"Jesus Christ, Tommy, what is that growing under your nose?" asked Bill. "What in hell are you doing here anyway? The last I heard you were freezing your ass off in Alaska."

McGuire answered, "I'm here to protect your boys. I'm with the 49th Fighter Group across the field. Bill, you've gotten so tan that I didn't recognize you. You look like a native."

"Don't pay any attention to that, it's the Atabrine tablets that make me look like this. Aren't you taking it?" said Bill.

"Yea, but I've only been here a few weeks," said McGuire.

Tommy and Bill walked away arm in arm leaving the other chess player sitting at the board without a partner.

With four Sebring boys stationed at the same field, plans were soon underway to have a "Blue Streak" reunion in New Guinea. On the appointed date Howard McDonald, Bill Dutton, John Bates, and Tommy got together. Howard towered over the other three, but there wasn't an ounce of fat on any of them. John Bates wore a striped polo shirt, sun glasses, and a army fatigue hat. They all sported short hair cuts and smiles.

They laughed and told stories. Four brothers couldn't have been closer. It was very special for McGuire. Often in the past he had acted as everyone's superior--now being the only officer in the group, he wanted to be their equal, and it came off just that way. Bill, John, and Howard recognized a new maturity in McGuire. They had hardly seen

171

him over the last four years, and he had grown and had a aura of authority about him.

Howard McDonald, McGuire, Bill Dutton and John C Bates on New Guinea. A "Blue Streaks" reunion halfway around the world. Even a bad photo can't hide the smiles.

They discussed the band, football, painting the Red Devil, golf with Captain Pringle, the sailing canoe, kite flying, pillow feathers, the war, and going home to Sebring. Dutton had his own airplane in Sebring, and had questions about flying fighters. McGuire said, "Next time we get together maybe I can take you guys for a ride in a P-38. We have a plane that has the radio removed, so there is room behind the pilot for a passenger."

The day ended too soon, but with a promise that they would all get together again as soon as McGuire returned from Australia with his new fighter group. John said, "I'll get in touch with my brother. Maybe he can get together with us next time."

A few days later, McGuire got the word that he was promoted to the rank of 1st Lieutenant. He thought it would never happen! For the last 17 months he had been bouncing around, never staying anywhere long enough to establish himself in a situation that would warrant a promotion. It was good to have the silver bar of a 1st Lieutenant before his move to a new fighter group.

McGuire was sorry to be leaving the 49th Fighter Group. They had great pilots and a good combat record. He had gotten close to the guys and he truly thought he would go places with them. Gerald Johnson and

Wally Jordan were lucky in their early combat flights, and both of them shot down a Japanese plane, before McGuire departed for his new assignment. They kidded McGuire unmercifully because he hadn't yet had a chance at the enemy. Wally particularly lorded it over McGuire every chance he got. As a parting shot McGuire said, "You guys better get as many Japs as you want before I get back to New Guinea. The 475th and I are going to clean this place up when we get over here!"

> TO: Capt. Malcolm Watters
> 14th Fighter Squadron
> Page Field
> Ft. Myers, Fla.
> USA
> FROM: 2nd Lt. Thomas B. McGuire, Jr.
> 0-437031 AAF
> 9 th Ftr. Sq. APO 503
> San Francisco, Cal.

May 14, 1943

somewhere in New Guinea

Dear Malcolm,

Well if the shock of getting this doesn't upset you, read on. I was sorry as hell to have missed you when I got back from Alaska but we just couldn't get together. I guess you are glad to be back from Panama and enjoying Florida, I would like to be there myself now. This place isn't so bad, it's a big change from the other place but could be worse.

Congratulations on your promotion, I hope one catches up with me someday. I have been a Second Lt. for 16 months now and am getting used to it.

Well give my best to all and how about a line to let me know you're still alive.

Yours, Tom

[1] McGuire's Log book
[2] Ibid.
[3] The original of this V-mail letter and other items shown in this book will eventually be deposited in the Sebring Historical Society.
[4] John C. Bates, SHS '38

24

"Unofficially the word went out, 'this is Kenney's baby, don't send any dead-heads.' As a result we drew some damn good people from the 49th, 8th, and 35th Fighter Groups."

---- a former 431st Squadron Commanding Officer

The formation of the 475th Fighter Group was a tribute to General George Kenney. Kenney had taken over a war-ravaged, demoralized, and disorganized Fifth Air Force and turned it into a valuable fighting force. General MacArthur did not believe in air power--had never used it, and had given it very little thought. Kenney quickly turned MacArthur's thinking around, even though his Fifth Air Force was equipped, in the main, with a ragged collection of obsolete and war-scarred aircraft.

The Fifth Air Force was soon known as "Kenney's Kids." They were a group that could get the job done, even though their equipment was sometimes held together with bailing wire, and many of the men were so young that they didn't shave regularly. In September, 1942, only weeks after Kenney had assumed command, he convinced MacArthur to let his "kids" move part of the 32nd Division from Townsville, Australia, to New Guinea.

MacArthur's staff was against it, but Kenney won the argument, and moved a company of the 126th Infantry Regiment to Port Moresby in one day without a mishap. Later he moved the entire 128th Infantry Regiment to Port Moresby in borrowed and commandeered aircraft after other parts of the 126th Regiment sailed over on a slower sea voyage. The 128th was in place two days before the remainder of the 126th arrived via the sea.

The move saved two weeks and played a vital part in an early attack that turned the Japanese back. It saved Port Moresby, one of the last remaining American strongholds on New Guinea, from a ground attack and certain capture. If New Guinea had fallen, Australia would have been the next target of the Japanese. It changed the minds of MacArthur and his staff about the Air Corps.

Now MacArthur conceded that a strong air force would be vital in the retaking of New Guinea. He confirmed his confidence in Kenney by authorizing a new long-range fighter group which could escort bombers on raids against Japanese bases far to the west at Wewak and to the north at Rabaul, New Britain Islands.

On May 14, 1943, General Kenney signed an order to form the new group. General Paul B. Wurtsmith, the Commanding General of the Fifth Fighter Command, picked leadership that could form the new group and have it ready for combat in a few short months. They would need leaders with combat experience. Major George W. Prentice, a combat-wise squadron commander, was chosen to be the new group commander.

A request was sent to the three fighter groups of the Fifth Fighter Command---"Submit names of fighter pilots and skilled ground personnel who can be made available to man a new P-38 group." Unofficially the word went out that "this is Kenney's baby, don't send any dead-heads." As a result the personnel drawn from the 49th, 8th, and 35th Fighter Groups were top-drawer.

Captains Meryl Smith and Albert Schinz were the new Group Operations and Group Executive Officers. Captains Franklin A. Nichols, Frank D. Tomkins, and Martin L. Low were going to be the new squadron commanders.

In mid-June the officers and men from New Guinea units arrived at Amberly Field, near Brisbane, Australia. The men had left the steaming jungles near the equator and traveled south in the southern hemisphere, where they were greeted by the cold of Australia's winter. The men were housed in tents where four blankets were not enough to keep them warm at night. They huddled under the covers in the morning while a brave soul got out of bed and built a fire in the wood-burning stove. Some men wished they were back in the jungle until warmer clothes were issued.

Ten days later a larger group of officers and enlisted men arrived from the United States, and by July 1, the last of the enlisted men from New Guinea. [1]

McGuire had known for some time that he was assigned to the 475th Group, but he remained in New Guinea to fly missions, until the new group was equipped with airplanes. The P-38s arrived in Brisbane aboard cargo ships and created a spectacle for the local citizenry, as they were towed behind trucks, winglessly, and on their own wheels, down the narrow roads, through country, town, and village to Amberly Field. The planes were then assembled by mechanics, many of whom had never seen a P-38 before.

In mid-July, McGuire and the rest of the pilots selected from the 49th Fighter Group left New Guinea and made their way to flat and dusty Amberly Field. They too grumbled about life in cold tents. McGuire assured them, "You don't know what cold is until you have spent a winter in Alaska living in a tent. At least here it warms up during the day and it's good flying weather."

Now that the 475th Group had a full complement of men, Major Prentice, the Group Commander, spoke to the new men in his command, "We are going to be a vital force in the retaking of New Guinea. I know some of you have been in New Guinea for 16 months or more, trying to keep the Japanese from taking the whole damn place. Hanging on and being pushed around are things of the past. With your help we will run the Japanese out of New Guinea.

"We will start at Port Moresby on the Southeast end of New Guinea and we will strike the Japanese hard and often. We will destroy their air force and soften their ground positions. When our infantry lands, we will cover their landings. When new areas are secured we will move up and extend our flying range still further. We will drive the Japanese off of New Guinea and into the sea 1,500 miles northwest of where we started." There were cheers and catcalls from the approving audience.

The Major continued, "General MacArthur has told the Philippine people that he will return. We are vital to that promise. With other fighter and bomber groups, and foot soldiers, we will drive the Japanese from New Guinea and put ourselves within striking distance of the Philippines. When MacArthur returns, we will have paved the way.

"I know that many of you came out of the jungles or the bush and haven't enjoyed any of the comforts of civilization or had a decent meal in months. Enjoy yourselves while you can. We will arrange for you to have as much free time as is consistent with the proper performance of your duties. As long as you do your work and don't make trouble for anyone else I don't care what you do. I know that inter-squadron rivalries are already developing, and I think that is fine. I hope they help us make contributions to the Group's success."

There was, at once, a feeling of cohesiveness in the new group. Everyone gave their all-out to get things rolling. In a few days the Squadron areas starting taking on the appearance of a real army camp with signs labeling everything and stones painted white outlining the walkways. Electric lights were installed in the tents--a real luxury if you hadn't had them for some months. Many of the troops converted wooden crates from the new aircraft into flooring to lift their tents off the cold ground.

Captain Nichols had S/Sgt. James Bell collect pay books and he arranged for a supplemental payroll. He knew the troops were short of cash and couldn't enjoy Brisbane or Ipswich without it. He also made arrangements for a truck to transport them from the squadron area to the other side of Amberly Field where they could enjoy a hot shower before embarking on the evening's activities.

As the P-38H airplanes were assembled and tested, the flying started. Each day activities picked up, and the group of strangers started looking like a part of the Air Corps. Every possible need had to be anticipated.

Equipment ranging from typewriters to engine stands had to be acquired and organized.

The men worked long hours and they were rewarded with time off which they spent among the friendly Australians. For the men from New Guinea, there was food. Fresh milk, eggs, steak, and beer were all devoured in excess to try and wash away the memories of dehydrated food and bully beef that had made up the bulk of their war-zone diet. The new men, from stateside, were just as eager to get acquainted with the local fare. Many of the men searched for female companionship, and some found it.

To show that he appreciated the way his men were working, newly promoted Colonel Prentice arranged for trucks to leave each afternoon at 5:30 p.m. for Brisbane. This let the men save their money for more important things, and they only needed to stagger their way back to the trucks at Lennon's Hotel, by 12:30 a.m., to avoid the slower trip to the base via milk-train and bus.

Although McGuire had been in New Guinea for only three months, it was a pleasure to be where he could go out for drinks and dinner. He had a new group of friends, much like his old buddies from Ga. Tech, that dined together.

Things were different for McGuire with his new squadron, the 431st. He arrived from an active war zone as a 1st Lieutenant with almost 600 hours of flying time. Although he was only 21 years old, he was no longer a neophyte, or among the "yardbird" 2nd Lieutenants in the squadron. He would certainly be able to fly in a lead position with this unit. The Squadron Commander, Captain Nichols, sent a message for McGuire to report to his office. They talked for a while and discovered that the Captain's wife, Harriet, and Marilynn knew each other back in San Antonio. Then the Captain got around to the reason he had sent for McGuire:

"They tell me you hang around the flight line long after everybody else is gone."

"Yes sir," said McGuire, "I enjoy being around the new P-38s."

Captain Nichols asked, "As long as you are down there anyway, how would you like to be Assistant Engineering Officer? We need somebody to keep track of compliance and to do test flying on new and repaired airplanes."

"I'd love to do that, sir," replied McGuire.

Nichols said, "Report to Lt. Bill Dallas in maintenance. He's expecting you, and will be glad to have the help."[2]

McGuire was excited to get his first squadron job, and it gave him a chance to get in more flying time. He never seemed to get enough flying time, and he was bored when he wasn't flying. He couldn't spend his spare time sleeping like many of the guys did. He just had too much energy for that. He wrote Marilynn: *"As you know by now I have been transferred to this outfit, it's a darn good one and should go places. Besides leading flights I have been made Asst. Engineering Officer doing test work etc. so you can see what I've been doing."*

As part of his new duties McGuire delivered new airplanes to the armorer's range where the cannon and machine guns were bore-sighted and adjusted to fire where the gun sight was aimed. While other pilots would find a warm spot and catch 40 winks, McGuire took an active interest in the procedure. He sat in the cockpit and fired the guns when the adjustments had been made. After a few days he had learned all of the jargon, and knew as much about adjusting the guns as the armorers. The men greeted him warmly and appreciated his interest. McGuire loved it.

Some officers of the 431st felt a little different about McGuire. They thought he was an "eager beaver," and accused him of "kissing-up" to the brass. Captain Nichols heard these comments but he knew better. He had given key jobs to other veteran pilots and he included McGuire in that group. He had seen McGuire work, and he knew that he had the energy to do a good job for the squadron.

McGuire heard the remarks too and ignored them, but deep down, it hurt. Just like high school days, and later at Georgia Tech, McGuire still seemed to have the facility of doing things that set him apart from the group. His mother and grandmother had said, "Remember who you are--you are not just one of the gang, you are somebody special." In his heart he knew it was true.

Fourteen new pilots from the States reported to the squadron on July 19, and the veteran pilots, including McGuire, set about training them for combat flying. Captain Nichols passed the word that the forming of the 475th Group had gone so well that they would soon move to New Guinea where they were desperately needed.

Mr. Mike Jacobsen spent a day telling the pilots about New Guinea. He had owned a farm at Salamaua, New Guinea, before the Japanese had overrun the area. He showed them pictures of the jungle so thick that foliage blocked out the sun, and of the impassable six-foot-tall kunai grass, which harbored deadly Typhus-bearing ticks. He instructed them on methods of finding their way by following animal trails, or by seeking help form natives who were generally friendly. Any pilot forced down in New Guinea would find the information useful.

Group activities continued each evening. Beer parties, basketball games, and even a dance with 50 WAAFs bussed in. The Group and

Squadron Commanders did everything they could to help the men enjoy themselves. The men appreciated the effort and it helped to meld them into a cohesive team.

The men understood that time was growing short when they were issued mosquito bars, gas masks, rifles or pistols, and shoe impregnite. McGuire and the other men who had served in New Guinea were issued atabrine tablets with instructions to start taking a tablet each day. Newer members would have to take them once they were in New Guinea and subjected to the malaria-carrying mosquitoes.

By the first of August the number of available airplanes caught up with the number of pilots in the group. P-38 assignments were made according to seniority--the higher ranking pilots got their aircraft assignments first. McGuire was well known by the enlisted men on the flight line. He spent many hours with them day and night to make the 475th Group combat ready, and he knew some of them from the 49th Group back on New Guinea.

On the third of August a sergeant stopped McGuire and said, "Lieutenant. Do you have a minute?"

"Yes, Sergeant. What is it?" asked McGuire.

"We've been keeping our eyes open, and we have a special plane picked out for you. The guys have checked it out real good," said the sergeant.

McGuire said, "You didn't need to do that."

"We wanted you to get a good one," said the sergeant. "If you have a name for it, I'll get it painted for you, sir."

"Let me think about it. I'll let you know." said McGuire.

McGuire thought about a name for his plane. Most of the guys had some tricky name like "Florida Cracker," or "Georgia Belle." Often they named the plane for their girl or their wife. It had to be something a little different. What was the nickname they called Marilynn back in San Antonio? "Pudgy," that was it. He never understood why they called Marilynn "Pudgy." He didn't like the name, and it certainly didn't fit her. It was different. That would be it. He would have the name "Pudgy" painted on his plane. McGuire went to the flight line, checked out his new airplane and took it up for a two hour and ten minute flight. In his log book he wrote: "I got Pudgy I today."

In preparation for combat flying Captain Nichols had a roster of 431st Fighter Squadron flying personnel issued. It listed all of the pilots and named the leadership positions in the squadron. McGuire was one of the leaders:

Commanding Officer - Captain Nichols

179

Operations Officer - Captain Hood
Flight Commanders - Captains Brown (A Flight)
      Captain Jett (B Flight)
      Captain Hanning (C Flight)
Flight Leaders - Lieutenants Kirby, Lewis, Lutton, and
  McGuire
Element Leaders - Lieutenants Allen, Bellows, Czarneki, Holze,
Houseworth, Mankin, and Wenige
Wingmen - 2nd Lieutenants Blythe, Champlin, Cline,
  Cohn, Duke, Dunlap, Elliott, Hendrick, Knox, Lent,
  McBreen, Morriss, O'Brien, Phillips, Richardson, Samms,
  Schmidt, Sieber, Smith, and Flight Officer Gronemeyer

A scant seven weeks after the first men had arrived at Amberly Field, they were ordered to pack up and move to the battle zone. On August 5, the ground support personnel and equipment, known as the "water echelon," were loaded on the Liberty Ship Joseph A. Lane to be transported to Oro Bay, more than 1,100 miles away, on the northern shore of New Guinea. A small group, known as the "advanced echelon," went ahead by air to make housing arrangements for the arrival of the main air group. This was a procedure which would be used time and time again when it became necessary for the Group to move forward.

The "air echelon," consisting of non-flying officers and administrative personnel, had several more days to partake of the treasures of Australia: food, drink, and companionship. On August 8, the remaining men of the 475th Group boarded C-47s, or strapped themselves into P-38 fighters, as McGuire did, and started the trip north--to war.

[1] Most of the information in this chapter came
 from the 431st & 475th Daily Histories
[2] Maj. Gen. Franklin Nichols

25

"It was one of the damnedest things that ever happened in Sebring. If you weren't there to see it for yourself, you'll never know the truth. People just don't talk about things like that in a small town like Sebring. Oh, they talked---but not the ones that really know what happened!"

----a resident of Sebring, 40 years later

In Sebring, Florida, at the Hotel Sebring, Gatchel Burton was worried about Polly McGuire. She had been in her room for several days and would not respond to knocks on the door. They had called through the door and tried to get her to take meals in her room, as they had done before. They had left trays of food outside the door, but she had not taken any of them in. In months past Polly stayed in her room for days. This time was different. She hadn't taken in a tray of food for a number of days, and her dog was making a fuss every time someone knocked on the door. In the past Polly would tell them to go away. This time there was no answer.

Vernon Higgins, who ran the hotel, agreed with Gatchel. It was different this time. Reluctantly he also agreed they had to do something to get in the room and see if she was all right. Gatchel said, "We have tried a pass key, but the door is bolted from the inside. We have been trying to raise her all day. We have no choice, I'll call the fire department, and have them raise a ladder to the window and we'll take a look."

Vernon Higgins thought for just a second and said, "We have to do it. It'll cause talk all over town, but that's a chance we will have to take. Gatchel, you are a member of the fire department, why don't you go up the ladder and look. The least we can do is keep it in the family."

It was late afternoon when Gatchel called the fire house, but in a few minutes a fire truck was parked below Polly's window on the front corner of the building. It attracted the curious as the firemen raised a ladder to the window, and by the time Gatchel started up the ladder a small crowd had gathered. He struggled with the window and finally got it open. He called into the room and got no answer. He stuck his head in the window and took a look. He turned and shouted, "Somebody get Dr. Boorom, it doesn't look good."

Polly was laying nude on the floor. As Gatchel crossed the room to open the door, he knew she was dead. The little Boston Bull dog was acting wild and the room had a stench about it. He had never expected this. It was a shock. Within minutes members of the hotel staff gathered at the open door to peek into the room. Gatchel and Vernon Higgins opened windows to air the room and they asked the hotel maid, who had looked after Polly for many years, to take the dog. They left everything in the room just as it was, thinking the police would want it so.

Dr. Boorom arrived and went into a rage. "Why did you leave her body laying here like this with every Tom, Dick, and Harry wandering in and out of the room? Doesn't anybody have any respect?" He took a sheet from the bed and covered the body.

Higgins explained, "We never expected to find anything like this. We didn't know what to do. We didn't want to touch anything."

"Somebody could have covered her," said the Doctor, "Get everybody out of here and let's close the door."

The story of Polly's death was all over town before dark. "She drank herself to death," said one old-timer. "She used to stay drunk for days in that hotel room."

Vernon Higgins searched and found names of relatives and notified them. Polly's body was taken to Stephenson's Funeral Home and later shipped to New Jersey for burial in her "room" next to her parents.

Higgins also phoned Marilynn. She was on the next train out of San Antonio. The two-day trip was a very sad one for Marilynn. She had developed a real fondness for Polly during her first visit to Sebring. She worried about the effect the news would have on Tommy. He and Polly had been so close.

Meanwhile, nobody knew how to notify Tommy. They couldn't find his address. When Marilynn arrived Vernon Higgins offered his condolences and said, "Don't go into that room. We are cleaning it, but it is still very unpleasant. Her family will be here tomorrow. By then we'll have it in better condition."

Mr. Higgins continued, "Marilynn, no one has notified Tommy. We don't know how to reach him. He may end up reading it in the paper. There are four boys from Sebring, stationed on New Guinea, and several of them get a local paper." Marilynn sent a wire to Tommy and sat down and wrote a long letter.

The next day Marilynn met Polly's brothers Robert and Charles, and her sister, Estelle. Marilynn felt uncomfortable with them. To them she was an outsider. She had never been involved in dividing a deceased person's belongings, but she tried to look out for Tommy's interests without offending anybody. It was a trying experience for a young lady. If somebody wanted something Marilynn let them have it. Vernon Higgins said, "Marilynn, you are being too generous."

Marilynn replied, "I think Tommy would do the same thing."

Stella particularly wanted a bible which had the family's history recorded in it. She knew Polly had gotten it from their parents. They couldn't find it in Polly's room, and Marilynn didn't remember it from her visit a few months before. Vernon Higgins told them that Polly had sold her house with most of her personal belongings "thrown in."

Stella went to the house down on Kenilworth Boulevard to ask the people who had bought the house if they would let her have the bible. She was unable to recover it. Tommy's guns, his large collection of oversized classical music transcriptions, and his clarinet were never found among Polly's relics. They must have been included in the sale of the house. Marilynn knew some of Polly's jewelry was missing. She concluded that Polly had been selling it to pay her expenses, and said nothing to the family.

The story of Polly's death was on everyone's lips in Sebring. There were even stories told and repeated about her dog biting her body, some said to try and wake her, while others said the animal had gotten hungry. Nobody who knows if these stories were true has ever been willing to talk about it, even after many years had passed.

This was easily the most sensational thing that had happened in Sebring since the twenties, when a man had murdered his family with an ax, in their home on the DeSoto City road. He had tried, unsuccessfully, to blame it on a Negro man who worked for him.

When the weekly newspapers came out there was a difference in the way they covered the story of Polly's death. **The Highlands County News** covered it in the typical fashion of a small town paper of the era. The story was devoid of anything that might embarrass the family:

> Mrs. Pauline R. McGuire, more
> familiarly known to her legion of
> friends as "Polly" was found dead
> in her hotel room last Thursday.
> Dr. M. D. Boorom, her physician,
> told a coroner's inquest that a
> heart attack caused her death. ....

The **Sebring American** was something different: It gave graphic details of the conditions of the room and the body, and told the story in a more sensational manner--like a big city newspaper might have done. Local citizens were shocked by the boldness and they considered it poor taste by the American's editor: "It's just like Rod Arkell to use a story like this to sell papers."

Marilynn called both newspapers and explained that Tommy had not been notified of his mother's death. "Tommy has just been transferred and no one knew his address until I arrived. Can you delay the mailing of your papers to servicemen in the Pacific for a week or two so my wire has time to reach him. I would hate for him to read about his mother's death in a newspaper."

The **Highlands County News** agreed, "It's old news by the time they get it anyway. They don't care as long as it's from home."

Rod Arkell at the **Sebring American** said, "We can't delay the paper for any reason. Tommy doesn't get the paper anyway."

Marilynn said, "Tommy knows three or four boys over there from Sebring, and they pass the papers around. Your story was so detailed. I hope Tommy never sees it."

She got no satisfaction from Mr. Arkell so she went to Joe Kinsey, a local lawyer who had done some legal work for Polly. Together they went to see Rod Arkell and Marilynn pleaded with him not to mail the paper for a few days. Rod Arkell took a firm stand, "I have the responsibility to exercise the freedom of the press and stand up to those who would censor the news. I have an obligation to my subscribers."

Kinsey spoke up, "This has nothing to do with censorship. The judge would be sympathetic to a young man whose mother has just died, while he is 10,000 miles away, in the steaming jungles of New Guinea, defending your rights as a free press. I can be back here in an hour with an injunction that will hold up all of your out-of-town mailings for months. We are just asking you to be reasonable and responsible."

Kinsey was a large, imposing figure of a man with jet black hair. He gave Arkell, a small man, a steely stare. He and Arkell had been involved in disputes before and Kinsey had proved a tough adversary. Marilynn and Mr. Kinsey left the office with an agreement that papers carrying the story of Polly's death would not be sent to the boys in the Pacific for a few weeks.

Marilynn had one more task before she left Sebring. She and Polly's brothers and sister went to the Tropical State Bank for the opening of Polly's safety deposit box.

The first item in the lock box was a paper concerning legal action Polly had taken, to be declared the sole beneficiary of her parent's estates. Her mother's will had never been revised and had divided the Watson fortune among all their children. Unfortunately there wasn't a fortune when she died. Polly had proven to the court that she deserved what little was left of the estate, for the years of relentless care she had rendered to her parents. The action gave her ownership of the house, the only place she had to live. There had been little else of value. The dispute had left Polly on the outs with her brothers and sister when she needed them the most. She had particularly missed her brother Charles after that because they had been so close.

Nothing else in the safety deposit box would be considered valuable to anyone but a divorced mother who had fought to keep her son and raise him normally. There was a letter from Tom pleading with her to give him another chance--to take a cruise in the Caribbean to recapture the love they once had together.

There was a copy of the divorce decree which outlined a harsh condition that Polly had agreed to under duress, to get the divorce. She had agreed to turn her boy over to his father when he was 14 years old. She had figured that he would be in prep school by that age anyway, and Tom could take over and pay for the boy's schooling. She would still see Tommy in the summer. Most likely Tom had hoped that his son would not be too old at that age to be introduced to the Catholic Church.

It was clear by the wording of another letter in the box that Tommy had been given back to Polly. The letter, signed by Thomas B. McGuire Sr., some years after the divorce, rendered the custody provision of the divorce agreement invalid. It was Polly's official "ownership papers" for her son.

One must wonder what Polly "had on Tom" to make him give up the future rights to his son. Money might have been involved. Tom had gotten the money from somewhere to start a Packard automobile dealership. He had sold a very fancy car, the Pierce Arrow, but he had never been anything more than a car salesman. Polly's parents probably furnished the financing necessary to start an automobile dealership, in consideration for the letter in the safety deposit box, which gave up all rights to the boy.

The other document was also a letter. It was from a summer camp child psychologist who had, at Polly's request, interviewed Tommy to see if he had been affected by having his family split by divorce. The letter described Tommy as a brilliant and engaging young man who had tremendous energy and curiosity. It further stated that the boy was unaffected by the divorce and was a tribute to his mother, who was doing such a good job of raising such an interesting young man.

These documents had been a great comfort to Polly over the years when she was feeling blue. They represented everything in the world that she cared about after her parents were gone--her home and her son. When her home and Tommy were gone, her life had become painfully empty. She had died alone in her hotel room surrounded only by a few of her cherished possessions and with the company of her little dog. The maid agreed to keep the dog, and Marilynn made arrangements to have some of Polly's dishes and lamps shipped to San Antonio. That was about all that was left.

* See Appendix A, How this book was written

185

26

8/18/43 ...Escort Wewak (2 Zekes, 1 Tony destroyed,
ack-ack heavy, Lost coin toss for 1 Oscar)
----a notation from McGuire's log book

Transport planes carrying the Air Echelon of the 475th Fighter Group made their way across the Coral Sea and were forced to low altitude by bad weather as they got close to New Guinea. They were running low on fuel and for a time it was feared that they would have to crash-land wherever they could find a spot. Each one eventually landed safely at one of the seven airfields in the Port Moresby area. The passengers of one plane, landing at Hood Point, got an eye-popping "National Geographic view" of a native village where life went on in a pre-historic manner alongside the runway. [1]

The fighter planes of the 431st Fighter Squadron made their way up the coast of Australia and spent the night at Townsville, and then at Mareeba, waiting for the weather to clear before making the final jump to New Guinea.

On August 10, as they took off from Mareeba, the squadron suffered its first fatality. Lieutenant Andrew K. Duke lost an engine on take-off and was killed trying to land his P-38 on one engine. No one could understand how an engine that had worked well the two previous days could suddenly quit at the most critical moment of flight and betray the unsuspecting pilot.

The rest of the three-hour flight was uneventful as they droned over the peaceful waters of the Coral Sea. Here the Navy had changed the course of the war when they thwarted a seaborne thrust at Port Moresby, 15 months before, in what was forever after to be known as "The Battle of Coral Sea."

The arrival of the olive drab P-38s at 12-Mile Strip was an exciting event for the advanced echelon, which had been working long hours to prepare for them. Things didn't go as well when the planes landed on the newly constructed field. One P-38 skidded off the runway and was destroyed, while another hit a tree and damaged a wing. The pilots were unhurt and despite the calamities, everyone was in a festive mood. [2]

Orientation flights started the next day, as every pilot took to the air to learn the surrounding area. McGuire resumed his testing duties making two or three local test flights each day. He inquired about the 9th Fighter Squadron and found that they had been in heavy combat over the Markham Valley since McGuire had departed their ranks. Richard Bong, their top ace, now had 16 victories to his credit. McGuire wondered how many he could have gotten by now if he had stayed with his old unit.

The 431st Squadron was selected to fly the first combat mission for the 475th Group. After being served lemonade by a young and attractive Red Cross lady, they took off on a mission to escort troop transports across the Owen Stanley Mountains to Tsili-Tsili. Troop carriers were forced to cross the mountains through passes, to avoid the 13,000-foot peaks. Rain and fog filled the passes on this day, and the mission was scrubbed.[3]

The next day both the 431st and 432nd Squadrons completed their first combat mission escorting C-47s to Bena Bena. There was no combat encounter and all of the planes returned safely.

On August 15, McGuire flew a four-hour mission escorting C-47s to Marilinan, and again there was no action. The following day he was given the day off, as other members of the 431st escorted transport planes to Tsili-Tsili and encountered 25 Japanese aircraft. It was a spectacular debut for 431st Squadron as they downed 10 fighters and two bombers. Two P-38s were damaged but they all returned safely. The camp buzzed that night with the excitement of the day's action.

McGuire was disappointed that he missed the action, but the next morning before dawn, he went on a five-hour flight with B-24 and B-25 bombers across New Guinea to the enormous Japanese airdrome at Wewak. This was the first American attack on distant Wewak. It had been out of range for fighter escort until the additional P-38s of the 475th Fighter Group came on the scene. The Japanese were caught by surprise and few of their planes left the runway to offer aerial resistance.

As the bombers and fighters approached the drop area large black puffs of anti-aircraft fire blossomed in front of them. They had no choice but to fly into the ominous clouds. McGuire remembered reading that Eddie Rickenbacker had gotten "air sick" the first time he had flown into anti-aircraft fire. McGuire gritted his teeth and flew on. The heavy ack-ack fire was scary but little damage was done. The bombers did massive damage to the giant airdrome, catching hundreds of planes on the ground. It was a great confidence builder for the young pilots.

McGuire had been in New Guinea for months before, but his flying had been limited to patrols. He marked the flight on August 17 in his log book as his "1st raid." It was the first time he had ever seen an enemy installation, seen bombs dropped, and had live ammunition fired at him. It hadn't been that bad and he felt better now that it was over.

That night the 475th Group had a briefing for the next day's mission. Spirits were so high that it resembled a college pep rally more than a military meeting. The day's raid had dealt a devastating blow to the

Japanese defense of New Guinea, and the briefing outlined the follow-up attacks to finish the job.

The field was still moonlit the next morning as McGuire and the 431st joined other P-38s from the 475th Group to escort a low level B-25 raid on Wewak. McGuire was anxious to get into action if the opportunity presented itself. This time the Japanese were prepared and sent up swarms of fighters. The 475th Group was in the center of the action and they met the challenge well.

McGuire was leading the last element of three planes. One man had returned to base because of engine trouble. They were at 8,000 feet when a Zero attacked them from 45 degrees. McGuire shouted into his radio, "Let's get this Zero at two o'clock!"

McGuire felt weak in the knees as he led his flight into a turn for a head-on attack. The Zero flashed by, and McGuire turned his plane quickly and fired two long bursts. As the smell of cordite, from the machine guns, drifted back into the cockpit all fear left him. The No. 3 man, Lieutenant Bill Sieber, saw the Japanese plane burst into flames and crash.

The No. 2 man, Lieutenant Francis Lent, shouted over the radio, "Mac, you've got a Zero on your tail!"

McGuire was like a football player who had taken his first hit in a big game. The butterflies were gone and he was ready to fight. He kicked his P-38 into an unbelievable turn to the left and engaged his pursuer. He fired several bursts as he chased the plane down toward Dagua Field. He hit the plane again, and again, around the cockpit and it started burning. Lieutenant Lent observed its crash and said, "You got him, Mac!"

Lieutenant Sieber was separated from the flight, but McGuire and Lent made a head-on attack on another Zeke. McGuire and the Zeke held a collision course, both firing everything they had at the other--neither of them gave an inch. A mid-air collision was inevitable. The P-38 passed under the Zeke and their left wing tips scraped each other. McGuire had hit the Zero with several good bursts and his wing tip, but it got away.

McGuire and Lent joined up again to chase another Zeke down to 1,000 feet, getting in several good bursts. Rather than stay at low altitude and become a target themselves, they broke away and started to climb. They spotted another Zeke and made a pass at it. As the Zeke pulled up to the left Lieutenant Lent anticipated the turn, and shot large pieces off the plane before it exploded and burned.

As they headed home with the B-25s, a fast Japanese Tony fighter appeared, and initiated an attack on the bombers. McGuire and Lent had used their ammunition judiciously and they still had enough left to ward off one more attack. McGuire lined his sights on the bright green, yellow and brown fighter. He gave it three good bursts, and it started down, smoking. The B-25 crews saw it crash in the jungle below.[4]

When the smoke cleared, 41 enemy planes had been destroyed, with the 431st accounting for 14 of them. The B-25 gunners claimed eight of the enemy planes shot down.

When they landed at Port Moresby, McGuire spoke to his crew chief, Sergeant Frank Kish, "Take a look at my left wing. I think I had a mid-air collision with a Zero. See if it did any damage."[5]

McGuire was elated when he went into the intelligence tent for debriefing. He had tangled with a number of enemy planes and he knew he had hit five of them. He claimed two Zekes (often called Zeros), one Tony, and one Oscar. He was able to get verification on three of the victories, but the fourth one was challenged. Another pilot had also hit the Oscar and thought that he deserved credit for it. Since Air Corps pilots in the Pacific theater did not divide credits, it was left to the flip of a coin. McGuire lost. He was credited with three Japanese planes shot down.

After debriefing McGuire returned to his plane. A small crowd had gathered to look at the smudge of Japanese paint on the P-38's wing. Sergeant Kish was using a pad of steel wool to remove the paint spot. He reported to McGuire, "Lieutenant, the collision didn't do any serious damage to the plane, but there are some 7.7mm bullet holes that will have to be repaired."

By nightfall the word was going around the base, "Did you hear about Lieutenant McGuire? He shot down three Japs, and tried to knock down another one with his wing tip. On top of that, he gave away another one on a coin toss." It was the start of stories about McGuire that eventually would portray him as a daredevil with nine lives. Later, he was awarded the Silver Star for gallantry, for this first day of aerial combat.

Three days later they visited Wewak again and the 431st Fighter Squadron was flying top cover for the bombers, at high altitude. The bombers were attacked and the P-38s were called down to drive off the enemy planes. They went into the swarm of Japanese planes with great confidence. McGuire got one of the 15 Zekes in his gunsight and made a deflection shot, at close range. The Zeke fell in a steep dive and crashed. He turned quickly and caught another Zeke mid-ship and it, too, went into a dive and crashed. He drove other Japanese planes away without engaging them.

The 431st made quick work of 11 Japanese planes with Lieutenant David Allen getting three and Lieutenant Francis Lent getting two. Only four Japanese planes got away as the bombers finished their mission unmolested. Lieutenant Ralph Schmidt was lost and was the object of unsuccessful search missions for the next few days. After his outstanding efforts in defense of the bombers, McGuire would later be awarded the Distinguished Flying Cross for "Heroism displayed in flight."

The 431st Squadron was forging a name for itself. They led the 475th Group in the number of enemy planes downed. Three of the pilots ran their totals to five that day, and earned the right to be called an Ace. Captain Franklin Nichols, Lieutenant David Allen, and Lieutenant McGuire now joined Captain Harry Brown with the distinguished title. Every fighter pilot wanted to be an Ace but few would obtain that title though they might spend months or years in a combat area.

The news of the 475th Fighter Group's early success was greeted with glee by General Kenney and his staff. It was vindication of Kenney's plan and execution. He and his people had begged for the planes, and picked the men to start a completely new twin engine fighter group. Kenney had signed the order to form the group on May 14, and just three months later they had jelled into a fighting organization which had proven itself in action.

Their success in the first 10 days of operation proved the ability of the P-38s to provide the long-range fighter escort so desperately needed by the bomber groups to strike Japanese strongholds. Just as importantly, it was validation of the 475th's leadership which had taken all of the components, wherever they could find them, and melded them into a fighting force with skill and spirit.

Never before, or since, in the history of aerial warfare has a new unit, formed in wartime, made such an auspicious beginning. They had destroyed over 40 enemy airplanes in 10 days with minimal losses of their own. The officers and men of the 475th Group were well aware of their accomplishments and it served only to give them added enthusiasm for the task ahead. General Kenney made sure General MacArthur knew of their outstanding success.

After their grand entrance into the air war over New Guinea, in which they had shot down 36 Japanese planes in three combat engagements, the pilots of the 431st Squadron were given several days off to rest up a bit. They explored the area and made jeep missions into Port Moresby. Others slept or tried to devise furniture for their tents. By the end of the first day they had grown restless with the lack of action. On the second day they took turns on stand-by, two flights at a time (eight airplanes), but Fifth Fighter Command never called for them.

The young Turks of the 431st Fighter Squadron, confident after a few weeks in New Guinea. L to R Fred Champlin, Buffalo, NY, Verl Jett, Lompac, CA, Tommy McGuire, Sebring, FL, Ed Hedrick, Monrovia, CA, William O'Brien, Sherman Oaks, CA. Four of them would become Commanding Officer or Operations Officer of the 431st Squadron.

The squadrons were getting their living areas and mess halls organized after moving into their new location. Food was a problem and they sometimes had to eat "C" or "D" rations, which were filling but not very appetizing. In the evening the group's movie theater, which was just a projector and a screen, opened up for the first time and showed the Carole Landis movie "Powers Girl." It brought hoots and howls from the troops who hoped that they would soon be on the USO circuit so they could see some females in the flesh.

During the off-days McGuire flew test flights, and wondered to himself if the events of the past few weeks had really happened. After the months of patrol missions in Alaska and later New Guinea, he was at last helping to win the war. He had dreamed most of his life that he would someday be a victorious fighter pilot, but it was hard to believe that it had come true, and that he had coolly shot down five enemy planes in his first two combat encounters.

He wondered how he had beaten the odds qualifying for cadets and surviving the training. How he had been selected to be a fighter pilot instead of bomber pilot? How he had arrived at this place at this time? He knew that he was meant to be where his country needed him, and he couldn't wait to get another chance at the enemy, just to prove to himself that it was all true.

He saw action the next two days, flying on a five-hour bomber escort mission to Wewak, and a four-and-a-half hour flight to attack Ack-Ack installations at Hansa Bay. There were no enemy planes in the air to test him on either mission.

* * *

On August 26, after flying a one-hour test, McGuire returned to the squadron area where he picked up his mail. There was a letter and a telegram from Marilynn that told of his mother's death. He sat down and wrote Marilynn: *"I just received your letter telling me of Mother's death. It is hard to express one's feelings at such a time but I appreciate deeply the considerate way in which you informed me .... I am glad that you were there to act for me and do what you could .... I received your wire same time as the letter .... I am happy my mother got to know you & love you before she passed on .... I have been very busy here and the hunting has been excellent. We have been in a big show lately of which you have probably read."*

With men dying around him every day, McGuire kept the news of his mother's death to himself. He was sorry that she would never know about his success in combat. He knew she would have been proud of him. He was sad, but the war was consuming every waking hour.

* * *

The next day he took a P-38 test flight and stayed aloft two-and-a-half hours. It was a chance to be alone with his thoughts. His family was gone; his Grandfather, his Grandmother, and his Mother. The house by the lake in Sebring was gone too. Thank God he had Marilynn! She was his family and that was where his home and heart were now.

The following day the 431st escorted bombers to Wewak again and expected little opposition. The raids of the last two weeks had devastated the Japanese, destroying several hundred planes on the ground and a hundred or more in the air.[6]

When they approached Wewak 20 enemy fighters were spotted and the 16 P-38s went into action. Lieutenant Harry F. Holze led the flight on an attack against the element of Zekes. After one pass McGuire and his wingman lost contact with each other, but McGuire turned his plane sharply and saw a Zeke that had just made a diving attack through the bomber formation. As the Zeke pulled up McGuire got him in his gunsight. He fired several short bursts following the aircraft until it burst into flames and spun out of control. Lieutenant Holze got his first victory as he shot down one of the Zekes, too.

McGuire quickly spotted an Oscar diving to attack the bombers and he met it with a direct head-on attack. He could see his bullets striking the Oscar but it flew on. McGuire kicked his P-38 into a turn and followed the Oscar as it tried to escape. Turning first one way and then another, McGuire fired deflection shots in short bursts into the plane's wings and fuselage until it began smoking and went out of control. With dozens of fighter planes still in the sky McGuire wasn't surprised to hear on his radio, "Mac, break! There are three Zekes on your tail!"

He checked his rear-view mirror, and started evasive action. One of the Zekes got in position and fired tracers in front of the P-38. McGuire racked the plane into a turn, but saw an explosion as his left engine was hit by a 20mm cannon shell.

Suddenly the engine belched black smoke and flames. This was serious! McGuire had a major fire in his left engine. He thought of bailing out, but there were still three Zekes following him. He'd have to do something to get out of their gunfire before he decided to stay in the plane or bail out. First, he took measures to control the plane and stop the fire.

He chopped the throttle of the left engine, moved the mixture control to "idle cut-off," feathered the propeller, and turned off the gas pump and the fuel tank selector valve to that engine. It only took a few seconds, he had practiced the procedure before and followed it without thinking much about it. He completed the procedure by closing the coolant and oil cooler scoops for the left engine. Sometimes just shutting off the fuel was enough to stop a fire---he hoped so this time. It continued to burn.

If he was going to stay in the plane he'd have to get away from the Zekes, and take some measures to extinguish the flames before they reached his gas tanks. He remembered talk of diving a plane to blow out the flames. He racked the plane into a cross-control maneuver by kicking in right rudder and left aileron. The left wing dropped and the plane went into a slip--falling in a diagonal path. A slip was normally used to lose altitude quickly on the final approach of a landing, and he hadn't done one since he was at Corsicana. He held the slip for 2,000 feet and the flames died out.

The Japanese were bewildered by the maneuver and broke off as McGuire guided the smoke-trailing P-38 into a cloud bank. When he emerged he was alone, the engine had quit smoking, and the propeller was feathered. Now if he could just get out of the battle area and make it to some place safe.

To stop the plane from yawing, he trimmed the rudder tab so he could fly without applying constant pressure to the rudder pedal. He set his good propeller to "fixed pitch" and flipped his battery switch to "off." The P-38H had only one generator and it happened to be on the left engine. With that engine no longer running he had to conserve his battery until he needed it.

He would not be able to cross the mountains on one engine, to get back to Port Moresby. He was a "sitting duck" if an enemy plane happened along, and he wanted to land as soon as possible. He checked his map and set a course for the nearest American air field, 250 miles away, at Marilinan. It was a remote field that had been opened a month before to support the advance on Lae.

Two hours later he carefully kept his air speed above 120 miles-an-hour as he made a straight-in approach at Marilinan. He remembered others who had spun-in when they tried to land a P-38 on one engine. One of the 431st's planes had crashed several days before, trying a single-engined landing at this very field. He exhibited superior flying skill as he landed the crippled plane without a hitch.

He spent the night at Marilinan and the next day caught a B-25 flight back to Port Moresby. "Pudgy" had been badly damaged and would have to be repaired where it was parked before it could be flown again. Later, McGuire was again awarded the Distinguished Flying Cross for: "Heroism in flight.....in the face of great danger above and beyond the call of duty," for his action on August 29, 1943, defending the bombers at Wewak.[7] Eventually, McGuire was awarded three Distinguished Flying Crosses and a Silver Star for his heroic accomplishment in aerial combat, during his first 11 days in combat, August 18 to August 29, 1943. The awarding of four medals of this magnitude in such a short period is unprecedented in Air Force annals.

[1] 431st Daily History

[2] Ibid.

[3] Ibid.

[4] McGuire's Combat Report

[5] Frank Kish, McGuire's crew chief

[6] 431st Daily History

[7] Citation for DFC

27

These hot shot pilots play a deadly game. Like the matador, they trick and try their deadly foe. They must strike and kill, and see no more. If they look too long they might see that the foe is another matador.

----- "They Play a Deadly Game" by Charles Martin

McGuire was lost without his own P-38. He had grown fond of "Pudgy," but the plane sat badly damaged at Marilinan where he had made the emergency landing. The stray 20mm cannon shell he had picked up at Wewak, and the resulting fire, had caused serious damage to many of the components in the engine nacelle. It was likely that the plane could never be flown again, and would be stripped for spare parts.

McGuire was flying whatever plane was assigned to him by the Operations Officer. He had confidence in his own mechanic and was unhappy flying somebody else's plane. He took off September 1, to fly an escort mission to Nadzab. Twenty minutes out he made a check of the aircraft's equipment and found his gunsight to be out of order. He had no choice. He had to return to Port Moresby.[1] Without a gunsight he would be useless on the mission.

When he parked the borrowed plane he was mad as hell and he spoke to the plane's mechanic, "Do you ever check the god damned gunsight when you service this plane? I had to scrub a mission in a perfectly good airplane, all for a fucking fifty-cent light bulb. Who knows what kind of trouble the bombers are going to run into over Madang! I might have saved a bomber from being shot down, but I can't do that sitting at Port Moresby!"[2]

"I'm sorry, sir," answered the mechanic. "There was no mention on the form one about the gun sight being on the blink. I'll check it out right away."

Several days later Captain Bill Haning, the 431st Operations Officer, assigned McGuire a brand new P-38H5, and it was promptly named "Pudgy II." Haning reasoned that the squadron's hottest pilot was entitled to his own airplane. McGuire flew the new ship on a three-and-a half hour mission to Nadzab. There was no aerial combat on the mission but the new plane was a sweetheart.

By the ninth of September, the new plane had been boresighted and set up the way McGuire wanted it. His gun fire was very effective strafing luggers at Alexishafer as he set one on fire. During the next few days he flew long escort missions to Wewak where the Japanese were still trying to repair and hold their air field, and to Hansa Bay where the

B-24s sank four ships. There were no Japanese fighters in the air to challenge them.

McGuire flew long hours almost every day but found the time on September 15 to write Marilynn a letter in which he said: *"You said to let you know next time I had leave and you would fly down to see me. I don't think you can make Australia, do you?"*

On September 21 he and other members of the squadron moved across the mountains of New Guinea to Dobodura, to be in position to cover landings at Finschhafen. The move was on. The crippling of the Japanese airdrome at Wewak was a vital step in the retaking of New Guinea. Occupying Finschhafen was one of the next steps.

McGuire did his part. The next few days he flew two missions a day--what the men called ass-busters. He spent over seven hours in his airplane on each day. There wasn't much action, but the hours were wearing. The P-38 cockpit was fairly comfortable, but to sit on heat-rash-covered buttocks and not be able to stand up or stretch one's legs for three hours, required special patience.

Most of the men carried a canteen of water, a poor tasting no-melt tropical chocolate bar, or a bar of pressed dried fruit to keep up their energy on these long flights. Bodily functions were one of the most pressing problems. Urinating was no problem, the plane was equipped with a relief tube. Bowel movements were another thing. The fighter plane made no provisions. Good eating habits and a strong will were the best answers to that problem.

For two weeks the pilots of the 431st had been flying long, boring missions without any action. On September 28, 15 P-38s of the squadron were flying cover, at 18,000 feet, for 40 B-24 bombers on yet another mission to Wewak. Led by Captain John Hood they flew ahead on a fighter sweep to clear any enemy fighters from the area. They found none, and returned to escort the bombers while they dropped their bombs. Suddenly a Zeke zoomed up at the formation and Captain Hood ordered his pilots into a diving attack. Lieutenant Fred Champlin piped in on the radio, "Somebody help me. I've got a Zeke on my tail and I can't shake it!"

Captain Hood said, "Hang on, Champ, I'm on my way!" He and his wingman broke from the squadron and chased the Zeke into a cloud. Suddenly, 30 enemy aircraft appeared from nowhere. They were from the bases at Dugua and But. Wewak had been bombed so heavily it was no longer suitable for flying of any sort. The single Zeke attack was no doubt a trick to distract the squadron until the 30 enemy fighters were in position to surprise them.

The B-24's flew on and their bombs hit the giant ammunition dump at Wewak, causing an explosion of such great force that it could be felt in planes at 12,000 feet. A column of black smoke rose to that height and the sky filled with a colossal dog fight.

McGuire made a pass on a Zeke but before he could get into position to fire, called to his wingman, "We've got two Zekes on us, you break right, I'll break left! It's each man for himself!" The Japanese pilots were skilled, but the sudden split by the two P-38s worked and McGuire headed for a Zeke which was on the tail of another P-38. He made a pass and drove it off its attack. The Zeke pulled up to the left. McGuire anticipated it and turned ahead of him, staying in position until the Zeke flew into his gun-sight. McGuire got several good shots, knocking off large pieces of the plane. The Zeke caught fire and went down spiraling.

Turning back and gaining altitude he saw a Zeke making an attack on a flight of P-38s. He headed toward it. The Zeke saw McGuire coming and turned for a head-on attack at McGuire. He wasn't fast enough and McGuire made a deflection shot from close range. His aim was perfect, and the Zeke started down and passed under the wing of his P-38--the propeller was just barely turning, and the plane was smoking and finally burst into flames.[3]

McGuire tried to initiate another attack but a Zeke was on his tail. He nosed the P-38 into a dive but the Zeke's bullets hit his left engine. The needles on the left engine's instruments bounced and started back toward the lower peg. His engine was badly damaged. His only chance was to outrun the Zeke in a dive. Luckily the engine didn't burn. The P-38 gained enough speed in the dive to out run the Zeke, and McGuire broke free before he ran out of altitude. Had the Zeke not given up so quickly he might have had an easy, single-engined P-38 as a target.

McGuire went through the procedure of shutting down all of the left engine controls. He had experienced the same fate a month before and it was familiar. He trimmed the aircraft and headed Southeast along the coast. Glancing over his shoulder every few minutes he left the battle area. The column of black smoke from the Wewak ammo dump rose to 15,000 feet, and could be seen from 50 miles away.

The air field at Tsili-Tsili was 250 miles away, but McGuire once more nursed his crippled plane the whole distance and landed safely. There was a P-38 which had been left at Tsili-Tsili a few days before, with minor mechanical problems. It had since been repaired and McGuire took it and flew back to Port Moresby by supper time. His fellow pilots kidded him that he was the first 475th pilot to leave for a mission in one plane and return in another.[4]

The squadron's record for the day was: a Tony and a Zeke by Captain Hood, a Zeke by Lieutenant Champlin, a Zeke by Lieutenant Lewis, and two Zekes by McGuire (his eighth & ninth). Three P-38s were damaged.

McGuire was the leading Ace in the 475th Fighter Group, and for this day's action he was later awarded the Distinguished Flying Cross for: "heroism in flight and exceptional and outstanding accomplishment in the face of great danger above and beyond the line of duty." Two days later he wrote Marilynn and almost as an after thought closed with this sentence: *"We got into a little fight recently and I got 2 more nips which makes nine now."*

McGuire had flown 72 hours in the month of September, doubling his flight time for the whole year. He was beginning to look drawn. It was apparent that he had lost weight from the poor food, constant heat, and long flights. Though no one else flew as much as McGuire, they were all tired and ill tempered.

On the second day of October, when there would be no flying for a few days, the pilots of the 431st came upon the good fortune of a sizable quantity of liquor and threw themselves a party. The pilots were allowed an ounce of liquor after each combat flight--it was carefully issued by the flight surgeon. There was talk that the "Doc" might have allowed the allocation to "build-up," against regulations, figuring that one good blast might do more good than a lot of sips.

Most of the pilots had earned at least a fifth of liquor in the last month of so. The singing and yelling lasted long after lights out. They celebrated their victories, but they had reasons to be troubled. They were risking their lives every day and some were losing the gamble. When successful they killed the enemy, but none of them was prepared to deal with the flood of conflicting emotions. They were "immortal" young men and though they didn't want to show it, they were affected by the loss of friends, and the death they had wrought, even if it was to their enemy. The liquor numbed them for a few hours of escape from the thoughts that raced through their brains every waking hour, and caused them to sleep fitfully, if at all.

[1]McGuire's log book
[2]Frank Kish, McGuire's crew chief
[3]McGuire's Combat Report
[4]431st Daily History

28

Legends are unverified stories which have been passed down through the ages until they are generally accepted as historical facts. Give me a "legend in his own time" every time. He has not benefited from time, which washes away the shabby deeds, and glorifies the real ones.

---------C. Martin

By October, 1943, McGuire had earned a reputation as an outstanding combat pilot. In two short months of combat he was credited with 10 Japanese planes, but everyone said he had shot down more than that. At any rate he was the 475th Fighter Group's leading Ace, and was spoken of in awe: "What a shot--he just points 'Pudgy' and shoots--there's no wasted ammo. I've seen him hit two or three Japs on a single run."

McGuire was accumulating flying time faster than anyone in his squadron. He had almost caught up with Major Nichols, Captains Hood and Jett, and a few others who had been around much longer than he. The pilots in the squadron were split. Some thought he was too eager, but others appreciated what he was doing and wished they could do the same.

While most pilots slept late on non-combat days, McGuire was up flying tests. One of the pilots said, "Why doesn't that son-of-a-bitch wait till 9 o'clock to fly? Every time we have a day off he's out flying at 7:30. Hell, I always think I've overslept and missed a mission."

Another replied, "You'd better be glad Mac's doing the testing. The way he wrings out a plane you know it's got to be all right." A third said, "Sergeant Clem Lewicki, one of the armorers over at Three-Mile Strip, says Mac sticks with each plane until they have it bore-sighted and then does the test-firing himself. He keeps his nose right in the middle of it. Lewicki says he's the only pilot around that knows anything about bore-sighting P-38s."

The 431st Squadron started October in the doldrums. They were kept out of action by bad weather and the movement of the squadron from Port Moresby to Dubodura. Their P-38s had provided long-range escort for the complete destruction of the Japanese forces at Wewak, far to the west. Now it was time to turn their attention to the powerful Japanese naval and air installation at Rabaul. The Japanese were dominating the Solomon Islands and the sea around them with their forces at Rabaul.

The long-range P-38s were vital to any mission against that stronghold, reportedly one of the most heavily fortified ports in the world. Rabaul was 450 miles north of New Guinea. Missions across the Solomon Sea to Rabaul on the northern shore of New Britain could only be flown from Dobodura, so the 475th Group was ordered to transfer across the mountains from Port Moresby to Dobo.

On October 2 the officers got a quantity of liquor and had a party which lasted late into the night. Shortly after they bedded down for the night the camp was awakened at 2:00 a.m. and told to pack. Everything was to be at the air strip by 7:00 a.m. As usual, there was a delay and loading didn't start until 10:00 a.m..[1]

On October 5, the squadron had its first payday in two months, followed by three days of rain, and the pilots wore out the seats in the alert-shack.[2] Large quantities of money flowed in a three-day non-stop poker game. Everyone was itching to get back in action. McGuire flew to and from Port Moresby each day to coordinate movement of the maintenance people and supplies.

By the eleventh of the month the weather had cleared. McGuire had gotten "Pudgy II" back from the service squadron where they had replaced the left engine and repaired the damage that had forced him to leave it at Tsili-Tsili two weeks before.

On October 12, the purpose for the move across New Guinea became a reality as the 431st and 100 other P-38s flew cover for 230 bombers making their first strike on Rabaul. The Japanese didn't expect the raid, but the sky was black with ack-ack. With little aerial resistance from the enemy, American bombers caught Japanese airfields glutted with planes and destroyed over 100 of them. In the harbor they laid waste to 120 vessels including three destroyers and three large cargo ships. It was one of the most important victories since the Battle of the Coral Sea.

The Japanese sensed another invasion was about to follow the Rabaul raid as it had the Wewak raids. They sent night bombers over Dobodura several nights in a row to damage the field and interrupt the sleep of the pilots and crews. Then, on October 15, they made an attempt to catch American forces marshalling in nearby Oro Bay, New Guinea. Controllers sounded a scramble at 8:30 a.m. An all-out effort was needed to combat 60 enemy planes coming in from Rabaul. While standby pilots taxied to the runway and took off in pairs, other pilots grabbed jeeps, and jumped on trucks in the tent area and raced to the revetments, and their own planes.

Fifty P-38s from the 475th Group entered the battle at some stage of the assault. The cooks, clerks, and ground crews who had spent day and night the last few months to keep the P-38s flying were now, for the first time, witnesses to the Group's onslaught. They watched and cheered as the P-38s destroyed a record 21 enemy bombers and 15 enemy fighters! The ones that escaped were badly damaged and estimates were made that six or less of the original force made it back to their home base.

The 431st Squadron accounted for 10 of the enemy planes with Lieutenant Lent getting three, and McGuire and six other pilots getting one each. The squadron lost a plane but the pilot was later found and returned to the squadron.

On October 17, McGuire's "Pudgy II" was out of service, when a large flight of Japanese bombers and fighters was spotted heading for the American shipping in Oro Bay, the same target they had tried unsuccessfully to hit two days before. The call came down, "SCRAMBLE---SCRAMBLE, get everything in the air that will fly."

Although he wasn't on alert, McGuire knew that every effort was needed to turn back the enemy attack. He quickly did a mental check of all available aircraft. As assistant maintenance officer he knew the status of every airplane in the squadron. There wasn't a plane to be had, except for Major Nichols'. The CO was at Fifth Fighter Command for the day, but his plane was in good order.

Major Franklin Nichols, the Squadron Commander, had the reputation for being a good sport. A week before he demonstrated this while on his way back to his tent after a shower. He was dressed in undershorts and Australian flying boots and was carrying a shaving kit and a towel. The players in a nearby field touted him into a touch football game already in progress. Nichols caught a pass and ran for a touchdown as his shorts slipped down, first around his knees, then around his ankles, and finally onto the ground. He proceeded across the goal line in his birthday suit and knee-high boots to the cheers of the players, including those on the opposing team. The opposition tried to get the play called back because the Major was "out of uniform."[3]

As good a sport as he may have been, the Major had one rule he insisted on: "Nobody flies my airplane without my permission."

McGuire had flown into battle with Major Nichols many times and knew the rule. In spite of this, he made a decision. He ran down the flight line and shouted an order to the Major's crew chief, "Get Major Nichols' plane started."

Major Nichols' crew chief said, "Sir, I have strict orders. No one flies the Major's airplane without his permission."

"I understand, Sergeant. I will take full responsibility. Right now, the Japs scare me more than the Major does--let's start the engines."

McGuire quickly attached himself to Red Flight led by Lieutenant Marion Kirby. They taxied to the end of the field, turned the planes, and without stopping, roared down the runway and pulled their planes up into the sky. There was time to get altitude before the intruders appeared. At 23,000 feet the enemy was spotted at a slightly higher altitude. Lieutenant Kirby ordered, "Drop your tanks, we'll go at them head-on."

Climbing slightly, the flight started its attack. McGuire picked one of the 15 enemy planes, a Zeke on the right side of the formation, and started firing. It started smoking and rolled off to the right into a dive. McGuire followed, firing a few more short bursts. At 18,000 feet, he decided that the Zeke was severely damaged and pulled up to return to the main force, above.

McGuire's wingman had only been able to drop one of his large fuel tanks and found himself unable to pull out of the dive. He followed McGuire's wounded Zeke down to 4,000 feet and saw it explode, before he could pull his P-38 out of its dive. He shouted to McGuire over the radio: "Mac, I can't shake one of my fuel tanks. I'm a sitting duck as long as I have this hanger--I'm heading home."

"Hit some clouds and get out of here," replied McGuire.

Alone, McGuire tried to rejoin the Red Flight at 21,000 feet, but saw two Zekes about to attack them from four o'clock. He shouted a warning on the radio and turned his craft and fired several short bursts to drive the Zekes away from the P-38s. Suddenly, McGuire saw four Zekes in his rear-view mirror, closing in to attack him. He pointed the nose of Major Nichols' plane toward the ocean below and pushed the throttles to the firewall, increasing his speed until the turbo warning lights came on. It was no time to worry about operating limits!

The Japanese followed, but McGuire pulled away. After a descent of 15,000 feet, he cut his throttles and started a gentle pull-out which left him only 1,000 feet from the surface of the ocean. He had gotten away using speed and he pulled the plane's nose up to convert the speed back into altitude. At 18,000 feet he was attacked from above by three Zekes. Again, he pushed the nose over into a dive, as one of the Zekes latched onto his tail, and he felt bullets hitting his airplane. Several slugs ricocheted inside the cockpit. He pushed the nose lower until the plane was diving vertically toward the sea.

A dive of this sort was very dangerous in a P-38 due to a problem called compressibility which could make it impossible to pull out. McGuire knew this, but the possibility of bullets hitting inside his plane again, worried him more. He pulled away from the Zeke, who broke off the attack. He returned to 12,000 feet where he saw seven Zekes chasing a crippled P-38, which was trailing black smoke from one engine.

It was a sure kill for the Japanese, and McGuire had no choice. As one Zeke closed in to polish off the ailing P-38, McGuire made a desperate 90-degree deflection shot. A shot from this angle was extremely difficult because it required great judgment in leading the target, but it had become a McGuire trademark. He gave a long burst and saw it hit the Zeke around the cockpit, causing it to break off its attack and explode into flames.

Pulling up to the right, he closed in behind another Zeke for a rare, direct tail shot. He flew right up the tail of the Jap getting within 100 feet before he began firing. His ammunition was limited and he had to make the best use of what he had left. He could see his bullets ripping large chunks from the Japanese plane, and it started burning and rolled slowly to the left and down. The pilot made no evasive move--he was dead.

Now that he had attracted their attention, and the wounded P-38 had escaped, the five remaining Zekes turned on the willing fighter. McGuire started evasive action, but could not get away from one of the agile Zekes which closed in behind him to a few hundred feet. He could see bullets striking his left engine, and black smoke started trailing from it. A cannon shell hit in the radio compartment behind his head and exploded, spraying shrapnel all over the cockpit. Only the armor plate behind his head had saved him from certain death. A 7.7mm shell struck McGuire in the wrist with a fierce sting and passed into the instrument panel. He felt the burn of shrapnel wounds in his hips and arms.

The Zekes had broken off, but his troubles were not over yet. McGuire pulled the yoke back to bring the P-38 out of a dive, but his controls were useless and he realized that the bullets passing through the cockpit had severed the control cables. He'd have to get out of the plane while it was still in a steep dive.

He chopped both throttles and pulled the emergency hatch release. The canopy ripped away in the slip stream. He released his seat belt and shoulder harness, climbed into the seat and jumped. The thought of that great knife-like elevator at the back of the plane flashed through his mind as he went into the blasting air of the slip stream.

Something was wrong! He dangled in the slip stream, somehow tethered to the falling plane. His parachute harness was caught inside the cockpit and he was unable to free himself. He was buffeted violently against the plane, which was now burning. Down, 2,000, 3,000, 4,000, 5,000, 6,000, 7,000 feet---struggling all the way to get lose. Then, bruised, battered, and stunned, he pushed free of the plane, clearing the tail with plenty of room.

He reached across his chest, to the parachute harness, and with a wounded hand, pulled the ripcord. He was still about 5,000 feet from the water. Another surprise! The "D" ring pulled loose in his hand, with just a small piece of cable attached. Nothing else happened. The chute wasn't opening as it should! The shrapnel which had showered through the plane's cockpit and peppered him, had severed the parachute cable too.[4]

With no reserve chute, he had only one chance as he tumbled toward the ocean below. In spite of his wounded wrist, he managed to reach behind his back, find the loose end of the broken parachute cable, twist it around his hand and pull it. The chute popped open and he felt the sudden jolt of the life-saving canopy blossoming above him.

McGuire was dazed, but he made a quick assessment. He had a few hundred feet before he would enter the water. He could see that he was many miles from shore, and there wasn't anything in the ocean below. A scan of the sky revealed burning airplanes, leaving columns of smoke, as they, too, plunged toward the sea.

Remembering his survival training, he released himself from his parachute as he entered the water. He felt relieved to be in the water. After all it was only water. He struggled with his one-man life raft, pulling the inflation tab. There was a loud hiss of CO_2 gas, but the small boat did not inflate! An inspection revealed that the boat was peppered with shrapnel holes.

He felt pressure and pain in his chest as he tried to inflate the yellow Mae West life jacket which was strapped around his neck and waist. It too hissed, as one side inflated and one side did not. One side was enough to keep his head just above the water. If it didn't start leaking, he would be all right for a while. To make himself more buoyant, he kicked off his prized Australian flying boots, and dropped off all excess equipment, including his 45-caliber pistol and shoulder holster.

He thought that it may not matter if the jacket kept him afloat or not. He was bleeding and the sea water stung his wounds. If he didn't lose enough blood to endanger his life, the blood might attract sharks which would do the job. If the tide took him away from shore, it may not make any difference anyway. There were ships in the area, but the action had been so fast and furious, it was unlikely that anybody had seen him bail out--after all he had fallen almost to the surface of the ocean before his chute had opened, and he had only floated in the air for a few seconds before hitting the water.

The odds weren't too good this time. Just the same he opened the dye-marker packet, saved from the raft, and sprinkled it on the water. It spread on the ocean forming a bright yellowish-green slick which would be visible for miles, from the air.

His chest hurt, and he knew he must have crushed some ribs. His thoughts flashed back to Lake Hopatcong, New Jersey, and the day he had taken the dare to swim to the raft. He had come close to drowning that day with his cousins and Paul Gustat. He had looked the grim reaper in the face that day, and it had scared him more than he had let on--more than this whole crazy day had.

As McGuire floated he applied pressure to the bullet hole in his arm to stop the bleeding, and fought off pain that almost caused him to lapse into unconsciousness. A half hour passed. Now he thought how mad Major Nichols was going to be and he said to himself, "He'll chew my ass real good when he finds out about his airplane--may not even want me in the squadron any more. I guess I've really cooked my goose this time."

The concussion of the cannon shell exploding in the radio compartment had induced ringing in his ears but he thought he heard the sound of an engine, and it seemed to get louder. He turned in the water to see a PT boat in the distance, and it was headed his way.

They had seen a chute above the water and knowing the Japanese didn't use them, came to see if an American was in the water. In minutes PT 152, under command of its Captain, Herbert Knight, pulled alongside and fished McGuire from the water.[5] As the crew helped him into dry clothing and dressed his wounds one of the crewmen spoke up, "Lieutenant, that was unbelievable. We saw you get the two Japs. Bang! Bang! Then we saw the Japs get you. Your plane didn't pull out--we thought you were dead. Then we saw a chute open near the water. The whole thing happened so fast that the two Japs, your plane, and your chute, were all in the air at once. You all hit the water at the same time. It's the damnedest thing I ever saw."

McGuire agreed, as one of the crewmen administered Morphine for his pain. They were 25 miles from shore and it would be a rough ride. Before night fall he was transferred to the PT tender Hilo, docked in Buna Bay.

Back at the base word got around. The Japs had sustained great losses, the 431st only one pilot--McGuire. There were reports that McGuire had been seen attacking seven Zekes, but nobody saw him go down. Search planes were sent out, but they found nothing. Communications were poor, and it was late in the evening before the squadron operations phone rang. It was the Fifth Fighter Command. "We heard from the Captain of a PT boat. They picked up McGuire 25 miles out to sea this afternoon. Mac broke some ribs and is wounded, but he will be O K."

Everyone in the squadron was relieved to hear that McGuire had been found. They hated to lose a comrade but it was even worse when a skilled pilot like McGuire got shot down. Young pilots wondered: if they got McGuire the way he can fly, what chance do I have? Knowing McGuire survived, renewed each pilot's spirits.

It was several days before the 431st could find their top Ace. He had been transferred to the Army's Tenth Evacuation Hospital, but the Navy didn't know where he had been taken. After a canvas of Army hospitals he was found and Major Nichols was the first to visit. The Major approached McGuire's bed to find him in a half sleep. He cleared his throat. McGuire opened his two blackened eyelids to reveal two blood red eyeballs.

"Where in hell did you get those eyes?" asked the Major.

McGuire told his story, "When I bailed out my parachute harness or something caught in the cockpit and I couldn't get loose. My goggles ripped off in the slip stream, and I felt like my eyes were coming out of their sockets. The plane must have been doing 400 miles an hour."

Nichols shook his head and said, "If you took better care of your airplane, things like this wouldn't happen."

"I'm sorry as hell about your airplane," said McGuire.

McGuire looked so bad and sounded so sincere that Major Nichols could only reply, "I'm just glad as hell to see you alive. They tell me you took on the whole Damned Japanese Air Force. You did the right thing, taking my airplane. A maximum effort was called for and you undoubtedly saved a few people's lives. Just don't do it again."[6]

A few days later Major Nichols recommended McGuire for his second Silver Star, for gallantry in action, and returned to the hospital to present him with the Purple Heart for wounds received in combat.

Thus it was that McGuire got a reputation for cheating death. Since entering combat with the 431st, two months before, he had survived a head-on collision with a Zero, and twice flown home hundreds of miles on one engine after slipping away from pursuing Japanese. Now he had been wounded, escaped a burning aircraft, been entangled and battered against the falling bird, opened a faulty parachute, floated in the ocean with no means of support, and escaped the wrath of Major Nichols after losing his plane.

He had downed 13 enemy planes, and had been awarded two Silver Stars, four Distinguished Flying Crosses, two Air Medals and the Purple Heart. Surely a man who could do all of this in two months was on his way to becoming a living legend.

Tommy wrote to Marilynn: *"I sprained my wrist a week ago and haven't been able to hold a pen. We have been in quite a bit of action lately so up until I hurt my wrist I have been quite busy. I have 12 confirmed victories to my credit now so feel pretty good about the whole thing."* (He had not learned of the third Zeke he shot down. His wingman, while trying to drop a hung wing tank, had seen the Zeke go into the sea, and had made the claim for McGuire.)

[1] 431st Daily History
[2] Ibid.
[3] Ibid.
[4] McGuire's Combat Report
[5] 431st Daily History
[6] General Franklin Nichols

29

"I always thought a lot of him, and regretted very much his being shot down and in the hospital just at the time we went on the Rabaul raids. We could have used him!"

........Capt. Robert L. Herman, 431st Fighter Pilot.

The 431st Squadron continued to escort strikes on Rabaul, and they were met with heavy ack-ack and large numbers of enemy fighters. In one battle McGuire's friend, "Pappy" Cline, had to break formation to escape a Tony fighter on his tail. When he landed at a refueling field on Kiriwina Island he counted over 30 bullet holes in his plane. The plane was unsafe to fly, and McGuire's tentmate, Lieutenant Champlin, who had also landed to refuel, offered him a ride back to Dobodura in his one-man P-38.

They shed their parachutes and Champlin sat on Cline's lap as they flew back to Dobodura with Champlin handling the throttles and the control column, and Cline working the rudder pedals. They were so proud of their accomplishment that they decided to buzz the strip at Dobodura before landing. Unfortunately they met Captain Harry Brown, the acting Commanding Officer of the 431st Squadron, coming in to land from the opposite direction. They narrowly missed a mid-air collision, and were restricted to their tents for a week for their stunt.[1].

On November 2 the 431st Squadron was involved in one of the fiercest battles of the war. Against overwhelming odds they fought off enemy interceptors with great gallantry. Lieutenants Kirby, Wenige, Champlin, and Hunt shot down two Zekes each, and Lieutenants Lutton, Lent, and Monk got one each. Losses were high as Lieutenants Lowell Lutton, Kenneth Richardson, and Owen Giertsen did not return from the mission.[2] The next day, just 16 days after he was shot down and severely injured, McGuire was warmly greeted back to the camp of the 431st Fighter Squadron. He was pale, had a bandaged right wrist, was still black and blue around his eyes, and was walking with a limp. He was asked, "How long will you be grounded?"

"I'm catching the Fat Cat out of here for a couple of weeks in Sydney," said McGuire. "I'll have a steak for you while I'm over there. After that I'll be ready to go again."

One of the pilots said, "It's too bad you're off flying status. We've been talking about it while you were in the hospital: you shot down 13 Japs in two months. Dick Bong is the leading ace in the Southwest Pacific with 19, and he has been out here a year. They are sending Bong home to sell War Bonds. If you were flying you could take over the 'ace race' while he was gone."

"Ace race?" asked McGuire.

"Yeah, that's what they are calling it. There are some other guys close to Bong but they've been out here a long time too."

"I had no idea I was just six behind!" said McGuire. "For now, all I care about now is getting my ribs healed."

This was the start of an unofficial comparison between McGuire and Bong that would last until both of them were out of combat for good. Other pilots, the press, and even the brass recognized the two of them as competitors, but neither of them promoted the discussions, and both of them would deny any interest in it.

McGuire moved around the camp and got the latest version of the "War is Hell" theme: "The tents are a mile from the mess hall, the bugs are bad, and the food stinks."

He dropped in to see Major Nichols. "Just came by to apologize about your airplane again."

Major Nichols said, "Forget about it, Tommy. Just relax and get your health back, don't rush it."

"I hear you folks took a beating yesterday," said McGuire.

"We thought we were getting ready for a landing at Rabaul, but I just heard that the Marines landed at Bougainville," said the Major. "That's the reason we have been hitting Rabaul so hard. We kept the Japs so busy that our Navy planes had no opposition when the Marines landed on Bougainville."[3]

McGuire talked his way into the co-pilot's seat of the next Australian-bound flight of the 475th's famous supply plane. The B-25, which was no longer considered suitable for combat, was completely stripped of its armament and armor plate, rebuilt with scrounged parts, and was used for unofficial "fat cat missions" to supply some of the finer things of life for the group. Since the plane returned from every "mission" loaded to the roof with food, liquor, and tobacco, it was often cartooned as a pregnant airplane. It was also known as "Fertile Myrtle". McGuire had been on the unofficial committee that named the plane, and he surely appreciated the name more than most.

When the "Fertile Myrtle" arrived in Australia, McGuire sent a dozen roses to Marilynn. She had received a telegram saying that he had been wounded, but she didn't know much else. She had gotten word through Major Nicholas' wife that Tommy was doing well. The flowers set her mind at ease--he was safe.[4]

This was one of only a few times McGuire would make it out of the war zone for some rest. He stayed at a house the officers of the 431st had set up for the purpose. Accommodations were not easy to find in Sydney, with the large numbers of soldiers moving about the country. Each officer of the 431st contributed a few dollars each month to rent the furnished house from a couple named Harris. A housekeeper named Vi kept the place in order.[5]

McGuire enjoyed having drinks and dinner in the evenings, and sleeping a little late in the mornings. He had time to write some letters. He had gotten several letters from his father since his mother had died, and he hadn't had time or known what to write to his dad. Now he told him about his war adventures. His father had shown great interest in his flying experiences.

He browsed the shops during the day and picked up some phonograph records for his wind-up record player. One of the records was "Jealousy" featuring Artie Shaw. He had always enjoyed Shaw and Benny Goodman because they played his favorite instrument, the same one he had played in the Sebring High School band, the clarinet.

Every day he felt stronger and before long he was itching to get back to New Guinea. If he didn't get back soon, he was afraid he would lose his place in the so called "Ace Race." More importantly, he had time to think and it made him nervous to sit around. He hoped that he hadn't lost his edge. His timing had been so good before he was shot down. Now that he had not flown for a few weeks he wondered if he could get his confidence back.

The longer he sat around the more time he had to remember the number of close calls he had survived. He had time to remember the crunch of his wing tip hitting a Zero's wing, and how it sounded to hear enemy bullets striking his plane. He remembered how it had been to return alone through enemy skies twice with only one engine, and how it had been to dangle in the air still tethered to his falling P-38.

He had been so caught-up in the daily activities that he had never had time to think much about all of these close calls. Now that he was removed from it all, and had no daily tasks to perform, the incidents seemed like a fantasy that raced through his mind over and over again. It was a lot to go through in two months, and he had seen other pilots completely shattered by less combat stress than he had experienced.

He vowed to himself that he would do what he had done on the football practice field back in Sebring. When he had been knocked down and hurt there, he had forced himself, each time, to get up and try again. Soon he had forgotten the pain and fear and had played football on sheer determination. Although he had lacked the skill and size to play the game, he had gained the respect of the other players because he wouldn't quit.

He would do the same thing now. He would return to combat determined to overcome his pains and fears. He was becoming a natural leader when he was shot down. People in the squadron were beginning to ask him for advice, and value his ideas. They would all be watching him when he returned, to see if he still had the daring and courage to go on as before. He would return and set an example for others to follow.

He wrote Marilynn: "*As this should get to you about December 4th, I will take this opportunity to wish you a Happy Anniversary!...Don't think so much of the fact that I am not there but rather that we will have many more happy anniversaries together...You probably read about all of the big raids over here a while ago. Well I was in on it. The nip hunting has still been good & I have 13 confirmed & two probable victories now.*"

The news from New Guinea confirmed that the 431st was still hitting the Rabaul area. Some of the pilots and ground crew were temporarily moved to the island of Kiriwina, in the middle of the Solomon Sea, to be closer to the action. The small strip was void of civilization except for a nearby native village which looked like a picture from National Geographic Magazine.

The GIs, having nothing else to do, installed a crude shower. It was a pipe, seven feet above the ground, that flowed fresh cool water. The troops were so eager to bathe that they couldn't wait for a bathhouse to be built. They bathed in full view of a path frequented by native women. The women were fascinated by the men's white bodies, and were completely uninhibited. They often stopped and watched, pointed, and made comments.

The squadron historian was inspired to record: "These women are prone to comment on the size of the sex organs, it is supposed that the remarks, 'Ugh, Ugh, big stick, good pom pom, was flattery of the first order.'"[6]

In McGuire's absence Captain Danny Roberts, CO of the 433rd Squadron and one of the most respected men in the 475th Group, took over the leadership in enemy planes downed. Unfortunately he was involved in a mid-air collision, and fell to his death minutes after shooting down his 15th Japanese plane. The quiet, religious man would never be forgotten by his men.

Three more 431st planes were lost as Lieutenants J. J. Durkin, Paul Smith, and Frank Monk were not able to make it through some violent weather while returning with Major Nichols and six other planes from an aborted mission to Rabaul. Monk and Durkin were later rescued and returned to the squadron.

On November 15, McGuire again talked his way back into the co-pilot's seat of "Fertile Myrtle" for the three-day trip back to New Guinea and the 431st Fighter Squadron. He was feeling fit---his ribs still felt tight, but they didn't hurt like before. His eyes were no longer bloodshot but his cheek bones still had a tint of yellow in the skin--the last trace of the horrible black eyes he had suffered. At first he had feared that he might have done damage to his vision that would prevent him from returning to flying status, but it was clearly established by now that he had not suffered any permanent eye damage.

McGuire was welcomed home by a sergeant as he stepped off the B-25 at the Dobodura Strip, "Welcome home Lieutenant. You missed a lot of fireworks while you were gone. They've hit Rabaul almost every day since you left, and we've downed so many Nips that Tokyo Rose calls us 'The Butchers of Rabaul'."

"Great," said McGuire. "I hope they saved some for me."

"I think they saved a few," quipped the Sergeant. "By the way, Bong got two more before he left for the states and has 21 now."

McGuire knew he would have a battle with the flight surgeon to get back on flying status. At least his weight was up as a result of the fine meals he had enjoyed in Sydney. He checked in with the 431st's flight surgeon, Captain George R. Smith, who said, "Sorry, Mac, you're three or four weeks away from flying yet."

"Come on Doc, I'm feeling fine. I'll go crazy sitting around here if I'm not flying," said McGuire.

"Come back and see me in two weeks," replied the doctor, "I'll see how you're doing."

McGuire went to see Major Nichols and pleaded for him to intercede with the medics to get him back on flying status. "Major, I think I'm ready to fly, but the surgeon said it's going to be three weeks. Can you do anything about that?" asked McGuire.

Major Nichols said, "I know you like to keep busy, but you have to remember that you were pretty beat up. I've got a couple of jobs for you on the ground. The 9th Fighter Squadron switched to P-47s and we got five of their P-38s. We cut cards with the 432nd and 433rd and we got first pick. We need these planes as soon as possible, but I want you to make sure they are in good flying condition, before we assign them to someone."

"Yes, sir. I'll have them checked. I'm sure we can have them ready in a few days," replied McGuire.

The Major continued, "We've lost eight planes in combat or to bad weather in the last two weeks. We've got to do a thorough check-ride with all replacement pilots when they come in. These kids are green, and we need to see what they can do before we send them into combat."

McGuire agreed, "These kids don't have much flying time. Maybe we can get them on some milk runs to start out. At least, I'm glad we aren't the ones switching to the Thunderbolts."

"You can say that again," replied the Major. "We've got the 342nd Fighter Squadron on the strip now. It's a P-47 outfit, straight from the states. They are going to stand alert while we're flying Lightnings on the long missions. We tell them 'A Thunderbolt is a meaningless noise that follows Lightning'."

"What do I do after we get those planes out?" asked McGuire.

"I've got another job for you, Mac," continued the Major. "The food in the mess hall has been terrible. As long as you aren't flying, I want you to be mess officer and see if you can't get some better food for the troops."

"I don't know anything about running a mess hall, but I'll do my best," answered McGuire.

"Give it a try, it couldn't be any worse than it is now."

A few days later Major Nichols announced that he would leave the Squadron soon for a long leave in the States and then a new assignment. It would signal the end of a name the 431st Squadron had earned: "Nick Nichols' Nip Nippers." Captain Harry Brown who had been at Pearl Harbor when the war started, and had become the 431st's first ace, was also going home.

Before he left, Major Nichols set a good example for future squadron commanders when he had the enlisted men gather and thanked them for their good work: "You men share equally in the credit for the squadron's excellent record. There isn't a pilot alive that could defeat the Japanese, if he didn't have an airplane that was properly maintained. Keep up the good work."[7] Captain Verl E. Jett who had been the Operations Officer was appointed the new Commanding Officer. Captain Marion F. Kirby became the new Operations Officer.

Dobodura hit the big time on November 19, as it hosted its first live USO show. The master of ceremonies was Gary Cooper, and he seemed uncomfortable with the job. He was nervous and shy, and knocked the microphone off of its stand several times. The GIs shouted "watch it" to no avail before he knocked it off again, to produce the biggest laugh of the night.

The two actresses with the troupe weren't pin-up girls but their efforts were appreciated. Una Merkel and Phyllis Brooks joined in songs and Andy Arcari played the accordion. Arcari played his instrument with his feet, and nose, and stole the show until Una Merkel sat down on the

stage and forgot to keep her knees together. The glimpse of black pant-
ies almost caused a riot as one GI jumped to his feet and went into the
old burlesque theater pitch: "A prize in each package. You see a picture
of a young couple in an innocent embrace, but when you hold it up to
the light you see the real picture!"[8] A good time was had by all.

Later, Gary Cooper looked uncomfortable as he folded his large
frame to fit into the small radio compartment, behind the pilot's seat of a
P-38, for an obligatory piggy-back ride. Afterwards, he smiled with
pride and satisfaction as he shook the hand of Colonel Prentice and
thanked him for the 20-minute flight. For the next few days the main
topic of conversation around the base was: "Who'd you like best, Una,
or Phyllis?"[9]

On November 22, the troops were surprised by a fine meal with food
furnished by the "Fat Cat" flight and it inspired the following poem from
the squadron historian:

> "Oh sing my tongue of taste's delight,
> in banquets such as that tonight,
> of fresh roast beef and mashed potatoes,
> white and soft, with dark rich gravy,
> cukes and rings of onions inspiced,
> with salt and vinegar deviced,
> to compliment the bread and meat,
> but best of all to top the treat,
> a piece of cake light as a dream,
> with two full scoops of cool ice cream,
> coffee to keep the sweets uncloyed,
> may cooks be ever thus employed."[10]

When Thanksgiving came most of the troops felt that they had little
for which to be thankful. The 24-hour-a-day heat and humidity had not
let up since they had been there. Everyone was suffering from a permanent case of athlete's foot and chronic jock itch. Some had fungus
growing under their finger nails and others fought fungal ear infections.

The Holiday meal was surprisingly good. It was just like home, with
turkey and all of the trimmings. The heat seemed to take their appetites
and it just didn't seem like Thanksgiving. Most of the men were unable
to eat all the food they took. They were not accustomed to the quantity
or quality of the food.

Lt. Colonel George W. Prentice, the first man activated in the 475th
Group, departed for home. He was instrumental in the early success of
the group. He picked the leadership, and set the tone which resulted in
the group's great start-up. Lt. Colonel Charles MacDonald, the Group

Executive Officer, and a truly gifted fighter pilot, took command of the group.

[1]Fred Champlin, 431st pilot
[2]431st Daily History
[3]Ibid.
[4]General Nichols later told Marilynn in person
  that he thought Tommy was through, because
  of his wounds, and would soon be coming home
[5]Robert L Herman, 431st pilot
[6]431st Daily History
[7]Ibid.
[8]Ibid.
[9]Ibid.
[10]Ibid.

30

"We all wondered if he could come back and have the same daring that he exhibited before being shot down. It takes something out of a man when he has been shot down, particularly when he has been wounded by the enemy. Others who had been shot down were never the same. We all wondered how McGuire would react--he had been so aggressive before."   -------- A 431st pilot.

McGuire received an early Christmas present. After weeks of battling with the Flight Surgeon he finally got permission to return to flying status on December 12. He popped into the operations office to see Captain Kirby.

"Hey, Kirby, guess what! I'm back on flying status. Have you got a plane I can fly?"

Kirby said, "Mac, I've got a plane. How about letting a new pilot tag along with you for a combat check ride?"

"Sure, I'd be glad to check him out," replied McGuire.

John Tilley had met McGuire a few days before in a bull session and knew his reputation as the squadron "hot shot." McGuire had not seemed very friendly and Tilley thought it was probably because he had just gotten out of the hospital.[1]

They met at the flight line and with little conversation, saddled up and took off in element formation with McGuire in the lead. When they reached altitude, McGuire threw his plane into a series of violent maneuvers that took the two planes all over the sky. They dived, rolled, climbed, and turned. Tilley hung on, although the "G" forces in some of the turns almost caused him to black out. One minute they were inverted. The next minute they climbed at full wartime power. It was a bewildering combination of banks, high-speed stalls, and semi-inverted flight, and it all seemed to be at tree-top level. Tilley thought to himself, "This crazy bastard is trying to kill me."

Tilley was good but the flight was more than he had expected. He had been an instructor stateside and had many hours of twin-engine flying time. He had come overseas hurriedly with limited P-38 time, none of it with a wild man leading the way. Tilley did all the maneuvers with McGuire and was quite pleased with himself afterwards because he then thought he might be able to survive the hazards of combat.[2]

McGuire had treated Tilley the way he had been treated when he reported to the 49th Fighter Group. McGuire had not liked it then, but the shoe was on the other foot this time.

McGuire wasn't reluctant to talk about combat flying with the younger pilots in the 475th. They had not been around when McGuire had been in his heyday, and some were not impressed by McGuire's demeanor or stature and one asked, "Who does McGuire think he is? I know he's some kind of hot-shot pilot who flies like a crazy man, but where does he come off with all the talk?"

An old timer replied, "He may come on a little strong but he's got more combat time than God, and he's one of the top aces in the Pacific. You'd be smart to listen to him."

McGuire returned to combat flying cover for Marine landings at Cape Gloucester, New Britain. He saw some Zekes on his second mission, but had to flee, when a supercharger failed and left him with a sputtering engine.

On the same day John Tilley flew his first combat mission and got his first kill, a Betty Bomber. Maybe Tilley would be another McGuire. He was a talented flyer and he had the daring. He and McGuire could have been good friends, but they got off to a bad start, and their relationship never seemed to get any better.

The Fifth Air Force sent word that McGuire was promoted to Captain. He had waited 16 months to make 1st Lieutenant. Now, six months later he was promoted again. Little was said, but the promotion upset some old timers in the Group who had waited a long time for their second silver bar. McGuire's two promotions in six months did not sit well with them.

For the rest of the month McGuire was back to the daily grind, flying two missions a day. He flew five and six hours each day and took it in stride. Late in December the 431st turned its attention back to Wewak where the action was once again hot and heavy. McGuire was in the thick of the battle but had no luck against the Japanese. The enemy pilots were tough, and he wondered if he had lost his touch.

Although Christmas was approaching, the climate and vegetation on New Guinea remained the same as it had for months. Being near the equator, the foliage remained green, the days and nights were hot, and the mosquitoes still swarmed. Only the calendar noted that Christmas was near. With the usual steam-cooker weather it was hard to get into the Christmas spirit.

On Christmas Eve, Captain Jett showed his appreciation for the enlisted men's efforts and furnished, from his personal stock, 10 quarts of gin, 10 quarts of whisky, and 10 gallons of GI alcohol for a party at the Enlisted Men's Club. The Captain made the mistake of waiting until the party was well under way before he dropped into the club to extend his greetings. The party had already advanced to the brawl stage and the

Captain went unnoticed even after he stood on the bar and waved his arms to draw attention.

Sergeant Ira Martin came to his aid and shouted, "Shut up, you bastards, and listen to the god-damned CO."[3]

Captain Jett only got a chance to say, "Merry Christmas" before the hordes drowned him out again. He sneaked out the back door quietly and went to visit other celebrations on the base. The Officers Club which now boasted newly finished murals on the walls, also had plenty of booze, a good dance band, and a bit of magic in the form of a number of Army nurses. News that nurses would attend the party had caused a scurry on the base among the officers to find a supply of Mum or Arrid deodorant, products which had not been in demand in those parts for some time.

It was a house warming for the Officer's Club. The party heated to a point where Captains Don Bellows and Marion Kirby took it upon themselves to quiet an obnoxious visitor who had been around men too long and used language which was deemed inappropriate in the presence of the women. Both Captains ended up with skinned knuckles, but the visitor got the message.[4]

A command car was driven into a creek when the driver, who had been celebrating, saw two bridges and picked the wrong one. A drunk pilot was later found face down in the middle of the road, and another one was found hanging over a rail fence. No one was seriously injured, although the party continued most of the night.

Most of the camp slept late in the heat of Christmas Day. The early morning patrol pilots and their ground crews stumbled to the flight line to put up the first shipping patrol of the day. McGuire was among those pilots, and he flew for three hours with a hangover so bad that he mentioned it in his log book.

Shipping patrols continued all day, as if the Japanese might be versed in American History, and might remember that George Washington and his men had defeated the Hessian Troops at Trenton, when they crossed the Delaware River on Christmas night, and caught them in a drunken state. In the afternoon some brave souls ventured back to the scene of the crime for some "Hair of the dog that bit them." They were sifting through the empty bottles for the dregs when one GI, from North Carolina, produced a bottle of Bourbon he had put away the night before. His pals cheered as he explained, "It's a poor dog that don't bury a bone for later."

The war resumed the next day as the 431st put up a full complement to support the advancement on New Britain. Over the sea near Cape

Gloucester they took several headings from ground controllers and saw nothing. Then they hit the jackpot.

"O K, men, Zeroes at twelve o'clock high, lets get 'em!"

The 16 P-38s started for the 30 Zekes and Oscars and then some one shouted, "Hey! Look below, the whole sky is full of Vals!"

The command came, "The first two elements take the Zekes! The last two elements get those Vals--they're going for our ships!"

Fighter planes from the 49th Group heard the call, too, and joined in the battle. McGuire and his wingman picked a Val and gave chase. McGuire caught the bomber with a perfect deflection shot, and the Val went out of control and crashed into the sea.

He racked his P-38 into a sharp turn and closed in on another dive bomber. He fired until it, too, exploded and fell into the sea. He then spotted a Val making a bomb run on a destroyer, and he chased it and blew it from the sky with a single long burst of machine gun fire. He completed the run by firing on another Val until it went into the sea. In two quick passes he had flamed four of the bombers.

The sky was filled with burning and tumbling enemy aircraft as McGuire gave chase to other bombers with no visible results. Thirty enemy planes went down in the 20-minute battle, and the 431st Squadron got 13 of them. McGuire landed and refueled and reloaded twice and flew combat a total of seven and a half hours[5]. In debriefing he got confirmation of four victories, but gave credit for one of them to a P-47 pilot when a dispute arose[6]. For the day's action McGuire was awarded America's second highest medal, the Distinguished Service Cross.

The word got around camp, "McGuire is back. He got four Vals, but felt sorry for a P-47 pilot who didn't get anything for Christmas, and gave him one of the Vals."

On December 29, McGuire got a late Christmas present. Capt. Jett called him into his office and said, "Mac, I've got good news for you. Captain Kirby is going home, and you are going to be our new Operations Officer."

McGuire was thrilled that his hard work had been recognized and left the Captain's office floating on air.

He finished December with 70 hours of flying time, although he flew only 15 days in the month. It was a month to remember: He celebrated his first wedding anniversary, was promoted to Captain, returned to flying status, shot down four Japanese Fighters, earned the D.S.C., and was elevated to Operations Officer. He wrote his wife: *"I am second in command of the squadron and am squadron's operations officer now. I have also been running the mess as it had been very poor & something had to be done. As you can see I have been busy.*

*We got into a little fight a while back covering the Cape Gloucester
landings and I shot down 4 dive bombers but only got official credit for
3 as someone else claimed the last one also. We cut cards and I lost. I
shot the plane down but as he didn't have any to his credit and we both
had been shooting at the bomber it was the only fair thing to do. That
makes twice I have not gotten credit for four nips in one fight. The first
time I lost a toss of a coin. This time it was cards. Must be lucky in
love, see what you cost me...This is a hell of a place to be at Christmas...Things look better over here now that we are really on the offensive..."*

The Army lexicon was always being enriched. It started with the
term "GI", which derived from the term "Government Issue" and described the troops themselves or anything the Army issued to them (e.g.
GI soap). Then "Gremlins" were invented, but no one's sure where these
invisible trouble makers came from. Next came the acronym "Snafu". It
was the GIs way of complaining about Army inefficiency: Situation
Normal, All Fouled Up. GIs used a different "F" word in the phrase.
The condition was thought to be caused by Gremlins.

Mechanical failures were the biggest problem any squadron had
when it came to daily flying operations. The P-38 was a complicated
machine, with hydraulic, electric, coolant, armament, and fuel systems
which were being serviced under adverse conditions. One of the Allison
engines alone had 7,000 parts--the whole plane had tens of thousands of
parts. One malfunctioning part could cripple a plane before it ever made
contact with the enemy.

GIs called any of these failures a "snafu," and the slang term soon
worked its way into the official jargon. Any failure, weather trouble, or
pilot error that caused a pilot to cancel a mission went into the records
as a "snafu." McGuire's job as Operations Officer was dedicated to the
elimination of "snafus."

In their first five-and-a-half months in combat the 431st Fighter
Squadron flew over 1,700 sorties towards the recapturing of New
Guinea. Simply put, 1,700 times one of their fighter planes went into the
air on a mission. About 15% of the time a sortie would end in a "snafu."

The year 1944 started like 1943 ended. McGuire, in addition to his
new duties, flew 27 combat hours in five days, spending eight hours and
twenty minutes in the air on the third day of the new year. He could
hardly stand when he got out of the P-38 after being strapped into the
seat for a full day.

Lieutenant David Mankin's transfer out of the squadron took another
one of the old timers out of action. He'd be missed. He'd been one of the
cornerstones of the 431st, and had been helpful to men like John Tilley

as they came into the unit. His departure also caused some friction between Tilley and McGuire

Mankin had let Tilley fly his "special" P-38 on a couple of missions. Mankin and his mechanic had removed the bullet-proof windshield from a wrecked P-38. They had mounted the thick glass behind the pilot's seat. It was the perfect shape to add extra protection for the pilot's head and shoulders without cutting down on rear vision or light.

When Mankin transferred, Tilley said, "Dave, now that you are leaving, I'd like to have your airplane."

Mankin said, "It's OK with me. I'll mentioned to McGuire that you'd like to have it."

McGuire wasn't settled into his new job yet and he apparently resented Tilley meddling in the assignment of the squadron's planes, and he told him so. "Tilley, I assign the aircraft to the pilots around here."

"OK, Mac," replied Tilley. "It doesn't make any difference to me. I just thought as long as Mankin was leaving, I'd like to have his ship."

"It's Captain McGuire to you,"[7] answered McGuire. "It makes a big difference to me. I assign the planes for the best interests of the squadron, not to suit individuals."

McGuire didn't want the men trading equipment to suit themselves and was protecting his authority. Tilley thought he overreacted.

Flying tapered off in mid-January. The Army was getting set for another big push. It was a perfect time for some of the pilots to go on leave. McGuire and a dozen of the 431st's pilots had a week of leave in Sydney. They tried to eat all the steaks and drink the country dry. Many of them found female companionship which they had long missed. When McGuire returned to New Guinea he learned that someone had wrecked Pudgy II while he was gone.

McGuire and Pudgy II had been through some tough times and her wings were bent from violent combat turns. Sergeant Kish had found rivets, which held the plane's skin together, had been popped, and men in the squadron told him that the plane looked lopsided in flight. Kish had frequently, at McGuire's request, adjusted the tabs on the control surfaces to compensate for it. Still, he was comfortable with the plane and its 16 Japanese flags painted on its nose, and he hated to lose it. He understood why Major Nichols had been so protective of his plane.

Captain David Allen and Captain Carl Houseworth, two more old timers in the squadron, transferred back to the states. With Hood, Bellows, and Kirby already gone, it left only a few of the original crew who had helped to mold the 431st into a valuable fighting unit. Allen had been one of the best liked men in the squadron, particularly by the enlisted men. His absence left more responsibility on those who remained.

221

McGuire was now a real leader in the squadron. He was one of the senior pilots and found himself in frequent conversations with the newer men, many of whom held him in awe. Unlike some of the older pilots, he would spend hours recounting each fight and each victory. He enjoyed the limelight and felt obligated to pass on his knowledge. A few veteran pilots, who hadn't enjoyed the success or promotions, but had put in their time, resented McGuire, and considered him a "show-boat" for talking about his own experiences. Most of the veteran pilots knew McGuire was the real thing and admired the way he had bounded back into action after his injuries.

On the last day of the month McGuire ran into his old buddy, Wally Jordan, who was still with the 9th Fighter Squadron. "Mac, you've learned how to shoot since you left us," mused Jordan.

"Wrong," replied McGuire. "We've just been where the Nips are."

McGuire hadn't seen Wally for six months and asked about their old buddies in the 49th Group. Jordan and McGuire came to the conclusion that the two of them and Gerald Johnson, who had also been in Alaska with them, were doing OK. All three of them were aces and were moving up in rank and in the command structure.

The Fifth Fighter Command had now moved its headquarters to Nadzab, north of Lae. Three distinguished fighter pilots were now assigned to duty there. On his return from a War Bond tour in the states, Richard Bong (21 victories) was saved from the "horror" of flying one of the newly acquired P-47s with the 9th Fighter Squadron, when he was assigned as the Asst. Operations Officer for the Fighter Command.

Lt. Colonel Tommy Lynch (17 victories), former C O of the 39th Fighter Squadron, returned from leave in the United States, and was assigned to the Fifth Fighter Command, too. Neel Kearby (21 victories), former C O of the 348th Fighter Group, was already assigned to General Wurtsmith's staff at the same command.

The three pilots at first feared that they were out of the war with their new desk assignments. It was soon apparent that this was not the case. It was an open secret that General Kenney wanted these three men in a position that would not restrict their flying activities. They were allowed to free-lance---to go where the action was, without the confinement of a permanent field assignment.

Bong's War Bond tour showed General Kenney the value of having one of America's top aces in his command. He realized that 21 victories were only five behind the number of conquests that had made Eddie Rickenbacker a national hero, and an international celebrity after WW I.

There was little doubt that the superior fighter pilots of WW II, equipped with devastating fighter planes, would soon eclipse Rickenbacker's impressive WW I figure of 26 victories (which included some observation balloons). Kenney didn't want to take a chance that Captain Don Gentile, an Army pilot in the European Theater, would exceed the mark first. It was bad enough that two Marine pilots, Joe Foss, and "Pappy" Boyington had already tied the score. He placed three super aces, each with attractive personalities, in position to forge ahead of Captain Eddie's record, and become a new national hero.

Kenney personally favored Bong for the accomplishment. In Bong he saw a young man with an infectious smile, a genuine down-home shyness, and tremendous talent as a fighter pilot. Bong had just gotten a million dollars worth of publicity on his bond tour of the United States, being interviewed on CBS radio's "Report to the Nation," by all the newspapers, and by **Collier's** magazine, which had described him as a rosy-cheeked cherub. Kenney was like a father to the young ace and felt that he would be good for the post-war Army Air Corps. He could visualize Bong charming a Congressional Committee as he testified that the Air Corps should become a separate branch of the service, known as the Air Force.

In early February, Bong and Lynch, with the approval of General Wurtsmith, started their free-lance escapades which they called the "Flying Circus," ala Baron Von Richthofen of WW I. They attached themselves to escort missions, made two-man fighter sweeps, and volunteered for reconnaissance missions. They showed up where the action was, and soon their totals started to grow.

There was resentment to these operations among aggressive fighter pilots all over New Guinea, which was typified in a story that made the rounds: A fighter pilot supposedly called on his radio, "Help! I'm alone and I've got three Nips on my tail."

A reply supposedly came back, "This is Dick Bong. Where are you? I'll come help you."

The first pilot answered, "That's OK, Bong. I've got them surrounded."

McGuire was among those who pined to have the same opportunities for glory as the "Flying Circus" was having. He was tied down by lackluster patrol missions and bad weather that caused many of the sorties to be a long ride for nothing. The 431st Squadron flew cover for the landings on Los Negros near the end of February, but there was no action. McGuire flew over 60 hours during the month but never saw a hostile plane in the sky.[8]

He had time to write his father and several friends to bring them up to date on his promotion and his new job. Marilynn wrote often and McGuire got one of the letters that had been mailed months before. She informed him that she had not fallen for his story about having a sprained wrist. Newspapers had carried stories about him being shot down and wounded on October 17.

He wrote to his wife: *"As to the letter incident, well they told me no word would be sent back about my being wounded so since I didn't want to worry you I didn't say anything about it. I wish I had now, but since it wasn't really serious I thought it wouldn't do any good for you to worry .... By the way, I have just received a promotion & it's Captain McGuire now, how about that? .... Don't worry about me, darling, I'll be back in a few months and we'll really take a holiday! I now have received the Distinguished Flying Cross, the Purple Heart and have been recommended for the Silver Star, the Distinguished Service Cross, and oak leaf clusters to the Air Medal & Distinguished Flying Cross. I can also wear a group citation device. How about that? I guess I was really lucky. If anyone else had the same opportunities he would have done the same .... I am very sorry that you worried & I didn't want you to worry at all."*

The month ended with a B-24 bomber blowing a tire on a landing and barreling out of control towards the 431st alert shack which was adjacent to the runway. The lounging pilots scrambled to escape as the bomber bore down on them, and ground to a halt a few feet from the building. It was the most exciting thing that had happened in weeks.[9]

The movie of the week was "DuBarry was a Lady," as the 431st Fighter Squadron moved its flying operation from the relative civilization of Dobodura, to Finschhafen.[10] The move put them back on the fringe of the battle zone, which had been moving steadily to the West. It would save hours of flying time for the P-38s. Comfort was the main casualty of the move, after eight months at Dobodura. They were moving to a more primitive area of New Guinea, which would also put them back within the range of Japanese night bombers, like "Reveille Charlie" who came over and randomly dropped a few bombs just before daybreak. They would really feel the hardships of war at the new location.

[1] John Tilley, 431st pilot

[2] Ibid.

[3] 431st Daily History

[4] Ibid.

[5] McGuire's log book

[6] 431st Daily History

[7] John Tilley, 431st pilot

[8] 431st Report of Pilot's Combat Time

[9] 431st Daily History

[10] Ibid.

31

"To win the war was a business with McGuire. He had eyes that could turn you cold, and at times you felt he was looking right through you. Yet, I have seen him almost cry when he had to write to the next of kin about the death of one of our men. No individual drove himself as hard as the Major did, and he never asked his men to do anything he wouldn't or hadn't done himself."

..... First Sergeant Harry Dixon, 431st Fighter Sq..

March 1944 came in with a sigh of boredom. There was heat rash, poor food, and a new location. What else is new? A number of men were hospitalized with Malaria, Dengue and the first cases of Typhus. In spite of the heat, the men were ordered to wear long sleeved shirts and long pants to avoid the ticks, mosquitoes and lice which transmitted these diseases, and were prevalent in the Finschhafen area.[1]

The pilots of the 475th Group were having trouble staying awake on their long missions. Enemy resistance was low, and a pilot was heard to say, "Well, I got five more hours toward my senior pilot rating today."

A second pilot said, "Don't bitch, you're five hours closer to going home."

The first pilot replied, "Yeah, but what good will it do me to go home if my ears rot off from fungus, because I wear earphones five hours a day? What girl would look at a man without ears?"

The second pilot answered, "I guess you're lucky, just losing your ears--jock itch is my problem."

Major Wexler, 475th Group surgeon, had long debunked the claim that atabrine, Australian Fruit Salts and "6-12" insect repellent were a panacea for tropical ills; "6-12" was even claimed to be a cure for the New Guinea "crud." It caused a sensation when Major Wexler was found secretly applying "6-12" to his own case of "crud."[2]

Early in the month McGuire led a mission to cover a PBY making an over-water search near the Admiralty Islands. After a boring hour with the lumbering old Navy seaplane the mission ended and the PBY cleared the area. To give his men a feeling that they were not "just putting in their time," McGuire led the four P-38s on a strafing mission of enemy positions on Silin Point.

When they returned, McGuire and Lieutenant Alvin Kidd agreed that the charts of the western end of Manus Island did not match the actual terrain. They redrew a map of the area to conform with what they had just flown over.[3] McGuire sent the new drawings to the 475th Group so new charts could be issued. Most pilots would not go to that trouble after flying a mission. McGuire considered it his job to correct the flawed map. Some of the pilots thought he was being an eager beaver. They recognized McGuire's work at Group Headquarters and felt he was showing willingness to shoulder responsibility--a sign of a future leader.

McGuire was called to a meeting with operations officers from 432nd and 433rd Squadrons. The Group Operations Officer, Major Oliver McAfee, said, "We have 15 new P-38J-15s coming in to service. One squadron is getting all of the new planes."

All three men groaned, thinking that one of the squadrons had already been assigned the new planes.

"Wait a minute," said Major McAfee. "We haven't decided who is going to get them, yet." The three squadron representatives perked up.

The Major continued, "The J-15s have new equipment on them, and the squadron who gets them will have to stock new parts. It'll be easier to get new parts in stock for one squadron than for three. You'll cut cards---high card gets the new planes."

Nobody had a deck of cards, so the three operations officers fished out coins to flip for the new airplanes.

"OK, the odd man wins the J-15s," said McAfee.

They flipped the coins and McGuire's did not match the other two coins: He had won 15 brand new fighter planes worth more than $2,000,000.[4]

"You son-of-a-bitch!" said one of the men. "You are as lucky with a coin as you are at poker. I thought we had a chance if we could keep a deck of cards out of your hands."

"Where were you guys when I was flipping for Zekes a few months ago? I lost twice. The 431st needs a little luck," said McGuire. "You guys have been getting all the juicy missions lately."

"Bull shit!" said one of the men. "The 431st shot down six Japs in February, neither one of our squadrons got a single one."

"Hell, last year we got a dozen in one day!" said McGuire. "The hunting has just been bad. The weather's been so bad and the Nips have been so shy I guess we'll never see days like that again."

Major McAfee broke in, "There is one thing I forgot to tell you about the J-15, Mac, they have new tanks in the outer wings which hold an extra 120 gallons of fuel. The 431st will get the longer missions until we can modify the J-10s with the extra tanks."

McGuire groaned, "I knew there was a catch. More ass-buster missions are all we need. Just don't tell my men about this. They'd run me off the island."

"Don't worry," said McAfee. "The J-10s will be modified to carry the extra fuel. The other two squadrons will get those planes. Everybody will be flying long range in a few months"

On March 11, McGuire scheduled 15 pilots for a single mission. They flew 15 old drab P-38J-10 planes to Dobodura. They returned, hours later, with 15 shiny silver planes. The new unpainted planes were many pounds lighter and faster, and they looked clean and sleek.

Daily routine had become so boring that it was a problem. McGuire called in Lieutenants John Pietz and Bob Herman for a two-man mission to locate a Japanese freighter. When Lieutenant Herman heard the word "shipping" again, he almost fell asleep. McGuire started explaining the mission, and Herman came back from his brief nap to ask, "What was that again?"

McGuire said, "You are looking for a Japanese aircraft carrier, two battleships and five destroyers heading for Alexishafen. If you spot them, you and Pietz strafe them."

"What did you say?" asked Herman.

McGuire had their attention and gave them the boring details of their mission to find the single Japanese merchant vessel.[5]

Sgt.. Richard Van Der Geest, Capt. McGuire and TSgt . Frank Kish with Pudgy III

On March 14, McGuire took possession of his part of the gambling booty, in the form of a brand new P-38J-15. He took Pudgy III up and wrung it out.[6] It was exciting to have a shiny new plane with straight wings, and a clean smell like a new car. Sergeant George Jeschke painted a large new "Pudgy III" on the nose along with 16 small Japanese flags and a large red "131." Solid red spinners finished the bright new design which was soon known all over the area as the trademark of the 431st Squadron.

The new airplanes invigorated the squadron as they flew them on a B-24 escort mission to Wewak. McGuire noticed that his outer wing gas tanks were losing gas. Air passing over the tank caps was siphoning gasoline at a rate that caused him to cut his flight short.[7] He called in a snafu and returned to the field.

He taxied back to the revetment and sent for Sergeant Kish. The gas tank caps were properly installed. They installed gas caps from auxiliary belly tanks and test flights proved that this solved the problem. It was later discovered that check valves between the fuel tanks on all J-15 model P-38s had been installed backwards at the factory, allowing fuel to flow in the wrong direction. McGuire wrote up a modification to correct the problem, and forwarded it to Group. It was adopted as standard procedure on all late model P-38s.[8]

Subsequent missions to Hollandia, a distance of 535 miles one way, were made without trouble. The missions could only be made with the full utilization of the new fuel capacity, which allowed the P-38s to travel the distance and have enough fuel to stay over the target and protect the bombers during the raid.

Tedious shipping patrol missions continued to be the order of the day. The P-38s were flown back and forth over the anchored ships for a four-hour period. They had been doing this for days and there was never any action. McGuire was so bored flying back and forth that he trimmed up his plane and was able to read the complete Perry Mason book, *The Case of the Counterfeit Spy*, in a single afternoon, just looking up from the book to make a turn.[9]

McGuire heard through the grapevine that Bong's victory total had risen to 24, and Major Lynch had upped his score to 20. It made him stew to think of them out there flying where and when they wanted to, while he was stuck with routine patrol missions.

The news about Bong and Lynch was followed by a shocking development: Colonel Neel Kearby, finding his 21 victories surpassed, apparently decided to re-enter the race. He had his own numbers to defend, and the reputation of the P-47 fighter he flew was on the line, too. He formed a flying group with two other Thunderbolt pilots, and went on a sweep over Wewak. They spotted three Nell bombers and quickly disposed of them. In the process a single Oscar jumped Kearby and sent him to his death.

It sent a shock wave through the Fifth Fighter Command. There wasn't a more able fighter pilot in the Air Corps. He was a wily veteran and an outstanding command officer. His 22 victories ranked second only to Bong, and his death seemed unnecessary.

Three days later Bong and newly promoted Lt. Colonel Lynch went on a "flying circus" sweep of Tadji. Finding no action in the sky they decided to use their ammunition on the shipping in Aitape Harbor. They attacked three luggers (large barge), setting one on fire. On a second run Lynch's plane was hit by small arms fire and he pulled up to 2,000 feet and attempted to bail out. His plane started to burn. He struggled to bail out, but the plane exploded near the water as Lynch jumped, much too low for his parachute to open. Bong circled the area in disbelief. There was no sign of Lynch. Bong lost an engine and was lucky to make it back to Nadzab on one balky engine. Over 80 bullet holes were counted in his plane. Bong and Lynch had surprised the boats on their first attack, but had drawn brutal small arms fire on the second run.

In four days, two outstanding pilots had been killed. Bong lost Lynch, the closest friend he had in the Air Corps. General Kenney had concerns about Bong being disheartened and ordered him on a mission which took him to Brisbane for 10 days. While Bong was gone another pilot flew his new "Marge" P-38, had trouble with it, and bailed out. Bong had just named the new plane and had it adorned with a large photograph of a young lady, Marjorie Vattendahl, whom he had met on his bond tour.

The 431st Fighter Squadron finally had their tents installed properly and were settling comfortably in their new camp which was in a very pleasant location. Then, the order came from Major Jett to break camp and prepare to move on to Nadzab. The troops had worked tirelessly for a full month to put the camp in order, and some of them said they weren't going. In the end they dutifully helped strike the tents and pack the equipment for the next move in this barbaric game of human chess. Their only consolation was the direction of the move. It was toward the west--the direction they must travel to eventually get home.

Shakespeare knew something when he said: "Beware the Ides of March." It had been a lousy month for the Air Corps on New Guinea.

Early in his duties as operations officer, McGuire realized that new pilots reporting into the squadron from stateside were unfamiliar with the fighter tactics being used in New Guinea against the Japanese. During the rainy days of February and March he worked on a manuscript which spelled out the fighter tactics he had learned. He asked the squadron's veteran pilots "Pappy" Cline, Dave Allen, "Champ" Champlin, and Bill O'Brien to made suggestions which were incorporated into the work. Then he added drawings to illustrate the formations used.

When the draft was completed he presented it to Major Jett for his comments and permission to have it mimeographed for hand-out to the squadron's pilots. Jett liked the idea and said, "Mac, I have a suggestion. I'd like to forward it to Colonel MacDonald. I think the Group could use this material for all of our pilots."

A few days later McGuire submitted his final draft and Major Jett forwarded it to Group Headquarters with his recommendation attached. Many days went by without an answer, and McGuire thought, "It's probably in some sergeant's in-basket, and I'll never see it again. I guess I might as well forget about it."

Later McGuire was having a casual conversation with Colonel MacDonald when the Colonel said, "Did I tell you about your tactics write-up?"

McGuire answered, "No, sir. I've been wondering if you had a chance to read it."

The Colonel said, "Oh yes. I've read it, and I liked it. I sent it up to the Fighter Command with a suggestion that they publish it. I'll let you know what they're going to do with it."

"Thank you, Colonel," replied McGuire. "Let me know what they think."

McGuire didn't act too excited about it, but he was secretly delighted that the Colonel had thought enough of his ideas to send his work up the chain of command.

The first April missions were long bomber escorts to Hollandia, a five-to-six-and-a-half hour round trip. The new P-38J-15s had range enough to escort the bombers, and again like Wewak and Rabaul, the Japanese were caught by surprise. Over 200 enemy planes were destroyed on the ground. McGuire and the boys saw few Japanese fighters in the air. They got in a few shots but observed no visible results.

On April 3, a massive armada of bombers was assembled to deal a knock-out punch to Hollandia. Dick Bong, who had just returned to Nadzab after 10 days in Brisbane, latched on to the 432nd Fighter Squadron for the mission. Over the target he quickly flamed an Oscar to bring his total number of victories to 25. It put him just one short of Rickenbacker's record.

McGuire was on the same mission but saw no action. He was frustrated when he heard about Bong's latest conquest and spouted off to Pappy Cline and Bill O'Brien. "Wouldn't you know it! Every pilot in the

475th has gone blind looking for Japs, and that damn Bong is back three days--flies one mission with the 432nd Squadron and gets an Oscar. There's no justice."

Cline and O'Brien looked at each other and shook their heads. Sometimes they felt the same way about McGuire. They'd often been on missions with him when they couldn't get an enemy plane in their gunsight--only to return home to find that McGuire had gotten one or two enemy planes. Some men had the knack. It had certainly deserted McGuire and the 431st lately. Fifteen Japanese planes were downed that day, and the other squadrons had gotten 14 of them--Lieutenant John Cohn of the 431st had gotten one.

The air space over New Guinea was under American control until a week later when the Japanese were able to put up a small force of zeros from Wewak which surprised and shot down three P-47s from the 58th Fighter Group. To prevent the reestablishing of a viable Japanese air arm, a fleet of B-24 bombers hit Hollandia. The 80th Fighter Squadron, attached to the 475th Group, and under the command of Captain Jay T. Robbins, was flying cover.

Robbins, with 16 victories, was one of the outstanding fighter pilots in the Pacific. "Cock Robbin's Headhunters" were an outstanding aggregation, even without their "guest" tail-end Charlie on this mission, Richard Bong. Robbins and Bong had arrived in New Guinea together in 1942, and Robbins had thought at the time that Bong lacked the "look" of a fighter pilot. That idea was long past, and Robbins was glad to have Bong along, as two of his 20 P-38s called in snafus and returned to their base.

The Japanese again sent up a force of Oscars and Tonys to surprise the American forces. The Headhunters were not surprised, nor was Bong. Flying without a wingman he bore in on the first enemy planes he saw, and after an hour-long battle that extended from one end of Tannemerah Bay to the other, he departed for Nadzab with the two confirmed kills that gave him his 26th and 27th victory. He had exceeded Rickenbacker's WW I record and was now America's new Ace of Aces. He claimed a third plane that day and later got confirmation of it for a total of 28 victories.

McGuire and the 431st Squadron had made the trip to Hollandia, too, with A-20 bombers, but saw no action. They returned to find Nadzab was in a state of jubilation over Bong's accomplishment. General Kenney promoted Bong to Major on the spot, and following a message from General "Hap" Arnold at the Pentagon, grounded him. Arnold did not want to chance their new hero being shot down. He had a growing concern about the high scorers staying in combat too long. He was reflecting the thoughts of many high Army officials about the recent loss of Kearby and Lynch.

Wires to Bong poured in from Eddie Rickenbacker, from General Arnold, and from General Douglas MacArthur in Brisbane. Captain Eddie kept a promise and sent a case of Scotch whisky to the man who had broken his record. Kenney matched it with a case of his own, and General MacArthur sent a case of Champagne.

Within a few days teetotalers all over the United States heard about the gift of strong beverages and one leader of the movement complained that, "It is a sin that an American hero is being rewarded with liquor, particularly in a war zone where a sober head is needed to protect one's life from the enemy." The prestigious Christian Science Monitor joined the outcry with an editorial on the subject.

General Arnold quickly took charge of the publicity disaster and issued a press release, "Today I am sending Major Richard I. Bong two cases of Coca Cola. I understand that he prefers this type of refreshment to others." When the coke arrived it was secretly accompanied by a case of Champagne.

McGuire had expected that Bong would break Rickenbacker's record but he was secretly disappointed when it happened. He had often hoped that he would be the one to do it. It would have meant so much to his Uncle Charles if it had happened. When Bong had been sent home McGuire was certain that he would have a chance, but the fates had dealt him a losing hand. Now it seemed that he would never get a chance to rival Bong for top ace.

When the liquor controversy broke out McGuire had something to say about it: "If Bong prefers Coke, tell him to send the booze over to the 475th, we'll dispose of it without harming anyone. We'd even go to his place to do it if we were invited." Most everybody at Nadzab eventually did help dispose of the booty.

Instead of fuming about Bong's success and his own inaction McGuire concentrated on being a good operations officer and it wasn't very glamorous. He had to know which planes and pilots were available to fly. Planes required routine maintenance, and many of them got damaged in combat or flying accidents. There were always more pilots than available P-38s.

He assigned pilots for each mission the squadron flew. He had to decide who would go on a mission, and who would remain on the ground. He had to decide who would fly and take the chance of dying, and who would stay at home and get a few extra hours of sack time. He often complained to friends that it was a hell-of-a-choice. It wasn't an easy job for a 23-year-old man.

He hardly ever pleased anyone when he posted the flying schedule. Some wanted to fly more, while others complained about flying certain types of missions. Few complained about having to fly, but some demonstrated that they weren't suited for combat flying. In that case, McGuire recommended to Major Jett that they be reassigned for more training or to less stressful flying somewhere else.

Every time McGuire made up a roster he wondered if he was sending someone out who wouldn't return. One pilot who almost always got an assignment was Captain McGuire. Maybe it was his way of soothing his conscience, but he was accumulating flying time faster than any other pilot in the group. He took the long missions. He took the boring missions. He took the dangerous missions. He was determined that he would never be accused of shirking his duty.

First Sergeant Harry Dixon knew how much it troubled McGuire when one of the men he had assigned to a mission didn't return. The sergeant was there each day and he could see the sadness in McGuire's normally steely eyes. He saw how McGuire agonized as he organized search parties for those who were reported missing, and how it pained him when a pilot's death was confirmed. He saw McGuire putting distance between himself and the other pilots---saw him acting more "official" and less friendly to them.

The sergeant had many more years in the Army than the young operations officer, and he tried to console him: "Captain, somebody has to assign these men to fly. If you don't do it somebody else will---there was a guy doing it before you got here, and someone else will do it after you move on. It's the nature of things in the Army. It's the war that's killing them, and the man who makes out the roster can't change that."

McGuire mustered a faint smile and replied, "I know you're right, Sergeant, but that doesn't make it any easier."

McGuire was concerned that new pilots in New Guinea were not prepared for the rigors of combat flying. In recent months a number of 431st pilots had died before flying 100 hours of combat---four of them had not even reached the 25-hour mark. If the Japanese didn't get them it was likely that the weather or a dumb flying accident would. He spent his time between missions training green pilots as they were assigned to the squadron. Twenty-six neophytes reported to the Group in April.

The constant rains and the boredom had the morale of the men at an all-time low, when a quantity of rum appeared one Friday night and most of the 431st "tied one on." Many of them had headaches the next morning, but they were ready for a big operation bright and early on Sunday, April 16. The 475th Group furnished cover for another raid on Hollandia. McGuire wasn't assigned to fly.

After a quiet bomb run, with no enemy resistance, the fighters and bombers turned for home only to find that a massive cold front had moved in behind them. Black clouds covered the sky from ground level to 35,000 feet, forming a wall that ran as far to the east and west as the eye could see.

Captain William O'Brien was leading the 431st and he knew from monitoring the radio that no one was having any luck passing through the towering clouds. There was mayhem and confusion and it was getting worse as more planes arrived in the area. Hidden in the clouds between these forlorn formations of planes and their home bases loomed high mountains peaks.

O'Brien ordered his men to tighten their formation and stick with him. He turned east, throttled down his engines, and picked his way through the overcast until he saw the New Guinea coastline. He turned south and lead his P-38s like a mother duck until they arrived at Saidor.

They found the field jammed and more planes were flying in from every direction. Aircraft flying on their last drops of fuel disregarded the control tower and landed in all directions. A P-38 and a B-25 landed on the same runway and collided. Ground crews pushed the burning wreckage aside with trucks so the next planes could land. Other planes bellied in alongside the strip.

Still possessing reserve fuel O'Brien ordered his men to look sharp, as they buzzed the field in a precision formation, before they entered the pattern and landed safely. Of the twelve 431st planes that had started out seven hours before, one P-38, piloted by Lieutenant Milton Mac-Donald, never showed up. [7]

Countless bombers and fighters milled around New Guinea for hours looking for any field they could find. Sadly, many of the 170 planes never found a place to land and crashed in the jungle or were lost at sea. Field phones rang and radios cracked in operations tents all night long as reports were filed regarding the whereabouts of bombers and fighters. In all, 31 planes and 32 airmen fell victim to the tragic events of the day.

The 475th Group, alone, lost six pilots and eight aircraft that day. Nature had imposed a higher toll on the Group in a single day than the enemy had ever inflicted. The 431st Squadron suffered fewer losses than any other unit involved in the day's action. April 16 was thereafter known as "Black Sunday."

The 475th Fighter Group lost a total of 16 planes during the month of April. Only one was downed by enemy action. On April 28, McGuire got a message to report to Colonel MacDonald at 475th Group Headquarters. He was nervous as he made his way to the Colonel's tent, and wondered if he'd done something wrong.

His fears were soon eased as Colonel MacDonald started to talk, "Mac, Major Jett has been out here 32 months. He's on his way home. You are the new commanding officer of the 431st Squadron."

McGuire was speechless as a smile covered his face.

The Colonel continued, "O'Brien will be your new operations officer. You take over officially on May 2. Meanwhile start getting in the groove. You're getting a good squadron. Don't screw it up!"

"Yes, Sir," replied McGuire.

"By the way," said the Colonel, "Your first job as CO will be handling a big move. We're moving all the way up to Hollandia."

"Great!" said McGuire. "Maybe we'll see some action!"

"I'd bet on it," agreed MacDonald.

[1] 431st Daily History
[2] Ibid.
[3] Ibid.
[4] Ibid.
[5] Ibid.
[6] Notation in McGuire's log book
[7] Ibid
[8] 431st Daily History
[9] Ibid.
[10] Ibid.

32

"The Squadron was always a good one. Under McGuire it became even better. He had a lot of energy and he couldn't stand his people being sloppy. Our flying improved. He insisted on it. When we flew formation we did it right, and when we came near other squadrons or flew over an air field he demanded that we tighten up and look sharp. He wanted everybody to know it was the 431st Fighter Squadron just by seeing us fly. Soon, all flight and element leaders were demanding the same kind of precision flying---it made you proud to be in Hades Squadron!"   .... A 431st Pilot.

The 475th Fighter Group had been searching for a name for the Group and each of its Squadrons. They had almost selected the name "The Sundowners" for the Group. The meaning was apparent to those who proposed it: The Japanese were "the rising suns," the 475th shot them down. The 475th Group were "the Sundowners."

Research killed the name. A Navy group somewhere in the Pacific was using the name. Then someone looked up the term in an Australian dictionary and found out that a sundowner was a person who always arrived at an out-laying camp at sundown to take advantage of the hospitality of the camp. In other words a sundowner was a kind of "outback panhandler."

A decision was made: The Group would be known as "Satan's Angels." The 431st Squadron picked the name "Hades" and the color red. The 432nd would be called "Clover" using the color yellow, and the 433rd would be "Possum," and use the color blue. Now, after all these months without names, the men of each squadron rushed to design emblems to be painted on their plane.[1]

The 431st Squadron came up with a design consisting of a red devil's head wearing a hat at a jaunty angle. Several members of the squadron took credit for the design. It looked suspiciously like the Avon Park High School red devil which McGuire had once helped paint blue. The devil was painted on the nose of each P-38, and the spinners and tail tips were painted red. The planes looked sharp, and identification in combat was much easier.

McGuire wrote to his wife, *"I have just had some pictures taken of myself & my plane. By the way all of my planes are named "Pudgy". This is Pudgy III. When I get back we are going to some resort....because I guess that later I will have to make some talks or something."*

Meanwhile the orders came from headquarters: "Pack everything. We're moving again." After 30 days at Nadzab the 475th was on the move again. It was a big move this time. They were going to jump over Wewak, Tadji, But, Boram and Dagua which had been bombed out of service. The Army wouldn't even bother to land in those areas. Instead they would leave the few hundred Japanese stragglers in the surrounding jungles and move all the way up to Hollandia, over 500 miles to the northwest. Air attacks on Hollandia had been so effective that the Army had landed and secured the air field. They would be in Dutch New Guinea for the first time, and would be within range of the western end of New Guinea.

On May 2, McGuire officially took control of the squadron. Except for the day he had married Marilynn, this was the best day of his life. He left Sebring to make a name for himself, and he'd done it. Even in his wildest dreams he hadn't dared to dream of this day. In recent months he'd let the dream of commanding the 431st creep into his conscious thoughts but he'd quickly put it out of his mind, as if thinking about it might keep it from coming true. This had come so suddenly--he still couldn't believe it.

The new 23-year-old Commanding Officer, 431st Fighter Squadron

After a farewell party for Major Jett, McGuire moved his things into the Commanding Officer's desk. He still felt uncomfortable when an Army photographer came and took a picture of him sitting at his new desk. He had his own ideas about running the squadron, but it would take him a little while to get used to being the boss of 45 officers, and several hundred enlisted men. He was only 23 years old.

There wasn't much time to think about it before the ground echelon moved to the port at Lae for the five day ocean voyage to Hollandia. The pilots and their ground crews remained at Nadzab, until Hollandia was in proper condition for them to fly in.

Major Dick Bong was on his way home for another hero's tour of the United States, and McGuire, Jay Robbins, Colonel MacDonald and Gerald Johnson of the 49th Fighter Groups all re-thought their positions in the "Ace Race." If the Japanese would just cooperate, maybe one of them could make a move to catch Bong. No one knew if Bong would be back again to defend his title.

While working his way into his new command, McGuire got some more good news: The Fifth Fighter Command published his paper on Southwest Pacific fighter tactics. It wasn't a hard-cover text, but at least it was in print. When McGuire saw the first copy of the modest publication he was elated. It would be handed out to all pilots in the Fifth Fighter Command, and every new pilot would be trained to know its contents. McGuire was established as an Air Corps combat tactician, not just as one of the hot-shot pilots.

On May 15 the pilots and ground crews of the 431st Squadron moved to Hollandia. The field was covered with wrecked Japanese airplanes. There were 380 wrecked fighter planes and bombers. Counting the enemy planes which had been shot down by allied air action in the area, Hollandia was the graveyard for over 450 imperial planes. McGuire, Jay Robbins and Cyril Homer wandered around the field to take a look at the wrecked Oscars, Tonys, and Zekes. They had only seen these planes in the air before and they were shocked at the primitive nature of these wrecked airframes. A UPI photographer, on the strip to photograph the remarkable rubble, had the three aces pose in front of a tangled pile of planes. Reporters wanted their comments about the war. With Bong gone they had to find others to write about.

Back at the staging area at Lae, the ground echelon was still living in temporary quarters, waiting for a transport ship to move them up to Hollandia. They spent most of their time over at the PX drinking cokes and having impure thoughts about the Red Cross girls which they watched for hours.[2]

The flying echelon was making temporary camp at Hollandia and it soon became apparent that a foxhole was a valuable asset. The first night there were six red alerts between midnight and dawn. Often the attacks never came, and when they did, they caused little damage. The main purpose of the Japanese raids was to make sure that no one got a good night's sleep.

There were still Japanese forces in the area and scattered small arms fire could be heard off in the distance, any time of the day. John Tilley remarked, "It's a good thing they don't have a few artillery pieces---they could really raise some hell around here." At night the enemy was known to be wandering near the camp area, making uneasy sleeping conditions. A trip to the latrine after dark required a four-man group armed with at least one submachine gun.

On their second day at Hollandia the 431st flew cover for B-24s hitting the Japanese on Noemfoer Island. The Japanese had not conceded defeat, and sent fighters to stop the raid. McGuire and Lieutenant Frank Monk led the squadron down from 15,000 feet to 5,000 feet where they split up four Oscars. McGuire got in a quick burst which flamed an Oscar. It turned and exploded. McGuire had broken a five month drought. He had squirmed while others had added to their scores---this was long overdue. After all, they were in the Pacific to fight a war, and since December, McGuire had been marking time and wondering if he was losing his edge.

John Tilley and Bill O'Brien both scored on the same mission. Only one of the Japanese planes got away. It was a much happier bunch of pilots who sat down with the intelligence officer for debriefing after the mission. That afternoon McGuire sat down and wrote to Marilynn: *"I can't tell you where we are but I can say that we have moved further North. It certainly looks as though the war in the Pacific is going all our way."*

American airmen in England flew their share of tough missions, but they were at least comfortable when they returned to their home base. A night or weekend in London was a thing of joy. If the war got boring, England did not. On New Guinea the war never ended. The men flew and lived in the war zone. McGuire and many other men hadn't slept in anything but a tent for over two years. They didn't have good bathing or sanitary facilities, and the food was lousy. Their bodies were rotting away with heat generated diseases, and this last move had put them closer to the Equator where they were even more miserable.

Their only joy was defeating the enemy. There had been too little joy for the 431st lately, and New Guinea had been wearing them down. McGuire felt an uplift from being able to do what he was in the war to do---destroy the enemy. Two days later on a B-24 escort mission to Manokwari, McGuire got another chance to do just that. Nine P-38s met eight Sons of Nippon. The Japanese had no interest in fighting and split up and fled. McGuire caught a single Tojo climbing away from his flight and hit it with two short bursts of machine gun and cannon fire. It started to burn around the engine, and McGuire saw the pilot leap from the cockpit. As the Tojo tumbled into the sea, its pilot floated down in a parachute. McGuire had never seen a parachute used by the Japanese. Up to now it was well known that the enemy pilots were not furnished with a chute. McGuire's score was now 18.

A few days later he wrote to Marilynn: *"Since I wrote you we have had a couple of fights & I was lucky enough to get one each time. One thing I know I will not want to do when I get home is go camping! Our Flight Surgeon's wife wrote him that she was planning that they should go on a camping trip when he got back & he wasn't the same for days. By the way, don't forget about laying in all the good bourbon you can 'cause the longer I stay the thirstier I get."*

The next day McGuire got more good news: he'd been promoted to Major. For the third time in one year he'd been promoted. Most squadron commanders carried the rank of Major, but he hadn't expected it this quickly. Unfortunately McGuire didn't have much time to enjoy the good news before he was forced to take to a sick bed. He felt it coming on but he thought he was just tired. Instead, he was stricken with Dengue, a tropical fever.

The infectious disease caused McGuire to writhe with joint and muscular pain so great the Flight Surgeon gave him morphine shots to ease the pain. The malady, also known as breakbone fever, caused such discomfort that the touch of a bed sheet was painful. McGuire was completely "out of it" for a week, and hardly ate anything. He lost a good deal of weight and looked terrible, but was up and taking nourishment by the ninth day, and flew a five-hour mission on the twelfth day after he was stricken.

At the end of May the air echelon moved to a permanent camp three miles from the air strip. It was extremely comfortable with an ice cold stream to bathe in. Being away from the air strip also put them out of the danger area for the nightly air raids, and everyone slept better. The 431st ground echelon was still waiting at the staging area at Lae. They were still hanging around the Red Cross girls--a month wasn't long enough for the novelty to wear off.

On June 6, 1944, as Americans halfway around the world swarmed onto the beaches at Normandy, McGuire lead eight P-38s on a A-20 bomber escort mission to Manokwari. They flew the 300 miles and encountered no enemy resistance, so McGuire led the P-38s on a search for targets of opportunity. They spotted a 1,000 ton Japanese freighter and McGuire ordered an attack. "Let's hit that freighter. Save your tanks, we may as well take them home."

Anytime air-to-air combat was encountered the first order was "drop tanks." Strafing this ship was a relatively simple job--diving at the ship, firing, and then pulling up and over. The auxiliary gas tanks made the plane a little less maneuverable, but this mission didn't require any fancy flying. Several planes made their runs at the ship and then 2nd. Lieutenant Pete Madison took his turn. Madison was new in the squadron and had only flown about 50 hours in combat. His attack went well, and he could see his machine gun and cannon fire hitting the ship around the bridge. He was pleased with the results but held his course just a little too long before pulling up.

As Madison pulled back on the wheel he knew he hadn't allowed for the plane's sluggish performance with full fuel tanks, and he felt the sickening mush of the P-38--he knew he was going to hit the ship. His right propeller struck the ship's mast and his plane was suddenly upside-down, flying--just a few hundred feet above the water. Recent intelligence reports claimed that the Japanese in the area had turned to cannibalism due to lack of food--Madison had a thought flash through his mind, "Am I going to end up being an Irish stew for a Japanese banquet?"

By sheer instinct he righted the plane, only to have the damaged propeller fly off of the engine, rise over the wing and head straight for the cockpit. Madison, again instinctively, ducked as the propeller shattered the canopy, causing a piece of it to strike him in the head and start a stream of blood down into his eyes. The propeller then struck one of the vertical stabilizers, reducing control, and knocking out most of the plane's electric systems and the radio.

He turned off all switches for the right engine and tried to gain altitude on the remaining engine--instead the plane sank nearer to the sea. He was in big trouble--he was too low to bail out. His radio was out and the urging of his fellow pilots to "drop your tanks" fell on deaf ears. Finally Lieutenants Hal Gray and Foch Benevent flew alongside, got his attention and one-at-a-time dropped their own tanks. Madison saw the tanks drop and followed suit. He was then able to control the plane well enough to struggle back toward home at 150 miles an hour. Stunned from the blow on the head, Madison had to cross-feed fuel from the right wing tank of his plane to the left side so his good engine would have enough fuel to get him home.

Hal Gray and Lieutenant Jim Moreing flew with him to protect him from possible attack. After a two-hour struggle to gain altitude they approached a 6,000-foot mountain range that had to be crossed to reach home base. The single good engine would not lift the crippled plane over it, so the three pilots chose to land at a small island air strip at Wakde, which had just been captured from the Japanese a few days before.

Madison landed with his wheels up and was so dazed that he sat in the smoking plane and started filling out the aircraft maintenance "form one" to indicate that the plane needed work before it could be flown again.[3] His buddies yelled, "Get out of there--it's going to burn." Madison got out of the plane OK, and spent the night on the island under the care of Army medics.

Three days later McGuire asked him, "How are you feeling?"

Madison replied, "I'm OK. Nothing is broken and the cut on my head is doing fine."

McGuire asked, "Do you feel good enough to fly?"

"Yes sir, I do," answered Madison, with surprise.

"Are you interested in flying?"

"I sure am!" sang out Madison.

"Check the roster tomorrow," said McGuire. "I'll speak to O'Brien."

McGuire, having been through a tough emergency or two himself, knew it was important for Madison to get back in the air as soon as possible. He was glad he didn't have to add Lieutenant Madison to the bottom of his monthly report as killed, or missing in action. The next day Madison was assigned a mission and after that was frequently asked to fly wingman for Major McGuire.

On June 8, 600 men and officers of the 475th Fighter Group ended a five-week vacation and cruise when they started unloading from the liberty ship Frances A. Wardwell in Humboldt Bay. It had been anything but a vacation. They had all been pawns in a large game of Army "hurry-up-and-wait" A cheerful sign at the staging area had read: "STAY WITH US WHILE IN LAE." They had indeed stayed--waiting 30 days before loading onto the ship. The 52-ship convoy had only taken five days to sail from Lae, but the ultimate blow was a three-day wait to unload.[4]

The new arrivals were subjected to one last obstacle before joining their comrades of the air echelon, the 23-mile trip from Humboldt Bay to Hollandia, which could take up to five hours. The greasy red clay road was mountainous and infested with snipers who shot at the trucks as they passed. By evening all the men were safely at the new camp and enjoying a bath in the nearby creek. They had their first good night's sleep in five weeks.

McGuire had a chance to make good on a promise he had made a year earlier. He learned that Bill Dutton's bomber outfit, the 3rd Bomb Group, was stationed at Hollandia. McGuire and the 431st had been escorting them on raids to Noemfoer. Dutton was an aircraft & engine mechanic and a crew chief on a A-20 bomber. When McGuire and Dutton had been together at Dobodura, McGuire had promised his old high school chum a P-38 ride.

Bill Dutton and Tommy McGuire, after a P-38 ride at Hollandia, New Guinea

Bill had a pilot's license and was eager to have the P-38 ride. He had learned to fly with Wayne Manard in Avon Park, Florida, long before Tommy McGuire had entered cadets. Later when he was in the Army and stationed at Savannah, he'd bought a 40-horse-power Taylorcraft, which he had flown to Sebring on leave. He had generously lent the plane to W. A. Wootten, assuming that he knew how to fly. Before the day was over Bill's plane had been flipped over, the wing spar and propeller shaft cracked, and the propeller and tail badly damaged. It ended

Bill's days as a pilot, just a few days before he had been shipped to the Pacific.

McGuire loaded his friend into a special piggyback P-38, the 475th Group always kept to give rides to visiting celebrities. It was a regular P-38 with the radio removed, and a special seat installed in its place, in back of the pilot.

They took off and flew South, away from regular air traffic. McGuire showed his friend how fast the plane could climb, and then demonstrated a roll and some other fancy maneuvers. At a safe altitude he calmly shut down the right engine and put the plane through its paces on one engine. Bill loved every minute of the flight, but no more than McGuire did! There was special satisfaction for each man, flying with his old friend.

Back on the ground McGuire said, "Remember how we used to keep Mrs. Campbell up all night playing ping pong? I wonder what she'd say to us today, if she were here?"

"I don't know," replied Bill. "It's a wonder she didn't call the police. I'll be heading home soon. Maybe I'll go by her house and apologize for all the noise we used to make."

"You lucky dog," said McGuire. "Tell Prof and everybody in Sebring that I said hello. I expect to be out of here myself before the end of the year and Marilynn and I will come visit."

"I've got to go see Prof and tell him about my experience in show business," said Bill. "I played trumpet for a Army show called the 'Jungle Juice Review.' We had some damn good musicians and we played for the Bob Hope show, too."

McGuire laughed and said, "Call me if you need a good clarinet player."[5]

The next day it was back to work as McGuire and his men escorted A-20 bombers from the 3rd Bombardment Group to Babo, an island north of Biak. General Kenney wanted to move his forces to Biak so they could control the western end of New Guinea. First he wanted to drive the Japanese from all of the islands that surrounded Biak.

Jefman Island, near the westernmost peninsula of New Guinea, was a great distance from Hollandia, but near enough to Biak to cause trouble for any new occupants. A plan was devised to hit Jefman. B-25 Mitchell bombers were equipped with bomb-bay fuel tanks for extra range. The P-38s would stage at newly captured Wakde Island where they would top off their tanks for the long flight. They would then fly past enemy held Owi and Biak to escort the bombers to Jefman. On the way home the planes would stop again at Wakde and refuel before returning to Hollandia.

On June 16 the three squadrons of the 475th Group, and P-38s from the 35th Fighter Squadron, under the able leadership of 475th Group Commander, Colonel Charles MacDonald, set out to escort B-25 bombers from Hollandia for the first raid on the air dromes at Jefman and Samate. MacDonald snafued early in the flight with electrical problems on his P-38, the "Putt Putt Maru." McGuire resumed command of the 431st for the rest of the mission and led them through some perilous weather. Six P-38s dropped from the mission before they rendezvoused with the B-25s.[6]

Over the Jefman Drome enemy planes were spotted taking off for an interception. McGuire ordered the remaining nine P-38s to drop their belly tanks and led his element in an attack on a climbing Sonia. They dived from 6,000 feet and McGuire took the first shot, hitting the Sonia with a good burst. His speed quickly took McGuire and his wingman, Lieutenant Enrique Provencio, past the enemy plane, but Lieutenant Gronemeyer was following closely, and he fired several bursts and the plane went down.

As the B-25s made low-level bomb runs on the air strip and dropped 100-pound parafrag bombs, McGuire and his wingman quickly turned and made a second pass.

"Stick with me, Ricky!" shouted McGuire. "Let's cut off those Oscars before they get to the Mitchells."

Provencio, one of the newest members of Hades Squadron, listened to his commanding officer as they lined up two of the 14 Oscars. McGuire gave one Oscar several short bursts and saw his bullets ripping large chunks from the fuselage. The plane burst into flames and exploded.

"Ricky, watch the other one!" coached McGuire. "If he turns left, nail him!"

Provencio watched, and when the Oscar made a left turn, he anticipated it, and aimed his guns to lead it. He fired two long bursts which hit the Oscar and quickly set it on fire.

"Great shot!" shouted McGuire. "Great shot!"

By now the whole squadron had broken into two-man elements and they pursued every enemy plane they could find. McGuire got on the tail of another Sonia and make quick work of it. The plane caught fire and crashed in the ocean.[7] Captain P. V. Morriss got two Oscars, and Captain O'Brien got one. Lieutenants Reeves and Monk also got an Oscar each. The 431st accounted for nine of the 18 enemy planes that they had encountered.

Over on the mainland B-25s were hitting the Samate strip and members of the 432nd, 433rd and 35th Squadrons were also having good success. The battles and bomb-runs lasted only 15 minutes but U.S. forces had decimated the Japanese forces. P-38s had downed 25 Japanese planes and the B-25s had downed 12. Photos later showed that 50 planes had been destroyed on the ground for a total of 87 planes destroyed. Lieutenant Stiles of the 433rd Squadron was the only American loss.

Major Oliver McAfee, the group operations officer, lost an engine and flew 600 miles to Wakde on his remaining engine. The men had gotten out of bed at 5:45 a.m. and had left Hollandia at 6:45 a.m. to fly this mission. The last plane landed at Hollandia at 1900 hours (7:00 p.m.).[8] It was one of the longest fighter missions of the war. Each man had flown seven hours and forty-five minutes confined to a cockpit that measured less than half the width of the front seat of a small automobile.

The next morning they loaded up again and made another trip to Jefman. It was apparent that they had dealt a fatal blow to the Japanese the day before. No enemy fighters rose from Jefman or Samate as the Mitchell bombers pasted the two fields again.

Ack-ack was heavy so the P-38s cleared the area. They followed standard operating procedures and flew along the coast where they set three barges on fire. On the way home they encountered an impassable front. To avoid another "Black Sunday" McGuire led his men to Owi, which had been occupied by American forces the day before. McGuire became the first American pilot to land on the strip. Men of the 860th Engineering Battalion who were working on the strip, welcomed them. They treated McGuire and his men like dignitaries--fed them, and put them up for the night.

McGuire wrote to his wife: *"Things have been busy lately. I knocked down two more Japs the other day and we have been damned busy. I have been a Major for about two months but just received the orders a week ago. Sure feels good, as if your work is appreciated. Since Dick Bong went home I am tied for the top ace now in the S.W.P.A. Not bad Huh?"*

[1] 431st Daily History

[2] Ibid.

[3] Pete Madison, 431 Pilot

[4] 431st Daily History.

[5] Bill Dutton, SHS '37

[6] Ibid.

[7] McGuire's Combat Report

[8] Ibid.

33

"McGuire felt that the most dangerous parts of a flight were taking off and landing, when a Japanese fighter might catch one of our planes with wheels and flaps down and make quick work of it. We practiced the pitch-out maneuver until we could put a plane on the ground, from level flight over the runway, in 20 seconds. It was tough for a P-38 pilot to switch hands on the wheel two or three times to reach the various controls. He looked like he was changing the settings on a pipe organ, but it left little time for an enemy attack."

------John Tilley, 431st Pilot

A tall civilian stood near the landing strip at Hollandia, watching the P-38s of the 475th Fighter Group returning from a mission. While a single P-38 orbited above, four red-spinnered P-38s of the 431st Fighter Squadron approached the field in tight formation and the element leader whipped his plane up and to the left. One by one the other three planes quickly followed their leader into a tight left turn which brought them single file in a circle, back to the end of the runway with their wheels and flaps extended. The pitch-out maneuver had the four planes on the runway in less than 30 seconds. The civilian was impressed.

The P-38s cleared the runway and the sky was quiet for a moment. Then came the low moan of twin Allison engines from the other end of the field. This P-38 with red spinners and command stripes on its booms, had circled above while the other P-38s landed, and now buzzed over the runway at tree-top level with engines purring, wide open. The civilian watched as the "Lightning" did three rolls before it reached the end of the runway.

Suddenly the P-38 pulled straight up into a loop at the end of the runway. As the plane rose toward the top of the arc a few hundred feet from the ground, the pilot extended the landing gear and the flaps as the plane continued to climb. At the top of the loop the plane flew inverted for a split second with its gear and flaps extended--then the engines shut down, and the plane did a half roll into an upright position just a few feet above the runway. The pilot masterfully eased the plane to a perfect landing.

The civilian was a factory representative for the Navy Corsair fighter, who had incurred a small accident on his first P-38 flight, a week before. He shook his head as he watched the P-38, with 20 small Japanese flags on its nose, taxi to the revetment area. Charles A. Lindbergh, the visiting civilian, turned to a young Army pilot standing next to him and said, "The last time I saw anything like that was in an air show! Who's that?"

"That's Major McGuire, our leading Ace," answered the Army pilot.

"He'll never live to be an old pilot doing that," said Lindbergh.

Word got around the airfield that Lindbergh had arrived unannounced. GIs and officers alike strolled past Colonel MacDonald's tent trying to get a glimpse of the legendary "Lone Eagle."

Later, McGuire was summoned to Colonel MacDonald's tent and reported there wearing his crushed 500-hour hat and with his trousers tucked into his Australian flying boots. Along with his mustache he was dapper and stood apart from the other men as he was introduced to Lindbergh. Colonel MacDonald explained that Major McGuire was CO of the 431st Squadron, and he added, "He'll go with us tomorrow."

McGuire had just been introduced to one of the most famous men in the world. McGuire, who stood less than five-feet-ten inches tall, looked up into the face of the six-foot-four Lindbergh in awe, as they shook hands. He said, "Glad to meet you, Colonel."

Lindbergh said, "I'm a civilian. You don't need to call me Colonel. I was down at the air strip this afternoon when you made that fancy landing, Major."

"Oh yes," said McGuire, as his face turned red. "I don't do that all the time. Just got a little bored today."

Lindbergh was dressed like any one of them, in khaki shirt and trousers, but wore no emblem of military rank. He was tall, tan, and though slightly balding at age 42, still an imposing figure. Lindbergh might well have been a colonel or even a general, but President Roosevelt had not allowed him to go on active duty when the war started.

Also present in MacDonald's tent was the 475th Group Deputy Commander, Major Meryl Smith. Colonel MacDonald explained that Lindbergh wanted to know more about the P-38 in combat operation. "I feel that the only way for him to learn is to go on a regularly scheduled mission. Maybe a four-man fighter sweep to Jefman Island."

It was apparent to McGuire, by the group assembled, that Colonel MacDonald did not plan to take any chances with his special student. A fighter sweep to Jefman would be safe. The last two missions had rendered it so. McGuire was amazed that he was standing next to his childhood hero. As they planned the next day's mission McGuire was uncustomarily quiet.

Lindbergh explained that he had worked several years for the Ford Motor Company helping to get B-24 bombers off their new assembly line at Willow Run. He had also consulted with United Aircraft in Hartford, and Vought-Sikorsky on improvement of the Navy's Corsair fighter plane. He had come to the Pacific as a Vought-Sikorsky factory representative to visit Navy and Marine Corps pilots and recommend operating procedures which would improve the Corsair's performance. There was interest in a twin-engine Corsair fighter and he had asked the Navy to send him to a place where he could see the P-38 in combat to get a feel for the future of such a design.

Lindbergh had led an unbelievable life since he had left his Minnesota home, in his late teens, to travel with a group of barnstormers. He disappointed his Congressman father by failing to complete his education, but saved enough money to buy his own airplane and travel the South, Southwest and the Midwest, supporting himself by selling plane rides in small towns. He qualified for Army flight training which brought him a Reserve Commission and official recognition as a pilot. This led him to the dangerous profession of Air Mail pilot where he often risked his life in poor equipment and bad weather.

He found sponsors, helped design and build the Spirit of St. Louis, made the New York to Paris flight against great odds, and won the cash prize and the admiration of people all over the world. He wrote a book, *We*, about his experiences, met and married Anne Morrow, and toured the world on a number of goodwill flights with his bride. Anne, a talented writer, produced several books about their travels before she gave birth to a son. Charles traveled to Latin America and to the Orient helping to develop air routes and long-range cruise techniques for Pan American Airway's famous Clipper ships.

Every event in the Lindbergh's lives produced headlines, but no story lasted as long as the tragedy of their son's kidnapping and murder. Eventually, a German immigrant was charged with taking the baby from his crib in the Lindbergh home and killing him, after demanding and getting a large ransom. The trial was controversial, long, and devastating to the Lindberghs. They withdrew from public life until rumblings of war began in Europe.

Lindbergh had standing invitations to visit the countries of Europe and took advantage of them to visit Germany five or six times and to see the massive air force they were marshalling in violation of World War I treaties. He was still a reserve Colonel in the Army and he dutifully reported this information back to the American War Department.

He did not stop there, but joined other prominent citizens to form a group known as "America First." They advocated keeping America out of the war which was sure to engulf most of the world. Lindbergh was their most prominent spokesman and he drew much criticism for this unpopular stand. With his German sounding name and his recent visits to Germany he was accused of being a Nazi sympathizer and it made headlines all over America. In speeches before large groups he accused the British, Jewish interests and the Roosevelt Administration of pushing America toward war. He was not popular with these groups.

When the war broke out he asked to go on active duty as a Colonel in the Army Air Corps but President Roosevelt personally turned him down, declaring that his prewar political stance had rendered him useless in a military capacity. Lindbergh joined the war effort with Ford and other aviation companies and never experienced any personal animosity from the servicemen with whom he came in contact. It was plain that nobody in the 475th Fighter Group had any ill feelings toward him. Instead, they admired him greatly.

Lindbergh stayed in Colonel MacDonald's tent to be near the airstrip for the next day's mission. After dinner, pilots from the Group dropped by to meet Lindbergh. They discussed fighter planes and tactics, and even the taking of prisoners. The pilots of the Satan's Angels had never had anything to do with enemy prisoners, but they told Lindbergh "war stories" about prisoners being killed. Some pilots said they would machine-gun an enemy pilot as he hung in his parachute. Though most of them had never seen a Japanese pilot use a parachute, they said, "The Japs have done it. Why shouldn't we?" They glossed over the fact that the opportunity had never come their way because Japanese pilots rarely if ever were furnished with parachutes. Lindbergh didn't like what he heard, and feared that the war had distorted some of their values. They talked until after midnight.

Colonel MacDonald, Major Smith, Lindbergh and McGuire were up at 5:45 the next morning. After breakfast they went to the 431st Fighter Squadron's operations tent where McGuire conducted a briefing for the mission. He pointed out the terrain they would fly over and the key points in the target area. A small group of enlisted men gathered and watched from the back of the tent as McGuire stood in front of aerial photographs of Jefman Island, and reported, "Gentlemen, when we hit Jefman several days ago we encountered heavy anti-aircraft installations in this area. We will stay clear of these areas today. We will be looking for any Japanese planes that might try to intercept us. With the damage reports we've seen, we don't expect much aerial resistance. In that case we will proceed along the coastline, here, in search of barges."

On the flight line, McGuire showed the excitement of a child as he told his crew chief, Sgt. Kish, "I can't believe it! I'm going to be flying with a man I've admired all my life."[1]

An early morning rain delayed their departure until 10:30. They set a direct course for Jefman Island and arrived there after flying three hours over an unexplored area of New Guinea. Jefman was quiet, as expected, except for anti-aircraft fire that was accurate enough to keep the P-38s

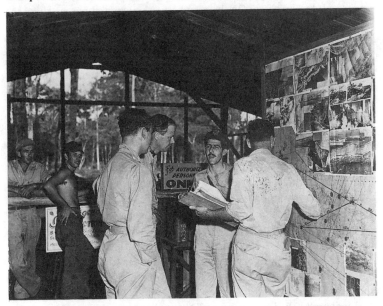

McGuire briefs Charles Lindbergh and Col. MacDonald for a mission to Jefman Island. McGuire had been on a mission to Jefman just days before. Also pictured front : Lt. Norris Clark. In the back: Sgt Victor Johnson and Sgt Edward Hall.

away from the airdrome. They headed out to the coastline in search of shipping targets.

They found four barges, one a large Lugger cleverly nestled in a small scalloped bay surrounded by steep hills. The attack, from a strafing circle, was difficult, each plane taking a short run and then pulling up quickly to clear the hills. They hit all three barges, and left the Lugger in flames. They headed for home, strafing every barge they saw on the way. They landed at Hollandia at about 6:00 in the evening.

Lindbergh was thrilled with the mission and took delight in spending the evening talking with his new comrades. He had used less fuel on the day's seven-hour flight than his associates, and expressed the opinion that the range of the P-38s could be greatly extended using techniques he had developed for the "China Clipper" when he was a consultant for Pan American Airways.

The next few days Lindbergh flew with various units of the 475th Group on all sorts of missions. He flew a mission on June 30 when McGuire and the other pilots tried their hands at dive bombing for the first time. They loaded 1,000-pound bombs on their P-38s and dropped them on Neomfoer. Only a few of the bombs hit the target. Nobody knew how to aim them. On the way home they strafed barges along the coastline, and left a number of them burning. They landed at Wakde because of bad weather.

On July 3 the 475th Group again escorted B-24 bombers to the Jefman-Samate area. Lindbergh flew as an element leader with the 431st Fighter Squadron. In all of McGuire's childhood dreams he had never once imagined that he might have Charles Lindbergh fly under his command. Here he was--his childhood idol--flying right back there over his shoulder, and following his orders!

Lindbergh planned to recheck his cruising technique on this mission. The plan was to fly directly from Hollandia to Samate and return to Owi near Biak for refueling. They saw no enemy opposition over the Samate area and after escorting the bombers clear of the area set off to use their ammo on barges.

After hitting a number of barges Colonel MacDonald led most of the flight back as pilots reported one by one that they were low on fuel. Lindbergh and his wingman stayed a little longer to make another pass, but the wingman orbited above the area while Lindbergh flew down and shot at a beached barge.

Lindbergh called on his radio, "Do you have a problem, white two?"

The wingman answered, "Yes, I do, white leader. I'm running low on fuel. I may not be able to make it home."

Lindbergh asked, "How much fuel do you have left?"

He answered, "About 175 gallons."

Lindbergh coached the pilot all the way home. He gave him engine and propeller settings and assured him, "You have plenty of fuel."

When they landed at Owi to refuel, the long-range technique had brought Lindbergh and his wingman home with a generous surplus of fuel. Lindbergh had 260 gallons left while his wingman still had 70 gallons.

That evening, the pilots of the 475th Group were asked to assemble and Colonel MacDonald introduced Lindbergh, "Gentlemen, give Colonel Lindbergh your attention. He has been testing cruise techniques on missions the last few days. Today, he was able to stay longer in the target area than most of us could. When he landed at Owi he still had 260 gallons of fuel on board. The rest of us were bone dry. He's going to explain how he was able to do that."

Lindbergh spoke in detail about his cruise technique of lowering engine RPM and leaning out the fuel mixture settings and concluded by saying, "A P-38, handled in this manner, can fly an 800-mile mission, stay over the target 30 minutes, at combat power, and still make it home with plenty of reserves. There is no reason why this plane couldn't stay in the air for 10 hours."

The pilots moaned, and one shouted from the back of the room, "Who needs an ass-buster like that?"

Everyone laughed, and then they went on to discuss the merits of the new information. Most of the pilots agreed that the present seven-hour missions were almost crippling, and that regular 10-hour flights would be dangerous due to pilot fatigue. When the meeting broke up McGuire went up to Lindbergh and said, "Colonel Lindbergh, the 431st Squadron will be implementing the new technique at once. I don't like the idea of 10-hour missions, but I do like the idea that we will have reserve fuel if we get lost or have bad weather."

The next day's flight proved Lindbergh's cruise theory, when every plane returned from the mission with hundreds of gallons of fuel in reserve. A new era of long-distance missions was about to be ushered in for Satan's Angels.

Charles Lindbergh stayed with the 475th Group for the early days of July and became "one of the guys." He flew often with various squadrons, and on his off-days recruited men to scout the local jungles with him. He had an inquisitive mind and wanted to learn about the natives and their culture. He even got Colonel MacDonald to go with him on one of these jaunts. To the delight of all, he cooked dinner one night in Colonel MacDonald's tent, when they arrived back too late for food in the mess hall.

The word came down from Nadzab that high command was unaware of Lindbergh's activities with the Army Air Corps. The word was straight from General Kenney in Brisbane, and it ordered him to discontinue his flying until he had come to Australia for a talk.

Lindbergh was embarrassed by the message. He had turned over his Navy orders to a Colonel when he arrived in the area under Army jurisdiction, and had assumed that his presence had been explained to the powers above. It was apparent from the message that the word had not gotten back to General MacArthur's headquarters through official channels but by word-of-mouth and they were steamed. Lindbergh had learned through his years of experience at the Ford Motor Company that politics in these matters could be very touchy. He packed his bags and headed for Brisbane to see if he could remove the monkey wrench from the works.

When he met General Kenney he knew that he had met a pilot's general. The General had flown in World War I and expressed admiration for Lindbergh's contributions to aviation. Lindbergh could see the glint of pride in Kenney's eyes when he talked about his prized child, the 475th Fighter Group. After a few minutes Lindbergh had an ally, and within an hour, Kenney was acting as his advocate with General MacArthur's Chief of Staff, General Richard Sutherland.

The problem was more than a matter of politics. Civilians were prohibited by regulations, probably the Geneva Convention, from engaging in combat. The Army was also worried about public reaction if something were to happen to Lindbergh while he was flying combat with the Army. They also feared that the Japanese might behead him, if they captured a civilian flying in a fighter plane in a combat area.

Kenney said, "You can return to the 475th Fighter Group anytime you want to, if you will agree to fly non-combat missions." Lindbergh rejected this, "General, I don't want to sit around while everyone else is flying combat. I need to see action if I'm going to learn anything."

"I understand," said Kenney. "I'm stuck behind a desk most of the time. I have to get over there every once in a while to see what's really going on."

"Can't we find a way of getting around the Army regulations so I can go back out there and get my work done?" asked Lindbergh.

"Meet with MacArthur," said Kenney. "I'll figure out something."

Lindbergh met with General Sutherland and later General MacArthur to plead his case. He had known both men before, in Washington, and was warmly greeted. Lindbergh had known MacArthur's wife before the two of them had met and married. Lindbergh inquired about MacArthur's wife and later visited her briefly to renew an acquaintance Lindbergh and his mother had made on an ocean voyage some years back.

Lindbergh explained to the Generals, "I'm studying fighter planes in combat so I can take back information for future designs. To do this, I need combat experience. Then I can make valid recommendations."

MacArthur listened as Lindbergh continued, "I've already told General Sutherland that I've learned how the operational range of the P-38 could be extended to 700 miles without any equipment modifications."

General MacArthur said, "It would be a gift from heaven if that could be done."

Lindbergh went on and explained his findings. MacArthur was enthralled and asked, "Are you in a position to go back to New Guinea and teach your methods of fuel economy?"

Lindbergh replied, "There's nothing I'd rather do, General."

In a few days Lindbergh was on his way back to New Guinea with a special designation as an "observer." He would be allowed to fly on any mission he desired. He wasn't supposed to fire his guns, but who would know? He agreed to train all P-38 pilots to extend their combat range, using his special cruise technique.[2]

McGuire wrote his wife, *"I am enclosing a couple of pictures. The one of Charles Lindbergh was taken when he was here lately. He seems like a hell of a fine man."*

[1] Frank Kish, McGuire's crew chief

[2] See Appendix A, How this book was written

34

"....Mr. Speaker, under leave to extend my remarks in the record, I am including a newspaper editorial describing the excellent war record of Capt. Thomas B. McGuire, Jr., a resident of the Seventh Congressional District of New Jersey.

---remarks by Hon. J. Parnell Thomas, Congressman
from New Jersey, for the Congressional Record.

In mid-July, McGuire and the 475th Fighter Group moved 300 miles further northwest, joining the 49th Fighter Group on the island of Biak where Japanese troops were still tunneled into coral cliffs along the coastline. The infantry had lost hundreds of men without ousting the enemy from their caves.

McGuire supervised the 431st Squadron's move and it went smoothly. The new camp near Mokmer Drome had been secured, but there were still Japanese troops in the area. It was a miserable spot which required the removal of tons of thick undergrowth before it could be made livable.

Infantry officers informed McGuire and other commanders that their men must be on guard, as Japanese stragglers were still in the area. McGuire ordered his men to dig fox holes and to keep side arms handy, particularly after dark. The men found coral just under a thin surface of top soil and it made fox hole digging nearly impossible.

The first night on the island was an adventure. The camp was in disarray and people were wandering around after dark still trying to erect tents or dig fox holes. Several times during the night enlisted men thought they saw Japanese soldiers in the camp area, and shot at them. Each time the shots woke everyone in camp, resulting in armed men surveying the area for a half-hour or more before returning to their beds.

The next day Colonel "Archie" Roosevelt, the son of Teddy Roosevelt, visited the camp and asked the commanding officers to instruct their men to be more careful at night. He and his 41st Infantry Regiment were nearby, and reported that random bullets, fired by the Air Corps, had ricocheted through their camp the night before. McGuire promised to talk to his men about it. [1]

The 431st Squadron reinstituted the buddy system for the purposes of going to the latrine. Carrying a submachine gun, one man would stand guard while the other used the facilities. One morning at daybreak Corporal Francis Robinson was on his way to the latrine alone when he tripped over a wire which was strung across the path. Wisely, he dove for cover, and was uninjured when a hand grenade exploded. The explosion woke both the Army and Air Corps camps. At first, it was thought that the Japanese had set a booby trap during the night. Later it was learned that our infantry troops set these traps each night to catch infiltrating Nips. They routinely removed the traps at daybreak. Unfortunately they hadn't removed the one Corporal Robinson discovered. They agreed to discontinue the practice.[2]

Back in San Antonio, Marilynn McGuire was working long hours at the phone company but she took time almost every day to write her husband. McGuire's Army records listed his home town as San Antonio, because his wife resided there. Since Polly McGuire had died, and McGuire had no family there, news stories by the AP or UPI made no references to Sebring, Florida. The San Antonio newspapers picked up stories about McGuire, but newspapers in Florida saw no interest in news stories about a pilot from San Antonio, and rarely ever published anything about him.

Marilynn was in touch with a few people in Sebring, and with friends of Tommy's she had met in San Antonio, like Paul Gustat and Herman Hancock. Bill Dutton, still on New Guinea, frequently mentioned McGuire in his letters home. Hayden Williams, the Tampa Tribune writer in Sebring, kept his ear to the ground and received a few second-hand stories about McGuire, from the Dutton, Hancock and Gustat families.

In New Jersey, it was a different story. McGuire's father was a member of the Pica Club, an organization made up mostly of newsmen. He passed on every bit of news he got about his son, and they in turn kept an eye on the teletype stories from the news services. The elder McGuire frequently dropped by the newspaper office or called on the phone to see if there was any news about his son.

Whenever a news item about McGuire came to the attention of the New Jersey newspapers, they carried the story and mentioned Tommy as a native of Ridgewood, New Jersey. After McGuire's outstanding accomplishments in 1943, New Jersey newspapers published detailed accounts of his deeds. Thus McGuire came to the attention of J. Parnell Thomas, the Congressman from New Jersey, and a long-time friend of Thomas McGuire Sr.

On March 9, 1944, Mr. Thomas rose on the floor of the U.S. House of Representatives and caused a newspaper editorial to be read into the "Congressional Record." It was devoted entirely to "Capt. Thomas B. McGuire Jr., a resident of the Seventh Congressional District of New Jersey." McGuire had not resided in New Jersey for over 15 years but that seemed not to matter. The entry was full of errors about McGuire's personal life (it said his wife's name was Marion, instead of Marilynn, said he played a cornet in the school band instead of a clarinet, had him graduating from school in New Jersey, and said he was a licensed pilot while in college, which he was not), but his war record was well portrayed.

On Biak, McGuire wrote his dad a letter:[3]

July 20th

Dear Dad,

I just received your letter of June 18th so sat right down to answer it. I am sorry about not writing more often and will try to do better in the future. As you can see by my new APO we have moved again.

We have the Nips on the run over here now. I expect we will keep right on going forward. I have been as busy as the proverbial one-armed paper hanger but now that we are settled down things are quieter.

There hasn't been much aerial combat lately. We had our last fight over Jefman last month but things should pick up pretty soon. I have 20 confirmed victories, 3 probables, and one more which blew up in front of me, in fact knocked a hole in my plane, but due to some mix up I never got official credit for it.

As far as ones destroyed on the ground we don't count them over here. I haven't done much strafing, but I have sunk a few barges and also the squadron strafed and sank a 1000-ton Jap freighter while I was flying. Tell the Pica Club the next one's for them. That's not for publication.

It sure made me feel good to learn about being put in the Congressional Record. I don't know whether I am worthy of all that but will do my best. I think I would like a regular Army commission but of course I don't think anything is being done about them these days. If you're interested I have received a Purple Heart, an Air Medal and two Oak Leaf Clusters, a D.F.C. and 2 Oak Leaf Clusters, a Silver Star and one Oak Leaf Cluster.

I have been recommended for 4 more clusters on the Air Medal, 3 more clusters on the D.F.C. and a Distinguished Service Cross. These should go through but it takes time. I have about 190 combat missions to date.

Not much more news. Don't send me anything for my birthday, things take so long to get here and besides I should be home before it would get here. As you see I am a Major, in fact have been one for two months now.

*I sent you a whole bunch of pictures by a Sgt. Bob Boucher
from Ridgewood, who is going home, so you should get them
soon. They have all been censored.*

*Charles A. Lindbergh was over here and I went on a flight
with him. Take it easy on that though it's a touchy subject as
you know. I have picked up some souvenirs, a Jap battle flag,
and a couple of swords which I will bring back. Not much
other news, give my best to all.*

Keep me up on all the news.

Love,

Tom

In late 1943 McGuire had written to Marilynn saying he expected to be home soon. Seven months had passed and he hadn't said much about it. Now, he told his father that he expected to be home soon after his birthday which was August 1. That date would come and go with no signs of McGuire heading home.

Charles Lindbergh worked his way from one P-38 squadron to another, training pilots on his long-range cruise techniques. After a few weeks he rejoined the 475th Group on Biak, and resumed combat flying.

One evening after supper Lindbergh asked McGuire to accompany him on a junket to explore the island's abandoned Japanese caves. They still had hours of daylight so McGuire got a jeep and the two of them set out for an area where the Japanese had just been extricated from their caves. They climbed up a battle scarred coral cliff past palms which had been splintered by cannon shells and defoliated by flame throwers. There were abandoned weapons and battle debris strewn everywhere.

They entered the mouth of a cave to find themselves staring down the barrel of a Japanese machine gun. The gunner was at his gun, but made no attempt to shoot because he was lifeless and decapitated. The bloating body was still tied to a post with ropes, apparently placed there to insure the soldier's resolve. It was a gruesome sight for the older man who cared so much for the human condition and for the young man who was not accustomed to seeing death firsthand.

There was a stench of death and rotting rice. The cave was littered with clothing, bags of rice, and large quantities of cannon shells and other ammunition. Further back in the cave they found huts on platforms where the enemy had slept. Twenty-five yards into the cave they found side passages with more supplies. A sound came from the back of the cave and Lindbergh and McGuire looked at each other with some trepidation. They didn't know if it was just an echo or a Japanese soldier waiting for them to come closer. Lindbergh suggested that they leave

259

since it was almost dark and they were at least a mile from any U.S. troops. McGuire agreed as he fingered his 45-automatic, still in his shoulder holster.

Neither man had much to say on the way back to camp. They had seen war and death in a way they had never seen it before. It had left a smell in their nostrils, and had burned an unforgettable image in their minds.

McGuire was up early the next morning and off the strip at 9:45 to escort bombers on a raid to Lolobata, Halmakera Isles. Lolobata strip was spotted at 12:35 and the air armada was unopposed as it entered the target area. Far to the Northwest a volcano was erupting violently as the B-24s administered an unhindered, devastating bomb run to the air strip. Lolobata was left in flames and shrouded in dark smoke which mingled with the volcanic smoke. A number of enemy planes, which had made no move to defend the base, burned alongside the landing strip.

As the bombers left the target area, several Oscar fighters appeared in the distance but they seemed reluctant to scrap. McGuire ordered flights one and two to follow him as they went after the Oscars. Flights three and four stayed with the bombers. McGuire warned that this may be a trick.[4]

McGuire led his P-38s in an effort to challenge the Oscars, but it became apparent that the Japanese were trying to lure them over an end of the Lolobata strip where large anti-aircraft guns were installed. It was an old trick, and McGuire and his combat-wise men recognized the ploy. They devised a plan to get the Oscars without getting in range of the heavy ack-ack fire.

They gained altitude and, on McGuire's command, moved into a string formation. McGuire made a solo dive at one of the Oscars. He drew within range and got off a short burst from slight deflection, and then quickly made a tight 180-degree turn. The sky between McGuire and the Oscar, where the Japanese had expected him to pursue, blossomed with black puffs of ack-ack smoke. McGuire's quick shot struck the Oscar around the cockpit and wing root and sent the plane into a spin. It crashed in the jungle below and exploded. This time the mouse had lost in the game of cat and mouse.

One by one the other P-38s of the 431st Squadron followed the lead of their Major and made a run at other Oscars, staying clear of the Lolobata strip. Each turned before reaching the ack-ack's range. Lieutenant George Veit made an attack and got his first kill. Lieutenant Foch Benevent used his dive flaps to make a turn with a fleeing Oscar and scored a victory when the enemy plane crashed on his own home landing strip.

When the squadron landed at Biak, there was a celebration. The 431st Fighter Squadron was now the home of the leading Ace in the Pacific Theater of War. With Dick Bong, Joe Foss, and "Pappy" Boyington no longer on active duty in the Pacific, McGuire's total of 21 enemy planes made him "king." The day's conquests had run the 431st Fighter Squadron's total to 141 enemy aircraft in less than a year of combat. Other squadrons, such as the 80th and 9th, had already topped the 200 mark, but they had been in combat a year longer than the 431st.

On July 29, maintenance crews were busy performing routine repairs on the planes of the 431st Fighter Squadron. S/Sgt. George Jeschke took a break and left the plane he'd been painting. He was tossing a football near the runway and signaled T/Sgt. Robert Applewhite to go for a "deep one" when they heard an unusual sounding airplane coming their way. They stopped and watched in horror as a P-38 veered off the runway with only one engine running. The plane flipped upside down as it passed over their heads. They fell to the ground as the P-38 descended toward the revetment where they had both been working, and where other men of the 431st Fighter Squadron were still working.

Ground crew members jumped from their planes and ran in all directions, as the errant F-5, a camera-equipped version of the P-38, crashed in an inverted position on top of two P-38s. One of them, No. 118, was the plane Jeschke had been working on, minutes before! The three planes broke into flames and the ammunition in the two fighter planes exploded like firecrackers.

Line Chief, M/Sgt. Steve Stanich, removed a hurt man from near the wreckage and Sgt. Jeschke helped drag him to further safety. The pilot of the "Photo Joe" had been killed instantly and the ground crews had miraculously escaped with only two men seriously injured. Fire fighting equipment was on its way but two undamaged P-38s in the same revetment were in danger of being set on fire and destroyed. Everyone cleared the area, fearing the live ammunition and further explosions of the three plane's gasoline tanks which held thousands of gallons of high test aviation fuel.

Major McGuire appeared from nowhere and motioned frantically for a bulldozer driver nearby to bring his equipment into the revetment. With total disregard for his own safety and that of the driver, McGuire jumped on the back of the bulldozer and shouted, "Let's push this wreckage to the side. My men will taxi the other two planes clear before they are damaged."

As flames from the wreckage bellowed up 30 feet into the sky and live ammunition zinged into the air, the bulldozer operator placed his machine's blade against the three twisted airplanes and pushed. He had to make several runs, pushing forward and backing up, and pushing forward again, before the wreckage was moved from the mouth of the revetment. McGuire held his position behind the driver until the path was cleared, and then turned and motioned to Lieutenant Kenneth Hart and Sergeant Kish who had started the engines of the two P-38s. They quickly taxied the two planes safely from the revetment area as the fire crews arrived to extinguish the fire. McGuire said to the bulldozer operator, "Sergeant, you are a very brave man, and one-hell-of-a bulldozer pilot! I want your name and serial number."

He went straight to the 431st Squadron's Headquarters where he wrote the bulldozer driver a commendation for the Soldiers' Medal, "for heroism, not involving actual conflict with the enemy."

S/Sgt. Jeschke picked up the football and said to T/Sgt. Applewhite, "A brave man, that Major Mac! A brave man!"

T/Sgt. Applewhite said, "You said it!" as he went out for a long pass.[5]

[1] 431st Daily History
[2] Ibid.
[3] Letter funrished by Joan Mallon
[4] 431st Daily History.
[5] See Appendix A, How this book was written

262

35

"I feel very close to Tommy McGuire because as you know we stayed in the same tent for a time on Mokmer Drome, and I flew with his squadron on a number of missions. He was a wonderful fighter pilot and a grand fellow besides."
                    ---- Charles A. Lindbergh, in a letter to General Kenney

The new camp at Biak finally took shape. It was near a steep bluff overlooking a group of native huts built on stilts over the water. Life was quite comfortable except for the nightly air raids and the poor food. The morale of the squadron was greatly enhanced by a notice of 64 long-overdue promotions which McGuire had posted on the 431st's bulletin board.[1]

Charles Lindbergh continued to fly combat with various squadrons of the 475th Fighter Group. Combat flying was at a low ebb with all Japanese air units forced from New Guinea. Missions to raid enemy air-strips on distant islands were being meted out to first one squadron and then another to keep things fair. Colonel MacDonald took Lindbergh flying whenever an interesting mission was assigned, regardless of the squadron which drew the mission. MacDonald was determined to get Lindbergh the combat experience he wanted, and he went along as a watchdog to be sure nothing happened to his celebrity guest.

Major Warren Lewis, the C O of the 433rd Fighter Squadron, invited Lindbergh, MacDonald and Captain Danforth Miller to join his men for a raid on the Japanese airstrips on the island of Ceram. They flew across New Guinea, and far south into the Banda Sea. The distance was so great that it demanded effective use of Lindbergh's technique to con-serve fuel.

Over Elpaputih Bay they engaged several Zeros and Lindbergh was in the midst of his first dogfight. It was almost his last as he barely avoided a head-on collision. He saw the Zero's machine guns flashing, but held his own finger on the trigger until evasive action was necessary to avoid a crash. The enemy plane rolled over out of control and crashed into the sea. Lindbergh had, almost by accident, shot down a Japanese fighter plane.

Everyone was ordered to keep quiet about Lindbergh's victory be-cause of his civilian status. No claim was put in for the downed Zero, but it was impossible to hide the facts and everybody knew about it. Even General Kenney back in Australia eventually found out about it, but said nothing.

Lindbergh was quietly elated about his victory and continued to fly a mission almost every day. Although he had taken a vocal and unpopular position to keep the United States out of the war, and frequently criticized American soldiers for having too much zeal in killing the enemy, he got caught up in the action and was eager to get more combat opportunities himself.

Over the next few days the weather over Ceram was bad, so Mac-Donald planed a long-range fighter sweep to Palau, north across the West Carolina Basin, in the South Philippine Sea. Four P-38s flew the long distance in hopes of surprising the Japanese where they reportedly had 150 airplanes stationed. Lindbergh for the first time saw the down side of combat flying as he found himself in the sights of a Japanese fighter. Tracers streamed past his plane as he tried without success to lose the Zero. Major Meryl Smith and Colonel MacDonald shot down the zero and several other enemy planes to save Lindbergh.[2]

In the rage of battle Lindbergh took a shot at a plane which turned out to be his wingman. Instead of remaining on Lindbergh's wing Major Smith had sneaked ahead to get a shot at a Japanese seaplane. Lindbergh mistook him for a Japanese plane and shot a long-range burst at him. Too late, he recognized the twin-booms of the P-38, and held his breath until his shots missed.[3] Fighting the Japanese in the air wasn't as easy as Lindbergh had found it a few days before over Ceram. His lack of combat training and aerobatics skills in the P-38 had jeopardized his life and those of the men with whom he flew. Everyone involved in the mission breathed easier when they got home safely with their "special instructor."

Word of the long-range mission got to Fifth Fighter Command and Colonel MacDonald was ordered to report to Headquarters on Owi. Fighter Command had been refusing to furnish fighter escorts on bomber missions to Palau. They had told Bomber Command that Palau was out of range for the P-38s. MacDonald's sweep to Palau proved that the fighters had plenty of range for such a mission. He had put Fifth Fighter Command in a bad light, and they were upset. He was reprimanded for making the long-distance fighter sweep without prior approval and two days later he was sent home on 60 days of well-deserved and long-overdue leave. Major Meryl Smith took command of the 475th Group until his return.

With MacDonald on his way home, Lindbergh had no place to stay, and accepted an invitation from McGuire to move into his tent. McGuire was living near the airstrip at Mokmer Drome. It was handy for the early morning flights, but dangerously near the target area of the nightly Japanese bomber attacks.

Instead of being awed by Lindbergh, McGuire had become very comfortable around the man. They had flown many hours together and had many long conversations in the evenings. McGuire now respected his guest more than ever. He'd seen the man fly long missions that were the bane of men half his age. McGuire admired him for putting his life on the line to collect information, instead of sitting around the camp asking questions.

Lindbergh was comfortable with McGuire, too. The young man was obviously a talented pilot, but more importantly, ran a squadron the way Lindbergh might have done it himself. The Major had a lot of energy, much as Lindbergh did. That was the reason Lindbergh had invited McGuire to search the Biak caves with him. He had often had trouble getting people to go on side adventures with him. In McGuire he found a willing participant.

The first night in McGuire's tent Lindbergh and McGuire were roused from their sleep by a red alert. They dressed in the dark and lay on their bunks and went back to sleep. Later a bomb fell nearby and Lindbergh tumbled to the floor tangled in his mosquito net. McGuire, being more accustomed to these night raids, didn't wake as quickly, but soon joined his guest on the tent floor. The two men talked of their families and their plans, and when the threat of danger passed, stood and watched searchlights follow enemy planes across the sky. Enemy bombs fell far from Mokmer Drome, and echoed from the distance like thunder.

The next day McGuire was struck a tragic blow. His Operations Officer, Captain William O'Brien, failed to return from a mission to Ceram. Other pilots reported that O'Brien had been involved in a mid-air collision with a looping Zero. There was hope--a parachute had been seen after the two planes exploded. O'Brien was not just the Operations Officer, he was also one of McGuire's best friends. He, too, was one of the charter members of the 431st Squadron and had helped McGuire run the squadron over the last few months. McGuire had assumed Bill would be the next Commanding Officer of the squadron.

Early the following morning McGuire led a 10-plane search party, which included Lindbergh. They searched the area where O'Brien had last been seen but saw no sign of their lost comrade. After searching the area again, McGuire was finally forced to order the planes back home.

The next few days were quiet. Only patrols were being flown because of poor weather conditions. McGuire and Lindbergh spent those days together and the older man, who years before, had suffered so with the loss of his young son, knew how disturbed McGuire was by the loss of O'Brien. He marveled at McGuire's maturity and resilience, as with much distress, he wrote to O'Brien's relatives to express his regrets.

265

Lindbergh spent his time writing, too. He wrote to his wife, Anne, and told her that he felt a comradeship with the young pilots of the 475th Group that he had last felt when he was a young pilot barnstorming and flying the early airmail routes. He enclosed pictures of himself with McGuire. Anne told friends that the pictures showed her husband smiling in a way she hadn't seen in 15 years[4] (since their son had been kidnapped and murdered).

Charles A. Lindbergh and Tommy McGuire on the flight line at Hollandia

It dawned on Lindbergh, after eating at the Officer's Mess for several weeks in a row, that the food was very poor. They were served canned "bully beef" and dried beans almost every day. In itself the food wasn't that bad. The men had been eating the same diet day in and day out for a year, and they just couldn't face it any more. Some of the men were living on peanut butter and bread, but often they didn't get fresh bread. When they did, it molded almost overnight. They could hardly tolerate the hard biscuits from the Army rations. Officers and enlisted men made regular contributions from their pay to a food fund. They were literally buying their own food in a combat zone, but the Fat Cat flight couldn't bring in enough to keep them well fed. McGuire, who normally weighed about 142 pounds admitted that he had lost 14 pounds.

Lindbergh asked McGuire to get some sticks of dynamite so they could go fishing. McGuire knew he could get it from the engineers but suggested that dynamiting fish would be dangerous. Lindbergh agreed and also thought it was a little unsportsmanlike, too, under normal circumstances. He explained that when men are hungry it might be OK to use whatever techniques they had available to feed them. McGuire wondered how they could tell whether the fish might be poison or edible, because he had seen some strange fish in these waters. Lindbergh suggested that they ask the natives, who certainly ate the fish regularly.

McGuire got dynamite, a rubber boat, and some diving masks. They floated their boat out to the edge of the reef, where the ocean floor dropped off. A look under water revealed hundreds of fish. Lindbergh lit and threw a stick of the dynamite. In a few seconds there was a underwater thud and a column of water rose 30 feet in the air. Lindbergh and McGuire put on their diving masks and slipped over the side of the boat to harvest their bounty.[5] They loaded a boat full of stunned fish. None looked like anything McGuire had ever seen in Florida.

The natives didn't speak English, but had no trouble telling the flyers which fish were the best. They rubbed their stomachs and grinned to indicate their choice of the catch. The wilder a fish looked, the better the natives rated them. As a thank-you, McGuire and Lindbergh shared the fish with the helpful little men of Biak. Supper that night for the 431st Squadron was fish, and the men devoured them. Even men who had never liked fish ate their share. McGuire and Lindbergh went fishing again the next day and offered their catch to other squadron messes.

The local natives had a problem of their own. The "titti bagus"(no good) Japanese had taken all of their women to the nearby island of Japen, for what the natives called "Pom-Pom." When the Japanese were driven from the area the Biakians had gone to Japen to recover their women, but the Japen natives refused to let them go. The Biakians, helpless when the Japanese had taken their women, were not about to stand by while the Japenians "Pom-Pomed" their women. It looked like war for sure!

An Army cook came to the rescue. "War painted" with aircraft paint, and beating on pots and pans from his mess, he led the natives on a war dance which eventually freed the Biakian women without bloodshed. The women didn't seem to care one way or the other, but their return to Biak insured peace in the region.

In the weeks that followed, native men often saluted American GIs and shouted "American bagus" (American good). They were appreciative that the GIs "no pom-pom perimpuon" (native women).[6] The GIs showed great restraint--they had been away from civilization so long that the Biakian women were beginning to look like good pom-pom material.

McGuire wrote Marilynn: *"Since my last letter we had a little fight over the Halmahera Islands and I got one more. Hon, your husband is now the leading ace in the S. W. Pacific---how about that---On that news item you read about the forced landing on Owi Island. The name was a misprint cause it was me. We were coming back from a mission when the weather got bad so we had to set down there...Please don't pull any wires on getting me home. Nothing would ruin my chances in the Army any more than that."*

Combat flying on New Guinea was winding down, but Charles Lindbergh provided the men of the 475th Group with a topic of conversation each day. Returning from a patrol mission Lindbergh had been separated from his wingman. He spotted three P-38s from the 431st Squadron and moved into the number four slot of their formation. A Second Lieutenant, who was leading the flight, and had no idea who the stray pilot was, admonished him to fly McGuire's way: "Tighten it up number four, you're flying with the 431st!" Lindbergh politely answered, "Yes, Sir!" and moved closer. Another time, after takeoff, a 431st pilot noticed that Lindbergh failed to retract his landing gear, and was having trouble joining up with the formation. He advised Lindbergh, "Get your gear up, Lindy. You're not flying The Spirit of St. Louis!"[7]

Lindbergh accompanied McGuire on a seven-hour fighter sweep to Halmahera, but it was just a dull day of flying with no action. It proved to be one of the last missions flown from Biak for a while, as weather conditions prevented more long-range missions.

McGuire and Lindbergh continued dynamite fishing until they had an accident. Lindbergh was the "powder man" on these missions, taking it upon himself to light and throw the sticks of dynamite. One afternoon as he drew back his arm to throw a charge, his shoulder became dislocated. Luckily, he flipped the dynamite far enough that no one was injured. McGuire took Lindbergh to see a flight surgeon, who got his shoulder, an old injury from his Air Mail flying days, to "pop back in."

Occasionally, when McGuire was otherwise occupied, Lindbergh took Lieutenant Chris Herman and others fishing. One evening Lindbergh had them clean the fish in front of McGuire's tent, although McGuire had complained about this practice in the past. McGuire had the only private refrigerator in camp---a symbol of rank. The men were reluctant, but Lindbergh insisted that they fill McGuire's refrigerator with the dressed fish since they would spoil in a few hours in the heat. McGuire came home after dark and smelled the fish in front of his tent.

He grumbled out loud, "This place smells like a God damned fish market!"

Men in the adjacent tents held their breath and listened as McGuire opened his refrigerator to get a cold beer. "Jesus Christ!" shouted McGuire.[8] The whole camp laughed in the dark.

McGuire and Lindbergh discuss plans for a mission

McGuire had been interested in Lindbergh since that evening in May of 1927, when he and his cousins lay in their beds at their grandparent's house and listened to the radio for news about Lindbergh's historic flight. Since the age of six McGuire felt as if he knew the "Lone Eagle," and he had noticed that he kept crossing paths that Lindbergh had taken years before.

McGuire and Lindbergh both had connections in New Jersey; McGuire had seen Lindbergh fly the "Spirit of St. Louis" over the Paterson factory which had built his plane's engine, and it was in New Jersey that the Lindbergh's had suffered the tragedy of having their son kidnapped and murdered. McGuire took his first flying lessons in Georgia, while a student at Georgia Tech. Lindbergh had taken his first solo flight in Americus, Georgia, where he had gone to buy a World War I surplus Jenny.

269

McGuire had taken Army Air Corps advanced flight training at Kelly Field, in San Antonio, and had felt lucky to avoid the "wash-out board" after ground-looping a plane. Lindbergh had also taken his advanced flight training at Kelly Field and had felt lucky to avoid the "Benzene Board." McGuire had been stationed at Meridian, Mississippi, a town where Lindbergh had cracked-up his Jenny landing in a farmer's field, a week after his first solo flight.

Lindbergh had bailed out of a mail plane and counted himself as a member of the Caterpillar Club, whose members had parachuted from an airplane to save their life. McGuire joined the club when he bailed out in battle over Oro Bay, the previous October.

McGuire had read Lindbergh's book, *We*, several times and he knew all about Lindbergh's adventures. When Colonel MacDonald, Major Smith and McGuire flew with Lindbergh on his first combat mission, McGuire felt that he had become a guardian of a national treasure. Later when they searched the Japanese caves and dynamited fish together, McGuire felt that he had joined Lindbergh as an adventurer. By the time Lindbergh had lived in his tent for a week, McGuire felt that he was with an old friend.

One day McGuire had a few pilots in his tent for a briefing and he casually asked, "Charles, will you pour me a cup of coffee?" Lindbergh thought nothing of it and handed McGuire a cup of coffee as the briefing went on. Some of the young pilots were shocked that McGuire would ask the "great man" to serve him a cup of coffee. Had they known how close McGuire and Lindbergh had become in a few weeks, they would have thought nothing of it. It was just a friend asking a friend for a favor.

Mid-August brought an end to combat flying in New Guinea, and Lindbergh did not want to wait for the Philippine campaign to begin. He packed his bags and told McGuire he'd love to hear from him when he got back to the states. McGuire treasured the invitation and knew he and his men would always be proud that Lindbergh had flown with the 475th Fighter Group.

McGuire made plans for some leave in Brisbane, before the big push on the Philippines began. Before he left Biak he wrote to Marilynn and answered some concerns she had written to him about:

"...Darling, I am not trying to beat anyone's record. I'm just doing my job, if I should happen to break it that's swell but I'm not out for a record. About getting home I can't give you a definite answer because I don't know, but I have a hunch that October might see me home."

In Brisbane, McGuire and his men soaked up the good things of life. They rested, dined, drank, and many of them looked up female acquaintances from previous trips. McGuire forgot that he was the Commanding Officer of the Squadron and he let the men go their own way. This was in marked contrast to the way he had acted on previous trips to Brisbane when he had often appointed himself the guardian of good taste. On those occasions he had spoken to the men about their dress and their activities, and they felt they were being watched and had to mind their P's and Q's when he was around. It is reported that on one of those trips some of the men devised a plan to tell McGuire something had gone wrong at the Squadron so he would go back to New Guinea. According to the story McGuire went back early.

This time McGuire learned that Major Lewis, the C O of the 433rd Squadron, was leaving for home in a few days. McGuire wanted to see Major Lewis before he left for home so he cut his leave short and caught the returning Fat Cat flight. The pilots of the 431st weren't nearly as eager to see him leave this time. When he arrived back in New Guinea McGuire found out that Major George Dewey of Group Headquarters had borrowed "Pudgy III" and damaged it beyond repair. McGuire loved the plane and was mad as hell that it had been destroyed. He couldn't say anything about it. After all he had lost Major Nichols plane himself, and he had only been a Lieutenant at the time. There was nothing to do but get another airplane, "Pudgy IV." He wrote to Marilynn: "...Not much to write about. Somebody tore up my airplane while I was on leave so I had to get a new one. Sure hated to lose it as it sure was a sweet ship, this guy really tore it up, so now it's 'Pudgy IV.' My tent is right on a cliff overlooking the bay with a beautiful tropical setting---if you like tropical settings. You would think it's a tropical paradise, but it damn sure isn't."

McGuire found little to do back on Biak, but his new quarters at the new camp were delightful and he listened to his Artie Shaw records all day long, practically driving the people in camp mad. He represented the 431st Squadron at the going-home party for Major Warren R. Lewis, the Commanding Officer of the 433rd Fighter Squadron. Lewis was an old-timer, and had 611 combat hours and seven Japanese planes to his credit. He and McGuire had been friendly rivals all these months. When it came to combat against the enemy they had been good teammates and it had forged a strong bond between the comrades. The party was wild.

There was no combat to fly now, and they stayed up late and did a lot of drinking. The whole 433rd Squadron area was involved in the party and they thought it was a good chance to strike a blow against the Commanding Officer of their rival squadron. A young pilot, Lt. Joe Price, had some Limburger Cheese he'd brought back from Australia. Nobody liked it and it smelled. Price saw McGuire's 500-hour hat lying on a table, and amidst the singing and many toasts, rubbed Limburger Cheese in the prized chapeau.[9]

McGuire got in his jeep and drove back to the 431st Squadron area. The road was muddy from recent rains and the jeep skidded on a curve and ran into a ditch. McGuire stumbled from the jeep unhurt, and fell in the mud. He left the jeep in the ditch and found his way back to his tent where he fell on his bunk and went to sleep in his clothes. He woke the next morning coated from head to foot with dried mud, and with the mysterious smell of the Limburger Cheese in his hat. He said, "Damn, those sons-o'-bitches at the 433rd play rough. Somebody shit in my hat!"

In the midst of the calm of mid-September, Dick Bong returned from the United States. Bong had met many high officials in Washington, had visited Eddie Rickenbacker, and had toured the United States. The press had followed him everywhere, and he was to be featured in several magazine articles.

There had been talk that he wasn't coming back, but he took gunnery training while he was in the States, and he was back to test out his new training. He was assigned to the Fifth Fighter Command as a gunnery instructor, which meant that he could fly anywhere he wanted to. He'd certainly go where the action was.

McGuire had hoped that he would pass Bong's record while he was gone, but there just hadn't been any action. It had been two wasted months. McGuire bristled when he heard that Bong met with Rickenbacker while back in the states. McGuire had always wanted to meet the man his uncle had known, but instead Bong had been given the opportunity. It was like rubbing salt into his wounds--being "number two" again.

McGuire was the top ace around while Bong was gone, and with Lindbergh there too, he saw the press often. Now that Bong was back and Lindbergh was gone, McGuire was sure that the reporters would flock back to Bong. McGuire said he didn't care---Marilynn had written that reporters were calling her for interviews, too. He wrote her: *"I hope the press is not too much for you....You see what I mean when I say we will have trouble having any privacy when I just get back."*

Since the first P-38 had gone into service in the Army Air Corps, pilots were warned to refrain from putting the plane in a high-speed dive. The plane had a problem known as compressibility. Simply, the plane might not pull-out of a high-speed dive. In late September, McGuire flew a new P-38L, equipped with dive flaps on the lower surface of the wings, which were supposed to solve the pull-out problem. McGuire took the P-38L to 25,000 feet and put it into a steep dive. The air speed indicator showed 550 miles-an-hour before he tried the dive flaps.[10] They worked beautifully and solved the compressibility problem which had plagued the P-38. It would make a high-speed dive a much safer way to escape from a Zero. He also tried the flaps to maneuver the plane. Although the controls were in an awkward position, he found that the P-38 could turn much quicker when the flaps were extended, and he knew he had a new trick to try against a Zero, in combat.

He wrote Marilynn: *"I can say I will be home for Christmas. ...Harry (*someone he and Marilynn had known in Texas*) looks good but he's getting a little fat. We got a little bit drunk when we got together and just sat & wished we were back in San Antonio...As far as I know, you can't apply for a regular commission now but I think I have a very good chance of getting one."*

At the end of the month McGuire wrote Marilynn: *"Got the day off...It's a damn good thing we had the day off too, as one of my boys got a case of Coca Cola from the Navy and since 'Pappy' Cline & P. V. Morriss who live in my tent each had a bottle of Aussie rum (vile stuff but potent) we had a party. It's that dark thick rum and gives you an awful hangover, of course this climate helps too. We all got up saying never again this morning. (There is a big bird that sleeps in a tree over looking our tent who starts making loud & very unmusical noises about 0600 so when he started we all got out our 45s & took a shot. I don't believe any of us came within 6 feet of the damned bird but at least he flew off & let us go back to bed.)"*

McGuire and his tentmates had awakened the whole camp with the gunfire. Enlisted men came from their tents carrying rifles and machine guns, thinking some isolated Japanese might have wandered into their camp. Instead they saw their Commanding Officer and some of the crack pilots of the squadron wearing only their shorts and their gun belts, wandering around the camp shooting at the tops of the palm trees. It was not a pretty sight.

[1] 431st Daily History
[2] 475th Daily History
[3] Ibid.
[4] *The Last Hero*, Walter S. Ross
[5] *The Wartime Journal of Charles Lindbergh*
[6] 431st Daily History
[7] Ibid.
[8] Ibid.
[9] Joe Price, 433rd Pilot
[10] 431st Daily History

36

"I don't think many people have thought of McGuire as a commander. The way the enlisted men were kept in that theater (many over 30 months), it took a sensitive person to really get the best out of them, and McGuire had that capability. ...I would say that McGuire and Jay T. Robbins, Commander of the 80th Fighter Squadron, were probably the best two commanders in the Fifth Fighter Command."

---- A long time pilot of the 431st Ftr. Sqd.

Not all of the men of the 431st Squadron fully appreciated Major McGuire as a commander. He was opinionated and decisive and sometimes landed pretty hard on his men. Lieutenants Merle Pearson and Kenneth Hart were assigned to work on the flight line with the maintenance crews for a week, for mishandling their aircraft. It was very much like punishment McGuire had seen "Uncle Jimmy" Hancock, the police chief in Sebring, hand out to troublemakers. Hancock, instead of charging them with a crime, once assigned a group of boys to sweep the city streets early each morning, after they had broken some city street lights. Some of the men thought this type of punishment was demeaning and inappropriately applied to officers.

Lieutenant John Tilley was another pilot who often felt the sting of McGuire's command. Tilley and the 431st had been flying boring patrol missions for several months. The only action they had seen was the "rat racing" on the way back to the base. One day Tilley flew his three-hour patrol and chose to make a test on the way home. He'd heard that a wing tank could be dropped in the sea and then incinerated by gunfire. He tried it and found that the sea became an inferno. He felt that it might be a good tactic to use on a small enemy vessel.

When Tilley landed, word got to McGuire that Tilley had dropped his auxiliary fuel tank and he had fired his guns. McGuire knew there had been no combat and he asked Tilley why he had dropped his wing tank and fired his guns. McGuire wasn't pleased with Tilley's answer and proceeded to give him a lecture on the cost of the wing tank and the importance of keeping them when it wasn't necessary to drop them.[1] The breach between McGuire and Tilley was widened when McGuire asked Tilley to clean the guns on his own P-38. Tilley, the son of a high-ranking Army officer, was sure his father would never treat his officers the way McGuire treated his.

Another time McGuire stood in front of Tilley's P-38 and gave him hand signals to rev his engines and taxi through a swale in a parking area of a new field. McGuire gave Tilley an impatient wave to advance his throttles. Tilley was irritated by the signal. He felt like an adult being directed into a parking lot by a Boy Scout who was too young to drive, but he advanced his throttles and taxied the P-38 forward into the dip. The angle of the ground and the low position of the plane's main wheels caused a propeller to hit the high spot his nose gear had just taxied over. McGuire was furious. The propeller only required a buffing to remove a rough spot, but McGuire gave Tilley some grief.

Another time Tilley was taking off for a mission when he suffered a malfunction. As his plane rose from the runway the canopy popped open on one side. Tilley grabbed the latch and tried to pull the canopy shut, but he needed one hand to fly the plane. As his airspeed increased, he had to let go. The canopy ripped off, leaving Tilley exposed to the elements. Tilley circled the airfield and landed safely. When McGuire returned he lectured Tilley about checking the latches before take-off. Tilley's mechanic always latched one side of the canopy and Tilley the other. He knew he was responsible and didn't need the lecture just then.

McGuire wasn't the only officer who had special forms of punishment. Colonel MacDonald once issued orders creating the "Japanese Air Medal."* It was a large, gaudy badge which was to be worn by "any member of the 475th Fighter Group who, by his conspicuous poor judgment and unyielding resistance to the dictates of common sense, has distinguished himself and has made a substantial contribution to the cause of Japan." The medal was to be called by its initials J.A.M., and anyone getting the award would certainly be in a jam. There is no indication that the medal was ever issued, but full particulars were distributed to all squadron commanders, and a medal design was published.

On September 23 enlisted men of the 475th Group donned "Class A" uniforms for the first time in over a year. They polished shoes and brass so they could stand inspection and serve as honor guards at a presentation ceremony. General Wurtsmith was going to present medals to the pilots of the group.

One corporal complained, "Why do we have to get all polished up like a bunch of USO commandos? None of the enlisted men will be getting medals today."

A sergeant replied, "If you want medals you should be in the Infantry. Our pilots have put their asses on the line. I guess it's a fair deal. They are the ones that are dying--they get the medals."

General Wurtsmith presented the medals, over 150 in all. McGuire received six Air Medals, four Distinguished Flying Crosses, and two Silver Stars. His total of 12 medals presented at this ceremony is truly a remarkable event, maybe never matched in Air Force history.

McGuire receiving one of 12 medals from General Wurtsmith

The General praised all members of the group. "This has been a team effort. You men on the ground have been just as important as the men who do the flying. We've got the Nips on the run, and nobody could have done it alone. It's been quiet lately, but that's going to change. You will be moving soon. I can't tell you where, but it will be nearer to Japan. Keep up the good work!"

That evening a little more equity was in evidence as Major McGuire threw a squadron party and invited all officers and enlisted men. It was the first time in the squadron's history that a party was held for all members of the squadron regardless of their rank. McGuire had acquired, through a Fat Cat flight, enough cheese and bread to serve cheese sandwiches to everyone. Lobster and caviar wouldn't have been appreciated more by these men who were perpetually hungry. McGuire also furnished lemon drink spiked with medical alcohol to wash down the sandwiches.

The lemon drink was like oil--it lubricated away feelings of discontent and soon the officers and enlisted men were singing arm-in-arm, like school chums. "Down by the Old Mill Stream" and "How Dry I Am" were the favorites along with their own special squadron songs,

276

"Beside a Guinea Waterfall" and "A Pilot in Sydney." Everyone wondered why they hadn't had parties as a unit before.[2]

The next morning Major McGuire was up early and proclaimed a day of rest for everyone in the squadron. It was an unprecedented action. Most of the men would have been of little use, as they still had the taste of lemon drink in their mouths. A new record was set for squadron sack time in one day, and the troops speculated about the upcoming move mentioned by General Wurtsmith. The Squadron Historian recorded the following conversation among the enlisted men at the barber shop:

"'I understand we're going to the Philippines,' said one.

'We can't be,' countered another. 'We haven't even invaded the Philippines yet.'

'I know that,' butts in the barber, 'but I got the straight dinkum. Honest, I can't tell you where I got it, but it's the dinkum..... We're going in on the 3rd wave!'

'Sure we're going to P.I.,' insists still another. 'Do you know what the Quartermaster issued to the 49th?'

'No, what?'

'Rubber prophylactics!'

'No kidding?'

'Yup--straight stuff.'--Here there was an exchange of meaningful glances as several rather relished the prospect of bathing their souls in impropriety."[3]

There was a group who thought the next move would be to Morotai Island of the Halmaheras Group. The Japanese had recently been forced to leave their installations there, and it would follow the pattern set over the last year of making small jumps forward.

Tokyo Rose knew as much about the 475th Fighter Group's future moves as did the enlisted men. She had broadcast about Charles Lindbergh's visit while he was still flying with the Group. Japanese papers found on Biak indicated that the Japanese had been breaking our coded messages. They had the complete plans for the American attack on Biak, before the invasion had begun. Tokyo Rose's secret was out---she wasn't intuitive, just well connected with some code breakers.[4]

Instructions came from the Fifth Air Force that a higher grade cipher must be used in the future to prevent the decoding of messages. Still the troops listened to Tokyo Rose each night to see if she had any ideas about their move.

McGuire wasn't feeling well. He was running a fever, and was having chills and sweating. The medics confirmed that he was having a recurrence of malaria. He was grounded until the disease ran its course. His weight dropped down to 119 pounds.

On October 5 the order came to start loading squadron equipment on the boats--almost everyone would be in the water echelon this time--only a few key people would be air echelon for this move. The pilots and a few mechanics would stay back until the new field was ready. This seemed to indicate that the move was going to be a long one, and that meant the Philippines!

The showers were taken down and loaded on the ship and everyone had to resort to helmet baths until the new base was established. The food was even worse than normal--the unbearable Aussie "bully beef" or some unrecognizable dehydrated vegetable concoction. It was no great loss when the mess hall was knocked down. The 431st Squadron started eating with 433rd Squadron, where the food was equally bad. The men could only hope that food would be more plentiful and more palatable wherever they were headed.

The water echelon of 431st was soaked by a rainstorm as they loaded aboard the S S Charlotte Cushman, a liberty ship, at 10:00 p.m. At 4:00 a.m. the ship sailed for Hollandia to refuel and wait for a convoy to form.[5]

McGuire remained with his pilots at Biak. He heard that Dick Bong had resumed flying with Colonel George Walker's 9th Fighter Squadron, Bong's and McGuire's old outfit. On his first mission Bong got two Japanese planes to bring his total to 30. McGuire just shook his head in wonder and said, "It figures! The whole time Bong's been gone Japanese planes have been as scarce as hen's teeth. When Bong gets back they show up again."

McGuire got the new P-38L he had asked for and Sergeant Jeschke did a masterful job of painting "Pudgy V" on the nose, making it a large, flamboyant insignia. He put the 21 Japanese flags in a spot which left plenty of space for more. He was sure that the move to the Philippines would bring plenty of opportunities for his Squadron Commander.

McGuire just couldn't stand by while Bong built higher totals. He'd been back on flying status for a week, and had been flying locally. The 431st Squadron was not assigned to fly, so McGuire flew three-and-a-half hours to Morotai, an island northwest of New Guinea, where fighters were staging for a long mission. The next day he tacked on with the 9th Fighter Squadron and flew a seven-and-a-half hour bomber escort mission to Balikpapan, Borneo. The B-24s had made several air raids on the Japanese-operated Pandasari refineries, and had suffered heavy losses.

The bombers had made their first raids without fighter escorts because the flying distance was 1,000 miles one way. Now the P-38s could make the distance from the newly captured and repaired field at Moro

McGuire and new PUDGY V with 25 Japanese flags and room for more

tai, with the addition of larger belly tanks, and full employment of the Lindbergh cruising techniques. A number of P-38s from the 13th Fighter Command had to turn back because they lacked the fuel to complete the mission.

Over the target they were intercepted by 50 Japanese fighters. Twenty Japanese planes flew high above the bomber formations and dropped aerial burst bombs, hoping the explosions would knock down the planes before they could reach their targets. McGuire was flying wingman for his old friend from his Alaska days, Major Gerald Johnson. He stayed with Johnson through two passes and then picked out an Oscar and blasted it from dead astern. The Oscar burst into flames and the pilot bailed out.

Next, McGuire used the dive flaps on his new P-38L to turn with another Oscar which he hit from 20 degrees deflection. It started smoking and fell off in a spin from 15,000 feet. He then turned and attacked a Hamp and saw large chunks of the plane's tail break away before it burst into flames and crashed.

After firing at several other Japanese planes without any visible results, he chased a Tojo from 14,000 feet down to 3,000 feet. The Tojo had a sizable lead and McGuire could only close the distance by placing his plane in a dive that raised his airspeed to 500-miles-an-hour. He fired several bursts which heavily damaged the Tojo, and finally at 1,500 feet he hit it again and sent it into the ocean below.[6] McGuire had downed four enemy planes, but he had no witness for the second one, and didn't get credit for it. He was able to confirm two victories for Jerry Johnson.

The enemy pilots were skilled and aggressive, but disorganized. A total of 35 enemy planes were brought down. A single B-24 went down, and a P-47 fighter was mistakenly shot down by a P-38, but the pilot escaped and was rescued.

Lt. Joe Forester of the 432nd Fighter Squadron shot down a Zeke and then came under enemy fire. A violent roll and dive freed him of the enemy plane and his dive flaps were a life saver as he pulled out so low that he had ocean spray on his windshield. His left engine was hit, lost oil pressure, and had to be shut down. He almost ditched at sea but firing his ammo lightened the plane. He then flew 900 miles, on one engine, with a vector relayed to him by Lt. Ratajki, flying 5000 feet above the Morotai GCI radar, which Joe couldn't raise on his radio from sea level. His new P-38, Florida Cracker, was so badly damaged that it never flew again--the parts being salvaged to keep other P-38s flying.

McGuire's total was now 24 enemy planes destroyed, and he was within six of Dick Bong, the closest he had ever been. Each squadron kept careful figures on their conquests, and the pilots of the 431st Squadron were disappointed when McGuire's three victories were credited to their rivals, the 9th Fighter Squadron, rather than to the 431st[7].

McGuire's new-found joy over getting back into action and increasing his score was short lived. Colonel MacDonald, who had just resumed command of the 475th Group, learned that McGuire had flown with the 9th Fighter Squadron and told him that he would be grounded if he pulled a stunt like that again without permission.

---

* The existence of the Japanese Air Medal has been challenged but it is described and pictured in the 475th Group History microfilm.

[1] John Tilley
[2] 431st Daily history
[3] Ibid.
[4] Ibid.
[5] Ibid.
[6] Ibid.
[7] Ibid.

37

"Leyte was the real war. For the first time we found ourselves living in a battlefield. The Japanese were so close that they were able to bomb and strafe Tacloban day and night. The landing strip was so crowded that we hardly had a place to park another airplane. The 49th Group was the first and only Air Corps unit in the Philippines for about a week, the other fields were too muddy to support any flying. We needed help, and a wave of excitement went through the field when we saw the red-spinnered P-38s of McGuire's squadron arriving. If we could have had only one more fighter plane on the field, we'd rather have had McGuire than anyone else we could think of."

------Robert DeHaven, Operations Officer 7th Fighter Squadron

"The following instructions from the Commander-in-Chief, Southwest Pacific area through the Commanding General, Far East Air Forces, are published for your information and necessary action:

'It must be understood by all that the liberation of the Filipinos is one of the purposes of the Philippine campaign. Liberation will not be understood by the Filipinos if their possessions, their homes, their civilization and their lives are indiscriminately destroyed to accomplish it. Throughout the far East our moral standing and humanity dictate that destruction of property and lives in the Philippines be held to a minimum in our military campaigns compatible with the insurance of success. Evidence is accumulating that the Japanese in some localities are leaving Filipinos in residence, evacuating cities, either compelling the Filipinos to stay, or failing to warn them. In order to insure our success, our objective in areas we are to occupy is the total destruction of hostile efforts. Aerial bombing offers by far the greatest destruction effect. Port facilities that we plan to use we must preserve to the extent possible. Our attack objectives are primarily shipping and air fields in the latter areas, not barracks, villages or metropolitan areas. Any hostile effort which may tend to strengthen resistance of our occupation objectives we weaken or neutralize in other areas'

----(Sgd MacArthur, Sgd Kenney)"

All members of the Army Air Corps were required to read and sign this statement. Few warriors in the history of warfare have ever been asked to exercise such care in a battle zone.

On October 16, 1944, the 431st Squadron water echelon sailed after sitting in Humboldt Bay for four days. Because of the many troops on board only two official meals a day were served, but the Navy cooks sneaked food to the men between meals. On Biak, where he stayed to command the pilots and their P-38s, McGuire wrote to Marilynn: *"Well, we got in some action at last. I shot down 3 nips over Borneo the other day. It was the longest fighter mission ever pulled...Col. MacDonald got back the other day from the states. I asked him when I would be going home and he promised I would be there by New Years, so about 2 more months and we'll be together again."*

Several days later he wrote to her again: *"Saw the General the other day after our decoration ceremony and he said I should get out around the last of Dec., so looks like a Very Happy New Year, Mrs. McGuire .... I checked out as 1st pilot on a B-24. Flies like a truck, I still like fighters."*

On October 23 the 431st Squadron water echelon and its convoy sailed into Tacloban harbor, on the northeastern end of Leyte, the Philippines. Immediately, Japanese torpedo and dive bombers attacked the 78-ship convoy. The airmen aboard the S. S. Cushman were petrified by the attack, which lasted three hours. None of them had ever been under direct attack, and there were no slit trenches to hide in. The ship was a sitting target and the Japanese attacked it often but with no appreciable damage. The Navy gun crew on the Cushman shot down two Japanese planes. One almost hit them but it crashed harmlessly aft of the ship.

For two days the ship sat at anchor and was attacked by the Japanese during the day and the night. This was Japanese-held territory and the U.S. Navy provided air cover for the convoy, and they were badly outnumbered. The men of the 431st Squadron wondered why their own P-38s weren't available to defend the ships. Weather was the answer. Days of rain had rendered the air fields at Tacloban and Dulag pools of mud, and unsuitable for fighter operations. On the fourth day mechanics from the 431st Squadron were put ashore to service carrier-based Navy planes. Their ships were disabled, and they had been forced to land at Tacloban or Dulag. Of the 65 planes, 20 nosed over and were seriously damaged while trying to land in the mud. [1]

The majority of the 431st men remained frightened spectators in the harbor as bombs missed the ship by as little as 30 feet. The closest one proved to be a dud. The men went crazy as they watched jumpy Navy gunners aboard the S.S. Cushman shoot down a U.S. Navy TBF torpedo bomber. They shouted and waved at the gun crews, to no avail. The noise of the battle drowned out their warnings. The next two days they instructed green Navy gun crews on aircraft identification.

On October 27 the water echelon of the 431st Squadron was put ashore to try and ready the strips for the arrival of their P-38s. The strips were subjected to air raids day and night, and Japanese soldiers were lurking just outside the camp. There were shooting incidents each night, and everyone slept with their rifle nearby, but they were glad to be ashore.

The 475th Fighter Group was scheduled to be the first fighter organization stationed in the Philippines, but their new field at Dulag was muddy and unusable. The 49th Fighter Group was able to move into their new base at Tacloban, thus being the first Army Air Corps unit to "return." Dick Bong was with them and on the first day at Tacloban, shot down his 31st and 32nd enemy planes. The next day he got two more to bring his total to 34. This put McGuire down by 10, and he was twiddling his thumbs back on Biak.

On November first, the 431st Fighter Squadron flew into Tacloban, from Morotai. It was a eight-hundred-mile flight across the Equator into the Northern Hemisphere, and the planes were low on fuel and the pilots tired and ready to land when they arrived over Tacloban strip on Leyte.

A call came from the Tacloban fighter control: "Hades Squadron! This is Tacloban control. We have reports of a bandit in the area. Be careful, you may be jumped when you try to land!"

McGuire replied, "Tacloban control. This is Major McGuire. I still have a little fuel remaining. I'm staying aloft while my squadron lands!"

As the 431st Squadron circled and landed, McGuire spotted a Tojo fighter and gave chase. In full view of the Tacloban air strip, McGuire attacked and shot down the enemy plane with one short burst. The Tojo crashed in flames just outside the air field boundaries. McGuire checked the sky. Finding no other enemy planes, he circled and landed on his last few drops of fuel.

He taxied to the parking area where pilots and ground personnel applauded like they had just witnessed a stunt at an air show. Many of them had never seen a dogfight or an enemy plane shot down--those things always happened at some distant place. McGuire climbed from his plane and said, "This is my kind of place! You have to shoot down Japs to land on your own field!"

Many of the new pilots in the 431st Fighter Squadron had never been in combat or even seen it before. Biak had been boringly calm over the last few months. One of the neophytes wondered how much McGuire had led the Tojo, and asked, "How many rings did you lead him, Major?"

McGuire answered, "I don't know. I didn't have time to turn on the gunsight!"

Later, armorers checked McGuire's ammunition, and found that he had used only 18 rounds of 20 MM cannon shells and an equivalent amount of ammunition in each of the four 50-caliber machine guns.

McGuire and the 431st Fighter Squadron had flown the great distance across the South Philippine Sea to deliver their aircraft to the 49th Fighter Group, as replacements for damaged aircraft. The Japanese had over 500 airplanes stationed in the Philippine Islands, and many of the 49th Group's 40 P-38s had been damaged on the ground by enemy bombs. McGuire was disappointed that his squadron was being defrocked by the high command. Replacement planes were needed but there wasn't room for the 431st Squadron to operate at Tacloban.

Because of McGuire's position as a squadron commander he was not obliged to surrender "Pudgy V," and he was allowed to fly with the 49th Group until the field at Dulag could be opened. After flying in from Morotai and shooting down an enemy plane, McGuire might well have called it a day. Instead he joined a four-man afternoon flight that was designated the "Fatcat." It deserved the title by virtue of its members: Major Gerald Johnson, Major Richard Bong, Captain Robert DeHaven and McGuire. At the war's end the four men would have accounted for a total of 114 enemy planes. No other American flight, in any war, has boasted four such sharpshooters. Only DeHaven scored on the flight, but McGuire was satisfied just to get oriented to the area.[2]

The return of American forces to the Philippines was one of the biggest events of the war. It had been declared so by General MacArthur when he had said, "I shall return." The press was there to cover it firsthand. The day after he arrived, McGuire was besieged by the press. They had been covering Bong, but they were eager to meet the man everyone said was trying to unseat Bong as the Number One Ace. The press had never had access to both Bong and McGuire at the same time. Bong had faced the Fourth Estate for a long time, and it had proved to be a challenge. Now it was going to be a problem for McGuire, too.

Reporters interviewed them both and tried to get them to say something about the other guy. Neither Bong nor McGuire would have any part of it. They both professed their friendship for each other. A reporter asked McGuire, "The Stars and Stripes has been carrying a box score on you two lately. What plan do you have to catch Bong?"

McGuire said, "Dick Bong and I are friends, and have been since we were in the 9th Fighter Squadron together. We are not about to get involved in some silly competition which might put our lives at risk. It isn't worth it. We're here to win the war, not some mythical title."[3]

McGuire posing for **Time** magazine with members of his old outfit, the 49th Fighter Group. L to R: Walker, Morrisey, Johnson, Mathre, Jordan, Bong, McGuire and DeHaven Tacloban Air Field, Leyte, P.I. November 2, 1944 (Photo from R. M. DeHaven collection)

The second day McGuire was at Tacloban, he posed in front of a P-38 with seven other flyers for a **Time** magazine photographer. He was among friends: Colonel George Walker, outgoing CO of the 49th Fighter Group, Colonel Robert Morrisey, Fifth Fighter Command; Major Gerald Johnson, incoming CO 49th Fighter Group; Major Wallace Jordan, CO 9th Fighter Squadron; Robert DeHaven, Operations Officer of the 7th Fighter Squadron; Lieutenant Milden Mathre, 7th Fighter Squadron, who had just shot down the 49th Group's 500th Japanese plane; and Richard Bong. These were among the best fighter pilots in the Pacific and the picture eventually appeared in **Time** magazine, on January 1, 1945. It wasn't the last time McGuire would hear from the national press. He would talk to them almost every day thereafter.

On the third day at Tacloban, McGuire and 13 other P-38s dive-bombed Japanese shipping at Ormoc Bay. They were flying at 8,000-feet on the way back to Tacloban when they spotted an eight-mile-long Japanese convoy on the Valencia-Ormoc road.

The 14 P-38s dropped down to tree-top level and strafed the trucks, tanks and troops. They made several passes, until all their ammunition was expended. They left 35 tanks and trucks burning. They later learned that they had stopped a full Army division from reinforcing Japanese troops which were engaging the American Army. The strafing cost the Japanese 3,000 casualties.[4]

There were no American losses, but on his last run, McGuire felt a sting in his buttocks, and moments later saw smoke pour from one of his engines. He feathered the prop and shifted over to single-engine operation, which he knew so well from past experience. He made the trip back to Tacloban and landed safely.

When McGuire landed he had to call for a tow on his airplane, since he couldn't taxi it on one engine. When he reached the parking area he was slow in climbing out of his plane. One of the ground crewmen said, "Major, it looks like you took quite a bit of small arms fire! Is there something wrong?"

"Yeah, the plane took a beating. There's blood in here and I'm not sure where it's coming from. I think I got shot in the ass!"[5]

McGuire crawled out of the plane slowly, and discovered that he had been sitting in a pool of blood. A small caliber bullet had passed between his buttocks and his parachute, just creasing him.

He said, "It doesn't hurt. How about keeping this under your hat. I don't want one of those saw-bones telling me that I can't fly! Hell, they can't even cure jungle rot."[6]

McGuire had inflamed heat rash, or jungle rot as it was called, so bad that his body was always painted purple with gentian violet, from his crotch to his armpits. McGuire wasn't alone with the purple armpits---medics painted so many GIs' bodies with the fungicide that they developed their own styles, and even signed their work like an artist[7]. With the jungle rot, and his new wound, McGuire waddled when he walked, and he couldn't sit down. He even stood up while playing a few rounds of poker. His friends thought it was just the jungle rot, as he kept the recent wound a secret, even from his own men.

The remaining members of the 431st Squadron flew in from Biak with 23 new P-38Ls. Most of McGuire's squadron was now on Leyte but they had no place to settle. They were shifted to Buri strip which had housed Japanese three days before. Even though he was in pain when he sat down, McGuire borrowed another P-38 and flew 12 hours over the next two days.

Several days later he was on patrol over Tacloban when he intercepted an Oscar. He maneuvered in close before shooting, because he was uncertain of the borrowed plane's gunsight, having never fired its guns. When he fired on the Oscar it turned into a ball of fire that exploded in all directions. He tried to fly clear of the flying wreckage, but unavoidably flew through a ball of fire and a shower of aircraft parts.

He saw a flash in front of his windshield, and was instantly stunned. He lost consciousness momentarily--and thought he had blacked-out. He had a sharp pain in the top of his head, and there was wind rushing into the cockpit. He felt his head and drew back a bloody hand. As he regained his senses, McGuire realized that part of the Japanese plane had hit the top of his plane's canopy. It had smashed the Plexiglas and had struck him in the head. The P-38 wasn't otherwise damaged. He returned to Tacloban without further complications.

When McGuire parked his plane one of the ground crew came onto the wingwalk to help him with his gear. He would normally have raised the canopy, but he saw that much of it was missing, and that McGuire had a bloody head. He said, "Christ! Are you all right, Major?"

"Yeah," replied McGuire. "I almost brought an Oscar home with me this time. Can you fix this plane? I'm too embarrassed to borrow another one."

"We can fix it. It's just the canopy. Don't you think you need to see the Doc on this one, Major?"

"No, let's keep this quiet, too. I got an Oscar today. I don't want to lay around while the hunting is so good."

That single victory, on November 10, tied McGuire with Eddie Rickenbacker's World War I victory record. It was a record McGuire had dreamed of breaking. He thought about it quietly. It was "old hat" now---Joe Foss, of the Marine Corps had matched the record, and "Pappy" Boyington, of the Marine Corps, and Bong had broken the record. It was special to McGuire. He knew his Uncle Charles would be particularly proud, as would his Dad.

Two days later McGuire was involved in the interception of five of the new, highly touted Japanese Navy Jack fighter planes. The streamlined Jack was thought to be a Japanese version of the German Messerschmitt, but it was not. "Pappy" Cline and visiting Colonel W.T. Hudnell of Headquarters, Far East Air Force, followed McGuire, in pursuit of the agile enemy planes. McGuire had to chase one of the Jacks from the Colonel's tail, and then dispersed one from the tail of visiting Major Jack Rittmayer, an old friend from his Alaskan days. The P-38Ls were able to turn as tight a turn as the enemy and McGuire flamed two of them quickly, while Cline and Hudnell got one each.[8]

These victories were exciting to the visiting Colonel who had never shot down an enemy plane, and to "Pappy" Cline who got his second victory. McGuire's victories were landmarks, although they would go largely unheralded. The victories made McGuire's total 28, and moved him ahead of Rickenbacker's and Joe Foss's total, and tied him in the Number Two Ace's position with "Pappy" Boyington. Only Richard

Bong, who now had run his total to 36, had ever shot down more enemy planes than McGuire, and he planned to catch Bong.

McGuire's ability to stay in combat after suffering personal injuries added to the folklore about him. He continued to be indestructible, and some started calling him the "Iron Major." General Kenney was one of the believers. He knew everything that went on in his command. Every time Bong or McGuire did something General Kenney heard about it. He knew McGuire had gotten his head creased and marveled that he had come through a tough spot again. Still, he thought it might be time to take some action. He wrote McGuire a letter and told him to refrain from dangerous missions such as strafing, and dive bombing, and glide bombing. He went on to mention that McGuire was too valuable to the Air Force, as a leader, to put himself in risk. The Army considered Bong "too valuable to risk" as a post war hero, and Kenney had restricted his activities on direct orders from General Arnold in the Pentagon. General Kenney put McGuire on his list of "too valuable to risk" and restricted his activities, too.

[1]431st Daily History
[2]Robert DeHaven's Combat Report
[3]An AP wire story carried in newspapers nationally
[4]McGuire Broadcast on CBS Radio
[5]Frank Kish, McGuire's crew chief
[6]Ibid.
[7]*Doctors at War, Eli Lilly Co.*
[8]McGuire's Combat Report

38

"On Leyte you could get killed real easy. A Jap plane might come over at anytime. They wanted to hit our planes on the ground. If you were working around the planes you were in dangerous territory, especially just about day break--that was their favorite time for an attack."

----Sgt. Frank Kish, McGuire's Crew Chief

"That was McGuire for you. He got the men to go back out there. They returned because he was 'McGuire' and he asked them to do it."

---Lt. Douglas Thropp, Pilot in 431st Fighter Squadron

On November 5, McGuire flew three missions and was in the air over seven hours.[1] In the evening he wrote to his wife, Marilynn: *"There has been quite a bit of action. I got one more, shot down a Jap fighter the other day. We have had a few bombing & strafing raids. The little bastards come over at dawn & dusk everyday & also all night, but after the first few days they quit coming over during the middle of the day. We all have nice deep holes next to our cots, really handy sometimes. We haven't had a good bath outside of using a tin hat, which is not too good a substitute...We eat 10-1 rations which is about the best emergency rations there is...It's pretty damp here this time of the year but a lot better than New Guinea. The people are very friendly and seem glad to see us...My plane, 'Pudgy V', got shot up a bit but she brought me home OK and can be fixed up in a few days. I am OK, picked up a small piece of shrapnel but nothing serious---a small piece of adhesive tape fixed me up. I am writing this so you won't start imagining things if you read about it in the papers. ... I still plan to be home New Years, things look damn good for it."*

Sergeant Frank Kish had been McGuire's crew chief almost from the start. Like McGuire, Kish was an "ex-49er"---they'd both been with the 49th Fighter Group before being drafted into the 475th Fighter Group. Kish was an old-timer with over 30 months in the advanced war zone. He wanted to stay as long as McGuire stayed, and he wanted to be McGuire's crew chief when they both got back to the States---McGuire had promised he would be.

Kish was from Sharon, Pennsylvania, a small town on the Ohio state line. He had joined the Army at Jefferson Barracks, Missouri, and had no idea he would end up in the Air Corps. He had good mechanical skills, but had not been sent to aircraft and engine school. Instead he had learned to be an aircraft mechanic with "on-the-job" training. He learned well and McGuire, who was very demanding when it came to the maintenance of his plane, was sure Kish was the best crew chief in the 431st Squadron.

Kish idolized McGuire and made sure "Pudgy" was always in the best possible condition. When McGuire landed after a long flight Kish would be waiting at the revetment to check the plane. While the engines were still hot he would open up the cowling and dowse the engines with aviation gasoline. The gasoline cleaned the engines down to the paint job, and gave Kish a good look at everything. He'd then go over every hose and every wire to be sure that nothing had been damaged in the flight just completed.

Kish kept the exterior of the plane just as clean, and he always kept a canvas over the canopy to protect the Plexiglas. Kish knew that McGuire liked a clean airplane and he tried to keep it that way. After a flight, McGuire might complain, "Frank, she ran a little rough today."

Kish would change the spark plugs, check all the wiring and make sure the engine purred for the next day's flight. When McGuire would return, he'd say, "Frank, you've got her singing today."

Kish was constantly bending trim tabs or making other adjustments to make the plane perform the way McGuire wanted it to. He was constantly trading for or begging parts to keep Pudgy in perfect operating order. In appreciation of his hard work McGuire would slip Kish extra food or a couple of beers he'd had brought in on the Fat Cat. When McGuire flew patrol, where combat was not likely, Kish would place his canteen full of water in the battery compartment in the booms of the P-38. After McGuire had flown at high altitude for several hours, where the temperatures were below freezing, the canteen would be icy-cold. This would afford Kish a cold drink of water--a rarity in the tropics. When beer was available Kish would put five or six of them in the battery compartment and enjoy cold beers after McGuire's flight.

It was in this spirit of cooperation between McGuire and his crew chief that a new idea was hatched. McGuire had said, "I wish I could get off the ground quicker when those Zeros come over the field. Here in the Philippines they can come at any moment and I'd like to get off the ground and get them."

Kish proposed, "Suppose we come down here before daybreak and pre-flight the planes. Then when we hear a warning, we'll start the engines--when you get here the plane will be ready to take off."

McGuire called his crew chiefs together in the evening and asked them to preflight all planes for their pilots. There were groans from the enlisted men. One spoke up, "Major, it's dangerous around those planes early in the morning. The Japs want to bomb them. If we're out there with the planes when they come over, our ass is in a sling!"

McGuire said, "I know you'd be safer in a slit trench, but this is important. I'm willing to put my ass on the line to shoot down the Japs--you guys should be willing to help us get off quicker. How else are we ever going to run those bastards off?"

Another crew chief replied, "If we had somebody who would let us know when the Japs are coming we could jump in a slit trench until they go by."

"O K," replied McGuire. "You've got a deal! I'll stand watch while you guys work. I'll warn you if they come."[2]

The next morning, before daybreak, McGuire stood in the middle of the runway opposite the 431st's P-38s and scanned the skies for enemy planes. He held his 45 automatic in his hand to fire a warning, but none was needed, while the men worked. Sergeant Jeschke said it again, "A brave man, that Major Mac!" Two days later, while the men pre-flighted the planes, a Japanese plane swooped in over the field and dropped a bomb on two of the P-38s. Six men were seriously hurt. Still they agreed to service the planes early, and the practice continued, making the 431st Squadron the fastest react unit in the Philippines.

Other air fields in the area were under the same sort of attack all during the day. Lieutenant Douglas Thropp, of the 431st Squadron, took off from his home base one morning when a squall line was moving in. After a short flight, during which his wingman never got off the ground to join him, Thropp found himself socked out of his own field. He landed, with a bad oil pump, at the home field of the 49th Fighter Group. He scrounged around and got an oil pump, but had to borrow tools and install it himself because no mechanic would touch his plane. They would work on aircraft from the 49th Group, but the flight line was too dangerous to work on a visitor's plane.[3]

Between the Japanese and the rain, life was miserable on Leyte. The only food was emergency rations, which they had brought from New Guinea. Men from the 475th Group and the 431st Squadron had been strewn over locations a thousand miles apart. Some men were still at Biak, New Guinea, while others were still aboard ships when they left Tacloban Bay to avoid a storm.[4]

The planes were at Tacloban while the ground crews were at mud-locked Dulag and Buri strips. The weather and enemy action made their future uncertain and they suffered from poor housing and food. The crew chiefs rose at 3:00 a.m. and were transported 30 miles from one of the unusable strips, where they were housed, to Tacloban to get the planes into the air by daybreak.

McGuire had cooked his own goose. He'd brought home two damaged P-38s in less than a week. Planes were in short supply. Poor field conditions and frequent Japanese air raids kept many of them grounded. While he waited for Pudgy V to be repaired McGuire hung around the flight line with his crew chiefs.

Early one morning, after the 431st had put up a patrol in borrowed P-38s, McGuire and Colonel Hudnell set about preparing breakfast for themselves and the crew chiefs. As they heated the 10-in-1 rations, they were interrupted by the snarl of four low-flying enemy planes. Strafing began and they jumped into slit trenches, half-full of water. As they crouched in the muck and mire McGuire muttered in frustration, "I wish to hell I was up there! You guys would have your breakfast before it got cold! I've got to get a ride somewhere."

For several days McGuire made the rounds looking for an airplane he could borrow. He had no luck. In desperation he flew three days as a B-25 co-pilot, putting in over 13 hours[5] as a member of a bomber crew. It wasn't a fighter plane, but at least he wasn't sitting on the ground being bombed or strafed.

On November 19, the field at Dulag was deemed suitable for flying. The engineers had laid a steel-mat runway to cover the mud. The remaining pilots of the 475th Fighter Group flew in from Biak and a new Group Headquarters was started at Dulag.

Filipinos were hired to clear the area, build the camp, and to do laundry. After a few days most of the tents were even tended by house boys who welcomed the "Yankee Dollar." The Filipinos were happy to be free again and they showed their appreciation by giving and selling the Americans food, which they badly needed.

During the month many 431st pilots lost their "virginity" in the skies over Leyte. Many of the men had come in as replacements while the squadron was peacefully resting at Biak. Major Dewey, Colonel Hudnell, Lieutenants Hart, Pietz, Koeck, Barnes, Oxford, Moreing, Du-Montier and Ekdahl got their first conquests. Hart and Pietz had three and Koeck and Moreing had two by the end of the month. McGuire had upped his total by four, and the squadron had knocked down 23 enemy planes in just 20 days of operation. One pilot, Lieutenant Erling Varland was lost.

[1]McGuire's Log Book
[2]Frank Kish, McGuire's Crew chief furnished much of the information in this chapter
[3]Douglas Thropp
[4]431st Daily History
[5]McGuire's Log Book

39

".... McGuire is 24 years old. He isn't exactly handsome except for a constant grin. His straight black hair is always tousled. He is almost the exact opposite of Maj. Richard Bong, the only American to better McGuire as a Jap killer. Bong is quiet--so reserved as to be almost cold. McGuire is a fast talking, joking, pilot like those in the movies. .... Properly approached McGuire will go through a play-by-play account, with motions...."

---- Special to **San Antonio Express**,
Copyright, 1944: **Chicago Tribune**

On November 28, during an early morning scramble, a P-38 caught fire and crashed shortly after take off from Tacloban. The pilot was killed instantly. As the morning sky brightened, a rumor buzzed across the field. The P-38 which had crashed was the airplane of Richard Bong, the leading ace in the Air Corps, and it was thought that he was dead. Within an hour it was learned that the plane had been flown by Captain John Davis, the Assistant Operations Officer of the 49th Fighter Group. He had been killed. Bong was safe on the ground.

The news of the accident reached General Kenney and he contacted Richard Bong to restate his concern that he might be staying in combat too long. The deaths of Tom Lynch and Neel Kearby were still in Kenney's mind, along with his instructions from the Pentagon to limit Bong's flying. He asked Bong to continue with his gunnery instructions, but to refrain from dangerous offensive flying.[1]

Richard Bong grumbled, packed a bag, and moved to Dulag to "instruct" with his friend Major Thomas McGuire and his 431st Fighter Squadron. McGuire had told Bong that he was welcome at any time. Bong no longer had an airplane at Tacloban so he decided to accept McGuire's invitation, where he would be out of the spotlight for a while.

Bong had already shot down 16 enemy aircraft when McGuire got his first victory on August 18, 1943. Now, 14 months later, Bong had 36 victories, and McGuire had 28. McGuire had "out gunned" Bong 28 to 20 during the months since he had arrived, and was Bong's only rival for the top position. The others had been killed or had gone home. Eight planes behind was a position McGuire had held almost constantly since March, 1944. He once sneaked to within six of Bong, but fell 10 planes behind in early November. McGuire once told General Kenney, "I guess after the war I'll be known as 'Eight-Behind-McGuire'."[2]

McGuire had suffered periods of inactivity while Bong was in the United States, and later had been ill while Bong was in the States again.

Struggle as he might, McGuire had never been able to take advantage of
Bong's absences. Bong, on the other hand, moved into the Philippines
with the 49th Group a week ahead of McGuire, and had upped his score

Major Richard I. Bong and Major Tommy McGuire 16 Nov. 1944
McGuire was almost gaunt from months of combat life(USAF Photo)

by three before McGuire appeared and increased his score to remain a contender. Now they were together for some toe-to-toe action.

Bong's move to Dulag did not pass unnoticed by the hordes of newsmen who were with the liberation forces in the Philippines. McGuire and Bong were cooperative and even posed together for news-reel photographers. It was a newsman's delight.

Japanese forces had been subdued during November to the extent that American airstrips were not attacked as often during the day. Each night the Japanese did send over enough planes to disrupt sleep. Then, in a surprise move, the Japanese landed hundreds of paratroopers near Dulag and the harassment took on a new danger. Everyone again had to sleep with their rifles nearby.

It was the Japanese by night and the reporters by day. In between, McGuire and his guest managed to get in some flying but they didn't see any combat. McGuire wrote to his wife: *"...Well today is our 2nd anniversary, even though it doesn't seem like it ...I may have to go to Washington. I expect to leave around the last of the month so keep your fingers crossed. ...Dick Bong is staying with me at the present & doing some flying with us. My squadron now has 182 confirmed victories! I am really proud of my outfit, in fact I think it is the best squadron in the Fifth Air Force ...Had a letter from Dad & he is looking forward to seeing us. That's about all the mail I have had outside of a dozen or so fan letters. ..."*

Yes, fan letters in a war zone! McGuire was beginning to get some press. After being mysteriously left out of a **LIFE** magazine article which listed America's 11 top aces, McGuire was now starting to be noticed by the national press. The fan letters were the result, as was the talk about having to make a trip to Washington--presumably on public relations business for the Air Corps.

On December 7, 1944, just three years after the bombing of Pearl Harbor, American fighter planes in the Philippines dealt the Japanese a crushing blow. The Japanese made new attempts to reassert themselves on Leyte, and the Air Corps rose to drive them back. The men at Dulag flew from dawn to dusk. Bong flew with the 431st Squadron as McGuire led them on patrol. They circled Ormac Bay to protect the landing of the Army's 77th Infantry Division. Earlier in the day a Japanese plane had intentionally crashed into an American destroyer and smoke was still rising from the fire on board. Bong spotted a twin-engined Japanese Sally bomber and went after it with his wingman, without bothering to call it in to the rest of the flight. He quickly closed in and set one of the plane's engines on fire. The plane crashed on an island moments later, and Bong rejoined the patrol.

McGuire spotted six Tojos approaching Ormac Bay, for a suicide attack on American shipping. The Japanese planes were being fired on by the Navy ships, but the ack-ack was not effective. McGuire could see that the Naval fire would never be able to hit all six of the Tojos in time to prevent an attack--only his flight could prevent an attack on the ships. He shouted over his radio, "This is Daddy Green leader. We can't wait-- that ack-ack isn't doing any good! Let's get in there after them."[3]

McGuire led his flight into the deadly anti-aircraft fire---picked out a plane on the left side and attacked it from the rear at 30-degrees deflection. The plane burst into flames and crashed before it reached the convoy. He quickly turned and bore in on a second plane, sending it down in flames, too. Lieutenant Floyd Fulkerson and Major Jack Rittmayer followed McGuire in among the black puffs of anti-aircraft fire and each one latched onto an enemy plane, and shot it down. Bong caught the tail-end Charlie, and made a head-on attack which sent it into the sea. Rittmayer also got a Kate bomber which flew into the area.

Later, Lieutenants Ekdahl, Thropp and Provencio, and Captain Champlin each downed an enemy plane. Lieutenant Hart shot down two. When the smoke cleared, the 431st Squadron had shot down 14 enemy planes. Marine and Army pilots shot down 75 Japanese planes before the day was over. It seemed fitting on December 7th.

McGuire wrote to Marilynn: "I got Pudgy V back from the service squadron .... Also Dick Bong & I got into a fight the other day. Dick bagged 2 & I got 2 more. That makes 30 now. Not doing bad .... Pappy, Champ, and myself have quite a shack---the boys built for us. 16 X 32 with sleeping quarters and a living room. We have a bar (not much to serve but at least a bar) and a built on shower, really quite a palace."

Some of the pilots of McGuire's squadron disliked having Dick Bong flying with their squadron. The squadron historian even took time to mention it in the official history of the squadron: "Visiting pilots also gave us a bit of trouble as they interrupted to a minor degree our established good flying technique. On one occasion a visiting pilot flying element (third man in a flight of four) broke away from his flight in attacking an enemy Sally bomber before he had called in the enemy to his flight leader. On another occasion, a visiting pilot flight leader ordered separation of his element in attacking and destroying two Jap fighters, thus forcing his second element to break up to protect the flight leader and his wingman in their individual attacks. Those pilots, not assigned to our squadron, that flew with our pilots, seemed more interested in running up their individual scores than in protecting

*themselves and their flight members and following our standard oper-
ating procedures."*

They reasoned that Bong had been freelancing most of the war ---
that he had gone where the action was, to build his score. The 431st
Squadron, and McGuire, had often sat for weeks at a time without any
action. Now that the squadron was in an area where the hunting was
good, Bong showed up to match McGuire's efforts. Although they respected Bong's accomplishments, they resented his methods of operation. A Lieutenant in McGuire's squadron was heard to ask, "How long
would one of us stay in this squadron if we pulled a stunt like Bong did
on that Sally?"

McGuire being strapped in for take-off in PUDGY V with 30 victory flags. His 500-hour hat is on
the head of Richard Van Der Geest, assistant crew chief, for safe keeping until his return
Photo from Richard Van Der Geest

Another pilot said, "That's the truth! I don't think Bong could carry Mac's shoes when it comes to flying a P-38. He can shoot, but I wouldn't want him on my wing in a dogfight. He'd be too busy looking for a score, instead of looking out for me."

One day, returning from a mission, 2nd Lieutenant Chris Herman, who was leading the squadron, chewed out a pilot who straggled behind the formation. He returned to the base intending to speak to the tail-end-Charlie who had not flown the tight formation usually flown by the 431st Squadron. He learned it was Bong and dropped the subject.[4]

Bong wasn't the only visiting pilot flying with the 431st Squadron. With the return to the Philippines, a number of pilots, mostly from higher command, started feeling the war slipping away. Fighter pilots don't get but one war,[5] and these men wanted a chance to fly combat--maybe become an ace or at least shoot down a Japanese plane before the war ended. Of all the pilots in the war less than one in a hundred would shoot down an enemy plane and even fewer would have the notation "Ace" in their war records.

McGuire's Squadron had its share of these people coming and going. Major Jack Rittmayer lived at the "Wheel House," the squadron VIP lodge, with Bong. He was on Temporary Duty from the Fifth Air Force. McGuire and Rittmayer had known each other when they were both stationed in Alaska. Rittmayer had come to his old friend, Major McGuire, to get in some combat flying before it was too late. McGuire took him under his wing and gave him every opportunity to become an ace before the war ended.

The men of the 431st Squadron forgave all when they learned that Bong was to be presented with the Congressional Medal of Honor. It came as a sudden shock to everyone. They'd heard rumors about it but nobody believed it would be awarded until Bong was back in the States. They had not counted on the resolve of General Kenney. General MacArthur agreed, as a personal favor to Kenney, to present the medal in person to Bong in a public ceremony. MacArthur had been awarded the Congressional Medal, as had his own father, and he had a reverence for the medal. He would have preferred a private ceremony in his office. Instead he agreed to a public presentation so the Air Corps could get the press they wanted and deserved.

Four P-38s were lined up at the Tacloban airdrome and a dozen fighter pilots were assembled. In a drizzling rain MacArthur, wearing his trench coat and gilded hat, pinned the medal on Bong's chest, placed his hands on Bong's shoulders, looked him in the eye and ignoring a microphone which had been set up, spoke in a resonant voice that was heard by all present:

298

"Of all military attributes, the one that arouses the greatest admiration is courage. The Congress of the United States has reserved for itself the honor of decorating those amongst all who stand out as the bravest of the brave. It is this high and noble category, Major Bong, that you now enter as I place upon your breast the Medal of Honor. Wear it as the symbol of the invincible courage you have displayed in mortal combat. My dear boy, may a merciful God continue to protect you."[6]

It was a moving ceremony and it touched even the hardest veteran among those present. The press overran the rare ceremony. Rare, because MacArthur made the presentation, but also rare because the Medal of Honor had probably never been presented in a battle zone. General Kenney had sought special permission to speed the presentation, avoiding the months or often years required for the award to be made. (After World War I, Eddie Rickenbacker waited over 10 years before being awarded the Congressional Medal of Honor)

Bong was now a true national hero, and a valuable commodity. He deserved his honors but the Army would exact a payment--one Bong would rather avoid. He had a reputation with the national press which had been developed by his two public relations trips back to the States. The Air Corps would certainly take advantage of his popularity. Rumor had him on his way home for another round of visits to Washington to promote a new postwar service branch--The Air Force! Bong would have preferred to go home to the farm and go hunting.

[1] *General Kenney Reports*, George C. Kenney

[2] Ibid.

[3] 431st Daily History

[4] Chris Herman wrote this to his sister in a letter

[5] Raoul Lufbury, one of America's top WW I pilots once said,
    "There isn't any *after the war* for a fighter pilot."

[6] 431st Daily History

40

"I never lived with McGuire, but I argued with him, dined with him, and flew with him. I also listened to him. Each of these activities was made pleasurable by his mental excellence--his quickness to grasp a thought, an idea, a line of action, the whole situation. He was ahead of those he was with, most of the time. This did not annoy me. It may have annoyed some others. McGuire on occasion might finish a thought for someone. Why not? He could do it pleasantly, with a smile, and life is too short to stand around listening to some clumsy guy trying to wrap up his routine concept."

------------ Lt. Colonel Danforth Miller,
Operations Officer, 475th Fighter Group

The 475th Fighter Group had been at Dulag for a few weeks. In the scheme of things, they usually felt at home in that length of time. In this case things were a little different. They had been delayed for weeks flying into Dulag because of muddy grounds, and things hadn't changed all that much since they had been here. A steel-mat runway had been installed, but it was short, and the rest of the field was still a pool of mud.

Danforth Miller, Group Operations Officer, was technically responsible for the airfield, but nature had been the boss. Everyone had worked hard to get the field operational but Danny had decided that things weren't going to improve much until the weather did. He was sitting in the operations office with his feet on his desk. After all he had been through in the last few weeks, he was contemplating the ceiling, in this case the underside of the roof, and wondering how much water would come through the small holes when it rained again.

Outside he heard the familiar voice of Major McGuire. He remembered the time McGuire appeared at the door of the operations tent with a grin and a sparkle in his eye. Without a word he had held up three fingers, given a little nod and disappeared. This was his way of saying, "I just got three more Japs!" Colonel MacDonald had done the same thing an hour later. They both acted like Fitzgerald characters who had just been out playing tennis.

When Danny heard McGuire coming closer, he thought, "McGuire was over at Tacloban yesterday when Bong got the Medal of Honor---he has a new idea to get more action so he can catch Bong." He admired McGuire's quick mind. They had often argued, and Miller enjoyed it---he thought Mac was one of the brightest minds around. He was considered rude, by some, when he leaped ahead in an argument, impatiently presenting a counter argument before a colleague had completely expressed his viewpoint. Danny often found himself listening when McGuire talked because he knew McGuire had given a lot of thought to a subject before he spoke.

McGuire entered the tent, walked about with his hands in his pockets. Miller with his hands clasped in back of his head, and his feet still on his desk, pretended to be asleep. Through the slits of his closed eyelids he watched McGuire walk around the office and pretend to read first a letter on a desk and then a chart on the wall. Suddenly, McGuire stepped in front of Miller's desk, looked him straight in the eyes, just like they were wide open, and said, "We've got to talk."

Miller opened his eyes, feigning sleepiness, and grunted, "About what?"

"About the way you've been giving the juicy missions to the other guys, while my boys are flying milk runs," said McGuire.

Moving as few muscles as possible, Miller pulled open the lower drawer in his desk, withdrew a bundle of reports in a binder, threw it on the desk, and said, "Show me!"

McGuire picked up the binder and looked at the cover. It was marked, "Mission Assignments." It was a carefully compiled list showing how the missions assigned by the Fifth Fighter Command or other high commands had been allocated. Miller tried to be fair and he kept complete records to prove it. He'd heard the scuttlebutt around the mess tent or over a drink, that one squadron or another was getting the best assignments. This report was designed to put those stories to rest, once and for all.

McGuire sat and studied the reports with great intensity--leafing back and forth. After about ten minutes of searching, he stood up, tossed the binder on Miller's desk and said, "You'd have to be a God damn CPA to understand this fucking thing. To hell with it! It's hot. Do you want fly?"

"What have you got in mind?" inquired Miller.

"Nothing serious, just some new guys that need indoctrination. I need a fourth. Do you want to come along or should I look for someone else?"

"OK Mac, I'll come along. Maybe we'll find some action that will get you off my ass."

"Come on," said McGuire. "We'll make our own action."

They wandered down to the flight line where two green pilots were studying an area chart on the bulletin board. Everyone knew they were new pilots, because they were wearing silk scarf maps around their necks. The veteran pilots put them up to it, and wouldn't be caught dead, wearing a survival map around their necks. They had all been tricked into wearing them when they were neophytes. The maps were in each pilot's survival kit. They were printed on silk to tolerate sea water if the owner found himself floating in a raft. After a few days the new pilots would notice that no other pilot wore the map as a scarf, and would quietly return it to the kit where it belonged.

McGuire gave the three pilots instructions: "Watch for my signal. When I tell you, we'll fly a ragged formation, like we are still learning, or haven't got good sense. If the Japanese buy it, maybe we can lure a few of them off the ground. They haven't shown much interest in combat lately---maybe if they think we are easy pickings, they will come after us."

An hour later they were flying near the island of Cebu. McGuire gave a signal and they went into a daffy string formation. They crossed over a field where they counted at least 26 Japanese air planes on the ground. They bobbed and weaved past the field at eight thousand feet in a disorganized formation, and at a slow cruising speed. When they were out of sight of the field McGuire signaled his pilots to close in and form up. Following his lead they quickly climbed to 18,000 feet and turned to head back toward the Japanese field in a tight, neat, 431st formation.

Sure enough, the Japanese had taken the bait--they were coming up to attack the ragged, disorganized flight. McGuire led his men in steep spirals which gave them all a chance to see everything going on below.

Major Miller could feel himself on the verge of a blackout from the violent maneuver but thought, "That son-of-a-bitch, McGuire, has got to have a remarkable circulatory system if he flies like this without blacking out. This must be the way he bends the wings on his planes. I hope these kids can take it."

The four P-38s got down to about 1,000 feet before the ideal opportunity presented itself. McGuire spotted a Japanese fighter climbing up from the field below--he lined up the shot quickly--the range was 400 yards, deflection was 65 degrees. He gave a two-second burst, increasing his turn to the right as he fired. If he missed, he would have a second shot. Miller eased his thumb onto the gun button, to take a shot, but before he got into position, the Japanese plane exploded in a giant orange and black ball of flame. Fragments of the plane rained into the jungle below.

This was a textbook attack--just the way an instructor would draw it on a blackboard. It only took seconds. It only took a single short run, with one quick burst of gun fire. It looked so simple, but took so much skill. McGuire used all of the elements, air speed, lead, and elevation so smoothly that it looked easy.

P-38s from the 475th Fighter Group on patrol over the Philippines (USAF Photo)

A slight turn to the left and the flight reformed. McGuire already had them on a course for home. It all happened so fast and looked so easy that the other three pilots couldn't believe it. "Let's make another pass," cried one of the rookie pilots.

"Another day," replied McGuire. "Another day."

Back on the ground at Dulag the young pilots rushed to McGuire.

"Why didn't we go back after more?" asked one of the scarf wearers.

"It isn't always that easy. We had surprise in our favor for one attack," McGuire instructed. "We counted 26 of them. There were only four of us. If you don't have surprise working for you under those circumstances you say, 'another day'."

The other bright-eyed pilot said, "Where were we?"

Danforth Miller shook his head, and walked back toward operations. He thought, "Things are never dull when McGuire is around."[1]

[1] See Appendix A, How this book was written

41

"That afternoon I went down to Dulag to see how the Airdrome was coming along. The engineers were trying to enlarge it, to give more dispersal area, as the planes were lined up wingtip to wingtip on each side of the runway, which was only a hundred feet wide to begin with. I stopped to chat with some of the 475th pilots, who were looking over their airplanes preparatory to going out on patrol. One of them told me that Bong and McGuire had gone on a Nip hunting expedition together that morning and each shot down a Jap plane. I got my jeep and drove over to the hut where McGuire was living with two or three other members of his squadron. I opened the door without knocking and walked in. Bong and McGuire, naked as the day they were born, were standing in a pair of tin washtubs, scrubbing each other's backs. They turned around, grinned rather sheepishly, and reached for towels. I sat down and, as they dressed, asked them what they had been doing that morning. McGuire took on the task of spokesman, while Bong kept nodding in confirmation as the story unfolded."

------General George C. Kenney
From *General Kenney Reports*

McGuire and Bong had taken a morning flight and were back at McGuire's hut enjoying a cooling bath. McGuire had extended unusual hospitality to Bong that morning--Bong had gotten his 39th victory while flying with McGuire's squadron. McGuire, contrary to the story on the flight line, had come up empty. The door to the hut opened and McGuire thought it might be one of his roommates, "Pappy" Cline, or Fred Champlin. Instead it was the Commanding General of all air operations in the Southwest Pacific, General George Kenney.

McGuire and Bong fumbled for clothing as Kenney tore into Bong, with mock anger, for unnecessary combat flying. "Dick, I've told you, General Arnold, himself, has been in touch with me. When he hears about the Nip you got this morning, I'll have to answer to him, personally. You're putting me in a bad spot."

McGuire quickly assumed the roll of spokesman for the two. "General, my boys needed some gunnery training. I've got some real green kids. Besides, those guys at Tacloban were getting peeved with 'Bing-Bang-Bong'--seems he was taking too many nips from them. All of a sudden they can't find any place for him--no airplane either. We figure we can take care of our own interests along that line. I told Major Bong that he's always welcome at the 431st."

Bong smiled and nodded in agreement as McGuire continued, "This morning the Major just happened to see me getting ready to take off for a sweep over Mindanao and said he thought he ought to come along to look out for me. I had a feeling he shouldn't come, but I couldn't be impolite. After all he is a guest here.

"We took a real good look, but Mindanao had been plastered so much that nothing was happening. We couldn't even find anything to strafe and we were on our way home. The Major got lucky and got an Oscar, and I'm behind by eight again. Guess the war will end before I get any closer."

The pilots in the Fifth Air Force loved General Kenney, and they congregated to visit with him, anytime he appeared. Word got around the base that the General had arrived, and while McGuire was talking, Colonel Charles MacDonald, Major Danforth Miller and some other pilots came into the hut. They listened quietly as McGuire continued with his story. MacDonald, who flew as much combat as any Group Commander ever did, had 21 Japanese planes to his credit. Everyone else in the room had only a fraction of the numbers of these three great fighter pilots. The small audience listened to one of the most successful pilots in the Pacific, McGuire, complaining because he had only shot down 31 enemy planes.

"General, you know I've never gotten a break when it comes to catching Dick. Why only last week we were up on patrol and he was following me like a shadow. I spotted a pair of Oscars on my side, and in an effort to keep the Major from engaging in any 'unnecessary combat', I spoke quietly, over my radio, to my wingman to follow me. Figured I'd get both Oscars so the Major won't be endangered. I got in one nice burst and I got the first one--thought I'd just swing over and get the other one. Unfortunately, Major Bong was eavesdropping on a private conversation and just as I lined up on the second one, it blew up. I thought I'd cut his lead by two, instead, I just stayed even."

Everyone, including the General, knew McGuire was putting on a little show for the crowd. Kenney knew these boys like a couple of sons. He was about to give them one last little lecture, for the benefit of the gathering, when McGuire spoke again, "General, we have half of a cold turkey in the refrigerator. Will you stay and have lunch?"

The General knew he had been "had" by an expert. McGuire had changed the subject with an irresistible invitation. Kenney asked, "Where in the world did you get a turkey? There hasn't been a turkey in the Southwest Pacific in over two years!"

McGuire replied, with a grin, "I just told my cook I'd like one, and he cooked it up. Maybe you'd better talk to your guy. If he can't get one, tell him to talk to us."

The pilots present, who had lived on "bully beef" for a year-and-a-half, hooted with laughter. Kenney called his aide in from the jeep and said quietly, "See if any locals are missing a turkey--if they are, pay them for it--if I'm going to enjoy the spoils I should make sure it isn't ill-gotten."[1]

The next few hours passed quickly with a lot of flying stories and a lot of joking around. Just about every pilot on the field dropped by and listened in as MacDonald and McGuire dominated the conversation. Occasionally somebody would get in a question for the General about how the war was going. The General noticed that Bong, as skilled with a knife and fork as with a P-38, seemed subdued--hardly saying a word. These men were the titans of the Southwest Pacific, in fact, of the Air Corps, yet they were acting like boy scouts. Except Bong, who remained quiet.[2]

When Kenney got up to leave he spoke to Bong, privately, "Dick, you've got 39 now, when you get number 40, you are done, and I really mean it this time." Bong nodded, and the General knew by the look in Bong's eyes that he was making a good decision.

Before he left, General Kenney heard that Bong and McGuire had been involved in a high stakes poker game the last few nights. "They say Bong lost $1,500 and McGuire lost $2,500, but they were doing pretty well---Bob Herman lost $3,500. They were playing with everyone else's money---they've been winning for days."[3] The General said, "Things never change, the stakes just get bigger."

A few days later McGuire was once again polite to his guest and allowed him "to go along" on another mission with the 431st. It was a repeat performance--Bong got another Oscar while McGuire came up empty. It had been McGuire who afforded the combat opportunity and confirmed Bong's 37th, 38th, and 39th victories. It was McGuire who confirmed his final one--number 40.

General Kenney, true to his word, called Bong in and said, "That's it Dick, you are going stateside as soon as I can arrange it. You and McGuire have probably shot down twice as many Japs as you have gotten credit for. What's the point of going for more?"

A few days after General Kenney visited his tent, McGuire wrote to Marilynn : *"... By the way, I received a letter from General Kenney forbidding me to strafe, dive bomb, glide bomb or skip bomb---in short I can only engage in aerial combat now---He said he considered me too valuable to take any chances and I didn't have to go on unimportant missions.*

"We got a hell of a surprise the other day. General Kenney came over & stayed 3 hours in our shack. He came over just to see me. I think I am the first Squadron Commander who has ever had the C.G. of F.E.A.F. come & visit him for 3 hours. By the way, while the General was here, our laundry girl, a cute little Filipino girl about 16, who has adopted Pappy Cline, came by. Pappy is a great favorite of hers and she calls him "Poppy". Pappy is 6'3" and the little girl about 4'10" so while we were sitting around, up to the shack comes Maria yelling 'Poppy', 'Poppy' with a big grin on her face. She came right in the shack. Pappy got up, very red in the face--trying to show her out--saying 'We have no laundry today'. The General never cracked a smile, but the rest of us sat around & howled."

General Kenney's visit to McGuire's hut was important to McGuire. Next to having Lindbergh live with him at Biak, it was the most satisfying event of the war for McGuire. Bong had been in the limelight for a year--had made two headline-generating trips to the States. McGuire had scratched his heat rash out in the jungle the whole time.

McGuire enjoyed the instant fame he had acquired when he flew into Leyte, but Bong had stolen it away. First he received the well-deserved Congressional Medal of Honor. McGuire agreed with the award--Bong had earned it! But then, Bong had come right into McGuire's domain, his own squadron, and outscored him against the enemy. Although he would never admit it, McGuire was depressed when Bong got one more victory while flying with the 431st Squadron than McGuire had gotten during the same period.

Since McGuire had arrived in New Guinea, he had out-shot Bong by a score of 30 to 22. Bong had a 16-plane lead at the start and McGuire had cut it in half. He wondered if he'd ever catch up. McGuire was tired and sick, and he wavered between his strong desire to beat Bong and wanting to get home to his wife whom he loved very much, and hadn't seen in almost two years.

General Kenney's efforts to keep Bong out of dangerous combat were well known. Kenney's letter to McGuire, about his combat flying, and the General's visit to McGuire's hut, were messages to McGuire, that he was vital to the new Air Force, too.

McGuire was aware of his value to higher command each time his expected departure from the Philippines was delayed. He'd told Marilynn that he'd be home by Thanksgiving, then Christmas, and finally by the New Year. The Generals kept moving that date back. McGuire had already sent several messages to Marilynn explaining that he was going to be delayed. General Wurtsmith and General Kenney wanted him to stay, but they hadn't explained why.

Colonel MacDonald once explained why some men went home early while others stayed for an extended period: "War isn't fair. You get some guy out here and he fucks up--what happens? He goes home because he's dangerous to his own people. The poor bastard who does his job well has to stay--because we need to get the job done. It's not fair, but who ever said things were fair!"[4]

No, it didn't seem fair to McGuire that he was having to stay. Yet, he was flattered, as any young man would be. He was vital enough to be kept long after the average man would have been sent home. Unlike the European theater of war, where a set number of missions flown, sent a man home, the Pacific theater had no set policy. Most pilots went home with about 130 combat missions and less than 400 hours of combat flying time. McGuire had passed those figures long ago. He now had 240 combat missions and 725 hours of combat flying, almost double the average!

The 431st Squadron had its share of seasoned veterans: Captains "Pappy" Cline and Fred Champlin, each with over 155 missions and more than 510 hours flying time; Captains Bill Gronemeyer, Bob Herman, Frank Monk, Lieutenants John Tilley and Wilson Ekdahl with about 140 missions and 480 combat hours each. They formed a backbone for the squadron, and McGuire felt that his leadership was no longer indispensable.

McGuire and Bong had become good friends during their time together. They respected each other, though they were cut from different cloth. McGuire was aggressive--couldn't sit still, and was more likely to use profanity. Bong, on the other hand, was quiet--almost stoic. He could sit with a group all evening and hardly open his mouth. McGuire was thin and drawn looking with a bony suntanned face--Bong had full pink cheeks and looked like he hadn't ever missed a meal. Neither was a large man, but McGuire was slightly taller. The two men had many things in common: both played clarinet, both played golf, both had handled their own rifles and shotguns as teenagers.

Bong had come from a large family which was waiting at home for his return--McGuire was an only child, and had lived with his mother and his grandparents, all dead now. McGuire had a wife--Bong had fallen head-over-heels in love and expected to marry when he got home.

There was no doubt that Bong and McGuire were the best fighter pilots in Air Corps history. They had both done their jobs well, in combat and on the ground. Bong had done public relations for the Air Corps even though he was uncomfortable in that situation. McGuire had suffered physically in combat and had commanded 350 men for the better part of a year.

When McGuire and Bong parted they knew a lot about each other. They had their differences, but they were friends. Bong left reluctantly, but was glad to be going home. McGuire was ready to go home, too, but had willingly agreed to stay a little longer. In their own ways, Bong, a Swede, and McGuire, an Irishman, represented the diversity in American people that gave the United States the strength to win a world war. Given a chance they could have been friends for a long lifetime.

William J. Dunn, a reporter for CBS Radio, talked with both men often and in later years made this assessment: "...You've never known two men more completely dissimilar in appearance, temperament and, above all, imagination. Dick was a blonde, placid, country boy whose great ambition was to get back to the farm. General Kenney, who was one of Bong's greatest admirers, once told me that Bong really didn't realize that there was a human being in each one of those planes he shot down and when he finally did get the realization through his head, it damned near killed him.

"Tommy, on the other hand, understood exactly what was going on but accepted it as part of warfare. He was certain he would emerge from combat with a higher score than Dick, and understood fully what that could mean in civilian life--Ace of Aces! ...Given a chance Bong probably would have gone back to Wisconsin and sharpened his plow."[5]

[1]*General Kenney Reports*, George C. Kenney
[2]Danforth Miller, Appendix A, Re: Chapter 40
[3]Bob Herman, 431st Pilot
[4]Col. Charles MacDonald. Interview at Miami Reunion
[5]William J. Dunn, CBS News

42

"There wasn't an airfield anywhere in the Philippine Islands that had room to park our bombers, so we had to fly all day to bomb in the area. These were 13- to 14-hour-long missions from the Palaus for our B-24s, and it was necessary for us to land in the Philippines and refuel to make it back home. It was during these refueling layovers in Leyte that we got to mingle with the P-38 pilots. McGuire took us under his wing. We were as green as grass and he let us know in no uncertain terms that we needed to take care of our assignments in the formation. Something in his manner of speaking impressed our gunners, and they listened to him when they wouldn't listen to us."

> ----Richard Graham, B-24 Pilot,
> 494th Bomb Group (Heavy)

The B-24s were lined up on the flight line awaiting refueling for their long flight home. The jubilant crews, happy they had survived their morning bomb runs, were served coffee and doughnuts. Most of them gathered in front of one of the big bombers, where a single thin, mustached pilot, with his trousers tucked into his Australian flying boots, and wearing a horribly crushed 500-hour hat, addressed the group.

"I'm Major McGuire, Commanding Officer of the 431st Fighter Squadron. We've been in combat constantly for 17 months, and we have one of the best kill records of any squadron in the Air Corps. I'm not bragging. I'm telling you this to assure you that we can handle our job of protecting bombers, and we expect you people to do the same.

"I know you gunners want to protect your planes, but several times, some of you guys have gotten jumpy and taken shots at our P-38s. Fellows, look over there at those P-38s. There isn't another plane in the sky that looks like a P-38. Study your spotter charts, and know what you are shooting at. When somebody shoots at us, we shoot back. I don't think you guys would like that--we have a better kill ratio than you people do.

"Another thing, you gunners all have assignments. Know them, and follow them. If your plane is on the right side of the formation, you must guard that side. If you fire to the left, you are firing among your own planes. The guys on the left side are taking care of that side. Your pilots tell me that you've been burning out the servo-motors in your turrets, turning too much. What good is a turret if it won't turn? If you take care of your assignment correctly your chances of getting home safely will be greatly improved. Any questions?"

Invariably there were questions and McGuire answered them. He wasn't assigned to make these speeches. He just talked to the bomber crews because he felt that he could help them do a better job of protecting themselves. He displayed the same energy which had caused him to fly on missions with other units when his own squadron wasn't assigned, and the same energy which brought him to check out in B-24 bombers on his days off, and to fly B-25 missions when he didn't have a P-38 to fly. Some people thought it was crazy to get involved in activities that weren't assigned by higher command. Others thought it was a sign of leadership. At any rate, when he spoke to the bomber crews he spoke with authority and they knew it and they paid attention.

People who knew McGuire thought he looked tired. He was 30 pounds underweight and suffering from the usual tropical skin disorders which caused him to scratch where it itched. He was also nursing a wound in the posterior. With his abundance of energy these maladies made him look like his nerves were shot, and some pilots, who had never met McGuire, would later say that they thought he should have been grounded.

With Bong out of action the last great fighter pilot duel of the Southwest Pacific and World War Two had came to an end. Richard Bong had pleaded with General Kenney to let him go for 50 victories, but the General had put his foot down--Bong and his new Medal of Honor were going to report to General Arnold at the Pentagon. After that he would be assigned to the experimental jet aircraft project at the Lockheed Aircraft plant in Burbank, California. Somewhere along the line Dick planned to marry his girl, Marge Vattendahl.

McGuire would stay behind and fight the war. If he could find enemy aircraft to fight, he would try to catch Bong. There were no guarantees that there would be opportunities or that McGuire could take advantage of them. The enemy had been hit hard and fewer and fewer of their planes were rising to control of the skies over the Philippines. There was talk that the next big aerial battles would be over Japan.

There had been long slack periods before, like the six months between December 26, 1943, and May 17, 1944, when McGuire had flown 205 hours without a serious challenge from an enemy plane. Most of those days had been spent on patrol missions which lasted five to seven hours, during which time the pilots suffered from physical discomfort and boredom, without any prospects of action. McGuire's temperament, like that of most fighter pilots, was not well suited for inaction. On the ground the pilots were subjected to heat, humidity, insects, tropical diseases, poor food, and harassing Japanese air raids which robbed them of a good night's sleep. Boredom made these conditions almost unbearable. When there was action against the enemy the physical discomforts of daily life seemed unimportant--they had a sense of mission.

When there was no action the long hours in the air became a physical and mental drain. The shoulder-wide cockpit started to feel smaller. The perspiration of low altitude heat caused them to shiver at high altitude. The harmonious purr of the P-38's twin engines, muffled by turbo-superchargers, could lull a man to sleep. Most pilots carried chocolate bars or pressed fruit bars to ward off hunger. The GI chocolate bars didn't taste very good but they wouldn't melt in the tropical heat. The fruit bars were to say the least an acquired taste.

During a long flight McGuire once read a whole Ellery Queen mystery, but his most successful weapon against boredom was an active mind. McGuire thought often about Marilynn and how much he missed her. He thought about his dad, and his Uncle Charles, who had first fostered his interest in aviation. When he thought of his Uncle he'd inevitably think about Eddie Rickenbacker.

Rickenbacker had been America's second ranked ace during World War I when Lieutenant Frank Luke, America's leading ace, had been killed. Rickenbacker, a latecomer to the war, then passed Luke's score, to become America's "Ace of Aces," just before the war had ended. It had made Rickenbacker a national hero and had opened up opportunities which eventually led to the manufacture of the Rickenbacker automobile, ownership in the Indianapolis Speedway, and eventually the Presidency of Eastern Airlines.

Now, McGuire figured he would do the same thing. With Bong gone maybe he'd have one last chance to increase his totals until he was the new "Ace of Aces." He'd need 10 more victories, but that could take a lifetime. How many chances would he have now that Japanese planes were getting harder to find? He'd have to see what fate held for him, and take advantage of whatever opportunities came along.

McGuire expressed his hopes to William J. Dunn, of CBS Radio, who later reported: "Ace of Aces--McGuire mentioned Eddie Rickenbacker as an example of what that distinction could mean and he left no doubt he intended to make the most of it. At the same time he never gave the impression of braggadocio. He was very confident of his abilities but in a quiet way."[1]   As December passed, thoughts of Christmas occupied the minds of the war-weary men of the 475th Fighter Group. The previous year, on New Guinea, the natives knew nothing of the holiday the GIs had celebrated. The Filipinos celebrated Christmas, and the talk of the upcoming day made the soldiers homesick. Things had been quiet for a while around Dulag, but the Japanese resumed nightly air raids, a few days before Christmas.

Aerial combat over the Philippines had also slowed, and McGuire wondered if he would see more action before going home. He concluded that there was no chance that he could catch Richard Bong in the "Ace Race." Time and the enemy were running out on him. Once again, when Bong was out of the picture, factors beyond McGuire's control seemed to be working against him.

Clark Field, the former American stronghold, was now a great Japanese bastion. Many Americans had died defending Clark Field in the days after Pearl Harbor, and now the Japanese were going to put everything they had into the defense of the field. The Japanese had coveted the Philippine Islands for hundreds of years and were not going to give them up without a fight.

On the radio Tokyo Rose was promising Japanese troops a Christmas present, the complete destruction of all American forces on Leyte. B-24 bombers had been hitting Manila for two days, where Army Intelligence said that Japanese forces were building up. On Christmas Eve, they reported that there were at least 400 Japanese planes assembled at Clark Field and nearby airdromes.

A Christmas Day raid on Manila was planned and the 475th and 49th Fighter Groups were assigned to fly cover. McGuire and his men were to help take Clark Field back and they would make the Japanese pay a price for every minute they held on to it. Now it was apparent that there was going to be action, and plenty of it! McGuire spoke to some of his men: "The P-47s got 33 Japs over Clark Field today. It looks like hunting season is open again. If those guys got over 30 planes, think what we can do!"

The news of the impending raid cast a pall on the men at Dulag. Planned parties went on as scheduled, but it was difficult to muster much Christmas spirit. Pilots and ground crews dropped in for a drink of cheer, but departed early and sober to get a good night's rest in preparation for their early morning activities.

Nonessential personnel stayed at the parties and after a few drinks tried to muster some Christmas spirit in the form of song. Seeing Filipinos prepare for Christmas had brought back memories of home and family, and it was hard, even with the aid of the spiked punch, to forget those better days back home. Some men were spending their third Christmas away from home, and many a ruffian was seen with a tear in his eye as they exchanged memories with one another.

As the singing and talking got louder, an all too familiar sound interrupted them--the sound of a red alert. Anti-aircraft fire replaced the music, as the men scurried for their trenches. The Japanese were not going to let them forget about the war. The pilots in their bunks rolled out and went to their shelters as McGuire grumbled: "We might as well have gone to the party. They aren't going to let us sleep anyway."

The pilots and party goers alike were forced to remain in their trenches for an hour as the raid continued. During the lulls some of the braver revelers, with their daring fortified by drink, sneaked back to the punch bowl to renew their supply of courage.

When the all-clear sounded the party resumed, but never got back to the degree of merriment it had before. The pilots were mad as hell. Not only were they missing the party but they were also missing the sleep they so dearly needed. One of the flyers was heard to mumbled a promise as he lay, wide awake, in his bunk: "You sons-of-bitches will pay for this tomorrow."

The pilots and ground crews of the 431st Squadron rose early Christmas Day, not to look under the Christmas tree, but to ready their planes for the day's raid on Manila. They were sleepier than usual, because of the air raid the night before. It did not keep them from a 7:55 a.m. take off. The 15 P-38s circled and moved into formation, with McGuire leading, and then flew towards Pulan to rendezvous with the B-24 bombers at 9:15 a.m..

They approached the target at 21,000 feet, above a thin layer of clouds that blanketed the earth at 15,000 feet. At 10:35 a.m. one of the pilots called on his radio, "Daddy leader, I see something coming at us from the sun."

McGuire ordered, "This is Daddy leader. Zekes coming in from the sun. Drop your tanks!"

Suddenly, 20 Zekes flew directly into their formation with their guns blazing. Several P-38s were damaged in the initial attack. Everybody was under attack, and the squadron broke into units to fend off their own attackers. The Zekes were the latest design, and their pilots were well-trained and aggressive.

McGuire used his maneuvering flaps and quickly turned on a Zeke and exploded it with a long deflection shot. His wingman, Lieutenant Alvin Neal, set a Zeke on fire and it crashed. Several pilots called for help and McGuire went to their aid. Lieutenant Robert Koeck's plane was hit in an engine and he radioed that he was heading South to bail out. Lieutenant Enrique Provencio was heard to tell Koeck to "hit the silk" before he, too, radioed that he was hit and going down.

Seven more enemy aircraft were seen to enter the fight, diving from above. Anti-aircraft shells started exploding all over the sky as the B-24s approached Mabalacat Air Drome, 10 miles northeast of Clark

Field. McGuire forced enemy planes away from the B-24s and, on one run, sent two more Zekes toward the ground, smoking and on fire. Both were seen to crash.

Every member of the Squadron was doing his part, and the Japanese planes were dropping like flies. Somewhere above, other Japanese planes were dropping aerial bombs, but they exploded without hitting either the bombers or the P-38s. Lieutenant Floyd Fulkerson radioed that he was leaving the area of Clark Field to bail out. His plane was critically damaged.

McGuire used his flaps again to bring his guns to bear on one of 30 Oscars that joined the fight from above. Now 57 enemy planes were spotted in the area. As McGuire pulled the trigger, his guns stuttered and quit. His turn was so tight that the "G force" made the bullets so heavy that the guns were unable to lift them from their trays.

McGuire struggled to reload his guns, flipping the reset control, time and time again. It was no use--he was without guns, in a sky full of enemy planes! He did the only thing he could, he dove on enemy planes to make them change their course. For 30 minutes McGuire continued to make attacks with an unarmed plane, forcing the enemy to take evasive action.

The B-24s left the area without a loss, and headed for home. McGuire's men had done their job well, but stayed to occupy the enemy fighters until low fuel supplies forced them to withdraw. They had engaged at least 27 of the 57 planes in the sky, and had shot down 16 of them in a 50-minute battle.

McGuire and three other P-38s were able to return to Dulag without refueling and landed at 12:45. Eight of the planes landed at San Jose, on Mindoro Island, to refuel. McGuire waited impatiently until 2:45. His worst fears were realized--three of his men did not return. He was particularly distressed by the loss of Lieutenant Provencio, who had often been his wingman. He could only hope his men had landed somewhere and were safe.

The 475th and 49th Fighter Groups had destroyed 42 Japanese planes, including three shot down by Colonel MacDonald. Yet, McGuire couldn't be happy over the day's score with three of his men missing. He went from man to man in the intelligence tent asking what each man knew about the men who hadn't returned. It was likely that Lieutenant Fulkerson was alive, but nobody knew anything about the other two men. It was the largest one day loss for the squadron since the raids on Rabaul, over a year before.

Filipinos brought gifts and food into the camp and invited some of the men to their homes for Christmas dinner. Before dark, the word was passed around that another mission was on the docket for tomorrow. The pilots took their combat rations of Bourbon whisky early and went to bed. The rations flowed freely, but the men needed their rest if the sky was going to be full of Japanese planes again tomorrow. The Japanese did not stage an air raid during the night but the parties did interrupt their sleep.

At the 431st Fighter Squadron, there was more of the holiday spirit around the breakfast table on the day after Christmas, than there had been on Christmas Day itself. A report had come in overnight that one of their comrades, Lt. Fulkerson, was safe with the Guerrillas on Luzon. The report gave them hope for Lt. Koeck and Lt. Provencio who had also been lost the day before.

The results of Christmas Day's action over Manila was the main subject of conversation. Besides McGuire's three victories, Lieutenants Pietz, Fulkerson, Oxford, and DuMontier had scored two kills each, and Lieutenants Neal, Gray, Martin, Tilley, Moreing and Ballard, and Captain Champlin had gotten one enemy plane each.

Those victories had put the 431st Squadron's victory total above the 200 mark, a goal they had set for year's end. Their monthly average of Japanese planes shot down, in the last 17 months, was the highest of all squadrons in the Southwest Pacific Theater, and their total put them in third place among all Squadrons, behind only the veteran 9th and 80th Squadrons. It had also helped put the 475th Group's total over the 500 mark. They had reached that level in fewer months than any other Fighter Group ever had. It was a remarkable accomplishment for a new fighter group, and the men of the 431st Squadron were justly proud of their part in it.

The ground crews had worked late into Christmas night to service the squadron's planes and they had 10 of them ready for the day's return mission to Manila. A good night of rest had boosted everyone's morale. The P-38s left the runway at 8:15 a.m., joined planes from the 432nd and 433rd Squadrons and headed for Masbate Island. Rendezvous with the B-24s and P-38s from the 49th Group took place as planned, at 9:00 a.m., and the armada proceeded toward Clark Field, at 18,000 feet.

They approached Clark Field at 10:40 a.m. and were greeted by heavy anti-aircraft fire that filled the sky ahead with ominous black puffs of smoke. Adrenaline coursed through the pilots veins as they entered the antiaircraft fire. Luckily the gunner's aim was poor and the bombers made their bomb run unhindered. No enemy aircraft were spotted until the bomb run was completed. Then, three Zeke 52s, the newest model Japanese fighter, appeared at 20,000 feet. One of them started a dive towards the bombers.

McGuire ordered: "Daddy flight, drop your tanks. Zekes at eight o'clock high, and they're headed for the B-24s."

As the bombers turned to head home, five more Zekes dropped through the thin overcast above, and initiated an attack from the rear of the bomber formation. McGuire and his P-38s were ready! One Zeke completed a run on the last bomber in the flight and a second one started in. There was no return fire from the tail gunner of the bomber. McGuire could see that the B-24 was a sitting duck. As the Zeke closed in McGuire was still at a great distance behind. He had only one chance to help the bomber--a desperation shot from 400 yards, and 45 degrees deflection. He fired a long burst and watched--his aim was perfect! It was a vintage McGuire shot--few fighter pilots could ever have registered a hit from that angle and distance.

The Zeke was hit around the cockpit but continued to trail the bomber. McGuire and his wingman, Captain Edwin Weaver, closed in to within 100 feet, and McGuire fired one short burst which sent the plane rolling over in flames before it exploded.

He turned on the third Zeke in the flight and fired at it from 70-degrees deflection, closed in and shot again from 60-degrees deflection, sending it down in flames. Captain Weaver, who was on one of his first flights with the 431st Squadron, had never seen shooting like that before.[2]

Three more Zekes joined the attack and McGuire turned to attack the closest one from 30-degrees deflection, and then again from 45 degrees. Again the Zeke was hit around the cockpit and it rolled over and fell 5,000 feet crashing in a dry river bed.

Captain Weaver had not been able to stay on McGuire's wing through the wild turns and McGuire found himself alone. A Zeke was streaking below, and McGuire turned, alone, and followed him down to 1,500 feet. From a difficult 40-degrees deflection, McGuire fired a burst into the wing root of the Zeke, and then hit it again from 60-degrees deflection. Lieutenant Chris Herman witnessed the shots and saw the Zeke burn and crash near the other Zeke in the dry river bed.[3]

McGuire attacked other planes but didn't see any results. Low on fuel he joined some P-38s from the 8th Fighter Squadron and they left the area. Other members of the 431st Squadron also scored in the 20-minute battle. Lieutenant Tilley shot down a Zeke, his fifth, and became an ace. McGuire's tentmate, Captain Champlin, got a Zeke for his ninth, and Lieutenant Horace "Bo" Reeves got a Zeke for his third victory.[4]

McGuire was exuberant as he landed at Mindoro, to refuel. It was all coming true, now. Just the way he had dreamed it would. He had just broken the "eight behind" jinx for good. He now had a total of 38 victories, just two behind Bong. As they waited for the planes to be refueled, McGuire chattered excitedly about the air battle they had just completed. He still suffered from "jungle rot," and he scratched as he talked. Some of the pilots, who weren't well acquainted with McGuire's energy level, thought he was "jumpy," and might need a rest. They just didn't know McGuire.

Back at Dulag, nine of the 431st's P-38s had returned directly from Manila, and the ground crews were already cleaning the gunpowder from the cowlings, and preparing the ships for the next day's mission. It was quiet. Then came the purr of a low flying P-38. McGuire flew Pudgy V straight across the field and put her into four barrels rolls ---one for each plane he'd shot down. When he climbed from his plane, pilots and ground crewmen crowded around to congratulate him.

Captain Edwin R. Weaver, a veteran pilot who had just joined the 431st Fighter Squadron, reported to intelligence after the mission: "I was flying McGuire's wing when we spotted the first Zekes. McGuire made an unbelievable shot--I thought he was just trying to scare the Jap off and was just wasting his ammo. I'd never seen McGuire shoot before and I couldn't believe it when his first burst, from 400 yards, hit the Zeke in the cockpit. Minutes later he pulled the tightest turn I've ever seen a P-38 make. I tried to go with him but I blacked out and fell off!"[5]

That night, McGuire and his pilots had a few cups of cheer, to make up for what they had foregone the last two nights. They were not scheduled to fly the next day. Other pilots dropped in to share the bitter-sweet occasion. They had defeated the Japanese in a big way but they had lost friends, too. In the midst of it all they had missed Christmas. It was late before the lights went out.

[1] William J. Dunn, CBS Radio
[2] Interview with Edwin Weaver
[3] McGuire's Combat Report
[4] 431st Daily History
[5] Interview with Edwin Weaver

43

"Tommy laughed but he didn't want to spoil anything for Dick, so it was OK... I said, 'Now that that is settled, how about having lunch with me?' Since I had acquired the former chef of the St. Francis Hotel in San Francisco as my cook, everyone liked to be invited to my mess. Tommy said he hoped my estimate as to the duration of his 'illness' was correct, and he couldn't think of anything that he'd rather do in the meantime than eat a meal with me."

---General George C. Kenney, in *WORLD WAR II IN THE AIR, The Pacific,*
Edited by Major James F. Sunderman, U.S.A.F.

In San Antonio, Marilynn was suffering the post-Christmas blues. For almost a year she had expected that Tommy would be home for Christmas. He had written to her several times and told her that he would be home by a certain date. Each time, he had written later to tell her that his plans had changed and his homecoming would be delayed. The latest letter had promised that he would be home for New Year's.

Marilynn wasn't surprised when she received a cablegram from Tommy. She'd been expecting it for sometime. The contents of the wire were a disappointment. Tommy had sent the wire two weeks before to tell her that his plans had been changed again. He promised a letter to explain everything. The wire was certainly no cure for the blues.

At Dulag, McGuire was being hounded by reporters, but took the afternoon to write a long letter to Marilynn. He told her about his recent combat victories, and apologized for canceling his New Year's plans. He said: *"This time, the General has promised me that I'll be home in February."*

On December 28, McGuire flew to Tacloban. He had orders to report to General Kenney. He also wanted to see Richard Bong before his departure for the United States. McGuire did not want to "give Bong the business" about his recent successes. He wanted Bong to do him a favor.

Relaxed and rested, Bong said, "You bastard, you're going to do it, aren't you?"

McGuire replied, "Dick, I don't even want to talk about it. I'm upset. I've had plans to go home for four months, now, and they keep moving the dates back on me. My wife must think I'm crazy. I want you to call her and explain everything, time you reach San Francisco."

Bong replied, "Give me her number. I'll be glad to call her. Meanwhile, if you want to get a message to her real quick, ask one of the newsmen to send her a wireless message. They did it for me several times. You're going to be seeing those guys, you're all they've talked about for the last couple of days."

"Good idea, I'll do that," said McGuire. "I'm going to see Kenney before I go back to Dulag, and I'll get an absolute date from him."

"After what you've done the last few days, he's going to be on your back to watch yourself out there," said Bong. "Lord only knows, he's sure been on mine for a while."

McGuire spent the night at Tacloban and had a chance to visit with his old pal, Wally Jordan, from the 49th Fighter Group. They had flown to the Pacific on the same plane after going through P-38 transition training together in California. They had talked the last few months about going home at the same time, but it wasn't going to happen.

Bong and Jordan were off the next morning, and McGuire, as he had been ordered, reported to General Kenney. He was not pleased with what the General had to say. General Kenney later reported the conversation in his book, *General Kenney Reports*: "I told McGuire that I was taking him off flying as he looked tired to me. Tommy protested, 'General, I never felt better. Besides I'm only two behind and---'

"'That's just it,' I said. 'You are tired and you won't be rested enough to fly again until I hear that Bong has arrived back in the United States and been greeted as the top scoring ace of the war. As soon as I get the news, you can go back to work. If I let you go out today you are liable to knock off another three Nips and spoil Dick's whole party.'

"Tommy laughed but he didn't want to spoil anything for Dick, so it was okay. He'd just take it easy, get a lot of sleep for a few days, and then--he hoped the Japs wouldn't run out on us for a while yet."

Back at Dulag, McGuire talked to the press every day. He asked several of them to send wireless messages to Marilynn. He was asked to be a guest on two live short-wave broadcasts that would be beamed back to the United States. Both networks promised they would get messages to Marilynn so she could tune in and hear her famous husband on the radio.

On December 28, McGuire turned over command of the 431st Squadron to his friend Captain Robert F. "Pappy" Cline. McGuire moved up to 475th Group Headquarters as the Group Operations Officer. It looked like a license to hunt Japs, since he would be able to fly with any squadron and go where the action was most promising.

On December 29, McGuire told Sergeant Kish to have Pudgy ready for a mission. Kish asked, "Haven't you been grounded?"

"Not exactly," replied McGuire. "The General told me not to fly until I felt better. I feel fine."

"Major, that's not what I heard. I heard that the General didn't want you shooting any planes down until Major Bong was safely back in the States," replied Kish.

"Look Frank, if I wait until Bong gets back to the States, all the Japs might be gone. If I happen to latch on to something we could just forget to tell them for a day or so. It looks like the only way I'm ever going to get home is to beat Bong. I figure I might as well get started. The sooner I do it, the sooner I'll be going home."[1]

He flew fighter sweeps on December 30 and 31. He spent seven hours over Luzon,[2] but saw no action.[3] It looked like he'd have to wait until the new year before pursuing his goals.

For months newspapermen of Northern New Jersey interviewed their friend Tom McGuire. They had known him for years through the Pica Club. In early January, 1945, reporters crowded into Tom's office to photograph him holding a picture of Tommy. One of the pictures taken that day was sent out by the wire services in anticipation of McGuire becoming the number one ace of the war. The caption for the picture read: "Thomas B. McGuire Sr., holds a picture sent to him by his son from the Southwest Pacific, where he has just become the number one Ace of WW II by outgunning Richard I. Bong." The caption said, "Hold for future release," but everyone agreed that it was just a matter of time before the report would come through the wire service from the Philippines that Tommy McGuire was the new Ace of Aces.

Richard C. Bergholz interviewed McGuire and filed a report that appeared in the **Washington Post** and other newspapers on December 27. It read in part: "In any other war theater, Tommy McGuire's record of 38 planes downed, including seven over Leyte and Luzon in the last 48 hours, would make him top dog.

"Not here in the Southwest Pacific. Major Thomas B. McGuire's achievement has been overshadowed until now by America's ranking Army air ace, Major Richard I. Bong, of Poplar, Wis. who has 40 to his credit.

"While Major Bong was on furlough after bagging 27 Japanese planes, McGuire plugged away to reach the 20 mark. Flying together over the Philippines, the two aces matched victory for victory, but no matter how hot McGuire flew and fought, Bong always stayed ahead.

"Another day like McGuire had over Clark Field, near Manila, yesterday may lift him to the top.

"The young man, who grew up at Ridgewood, N.J., and Sebring, Florida, lives to knock them down.

"'For a time Mac used to be courageous to the point of being dumb,' his commander said. 'But now he's seasoned and knows his plane's limitations. He still has so much guts it makes it hard for his wingmen to stay with him.'

"The short, dark-mustached ace, whose wife lives in San Antonio, Tex., has flown 720 hours, and more than 240 combat missions ..."

The word went out over the Philippines: "General Kenney has grounded McGuire--doesn't want him going ahead of Bong before he reaches the States." In spite of "the word" McGuire continued quietly flying combat. He flew B-25 escort to Floridablanca on January 2, a five-hour and fifteen-minute mission--with no enemy action. Again on the sixth he flew a fighter sweep to Negros and Panay with no action. McGuire felt that time was running out. There just didn't seem to be any Japanese left to fight.

Pudgy V was seen leaving the runway every day but nobody thought anything about it. Everyone assumed that someone had borrowed Pudgy for a mission. Reporters were looking for McGuire every day and it was remarkable that none of them knew he was flying.

James Hutcheson of the Associated Press wrote: "Satan's Angels have become the second 5th Air Force group to pass the 500 mark in bagged Japanese planes.

"The Angels---the 475th group---have been labeled by Tokyo Rose as 'The Butchers of Rabaul'.

"They reached the 500-mark Christmas Day and now are raising that total rapidly.

"The outfit's top ace is Maj. Thomas McGuire Jr. of San Antonio, Texas, who has shot down 38 planes, only two planes under Richard I. Bong of Poplar, Wis. ..."

Hutcheson's story ran in newspapers with headlines like: "SATAN'S ANGELS, HEADED BY TEXAN, PASS 500 MARK," or "TEXAS ACE HAS 38 VICTORY RECORD IN PHILIPPINE AREA."

Because McGuire's home was given as San Antonio, newspapers in Florida didn't even print the story, and McGuire's friends in Sebring didn't see the latest news about their hometown boy.

In Chicago, a story ran under this headline: "ACE DISLIKES THE TITLE; SAYS IT'S ALL TEAMWORK." The story read: "The Major who had been leaning against the tent pole while his squadron of fighter pilots was being assigned its mission for the day, straightened up on assuming command.

"'Listen, you guys,' he said. 'There's been a lot of talk around here about aces. Every time a plane goes down it goes down because of the whole squadron, not one man.

"'I want you to remember that and anytime an ace develops in this squadron he is going to get thrown on his ear.'

"The Major is Thomas B. McGuire of San Antonio, a veteran of two years in the Pacific air. As squadron commander he is serious and thoughtful. As the 'Joisey Kid' he is the laughing fighter pilot who is credited on the records with shooting down 38 Japanese planes.

"In the last few days there has been considerable reference to McGuire himself, as an ace, especially after a day over Manila in which he--or, as he called it, his squadron--downed seven Jap planes.

"This reference embarrasses McGuire, 'The Joisey Kid,' no end and makes more difficult the persistent teamwork sermons of McGuire, the Major.

"McGuire is 24 years old. He isn't exactly handsome except for a constant grin. His straight black hair is always tousled. He is almost the exact opposite of Maj. Richard Bong, the only American to better McGuire as a Jap killer. Bong is quiet--so reserved as to be almost cold. McGuire is a fast talking, joking pilot like those in the movies. When it comes to flying both are conscientious, both insist on teamwork.

Tommy McGuire January 4, 1945 at Delug Air Field in the Philippines. McGuire looked healthy and rested compared to pictures taken months before. (USAF Photo)

"If properly approached, McGuire will go through a play-by-play account, with motions, of how the 38 planes were shot down. ...He doesn't try to explain why he is such a good shot. He grew up in Ridgewood, N.J., which he apologizes, had neither squirrels or deer for him to

323

practice on. ...'You just get him in your sights, press the trigger--and, puff,' he says. ..."

The pilots of the Fifth Air Force probably would have laughed if they had seen the articles. None of them had ever heard McGuire express his disdain for aces or insist on teamwork. Each reporter had his own point of view about McGuire and each developed a story about him as they saw him. They were pleased to have a new hero who would talk to them and seemed to delight in the differences between McGuire and Bong. The invention of the "Joisey Kid" was an attempt to contrast McGuire the "city kid" with Bong the "country boy." The characterization of Bong as "quiet and withdrawn" were not totally true either. Bong had been interviewed so many times that he figured he had said it all before and didn't need to repeat it.

The radio networks were particularly pleased to find that McGuire was a talker, and several of them asked him to do their radio programs which would be beamed back to the United States, via short-wave radio, for live broadcast. McGuire made but one request--he wanted Marilynn and his dad notified so they could hear the broadcasts. He also asked the networks to tell Marilynn that he wouldn't be home for a while, yet, and he was writing her to explain why. The networks agreed to contact her.

Marilynn received a wire from the CBS radio station in San Antonio, asking her to come to their station, for the broadcast, and then consent to an interview on air afterwards. Marilynn was at the station for the broadcast of CBS Reports, but she was disappointed. Live broadcasts were transmitted from New York by long-distance telephone lines. That particular morning the station in San Antonio did not receive the live feed because of trouble with the long-distance phone line. They told Marilynn the network was making a recording of the broadcast and they would ask them to send her a copy. Marilynn appreciated their good intentions but she was sure she would never hear the broadcast.

The rest of the nation heard the following broadcast by John Adams of CBS:

"There's a P-38 lightning fighter here on Leyte Island in the Philippines, with 38 Japanese flags painted on the fuselage, each representing one Japanese plane that will never fly again. In the studio today is the skipper of that plane, Major Thomas B. McGuire, Jr. of Ridgewood, New Jersey, top ace of the 475th Group of the Fifth Fighter Command, and ranking second only to Major Richard I. Bong, among all U. S. aces. Bong has 40 Jap planes to his credit, but it may take only one day like Christmas Day over Manila, for McGuire to set up a

new record. How long has it taken for you to run up this score of 38 Jap kills, Major?"

McGuire: "Just 17 months, but 14 of the kills have been made here in the Philippines in the last two months I got my first plane back in August of 1943 on a mission to Wewak. I've flown 740 combat hours and 246 missions since coming out to the Southwest Pacific."

Adams: "Do you think they are coming easier now, Major?"

McGuire: "Not exactly that. Some days you run into a lot and have good shooting. On my last two missions over Manila we didn't raise any."

Adams: "What's the fastest period of action you had Major McGuire?"

McGuire: "Last week just after Christmas we had a tough one up over Manila. The bombers had just completed their run and were starting for home when we saw five Nips coming down out of the clouds. One was just about 50 yards off the last bomber's tail and I took a long shot---about 400 yards---which hit him about the cockpit and he burst into flames. I caught another coming in from the left by a deflection shot and saw him blow up, turned sharply and took a shot at one of four coming in from the right, but he dove underneath and I couldn't see what happened to him. Then I dove down at some Zekes coming up and hit one around the cockpit. He rolled over and went down to crash in a dry river bed. I made my fifth attack at about 1500-feet and hit him in the wing gas tank, and he burst into flames. All of this happened in three or four minutes, and I don't mind telling you I was pretty excited."

Adams: "And you didn't pick up any Jap bullets during all of this?"

McGuire: "No, I was pretty lucky. But, about two months ago over Ormoc, I ran into some trouble and got a small shrapnel wound. We had been dive bombing a convoy and on our way back saw a Jap division moving along the Ormoc road. There were 14 of us dropping down from 8,000-feet to tree top level to strafe troops, tanks and trucks along about eight miles of road, between Ormoc and Valencia. Later we learned the action stopped a division. We left 35 vehicles burning and about 3,000 enemy casualties."

Adams: "Well, that's not a bad record for fighter pilots, Major, but what about that close call you had in New Guinea?"

McGuire: "That was back at Oro Bay when the Nips sent in about 75 planes. I got separated from my squadron and jumped seven Nips. It was a bad mistake. I guess I'd gotten a little too cocky and I tried to fly right into them. I got one from a hundred feet behind, then turned to pull up to get another one. I felt my whole plane start shaking---the left engine blew up---the right engine was fading, and the controls were shot up. Found I couldn't pull out of the dive and I tried to bail out, but couldn't get free of the cockpit for about 5,000 feet. Then my parachute didn't open until I was about 800 feet from the water. The boys on the PT boat that picked me up said the whole thing happened so quickly that the three Nips I shot down and my own plane were in the air in flames at the same time. I had about six pieces of shrapnel and a couple of 7.7 slugs and a few other scratches. That was about my luckiest day, I guess. I spent three weeks in the hospital and two months later I was back in action."

Adams: "Did that upset your sighting eye or your trigger finger, Major McGuire?"

McGuire: "Well, I was a little over-cautious at first, but as soon as I got back into the fight I found that I hadn't lost the edge. We got the formula for fighting back in training school. When you run into the Japs it helps a lot if you can fire on them instinctively, like hunting duck or game birds. Hunting Japs is the most dangerous kind of hunting there is. If you don't have good teamwork from your wingman you're liable to be the dead duck instead of the Jap. Teamwork enabled our outfit, the 475th, to run up a total of 507 Jap planes to date."

Adams: "Thank you, Major McGuire and I hope you get a chance to run your own total up to 40 or 41 on your next trip against Japan. This is John Adams now in the Philippines. I return you to CBS in New York."[4]

Another broadcast featuring McGuire was made by William J. Dunn for a CBS program, and NBC aired a similar interview. There was no doubt that McGuire would return home as a celebrated ace, just as Bong had. The pilots around Dulag were certain that before he departed, McGuire would be awarded the Congressional Medal of Honor for his two outstanding days of action on December 25 and 26, and they expected General MacArthur would make the presentation.

[1] Interview with Frank Kish
[2] McGuire's Form 5, Individual Flight Record
[3] McGuire's Broadcast on CBS--printed in this chapter
[4] The recording of this interview is in the Sebring Historical Society

44

"Please accept my most sincere condolences on the death of your son... You can rest assured that he had the makings of a most outstanding officer, because battlefield promotions were not too easily won. It is a tragic thing, of which he is one of the examples, that many of the men so promoted, and also many men decorated, become casualties through, perhaps, an undue desire to demonstrate to their comrades that they were worthy of the distinctions they had received. Of course, that is the stuff of which heroes are made, and, personally, I am a great admirer of heroes." ------------G. S. Patton, Jr., General, U.S. Army

To a father, in Buffalo, N. Y., whose son was killed after receiving a battlefield commission

McGuire, with his friend Major Jack Rittmayer in tow, met Sergeant Frank Kish, McGuire's crew chief, in the evening at the outdoor movie theater and McGuire said, "I just got the word from General Kenney. He's turning me loose. Dick Bong is in San Francisco and I won't have to sneak around any more."

Kish asked, "Are you going out tomorrow?"

McGuire answered, "I'm setting up a sweep for tomorrow morning."

"I'm taking a three day pass, but I'll stay if you are flying," said Kish.

"Take the pass. I won't be flying Pudgy," replied McGuire

"Is there something wrong with Pudgy?" asked Kish.

"No," answered McGuire. "She's in good shape. Maybe my luck has run out in Pudgy. Those flags on the nose may be causing the Japs to avoid me. Maybe I'll do better in another plane."

"Who's plane will you fly, sir?" asked Kish.

"Champ's lending me his plane for a few days," replied McGuire.

"Major, do you want me to stick around and service Captain Champlin's plane for you?" asked Kish.

"No, you go ahead and enjoy your pass. Champ's people and Van Der Geest will take care of me," replied McGuire.

"I'm glad Bong's home," said Kish. "I wish we were on our way."

"Don't worry, we'll be heading home soon," laughed McGuire. "You'll have to learn about jets. That's probably what we'll be flying."

"Yes, sir. I'll learn," nodded Kish.

"I'm sure you will, Frank," McGuire said. "Enjoy your pass, and look out for those Philippine women."

"I'll take care of myself," said Kish. "You do the same."[1]

McGuire was no longer the Commanding Officer, or even assigned to the 431st Fighter Squadron. He was now the Group Operations Of-

He had two men set for the mission and was looking for a fourth. He saw Douglas Thropp and said, "I just wrote you up for your first kill, didn't I? You want to go on a sweep in the morning ?"

"Hell, yes!" volunteered Lieutenant Douglas Thropp.[2]

"O K," said McGuire. "We're going to catch the early birds who've been hitting us at daybreak every morning. It's me, you, Major Rittmayer and Captain Weaver. We'll leave at 0630."

Second Lieutenant Thropp had joined the squadron in August and had accumulated 130 hours of combat time. He would be the junior man on this flight but was by no means a rookie.[3] McGuire had confidence in him and had verified his first kill, weeks before, on December 7.

Captain Edwin Weaver was a veteran pilot who had recently transferred into the 431st Fighter Squadron, after a stint of duty in North Africa, where he had put in flying hours but had not seen combat. He had flown McGuire's wing the day after Christmas and had witnessed his four victories. Although McGuire didn't remember it, Weaver was the same Edwin Weaver, who as a cadet in San Antonio, had once been dressed down and given demerits by an upperclassman, Thomas B. McGuire, Jr. Ed Weaver had never forgotten or forgiven the fact that McGuire had personally caused Weaver to "walk a tour" while his classmates were enjoying Saturday afternoon in San Antonio.[4]

Major Rittmayer, TDY from the 13th Air Force, had flown with the 431st Squadron for several weeks. He'd been on most of the missions McGuire and Bong had flown together. In that short time he had gotten four enemy planes. McGuire had promised Rittmayer he'd be an ace, and he just needed one more victory to make it.

The next morning, "Daddy Flight" left the Dulag airstrip at 6:20 a.m., McGuire in the lead and Weaver flying his wing. Rittmayer and Thropp formed the second element. They climbed to 10,000 feet and set course for Fabrica Airdrome on Negros Island. The air was smooth as they flew above a thick layer of gray clouds which completely shut off any view of the earth below. At about 6:50 a.m. McGuire estimated that they were near their target and led them down through several bumpy layers of clouds before breaking out of the overcast at 1,700 feet.

They were 10 miles from the target and they turned and flew towards it. They arrived over Fabrica Airdrome at 7:00 a.m. and circled the field for 10 minutes. No Japanese planes rose to challenge them so McGuire led the flight towards another field about 10 miles away. A few minutes later Captain Weaver called on his radio: "There's a Zeke at 12 0'clock, low." McGuire started a sharp turn to the left with Weaver on his wing. Thropp and Rittmayer had become separated during a descent through a layer of clouds and trailed by some distance. McGuire intended to bring his guns to bear on the single enemy plane. Just as the other members of the flight were preparing to drop their belly tanks McGuire ordered: "Save your tanks."

This order was contrary to normal combat procedure. Usually "drop tanks" was the first order when entering combat. McGuire thought the Zeke would flee without challenging the four P-38s.

Unbelievably, the Zeke made a quick turn and Lieutenant Thropp could see the enemy's guns flashing as he was being fired upon. Thropp threw his plane left and right, up and down to make the shots miss.

Major Rittmayer was to the rear, and fired a quick burst that caused the Zeke to break off his attack.

Weaver found himself the target and called for help.[5]

McGuire threw his plane, still heavily loaded with external fuel tanks, into an emergency turn with full power. He'd have to fire quickly to save his wingman! His P-38 shuddered violently--he was about to stall. He'd felt this before, but this time it was different. McGuire knew he was in trouble, but he continued his turn until he forced the Zeke to break off his attack.

Suddenly, McGuire's plane snap-rolled to the left. He was up-side-down, only a few hundred feet from the ground--not high enough to recover or bail out. His plane hit instantly in the inverted position, and there was an explosion. There was no chance he could survive.

McGuire's plane went down with both engines going full speed. Full speed was the way he had lived. He saved his wingman's life with his final effort. Enemy bullets did not take his life--his plane had not been hit. He died for trying too hard. He would not have been blamed if his wingman had been killed. No one would have called him a coward if he had boarded the plane with Richard Bong and Wally Jordan to go home--or he could have stayed in bed that morning back at Dulag, like most of the pilots.

What had started as an innocent fighter sweep ended the life of a young man who just wanted to prove himself. In Sebring, as a teenager, when his feelings had been hurt, he had said: "Some day, I'll show you all! I'll do something nobody else has ever done!"

What a show, Tommy! You did it!

[1]Frank Kish, in an interview at his home in Sharon, Pa., in 1987.
[2]Douglas Thropp, in a 1998 interview
[3]Thropp was not a helpless rookie as is often reported. His combat time is recorded in: 431st Fighter Squadron Report of Pilot's Combat Time. On file in the National Archives
[4]Ed Weaver in an interview in 1980.
[5]See Appendix A, How this book was written

45

There was no room to clear a sword--no power to strike a blow.

----Rudyard Kipling

The mission of January 7, 1945, which cost McGuire his life, also claimed his friend Jack Rittmayer. The combat lasted only seconds and everything went so fast that Weaver and Thropp, the survivors, hardly knew what had happened. Thropp, Rittmayer, and Weaver had all been fired on by a Japanese plane. Rittmayer was killed but Weaver and Thropp returned to the base ten minutes apart with different ideas about what had happened.

The Japanese fighter pilot seemed to be superhuman. He had attacked the P-38s as if by magic. Later it was learned that more than one Japanese plane was involved in that fatal day of combat. This fact eluded the two survivors because of the furious nature of the battle. [1]

The question every pilot in the Philippines was asking: "Why did McGuire order his men to keep their heavily laden external fuel tanks, when a combat situation was apparent?" He violated three of his own rules: "Never enter combat at low altitude. Never enter combat at low speed. Never enter combat without dropping your fuel tanks." No one knew the answer.

Sergeant Frank Kish, McGuire's crew chief, had taken his three-day-pass as McGuire had told him to do. He and a couple of pals had gone to a nearby town for several days. The last day of the leave they drove their jeep through areas where Japanese stragglers still roamed the countryside. They stopped at the 9th Fighter Squadron, their former outfit, and ate supper. After dark as they traveled the last 20 miles they sang American songs at the top of their voices so they would not be mistaken for Japanese. When Kish entered the 431st Squadron area he was met by his assistant crew chief, Corporal Richard Van Der Geest.

He said, "Frank, something real bad happened while you were gone. It's Mac. He didn't come back."

Kish said, "Hell, that's happened before---he'll be back."

Van Der Geest interrupted, "Frank, he's not coming back this time."

They went to Van Der Geest's bunk where they sat and talked. Van Der Geest produced McGuire's crushed 500-hour hat and said, "I've got his hat. He put it on my head, like he always did, when I was strapping him in. I don't know what to do with it."

With tears in his eyes, Kish said, "Give it to me. I'll be going home, now. I've been out here for over three years. I was just staying to take care of him. I'll see that his dad gets it." [2]

A young 431st Squadron pilot, Lieutenant Chris Herman, wrote home to his sister: *"I guess you've read about Mac 'missing in action'. It was quite a shock to us--sort of took the spark plug out of the squadron. Just one lousy little Zeke did the job--got two P-38s, shot up a third one--and got away! ... Our red-nosed planes are known all over, and wherever we go, we're asked, 'What happened?'"*

Dick Graham, a B-24 pilot, learned of McGuire's death five days later and was saddened by the news. Graham remembers: "McGuire's squadron protected us on Christmas Day over Manila. We witnessed two of his kills that day, and saw him and his men drive many enemy fighters away from our formation. The P-38's never had the same 'class' after Bong and McGuire were out of the air."

No one was more shocked by McGuire's death than General Kenney. He had seen men die in the air since his days as a active pilot during World War I. It never got any easier. McGuire was special; he had begged Kenney to get him back into combat. Kenney had come to believe what many people had thought about McGuire: that he was indestructible! Kenney never forgave himself for not sending McGuire home. He'd been swayed by the twinkle in McGuire's eyes. It had convinced him that McGuire would stay and beat Bong's record, and go home as America's Ace of Aces for all times.

Within a few days, an air field on the island of Mindoro was named McGuire Field. A few weeks later the Fifth Air Force published a collection of letters written by their top combat pilots. In McGuire's letter, written just before his fatal flight, he stated:

"...A fighter pilot must be aggressive. The enemy on the defensive gives you the advantage, as he is trying to evade you, and not shoot you down. Never break your formation into less than two-ship elements. Stay in pairs. A man by himself is a liability, a two-ship team an asset. If you are separated, join up immediately with other friendly airplanes. On the defensive, keep up your speed. A shallow, high-speed dive or climb is your best evasive action against a stern attack. You must never reverse your turn; that is asking for it. Try to make the Jap commit himself, then turn into his attack. If forced to turn, go to the right if possible. Go in close, then when you think you are too close, go in closer. At minimum range your shots count and there is less chance of missing your target. On deflection shots, pull your sight through the Nip. Most shots in deflection are missed by being over or under rather than by incorrect lead. Never turn with a Nip past the point where you can hold your lead. Don't let the Nip trick you into pulling up or turning until you lose your speed ..."

McGuire died because he lost speed in a turn.

On January 17, 1945, an official U.S. Army letter arrived at Marilynn McGuire's home. She did not worry as she opened it--she had gotten a number of letters from the Pacific--each one telling of a new medal being awarded to Tommy--besides bad news always came by Western Union with color coded stars on the envelope. She was stunned by the news that Tommy had been killed 10 days before. General Kenney assumed that she would be notified before his letter arrived.

HEADQUARTERS
ALLIED AIR FORCES
SOUTHWEST PACIFIC AREA
Office of the Commander
8 January 1945

Dear Mrs. McGuire:

The word that Tommy had been shot down brought me one of the worst of a number of bad moments I have had to face since the war began.

I have always had a lot of confidence in Tommy. I felt that he would make a name remarkable for command as well as for leadership and great personal courage. Highly intelligent and quick thinking, he had brought himself and his men out of trouble many times when others failed to come through. The accident which left him vulnerable on January 7, in which he met his death, was sheer chance, as Tommy was one of the most capable fighter pilots I have ever known.

I cannot express the depth of my regret. My heartfelt sympathy goes out to you. Your husband was one of the men the Air Forces can never forget. He has done as much as any other single fighter pilot in this theater of war to seek out and destroy the power of the Japanese. We will find it more difficult to carry on without him.

If at any time there is anything I can do to be of assistance to you, please let me know.

Sincerely,

GEORGE C. KENNEY
Lieutenant General, U.S.A.
Commanding

332

It was a terrible blow to Marilynn. She and Tommy had dated such a short time--had been apart for a year and then married. Their nine weeks together was a wonderful honeymoon, but hardly a marriage. Marilynn had dreamed for two years of having Tommy back home so that they could really be married. Tommy had said, "Let's think about children later; I want to be around when my children grow up." Marilynn had agreed.

Tommy had gone to war as just another pilot. By January of 1945 it was obvious to Marilynn and everyone else that she was married to a national hero. Although Marilynn never really thought about it, the prospect of having Tommy come home under those circumstances was even more exciting. Now, he wasn't coming home. There would be no homecoming. No marriage. No children. It was devastating to the young bride.

She went through a bad period when she wondered if she should have insisted on going to California with Tommy, or maybe she should have had a child. At least she would have had some part of Tommy with her. She looked around her apartment and saw the items she had brought back from Sebring when Polly died. She had brought them back because she thought Tommy would enjoy having them. Now the lamps and dishes were a reminder of what seemed like a strange dream.

Dealing with the Army had a way of bring one back to reality. From the moment of Tommy's death there were a string of blunders which would add frustration to her grief. Poor communications facilities from the Southwest Pacific delayed notification to her, and the destruction of Tommy's service records by a Japanese air raid on Dulag added more problems.

It all started when Marilynn received the letter from General Kenney. The General, being a caring man, had taken Tommy's death very badly. He had seen many young men die but he had known Tommy like a son. Yet, he had let him stay in the war long after he deserved to go home. He let him stay because Tommy wanted it. He had also fallen prey to the mystique that had grown around McGuire--that he would always survive. Now in an attempt to tell Marilynn how much Tommy had been valued and how badly he felt, he had unwittingly announced Tommy's death to her.

Tommy had gone down on the seventh of January and by the next day it was known for certain that he could not be alive. General Kenney had written his letter that day. It arrived in San Antonio on January 17. Marilynn had to call Tommy's father, whom she had never met, to tell him that his son was dead. Then she had to face the press and tell them.

333

The story was carried on the front page of the **New York Times** and still, no official notice arrived.

A few days later an Army officer arrived at Marilynn's home. Instead of an official expression of grief, which Marilynn might have expected, he asked her to surrender the letter from General Kenney. He would not tell her why he wanted it. It was all she had and she would not even let him see it. The reason that request was made has always remained a mystery.

On January 19 a letter arrived from Superior, Wisconsin. It read:

Dear Marilynn:

"Through my fiancee, Major Richard Bong--with whom your husband lived and fought--I learned what a truly fine person your husband was. He will always remain as such to those who loved him."

It was signed: Marge Vattendall

On February 27, 51 days after Tommy went down, a telegram arrived from the War Department. It said:

I regret to inform you that your husband, Major Thomas B. McGuire, Jr., 0437031, Air Corps, has been reported missing in action over Negros, Philippine Island since 7 January 1945.

A few days later Marilynn was almost sent into shock by a letter that arrived in the mail. It was addressed to her in the familiar handwriting of her husband. It had been mailed December 31. It read in part:

"This is a hard letter to write. I had been expecting to send you a cable telling you to expect me home but my plans fell through. I went up and saw the General and got his promise that if my going home got balled up again, he promised to get me home the last of February. Dick Bong left two days ago and will call and tell you the story. He stayed with me his last two weeks over here and promised to call as soon as he hit Frisco. I had been waiting to cable you when I got the news that I would not be going for a while as I heard it the day before Dick left. I made him promise to call you as soon as he arrived---Wally Jordan with whom I came over and with whom I had expected to return left today and he also promised to call. I wanted to get back so badly, but I guess the cards were stacked against me this time. At least I have the General's promise so it should be definite this time.

"By the way, as you probably know by now, I knocked down seven planes over Manila the past few days and now have 38 to my credit. I was called today and told I was to make two broadcasts to the states---one New Year's Eve for NBC---the other on the third for CBS. They promised to cable you so you could listen. A cable from me would take about two weeks but they get out by wireless and can reach you in a day. Lee Van Etta of INS also promised to cable you via press radio to let you know I wouldn't be home right away."

Marilynn had gotten a wire from CBS, but no phone calls or other cables. On March 15, a letter arrived from The Adjutant General, Major General J. A. Ulio. It said Tommy was missing, and it gave graphic details about Tommy's last mission.

Marilynn was devastated by the experience and was feeling very low. In a few weeks a hand-written letter arrived that read:

April 28, 1945

Dear Mrs. McGuire:

Twice before, I have written to you since your husband's death; and each time, I have torn the letter up for it did not say what I wished to convey to you. Now, within a few days, I must leave on an unexpected mission into the European area, and I do not want to leave without writing to you however inadequate the letter may be.

It is not that I had known Major McGuire for a long time or that I could number myself among his closest friends; but friendships made in such places as the army camps of New Guinea and under combat conditions, take on a quality of their own which cannot be measured in the ordinary terms of time.

I flew with your husband on a number of missions when his squadron was based at Hollandia, and again after he had moved his group to the island of Biak. At his invitation, I stayed with him in his tent for a number of days near Mokmer drome. We went through the Biak caves and dynamited fish together to get fresh food. He was one of the ablest officers I have known and one of the finest pilots I have ever flown with. He often spoke of you during the evenings in his tent, and I know that he expected to return home within a few weeks of the time I left--that was late August. I think the Philippine campaign, and the op-

335

portunity of taking part, as he did so brilliantly, probably caused him to postpone his plans for returning to the United States.

I had hoped to see your husband again in this country, and to continue the friendship which began in that Hollandia jungle camp. The announcement of his death came to me as a great shock; and with it, I felt a keen personal loss.

I think there is no need for me to tell you that you have my deepest sympathy.

Sincerely,

Charles A. Lindbergh.[3]

(Lindbergh was on his way to Germany, at the request of President Truman, to assess the German rocket and jet aircraft programs)

A few months later Marilynn received word that Tommy was to be posthumously awarded America's highest honor, the Medal of Honor, for the action on December 25 and 26, 1944, when he had shot down seven Japanese planes and risked his life to fend off other attackers even after his guns were hopelessly jammed. Marilynn called Tommy's father and they started making plans for the ceremony.

Sometime later Marilynn received a large flat package from the Columbia Broadcasting System. She opened it to find a recording of Tommy's radio broadcast from Leyte. It was the broadcast she had missed in San Antonio, because of transmission problems. The people at CBS had been true to their word and had sent the record so she might hear her husband's broadcast. They had no idea that Tommy had died when they sent it. It was difficult for Marilynn to listen. The sound of Tommy's strong and confident voice has haunted her over the years.[4]

[1] See: The Fatal Mission, in this book
[2] McGuire's hat was presented to the Air Force Museum, Dayton, Ohio, by Marilynn McGuire. It is displayed in the Bong and McGuire exhibit
[3] Charles Lindbergh's letter is published here for the first time
[4] This recording resides in the Sebring Historical Society, a gift of Marilynn McGuire Beatty

EPILOGUE

"With gallant initiative, deep and unselfish concern for the safety of others, and heroic determination to destroy the enemy at all costs, Major McGuire set an inspiring example in keeping with the highest traditions of the military service."

----from McGuire's Medal of Honor citation
Signed by Harry S. Truman

May 8, 1946, was the date selected for the presentation of Tommy McGuire's Medal of Honor. The Medal was to be presented to Marilynn and she could pick a site for the ceremony. Any one of the military installations in San Antonio would have done a beautiful job. Instead, out of respect for Tommy's father, she allowed the ceremony to be held at the City Hall in Paterson, New Jersey.

The Medal of Honor ceremony was a formal affair held at three o'clock p.m. in the City Council chambers, and Tommy's father and the Mayor of Paterson, William Furrey, wore tails. Color Guards entered down the center isle. After the invocation Mayor Furrey introduced the distinguished guests: William Edge, Governor of New Jersey; Albert Hawkes and Alexander Smith, U. S. Senators from New Jersey; J. Parnell Thomas and Gordon Canfield, U. S. Congressmen from New Jersey; John Barbour, Charles Barton, State Senators; Lloyd Marsh, Secretary of State for New Jersey; Judge Wendell Furrey; William Rurode, Mayor of Ridgewood; and Colonel Charles A. Lindbergh.[1]

General Kenney made the presentation speech and repeated the statements he had made in his letter to Marilynn: "Major McGuire is a man the Air Force can never forget. We find it difficult to carry on without him." Then Captain Quinn of the Air Corps read:

THE WHITE HOUSE
WASHINGTON
The President of the United States takes pride in awarding
the MEDAL of HONOR posthumously to
MAJOR THOMAS B. MCGUIRE, JR.
AIR CORPS, UNITED STATES ARMY
for service as set forth in the following:
CITATION
"Major McGuire fought with conspicuous gallantry and intrepidity over Luzon, Philippine Islands, on 25 and 26 December 1944. Voluntarily, he led a squadron of fifteen P-38's as top cover for heavy

337

bombers striking Mabalcat Airdrome, where his formation was attacked by twenty aggressive Japanese fighters.

In the ensuing action he repeatedly flew to the aid of embattled comrades, driving off enemy assaults while himself under attack and at times outnumbered three to one and, even after his guns jammed, continuing the fight by forcing a hostile plane into his wingman's line of fire. Before he started back to his base, he had shot down three Zeros. The next day he again volunteered to lead escort fighters on a mission to strongly-defended Clark Field. During the resultant engagement he again exposed himself to attacks so that he might rescue a crippled bomber. In rapid succession he shot down one enemy aircraft, parried the attack of four enemy fighters, one of which he shot down, single-handedly engaged three more Japanese, destroying one, and then shooting down still another, his thirty-eighth victory in aerial combat. On 7 January, 1945, while leading a volunteer fighter sweep over Negros Island, he risked an extremely hazardous maneuver at low altitude in an attempt to save a fellow flyer from attack, crashed, and was reported missing in action. With gallant initiative, deep and unselfish concern for the safety of others, and heroic determination to destroy the enemy at all costs, Major McGuire set an inspiring example in keeping with the highest traditions of the military service."

It was signed by Harry S. Truman, President of the United States.

General Kenney placed the Medal, which hung from a blue and white ribbon, around Marilynn's neck. She towered over the pint-sized Three Star General. Then a pair of army buglers, one in the room and one removed to a far part of the building, played taps. Marilynn and Tommy's father were still crying when the color guard withdrew with the flags.

Charles Lindbergh had sat quietly in the back of the chamber unrecognized by most of those in attendance. During the reception Lindbergh came forward and helped Marilynn escape from the photographer. He spoke to her quietly and asked, "Have you had enough of this?" Marilynn agreed and Lindbergh said, "That's enough boys."

Several years before Lindbergh had stopped appearing at public events saying, "I am most anxious to continue living and working quietly, and experience has shown that I cannot do this and at the same time take part in even semi-public occasions."[2]

Lindbergh had come to this public affair only because of his high personal regard for Tommy McGuire and to have a chance to express those feelings to Marilynn. In the South Pacific he had seen McGuire fly fighter missions, run a squadron as its Commanding Officer, and deal

Lindbergh and McGuire. Great friends in a short time

with the tragic death of men under his command. All of this from a man only 24 years old---about the same age Lindbergh had been when he helped design, build, and fly the Spirit of St. Louis into the history books. He couldn't help but admire this young man and he had to come and tell Marilynn. He expressed his admiration and told her that Tommy had spoken of her often and was anxious to return home and resume his life with her. He then slipped quietly from the crowd leaving Marilynn with strangers.

[1] From the official program of the ceremony

[2] A quote written in a letter from Gen. George Kenney
to T. B. McGuire, Tommy's father

THROUGH THE YEARS

There was an Army air field at Fort Dix, New Jersey, 30 miles east of Philadelphia. It was called "the air field at Fort Dix." During World War II it became a very important port of embarkation and during the Berlin Airlift it became invaluable for air shipments to Europe. It was apropos then, when the Air Force split from the Army, that the air field be given a name. The timing was right and it was named McGuire Air Force Base, after a native son.

Many United States Air Force Bases are named for people who died in training flights. Some are named for true flying heroes. Each base has obtained its name in a different way. Tommy McGuire is one of the most deserving to have achieved this honor. Had it not been for Congressmen Gordon Canfield and J. Parnell Thomas from New Jersey, the base may never have been named McGuire Air Force Base. These two men knew Tommy's father and both had read Tommy's war record into the **Congressional Record**. Richard Bong was similarly honored with an air base in Wisconsin, but Bong Air Force Base was closed shortly thereafter, as surplus.

The Air Force contacted Marilynn, now married and a mother, and ask her if she could come to New Jersey on September 17, 1949, for the dedication and naming of the air base. "We will fly you from San Antonio and we will billet you in the base Guest House." Marilynn told them that she would be happy to attend. Months went by and the event was nearing but she never heard from the Air Force again. Marilynn made several calls to the Air Force about the trip but got no answers except that the ceremony was going on as planned. She made her own airline and hotel arrangements and headed to New Jersey. When she arrived at the base for the dedication, she was shocked to find that they did not even have a seat for her on the reviewing stand. Every politician in New Jersey was on the stand with Tommy's father and the military. Through some misunderstanding Marilynn had been left out of all of the proceedings at the base and after some scrambling around she was given a seat in the front row of the audience.

General Kenney, now Commander of the Air University at Maxwell Field, made the dedication speech to name McGuire Air Force Base. Tommy's father was called upon and he gave a brief speech before unveiling an oil painting of Tommy which he presented to the base. Marilynn almost fell off of her chair. She had paid $350 to have the painting made, right after the war. It had hung in her home until she remarried. Feeling then that Tommy's father might like to have it she had given it to him for Christmas. He presented it to the Air Base without ever mentioning where it had come from.

During the ceremony General Kenney spotted Marilynn in the front row and made hand signals which asked her why she wasn't on the reviewing stand. She shrugged her shoulders and signaled back, "search me?" It would be years later before Marilynn would understand why she had been snubbed by the Air Force.

In late 1949, Tommy's remains were finally found, not at sea, as had been reported, but on land, near the village of Cadiz on Negros. Identifications were made by dental exam and the aircraft wreckage. It carried the serial number of Fred Champlin's P-38, which McGuire had borrowed for his fatal mission.

McGuire's remains were returned to the United States for burial with full military honors, in Arlington National Cemetery. In May of 1950, Marilynn once again accepted the Air Force's invitation and once again Thomas B. McGuire Sr., being a constant influence with the people at McGuire Air Force Base, assured the Air Force that no arrangement need be made for Marilynn. She was not provided with accommodations of any sort before or after the ceremony. She asked the Air Force to provide transportation to the graveside and they arranged for her to ride with Tommy's aunt, Estelle Tolson. Stella was pleased to have Marilynn in her car and couldn't believe proper arrangements hadn't been made.

Marilynn, having been raised in San Antonio, knew a lot about military etiquette and she was shattered by her experiences with the Air Force. She had tried to donate Tommy's medals to McGuire Air Force Base but had never received a reply from them. Mr. McGuire once came to her home in San Antonio, and asked for the medals, "for the base," but she had never heard from the base and did not turn them over.

When Tom McGuire died, Joan Mallon, his long time girl friend, came into possession of Tom's files from the VIP apartment at McGuire Air Force Base where he had spent every weekend for 20 years. Joan sent one of the files to Marilynn. The Air Force had entrusted Tom McGuire to act as a go-between with Marilynn and the old man had systematically eliminated her from each invitation list out of a false sense of loyalty to his son, presumably because Marilynn had remarried. All the letters from Marilynn to McGuire Air Force Base, offering the medals, were in his file. They had turned over the letters to Tom McGuire because he had told the Air Force he would handle things.

Life went on for Marilynn. She had a husband and a son to look after, and she helped run their business. She got regular requests for information about Tommy and she donated a number of Tommy's things to the Air Force Museum in Dayton, Ohio. She sent them Tommy's log book, a treasured record of every flight he had made, his famous 500-hour hat, his Bible and his medals. The Air Force Museum was delighted with the gifts and thanked her properly. The items are in the museum's Bong and McGuire exhibit which explores the relationship the two Aces enjoyed.

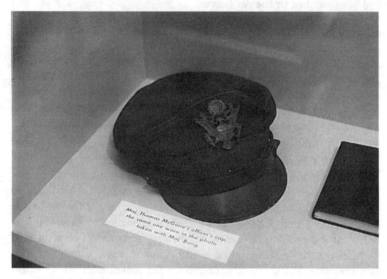

McGuire's famous hat. Displayed in the Air Force Museum Bong and McGuire exhibit

Fortunately, after many years Marilynn would have a more pleasant experience with McGuire Air Force Base. Her second husband, Clem Stankowski, had died after a 35-year marriage. After a few years she met and married Robert Beatty. In 1981, Marilynn heard from McGuire Air Force Base again. "Mrs. Beatty, this is Colonel Leete, at McGuire Air Force Base. I've been searching for you and finally got your name from a neighbor of mine, Charlie Martin. Our wing commander, Colonel Wright, has acquired a P-38 for permanent display on our base. We plan to have a dedication when the project is completed, and we'd like you to be the guest of honor."

Marilynn said, "I'd love to be there. When will it be held?"

"I'm not sure," said Leete. "But we will let you know as soon as a date is set. We will fly you up here and of course we will have housing for you at the base." It all sounded so familiar.

This was a well-intentioned offer, and Colonel Leete stayed in touch with Marilynn for a while. The project to move the P-38 from California to New Jersey didn't go as well as hoped. The plane was damaged en route but did arrive in time to be repaired and refurbished for the open house on May 25. Time prohibited the plane from being placed in its final display area but it was displayed on the flightline with other World War II airplanes. (See: "Securing a P-38," in this book)

Colonel Leete was transferred and the memorial project was left in the hands of a local business man, William Demas, who assembled the materials and people to complete the memorial. The project cost $500,000, and was completed without government money. In May 1982, the P-38 was placed on a mount, in a flying attitude, in the center of a traffic circle which is halfway between the main gate and the main air terminal building.

Demas called Marilynn to tell her the dedication was being delayed in hopes of getting President Reagan to give the dedicatory speech. Five years passed after the P-38 was obtained, and there was no dedication. In 1986, Demas and his committee arranged for Secretary of Defense Casper Weinberger to make the dedication. A November date was set. Marilynn and Robert were picked up at their home by a Air Force staff car and delivered to the San Antonio airport for a commercial airline flight to New Jersey. It was the beginning of a near perfect trip that would bring Marilynn the satisfaction that had eluded her for 40 years.

They were met at Newark Airport by Lieutenant Fox and a staff car driven by Airman Hawkins. The Lieutenant would escort them to McGuire Air Force Base, and look after their needs for the next 48 hours. They were housed in the McGuire Suite at the base guest house. The suite consisted of a sitting room, bedroom, and a kitchen generously stocked with refreshments and snacks.

Lieutenant Sherry Fox, a recent graduate of the Air Force Academy, was a perfect companion for the couple. Marilynn appreciated the young officer for her accomplishments as much as her help. The Lieutenant was not a public relations specialist, but an Air Force pilot who wore the same silver wings that Tommy had worn, and whose regular duty was flying the Atlantic Ocean as a pilot of a giant four engined C-141 transport plane.

Marilynn and Robert were escorted to the memorial site to view the P-38 and the plaques mounted below. At 6:30 p.m. there was a cocktail party at the Officer's Club. The room was filled with members of the Memorial Corporation, local Air Force Association members, military personnel, and members of the 475th Fighter Group, Tommy's old outfit. The men of the 475th Group, now in their late sixties or seventies, were particularly happy to be able to greet and honor Marilynn after all the intervening years.

One by one members of these groups worked their way toward Marilynn to introduce themselves, heap praise on Tommy, or tell their relationship to the project. Robert Beatty stood in the background and watched lovingly as Marilynn enjoyed the spotlight.

During dinner the guests enjoyed classical music from a string quartet of Air Force musicians attired in formal dress uniforms. Marilynn sat at a table with Pete Madison and his wife and other members of the 475th Fighter Group. She was delighted to meet some of the men who had known Tommy in the Pacific.

After the meal there were introductions and speeches explaining how the memorial had been built. General Larry Wright, who had been the Wing Commander at McGuire AFB, explained his part in acquiring the P-38 for the Memorial. Then he paid tribute to the veterans of World War II, saying: "They sacrificed so much to preserve our American way of life. Our generation owes them a great deal. If they had not been willing to lay down their lives in battle, there might be a Japanese Zero or a German ME-109 on the pole out there in the Memorial."

Pete Madison, the owner of a California printing business, related to the group how he had flown wing for Major McGuire: "I was one of the new guys. Mac always took on one of the new guys as a wingman. What better way for a young man to learn combat flying than to fly as McGuire's wingman? McGuire said, 'I do the shooting, you protect my backside. That's the way it works. I can't do my job unless I know that a Jap isn't on my tail--your chance will come later.' I was 19, the 'Iron Major' was all of 23 years old. I can't believe we were ever that young."

Pete Madison then said, "I am proud and pleased tonight that I am sitting with Marilynn Beatty, formerly Mrs. Tommy McGuire. Marilynn, will you please stand--would everyone please give her a hand." Everyone rose and gave Marilynn a standing ovation. It was her first public recognition as the widow of Tommy McGuire since she had received the Medal of Honor for Tommy, 40 years before. She smiled and waved through a few tears.

Friday morning Marilynn and Robert visited the McGuire Museum and looked over the memorabilia displayed there and saw a 10-minute slide program on Tommy's life, written by the author of this book. Then Marilynn made a presentation to the museum of pictures and the hat she had worn when she received the Medal of Honor in Paterson, New Jersey, in 1946. The hat, a John Frederick original, was of brown straw, and had a broad brim with gold mesh and gold feathers around the open crown. The designer hat had cost $65 in 1946 and matched the Nettie Rosenstein dress she had worn.

Marilynn was impressed by the artwork displayed in the museum, but she was visibly shaken by a bronze bust which had been commissioned by a citizen's group from Ridgewood, New Jersey. The bust was displayed with a spotlight positioned above and slightly behind it. The light caused the bust to have a macabre look.

At 2:00 Friday afternoon, 1,200 invited guests assembled at the P-38 Memorial where there was a seat for each person. One-star and two-star generals were almost commonplace as the Fort Dix Army Band played a prelude of marches. The base had been closed for security reasons at noon and the crowd consisted only of invited guests, the participating military personnel, and several busloads of children from nearby North Hanover schools. Marilynn and the other dais guests moved into place.

P38 McGuire Memorial at McGuire Air Force Base, New Jersey

The sky was gray and overcast when the program started at 2:30 with the formal entrance of Secretary of Defense Casper Weinberger, and New Jersey Governor Thomas Kean. They entered through an honor guard of people from all branches of the services. The band played "Ruffles and Flourishes," and "Stars and Stripes Forever" as the crowd stood and all military personnel rendered a salute during the presentation of the National Anthem.

Col. Jerold L. Weiss, 438th Military Airlift Wing commander, introduced the honored guests which included six Medal of Honor winners from New Jersey and the nearby area, and the 28 members of the 475th Fighter Group, some of whom had come from as far away as California. Edwin Weaver, who had been on McGuire's last mission, lived nearby, and was invited to the ceremony, but died shortly before the event.

New Jersey Congressman H. James Saxton spoke and mentioned that he had recently placed information about the memorial and Tommy McGuire into the **Congressional Record**. Governor Kean mentioned that he had declared November 7, 1986, Major Thomas B. McGuire Jr. Day in the State of New Jersey. Secretary Weinberger next spoke with a quiet passion. He greeted Marilynn and thanked her for being in attendance. He then recognized the six Medal of Honor holders sitting in the front row: "Anyone who speaks in the presence of a winner of the Medal of Honor has to be deeply moved. The man we honor today, Major McGuire, was also a winner of the Medal of Honor--so I am particularly honored to have the opportunity to participate in this very inspiring dedication. For a Secretary of Defense there certainly can be no more welcome or appropriate task than to salute an American Military Hero and the many other heroes, perhaps some of them less celebrated, that he epitomizes. ...I can't help injecting a personal word here--this is the P-38 plane that the Major flew. When I was in New Guinea as a member of the infantry, far, far below where these planes went over, I can't tell you how comforting it was for those of us in the infantry, and usually in the mud, to see this very distinctive silhouette. For one thing we knew it wasn't a Zero, and we also knew that it was manned by some extraordinary able and capable people who were helping us. And so it's a particular personal pleasure to come here today for this very appropriate, very fitting, very beautiful memorial and see this plane here. Also to be a part of New Jersey's salute to America's Armed Forces.

"...This memorial is really a very stirring tribute to a true American hero, because Tommy McGuire was the consummate combat leader. He was daring and yet careful of his men, he was proud--not boastful. He was decisive, yet flexible. He was caring, yet exacting, as a leader has to be. This is leadership born of deeds, and uncommon valor. Shakespeare wrote that 'Courage mounteth with the occasion.' Such was certainly the case with Tommy McGuire as he racked up his remarkable aerial victories, helping American forces to push the Japanese back across the immense expanse of the Pacific Ocean.

"And of course his final response to danger is characteristic, as we have heard, not only a volunteer mission--a fighter sweep through savagely infested skies over the Philippines, but indeed a mission in which he gave his life saving a friend. Courage has been called generosity of the highest order. And of course never was it more so than in Tommy

346

McGuire's final act of gallantry. Several months before that final flight Tommy McGuire wrote of fighter pilots as 'those whose faith in each other must be complete.' McGuire risked death rather than break that faith. And he lived and died in the brotherhood of American fighter pilots--the same brotherhood that has sustained all of our soldiers and sailors, airmen, and marines. President Reagan sometimes asks, 'Where do we get such men and women? What is it we do that produces them when we need them? What moves young men to such noble acts?' Well the poet talks of courage as the highest gift--'courage is an independent spark from heavens bright throne by which the soul stands raised triumphant and high alone, courage the mighty attribute of powers above, by which those great in war are great in love.' And it's for heroes like Tommy McGuire that memorials such as this are rightfully built and in celebrating one courageous patriot we honor of course countless others who also sacrificed for their country.

"Warfare and the world have changed very greatly in the decades since the P-38 fighters tangled with the Japanese Zeros across the Pacific, but the backbone of America's might has not changed. It is still the individual soldiers, sailors, and airmen, and women, and the marines and their spirit, their fortitude, their resilience, their bonds, and especially their team work. Tommy McGuire would be the first to share his fame with the ground crews that kept his plane flying and that tradition of teamwork and cohesion thrives with today's armed forces."

Weinberger went on to say that time to mobilize is no longer an ally in modern war. "It is so vital that we do the preparation in advance so that if we do it well and do it right we'll never have to use it. ...We can not wait until the bombs fall to train today's Tommy McGuires. ...Our goal has been and still is to be so well prepared that (in the future) the only memorials we will dedicate and visit will be those of America's past wars."

At the conclusion of Weinberger's speech he and Marilynn placed a wreath at the base of the Memorial and returned to their position on the platform. The 3rd Brigade firing team from Fort Dix gave a three volley rifle salute. It was too familiar to Marilynn--she had been through all of this at Arlington Cemetery 36 years before. Then came the part Marilynn had dreaded for days--the playing of "Taps." As the bugler blew the quivering notes an echo from afar came back from a second bugler. Marilynn's hand trembled with emotion. Secretary Weinberger saw this and took Marilynn's hand in his until "Taps" ended.

From the gray horizon came the roar of four F-4 fighter planes from the 108th Tactical Fighter Wing of the New Jersey Air National Guard, stationed at McGuire Air Force Base. It was the missing man formation fly-by. As the four planes arrived over the base one plane from the middle of the traditional "V" formation pulled up and out of the formation. The rising plane's afterburner kicked in, and the craft went straight up through the thin clouds, out of sight into the heavens. Momentarily, the sun brightened the sky and then vanished behind the gray clouds again. There were many tear-glistened eyes in the crowd as their faces turned from the sky back to earth.

A sergeant from the firing team came to the stand and presented Marilynn with a small dark green pouch, with "M A F B Nov. 8, 1986" embroidered on it. He made a snappy salute, did an about-face, and returned to his men. Secretary Weinberger explained to Marilynn that the sergeant had presented her with the 21 brass shell casings from the saluting rifles as a memento.

A reception followed at the Officers Club. Marilynn and Robert stayed for a while before retiring to the guest house. It was the end of two emotion-packed days. Just before their limousine arrived, Marilynn and Robert sat quietly in the McGuire Suite with three friends, Charles and Antoinette Martin, and Lieutenant Fox. They lifted their wine glasses in one last toast to Tommy.

SECURING A P-38

Because McGuire had flown all of his combat missions in a Lockheed Lightning P-38, such an aircraft had been sought by McGuire Air Force Base since 1966, but every attempt to get one had failed.

Once, one was located just 50 miles south of McGuire Air Force Base, in Wilmington, Delaware. The Committee had dickered with the owners but couldn't come up with the asking price on the spur of the moment. If the owners had given them some time they could have raised the money, but a quick sale was being sought. The plane was sold to two young men, with no P-38 flight experience, who promptly flew it south where they crashed. Both men were killed and one of the last flying P-38s was destroyed.

Somewhere along the line someone came up with the idea of recovering a P-38 that still lay where it crash-landed during WWII, on the tundra in Alaska. The plane could only be reached during the summer months. The committee prevailed on the Air Force Commander in Alaska and he sent a crew to the site to assess the plane's condition. It was in fairly good shape and recovery was feasible but expensive, and the project fizzled. Other P-38s were known to be frozen in ice near the Arctic Circle but the recovery of these was also dismissed as too costly.

Finally, on February 12, 1981, Colonel Richard L. Upstrom, Director of the Air Force Museum, Wright-Paterson Air Force Base, Ohio, contacted Colonel Larry Wright at McGuire Air Force Base and asked if they were still interested in having a P-38.

Colonel Wright replied at once that McGuire Air Force Base would love to have the plane, and appointed Lt. Colonel Edward Leete as project officer. Colonel Leete had recently completed an assignment at the Air Force Museum and knew the people he would be dealing with on the permanent loan of the plane to McGuire Air Force Base.

The project was going to require the solving of many problems. The P-38 was in the hands of RMP Aviation in California who had owned it. The Air Force asked Dave Tallichet, a well-known aviator, who had once owned the rare bird and was one of the few remaining qualified P-38 pilots, to fly the plane to McGuire Air Force Base. He agreed to do it with one proviso: He would have to fly in VFR conditions. Visual Flight Rules were necessary because the P-38 was no longer equipped with instruments for foul weather flying. His time was valuable--he wanted the Air Force to get their strategic weather boys involved so three days of good weather could be assured for the flight.

A top priority project was undertaken by the Air Force weather people---"Let's get McGuire AFB the three good days they need." They

349

were watching for a weather system moving across the country, clearing the skies behind. The P-38 could just follow the front for three days and make the trip safely.

The proper conditions arrived and Dave set out on the trip. On the second day he landed at Memphis to spend the night. Early the next morning he had the plane refueled and he checked the weather. Everything was still "Go." As he taxied the plane toward the end of the runway for take-off, the 35-year-old nose gear jumped beyond a worn stop that would normally restrict the angle of turn. The nose wheel turned to 90 degrees, or perpendicular to the travel of the aircraft. The nose wheel shuttered, and collapsed. The nose of the plane fell and both propellers made a sickening clatter as they slashed against the concrete.

The plane wasn't seriously damaged but both propellers were badly bent. Colonel Leete called his friends at the Air Force Museum and asked to borrow the propellers from their P-38. This request fell on deaf ears, "Colonel, we trusted you with the P-38 and you didn't even get it to New Jersey safely. There is no way you are getting our good propellers. You will have to solve this one yourself and get the plane in flying condition, it still belongs to us, and the loan agreement calls for you to keep it in flying condition."

Colonel Leete was resourceful, and he located another P-38 on display at another Air Force Base. He called the Commanding Officer and begged for the use of the plane's propellers for a few days, just to fly the plane to New Jersey. He said, "Just take the props off of the P-38 and have them ready. I'll get the next C-141 transport plane heading to McGuire Air Force Base to stop at your field and pick up the propellers. We'll have them back to you within a week."

Members of the New Jersey National Guard were flown to Memphis and the P-38 was equipped with the borrowed props. They repaired the broken landing gear, and checked the engines. Everything was in order. The borrowed propellers worked, although they had not been used for 30 years.

Dave Tallichet once again checked the weather on the eastern seaboard and started the final leg of the trip. When he got into the air the P-38 seemed to be operating all right, so he pointed it to the northeast, toward New Jersey. He was headed for the Naval Air Station at Lakehurst. The plan was for him to spend the night on the Navy base, and on the following morning fly the plane the scant 20 miles to McGuire Air Force Base where the press and television people would be prepared for the arrival.

On the way to New Jersey, Dave started thinking about landing at Lakehurst, which of course had been the sight of the famous Hindenburg Airship crash, May 6, 1937, in which a number of people had been killed or injured. He also thought how lucky he had been that the twin Allison engines in the P-38 were in good enough condition after the Memphis accident, that they had gotten him this far. He also considered the 40-year-old propellers they had borrowed for the flight. How much longer would everything hold up? He got cold feet, and when he was near Philadelphia, called the McGuire Air Force Base control tower and told them he was coming directly into the base. Only an Air Force photographer and a few dozen people saw the rare twin-boom P-38 settle gently onto the runway, late in the afternoon.

Lt. Patricia Haten and Col. E. M. Leete. Leete got the plane Haten supervised its refurbishing

At a small hanger located in the midst of sprawling McGuire Air Force Base, a frantic effort was put forth by Lt. Patricia Haten and her seven maintenance people. Thousands of man-hours were put into the repair of the plane, with many of the people putting in 16-to-20-hour days. First, they had to strip the plane of its olive drab, European theater, paint job. They spent many hours repairing the damage to the nose and hammering out the damaged props so that they could be remounted on the plane. Finally a civilian volunteer, Don Sperling, an aircraft antiquities expert from nearby Mt. Holly, New Jersey, painted the P-38 to the exact specifications of McGuire's last plane, "PUDGY V."

351

Colonel Leete had the borrowed props returned at once, but still got a phone call from the Air Force Museum, "What in hell are you doing with our propellers? The plane you borrowed them from belonged to us, too. We would never have given permission for you to use them."

The P-38 was finished in time for the open house on May 25 and was a big hit with the public that crowded onto the base that day. Not the least of these was a balding gentleman in his late sixties, and in failing health, who took a tour of the plane with Colonel Wright and Major General Thomas Sadler, the Commander of the 21st Air Force. Frank Kish had traveled from his home in Sharon, Pa., near Pittsburgh, to see the reproduction of "PUDGY V," the plane he had crew-chiefed for Major McGuire.

He inspected the plane from one end to the other, and touched it with reverence. It was so familiar to him, although he hadn't seen a P-38 for 35 years. He was pleased to see his and Richard Van Der Geest's names painted on the right side of the nose, just where they belonged. The old sergeant's eyes glistened with tears as the memories of the young Major flooded over him. The young man he had loved and idolized remained 24-years-old in his memory and now seemed like a son to him. He walked under the wing of the P-38, sat on the wheel of the main landing gear and wept into his hands.

THE FATAL MISSION

Over the years since McGuire's death one question has been asked over and over: Why did McGuire order his men to keep their heavily laden external fuel tanks when a combat situation was apparent? He violated three of his own rules: "Never enter combat at low altitude. Never enter combat at low speed. Never enter combat without dropping your external fuel tanks." The order certainly caused his own death and made little sense. Or did it make sense?

It was an instant decision to keep the tanks, but not a decision without reason. John Tilley remembered, 40 years later, that McGuire once "chewed him out" for what he considered the wasting of a belly tank, on the basis that they were costly and might be needed for future missions. This decision to save the tanks was much more complicated than that.

The mission itself was at stake. Fuel was needed to complete the mission--drop the tanks early in the mission and it meant an immediate return to home base. Why let one stray Japanese plane cause the whole mission to be scrubbed?

Charges have been made over the years that McGuire was blinded by greed and thought only of getting aerial victories enough to beat Bong. No doubt McGuire wanted the victories, but simple greed would have dictated that he drop the tanks, forget the mission, and go for the single "easy kill" that would have moved him one victory behind Bong. Saving the tanks had only one purpose: McGuire intended to complete the mission they had set out on instead of going for a quick victory.

Instead of greed--pride may have been a contributing factor. Believe it or not, American P-47 fighter pilots and some high level horse-play, may have had more to do with McGuire's fatal wing tank decision than the enemy's action. To understand how this might be true we must go back in the war to a time when the P-47s first came into the Southwest Pacific war. In an attempt to prove the value of the P-47, high officials had instead, generated a competitiveness between P-38 and P-47 pilots that almost boarded on hatred.

In March of 1943, General Kenney, with the blessings of General MacArthur, made the rounds in Washington, DC, pleading for more airplanes. He talked to everyone, including President Roosevelt, and did get commitments for enough airplanes to equip three new fighter groups. Two of these fighter groups would be equipped with P-38s and one with P-47s. The two fighters were apparently not wanted in the European theater where the "Spitfire-like" P-51 had become the favored fighter plane. Kenney needed planes. Some of his pilots flew P-38s and had come to love the airplane. Kenney was sure that they could also make good use of the giant, single-engine Republic P-47s.

The new allocation of P-38s arrived first and were used to form the new 475th Group, with Lieutenant Thomas McGuire a charter member. The P-47s were delayed some months due to engine problems. The word of the engine problems preceded the aircraft to the Pacific and the planes arrived in Brisbane under a cloud of distrust. The P-47 had been named the Thunderbolt, but the troops had nicknamed it the "Jug".

Colonel Neel Kearby was to head up the new P-47 fighter group and was given the job of establishing a reputation for the "Jug" as a competitive fighting plane.

General Kenney recounted in his book, *General Kenney Reports*: "I sent for Kearby and told him I expected him to sell the P-47 or go back home ... regardless of the fact that everyone in the theater was sold on the P-38, if the P-47 could demonstrate just once that it could perform comparably I believed that the 'Jug', as the kids called it, would be looked upon with more favor. I told him that Lieutenant Colonel George Prentice would arrive that afternoon from New Guinea to take command of the new P-38 group which I had formed (the 475th) and had started training out at Amberly Field. He would probably celebrate a little tonight. I told Neel to keep away from Prentice, go to bed early, and the first thing in the morning to hop over to Amberly in his P-47 and challenge Prentice to a mock combat. Neel Kearby was not only a good pilot but he'd had several hundred hours playing with a P-47 and could do better with it than anyone else. Prentice was an excellent P-38 pilot, but for the sake of my sales argument I hoped he wouldn't be feeling in tip-top form when he accepted Neel's challenge.

"The combat came off as I had hoped. Prentice was surprised at the handling qualities of the P-47 against his P-38 and admitted that Kearby 'shot him down in flames' a half dozen times. He still preferred his P-38 but began warning everyone not to sell the P-47 short. At the same time he wanted to go to bed early that night and 'have another combat with Neel tomorrow.' I interfered at this point and said I didn't want any more challenge foolishness by them or anyone else and for both of them to quit that stuff and tend to their jobs of getting a couple of new groups into the war."

Needless to say, the competition didn't end there. Instead, it built over the months with barroom comments like this by two P-38 pilots: "Do you know what a Thunderbolt(P-47) is?"

"Yes I do. It's a meaningless noise that follows the Lightning (P-38)!"

Two P-47 pilots might say: "Do you know why they have two engines on a P-38?"

"Yes, the Allison Time Bomb (the P-38's engine) is so bad that they take two along---if one quits they still have one to come home on."

Shortly after his challenge dogfight with Colonel Prentice at Amberly Field, Kearby took his act to New Guinea. He challenged Richard Bong to a mock battle between his P-38 and Kearby's P-47. Kearby wanted to beat Bong, the top ace in the Pacific, and convince the rest of the pilots that the P-47 was a top-notch fighter plane. Most witnesses to the battle thought it was a draw, or a victory for Bong and the P-38.

Nevertheless, when Bong returned from his war bond tour of the United States in February of 1944, he found that his old outfit, the 9th Fighter Squadron, had reluctantly switched to the P-47 months before. The pilots disliked the plane and found themselves the object of the same ridicule they had handed out before, to P-47 pilots. Bong escaped to higher command to do his flying and stuck with the P-38. Soon the 9th Squadron switched back to the P-38, using the justifiable excuse that maintenance was difficult for the P-47s when the rest of the 49th Fighter Group had P-38s.

In early December 1944, a P-47 pilot lost control of his plane and flew into the area where McGuire's 431st Fighter Squadron P-38s were parked. The plane plowed through and completely destroyed four of the P-38s. The P-47 pilot was killed. Everybody felt bad about the pilot's death, but some cross words were passed between P-38 and P-47 pilots anyway.

Someone said, "It took the Japs six months to get four of our P-38s. That damn P-47 just took a minute to do the same thing!"

On December 10, four P-38s from McGuire's squadron were on a fighter sweep to Santa Teresa when they were the victims of some dangerous horseplay. The P-38s were "bounced" in a surprise attack. Tracers flashed in front of the flight, resulting in an order from the P-38 flight commander, "Drop your belly tanks."

The mission report stated: "Eight belly tanks were dropped when a P-47 fired on our flight. One P-47 of a flight of four with black bands on the left wing, fired on our 4 plane flight at 1,000 feet at 1555/I over area just North of Esperanza. A long burst was fired from directly astern of our flight. Radio conversation between the P-47s later asked, 'Number fourteen, did you fire at those P-38s?'"[1]

It was a sick joke. There was no question of the P-47 thinking the P-38s were enemy planes. The P-38s were distinctive with their two engines, twin booms and twin tails, and bright silver color. Japanese

Zeke, Oscar, Frank and Jack planes were all single-engined and usually painted green.

P-47 pilots were heard to remark that the P-38 pilots were afraid of their own shadow and had dropped their tanks for combat when the only other planes in the air were a flight of friendly P-47s. The implication was that the P-38 pilots couldn't tell the difference between a P-47 and a Zero. McGuire and his pilots were angered by the remarks.

The friction between P-38 pilots and P-47 pilots reached its peak when squadrons flying the two types of planes were stationed near each other in the Philippines. A December 21, 1944 mission report from the 431st Fighter Squadron recounts: "Over Carigara Bay at 8,000 feet at 0945/I, one flight of four P-47s, with a red vertical stripe on the rudder, made a rear overhead pass at our four plane flight. Previous to this enemy-like pass, radio intercepts stated, (a) 'Those are Uncles.' (b) 'I'm going over and make a pass at them and give them a good scare.' Our leader said, 'If you make a pass at me, it may be the last pass you'll make.' This warning by our flight leader was unheeded and it became necessary for him to feint the P-47s away." [2]

As an aftermath of these incidents, relations between the two groups became more strained than ever--resulting in heated arguments and a few fist fights between the pilots of the two different types of aircraft.

On that bleak morning mission, McGuire must have remembered the needless tank-dumping incident and had it in the back of his mind when he saw the single Zero. He didn't want to return to the base with the story that they had dropped their tanks because of a single Japanese aircraft that got away before they could catch it. It certainly would have left him and his P-38 pilots open to more ridicule from the P-47 pilots.

The flight of four P-38s were completely surprised by the lone Japanese plane that came at them head-on from a gray, early morning sky. The Oscar, returning from patrol, was just as surprised. McGuire thought the lone plane would run for his life and ordered, "Daddy Flight! Save your tanks!"

McGuire surely expected the Zero to be frightened off by the four large P-38s. In recent months the Japanese had not shown much interest in combat, particularly when they were outnumbered.

Since the Japanese plane and the P-38s were both cruising near 200 miles-an-hour when they zipped past each other, the rate of closure was over 400 miles-an-hour. This meant that the Oscar could be long gone before the larger P-38s could drop their tanks and make a turn to pursue. Even if they could have dropped their tanks and turned the P-38s in 10 seconds, the Oscar could already have a mile-and-a-half lead, and would need only to pull up into the overcast to be completely out of danger. Chasing an Oscar, at combat speed, would use the remaining fuel, with little chance of catching it. It would have made no sense.

The fact that the P-38s turned at all was a knee-jerk reaction by experienced combat pilots to see what the Oscar was going to do. The order to "save your tanks" is proof that McGuire never expected to have combat with the Oscar. He knew better than anyone else that the tanks had to be dropped for combat--he'd flown 250 combat missions, a total of 750 combat hours, and had preached it to his men, and had written about it more than once.

It made no sense that the Oscar would turn and attack the four P-38s. McGuire's logic made good combat sense--both the Oscar and the American planes would go on their own way. For years it has been thought that the Oscar pilot turned to engage his enemy, figuring he would die in glory.

When Captain Weaver called, "Daddy Leader! He's on me now!" McGuire turned, trying to bring his guns to bear on the enemy. McGuire had been cheating death for a year-and-a-half. He was supremely confident of his flying ability and felt he could always get out of a dangerous flying situation. He'd broken the rules in combat when it seemed necessary. His airplanes always reflected his heavy-handed combat flying style, with their popped rivets and wrinkled wings. He would just ask his P-38 for everything it had--it had always been enough to pull him through. This time he had a friend to save, and that he did. He asked too much of his plane--it stalled. It cost him his life.

For years it was believed that the Oscar turned and single-handedly caused the death of two experienced fighter pilots. Years later Carroll Anderson, a pilot from the 433rd Fighter Squadron, examined the Japanese Air Force's records and discovered that a second Japanese plane, a high performance Frank, just happened on the scene and surprised the Americans, who were making a low-speed turn at low altitude, with full fuel tanks. Anderson discussed this new information with Ed Weaver and Douglas Thropp, the two surviving members of the mission.

Things had happened so fast that morning that Thropp and Weaver were confused about the action. That was not unusual under difficult combat conditions. Thirty years after the incident, it was more clearly understood than ever. **Air Force** Magazine, printed Anderson's article in January, 1975. It showed that McGuire's judgment was correct--the Oscar did run for his life. A second Japanese plane happened on the scene and caused the death of McGuire and Rittmayer.

Shortly before his death, I talked with Ed Weaver for several hours. He started out by telling me he didn't want to discuss McGuire's last mission--after 40 years it still bothered him. Weaver had vivid memories of McGuire, starting with the day he met Cadet McGuire at Randolph Field. He recalled that he wasn't sure it was the same person when he first met McGuire as the Commanding Officer of the 431st Squadron because McGuire had aged so much and was so thin. Weaver said, "He was eaten up by jungle-rot and his skin had that tinge of color caused by long-term use of Quinine. I don't know what kept him going--most guys would have checked in with the medics and gone home. But I must say, it never affected his flying or his shooting ability. I never saw anybody else who could shoot like McGuire the day after Christmas, when I was his wingman and he got four Japanese planes."

Douglas Thropp and Charles A. Martin, summer 1998 (Photo Teaky Martin)

In spite of his prohibition on discussion of the last mission, Weaver started to trust me and we did talk about it. He said, "I think about it everyday--it will never leave me. To tell the truth, it all happened so fast that we really didn't know what happened. You know witnesses at a car wreck never tell the same story. They all see it from a different spot. In our case it was impossible to explain how that Jap turned on us so quickly. I understand it better today than I did then. If you've read Anderson's article---that's the way I think it happened."

Years went by before I had a chance to talk with Douglas Thropp. In the summer of 1998 we sat together and talked for several hours. His memory at age 75 was remarkable--he still worked everyday as a financial consultant--had been working with computers for years. He was sharply dressed for a later business meeting and was still straight as a ramrod, reflecting his years of military schooling and service.

Thropp said he thinks about the mission often. He and Rittmayer were bringing up the rear. They had lagged back when descending through the gray clouds because Rittmayer, who was leading the element, was uncomfortable about hitting the lead aircraft in the formation which they had lost sight of in the clouds. McGuire urged them to latch on to the lead planes and Rittmayer suggested that he had a balky engine. McGuire asked Thropp to take over and lead the element. They had not caught up when the enemy plane was "called in."

During the combat which ensued Thropp and Rittmayer were both fired on with Rittmayer going down and Thropp developing a smoking engine. Thropp saw a flaming wreckage on the ground and then a second wreckage in flames on the ground. Buying into the McGuire mystique, he expected that Weaver and Rittmayer had been shot down and called for McGuire several times on the radio and got no answer. Finally he heard a voice say, "It's Weaver here."

Thropp cited his engine problem and said he was leaving the area and suggested that they pair-up and leave together. Weaver was reluctant to spend the time finding each other and suggested that they leave alone and make their own way back to the field. Thropp was below the gray strata when just above him a large turning propeller jutted down below the bottom of the clouds. He knew it was the Japanese plane because it was a single propeller instead of the two propellers a P-38 would have had. With a problem engine, he quickly turned and left the scene.

Weaver and Thropp arrived back at the field 10 minutes apart. They were both debriefed on the mission and were later summoned to Colonel MacDonald's tent for an interview with the Squadron Commanders present. Amazingly Thropp and Weaver never discussed the mission with each other. Years later Weaver referred me to his combat report for information. Thropp talks as if the mission were just yesterday but his memory doesn't always match his combat report. His and Weaver's combat reports state that they were on a fighter sweep of Negros but Thropp says the flight was designed to fly near a Japanese fleet, hoping that it would bring a defensive response from nearby Japanese air fields. Thropp and Rittmayer trailed by some distance and never saw enemy planes at Fabrica Airdrome as Weaver reported

Weaver eventually became the Commanding Officer of the 431st Fighter Squadron. After getting out of the service he flew for many years with the Pennsylvania Air National Guard, was an executive with Bell Telephone and was active in church work. He died in the mid 1980s shortly before the P-38 dedication at McGuire Air Force Base.

359

Thropp, who had attended Valley Forge Military Academy for six years, and was a 2nd Lieutenant at age 18, later survived a crash landing in a Philippine vegetable garden after foregoing a wheels-up P-38 landing on a steel matted runway. He has been a business consultant for years but failing eyesight has kept him out of the cockpit. In the late 1970s he made an attempt, using an overseas phone company interpreter, to talk with Mazunori Fukuda, the Japanese pilot involved in this mission but he could not make any sense of the conversation.

When I asked Thropp why he thought McGuire had ordered his men to save their belly tanks, he said, "We would have ended the mission right there. That wasn't what McGuire wanted. He wanted to get three more victories so he could go home as our number one ace."

Thropp resents the often repeated statement that McGuire was flying with "green pilots" on his last mission. Thropp had flown 53 Combat missions and had over 130 hours of combat time before this mission.

On July 14, 2000, Douglas Thropp participated in a program with me about Tommy McGuire on stage at the Air Force Museum, Dayton, Ohio. This was the day before McGuire was inducted into the National Aviation Hall of Fame. Thropp sat quietly while I gave a much too lengthy description of this book. One of the first questions from those gathered was about McGuire's last mission. Thropp answered every question asked in a discussion which lasted about 40 minutes.

As of November 2000, an MD-11 airline captain, David Mason, an Air Force veteran, is planning an expedition to find the remains of McGuire's crash site, on Negros. Mason, who maintains a home in the Philippines, hopes to find something which might clear up some of the unanswered questions about that fatal mission. A Philippine veteran's group plans to place a monument on the spot which will read as follows: *ON THIS SPOT AMERICAN P-38 PILOT MAJOR THOMAS B. McGUIRE, Jr. WAS KILLED ON 7 JANUARY 1945. IT IS ETERNALLY ENSHRINED FOR WHEREVER A MAN HAS SHED HIS BLOOD FOR TRUTH, JUSTICE, PEACE, AND FREEDOM, THERE IS SACRED GROUND. THE SUN CANNOT BLEACH, THE WIND CANNOT BLOW, THE RAIN CANNOT WASH THAT SANCTITY AWAY. FROM GROUND LIKE THIS SPRINGS THAT WHICH FOREVER MAKES MEN GREAT.*

Charles A. Martin

[1] 431st Mission Report # 1-596, 10 Dec. 1944
[2] 431st Mission Report # 1-636, 21 Dec. 1944

APPENDIX A
HOW THIS BOOK WAS WRITTEN

CHAPTER 11 The firehouse conversations were constructed from stories told to me by a number of people, some of whom asked that they not be quoted. The subject matter was covered in this manner without mentioning actual names.

CHAPTER 14 The conversations between Tommy and his Uncle Charles are recreated from stories told to me by a number of people. The stories related are true, the actual conversations are not. This is a method of laying a foundation for events later in this book where Lindbergh's background and Lufbery's "circle" played a key role in Tommy McGuire's life and death.

CHAPTER 25 It took years to get people in Sebring to discuss Polly's death. I had to promise some of them that I would not quote them. Four or five people told me the story and they all told it about the same way. I was 13 years old when this event took place and I remember it about the way everyone else does. Marilynn McGuire Beatty furnished much of the information in this chapter.

CHAPTER 33 The events in this chapter are recounted in Charles A. Lindbergh's book: *The Wartime Journals of Charles A. Lindbergh*, George C Kenney's *General Kenney Reports,* and confirmed by Tommy McGuire's log book and the Daily History of the 431st Fighter Squadron and the Daily History of the 475th Fighter Group. This was supplement by personal conversations at reunions of the 475th Fighter Group and the 49th Fighter Group.

CHAPTER 34 The events in this chapter re: Lindbergh and McGuire searching the Biak caves is recounted in *The Wartime Journals of Charles A. Lindbergh.* Frank Kish, McGuire's crew chief, also related conversations he had with McGuire about the search. The story of the F-5 crash into the revetment was told to me and later confirmed in writing by George Jeschke, the squadron's aircraft painter. This event is also confirmed in the 475th Group's Daily History.

CHAPTER 40 For an understanding of how this book was written, a letter from Danforth Miller, a wartime friend of Tommy McGuire, is reproduced below. Chapter 40 is based on this letter. It does not take a great leap of faith to believe the conversations in the chapter after you have read this engrossing letter. Some people didn't like McGuire---others genuinely admired and liked him. This letter explains a lot about people's feeling when it came to Tommy McGuire.

18 Feb 81

Charles A. Martin
105 Canterbury Rd.
Mt. Laurel
New Jersey, 08054

Dear Charles:

Of course, I don't know what you mean when you say that Tom McGuire, as a boy, was a controversial personality, I know nothing about his boyhood. I haven't a clue what he was interested in when he was in school, or what his extracurricular activities were. But I will bet you a new dictionary that his school-recorded IQ was at least 130: get permission from his family to check-out that piece of privacy! High IQ kids are often objects of misunderstandings, envy, wonder, hostility, and, sometimes, shabby, stupid treatment by society in general.

I never lived with McGuire, but I have argued with him, dined with him, and flown with him. I've also listened to him. Each of these activities was made pleasurable by his mental excellence - his quickness to grasp a thought, an idea, a line of action, the whole situation. He was ahead of those he was with, most of the time. This did not annoy me. It may have annoyed some others. McGuire on occasion might finish a thought for someone; why not? - he could do it pleasantly, with a smile, and life is too short to stand around listening to some clumsy guy trying to wrap up his routine concept.

With McGuire I felt at ease on a higher level. When the 475th was at Dulag, he one day came into group ops, where I had my feet up on my desk, contemplating the ceiling (roof). He had a sly grin on his face, which he dismissed as he sat. He said he wasn't sure his squadron was getting its share of the missions on which most enemy action could be expected. I took my feet off the desk and opened the bottom drawer, where I kept records showing how I made sure that each of the three squadrons took its turn in being assigned the "best" of the daily missions allocated by Fifth Fighter Command or higher headquarters. McGuire looked carefully at the data, and then thrust it at me, saying, with his accepting smile, "Ah, the hell with this! Let's fly!" We went down to Dulag Air Field (I have to call it that because I was responsible for it, as its executive officer, so duly-appointed by Col. MacDonald) and picked up a couple of relatively new 431st pilots, who, wearing silk-scarf maps about their necks, were studying other posted maps, and aircraft data. We flew over Cebu, a mere 100 or so miles from Dulag, in a raggedy string, as though we didn't have

362

good sense, at cruising speed and at only 8000'. After we passed out of view of a strip on which some 26 Japanese fighters rested, we suddenly tightened up and climbed rapidly to 18,000' as we turned back to the strip. (I may not be right about that 18,000 it might have been something less.) Sure enough, they were taking off after us! McGuire led the way down in steep spirals that let us see everything, but which nearly blacked me out (McGuire must have had a great circulatory system, also!) We got down below 1000' before the ideal opportunity came up: on our course for home, or close to it, a fighter which had just taken off was in a slow climb. The angle was about 65 degrees, the range was about 400 yards: McGuire fired a burst of about 2 seconds, beginning or increasing a turn to his right as he did so (in case he missed he might then have a second shot). I thought, "He's missed!" but as my thumb began to press the gun button the fighter blew up in a great orange-and-black ball of flame, fragments crashing into the trees beneath. Another slight turn to the left and we were en route home. Let's make another pass!" cried one of the new boys. "Another day!" replied McGuire, cheerily, thus imparting another valuable bit of wisdom to those on their first orientation, or first bona fide combat orientation mission. "That was great!" one of them exclaimed, eyes bright and full of enthusiasm, after we landed, "Where were we?"

Once I had dinner with both Bong and McGuire, I think it was Christmas dinner, but it might have been Thanksgiving or something else. MacDonald was there; he was the host! Others were there, Merl Smith and other squadron commanders. For what seemed like over an hour, Bong said next to nothing. Perhaps Smith, MacDonald and McGuire did most of the talking. I don't think I understood Bong. It has occurred to me that Bong must have been carrying both unusual motivation and unusual experience.

I last saw McGuire when he came thru gp ops with his guest, a Major from 5th Fighter Command or some other headquarters. He was wearing that crushed cap, a .45 (as I recall), and that sly-but-friendly grin. He said, "We're gonna go fly!" or something like that. I asked a question as they moved along to the exit. An orientation flight! (the major needed orientation, and so did the two they met at the strip). I thought to myself, "They look like Fitzgerald characters going out to play tennis." They never returned.

I don't know how other aces reported their victories. Both McGuire and MacDonald had a friendly way of appearing in the ops doorway and holding up one or more fingers, grinning wordlessly. One day McGuire appeared first, holding up three fingers, and I felt a little sorry for MacDonald. But an hour or so later he was there also, grinning and holding up three fingers.

My chief regret of two tours in the Pacific, with 13th and 5th, was that I did not become an ace. My second regret is that I didn't get to know McGuire better. If anything I have said at all surprises you, you might look at it this way: McGuire may have found himself; in man's ultimate arena,

where man must mix the best and the worst in order to
survive. But I really doubt that. I believe he was a great
guy, if unrecognizable as such, as a teenager, and that he
did some of his characteristic thinking, was alerted by in-
sights, when in Alaska. And I'll bet you a dictionary, new
or used, that his IQ, as measured or indicated by any
standardized test, was a couple of standard deviations above
the mean.

Good luck, and press on!

Danny Miller

CHAPTER 44 This mission and the conversations are reconstructed
from Combat Reports of Edwin Weaver and Douglas Thropp, and
interviews of both parties. Weaver's version of the mission was covered
in **Air Force Magazine**, January 1975, and Thropp's version was
covered in **Air Classics**, June 1992. The truth probably lies somewhere
in between.

APPENDIX B
Honoring Tommy McGuire

Here are many of the awards and honors which have been bestowed on Tommy McGuire. He is one of America's most decorated heroes of all time but his name remains unknown to most Americans.

An Army airfield on the south coast of Mindoro Island, The Philippines, was named McGuire Field, a few days after McGuire's death in 1945.

The Army Air Field at Fort Dix, New Jersey, was named McGuire Air Force Base. An oil painting of McGuire, commissioned by his wife, Marilynn, hangs in the main terminal. A bronze statue of McGuire is in front of the McGuire Museum, and a bust of McGuire is in the McGuire Museum on the base.

Awarded the Medal of Honor, posthumously, May 8, 1946, at Paterson, NJ --Charles A. Lindbergh attended the ceremony. McGuire also was awarded the Distinguished Service Cross, (3) Silver Stars, (6) Distinguished Flying Crosses, (15) Air Medals, (3) Purple Hearts, (2) Distinguished Unit Badges. He also would be entitled to wear a number of national defense, theater, and battle citations. He is no doubt one of America's most decorated soldiers of all time.

A P-38 Aircraft Memorial, in a traffic circle at the entrance to McGuire Air Force Base, New Jersey, was dedicated to Major McGuire. Casper Weinberger, Sec'y. of Defense, a New Guinea war veteran himself, gave the dedication speech. 1986

The V.I.P. Guest Apartment at the Guest House, McGuire Air Force Base, is named The McGuire Suite.

Major Thomas McGuire Memorial Scholarship, 1985, Florida Highlands Air Force Association, a full four-year college scholarship for student studying engineering or science and taking ROTC at Ga. Tech[1]

Tree planted in Florida Medal of Honor Grove, Sebring, Florida

Highlands County Health Building, renamed the Major Thomas B. McGuire, Jr. Building, Sebring, Florida

A plaque marks the spot where the McGuire/Watson home stood on Kenilworth Blvd., Sebring, Florida.

Display of McGuire medals and memorabilia, personal papers and sound recording at the Sebring Historical Society, Sebring, Florida 1994

A McGuire Reading Room, with a portrait, at library of the South Florida Community College, Avon Park, Florida

Commemorative Plaque on the Georgia Tech campus, Atlanta, Georgia, 1984

Enshrined in the New Jersey Aviation Hall of Fame at Teterboro Airport, New Jersey, (just a few miles from his birthplace) 1982

A chapter of the Air Force Association in New Jersey is the Thomas B. McGuire, Jr. Chapter.

Enshrined in the Georgia Aviation Hall of Fame at the Museum of Aviation, Robins A F Base, Warner Robins, Georgia. May 17, 1997

A display of McGuire's "500 hour hat," log book, his bible and his medals--in a shared exhibit with his friend Major Richard Bong, at The Air Force Museum, Dayton, Ohio.

A McGuire/Bong display at the Aviation and Aerospace exhibit, Smithsonian Institute, Washington, D. C.

Tree planted in Medal of Honor Grove, Freedom Foundation, Valley Forge, Pa. Trees are planted in the Florida and New Jersey Grove.

New United States Air Force Logistics Building named the Major Thomas B. McGuire, Jr. Building, Lackland A F Base, Texas. 1997

McGuire Exhibit at 475th Fighter Group Museum, March Field, CA

McGuire Model Show at Hendricks field, Sebring, Florida

A P-38 model airplane manufactured by Revel Plastics has McGuire's plane, "PUDGY V" pictured on the box.

The McGuire Museum at McGuire A F Base features a slide show about McGuire's life, with a script written by Charles A. Martin, the author of this book. The exhibit includes a bronze bust of McGuire commissioned by the citizens of Ridgewood, New Jersey. A number of documents are on display regarding the naming of McGuire Air Force Base. One of the citations for the Medal of Honor, signed by Harry Truman, is on display. Marilynn McGuire Beatty donated the hat she wore when she received the Medal of Honor in Paterson, New Jersey.

McGuire is buried in Arlington National Cemetery, Virginia. He has a simple "GI" stone with the CMH etched into the stone.

McGuire is featured in the Randolph Field, San Antonio, Texas, Hall of Valor, located in Building 100.

McGuire's bailout over Oro Bay, New Guinea, was portrayed in a King Features Comic book in the late 40s.

On Memorial Day 2000 a large bronze plaque honoring McGuire was placed on the wall of the ROTC building at Ga. Tech by his classmates, the Class of 1942. No mention of aerial victories was allowed but there are 38 rosettes across the bottom of the plaque.

On July 15, 2000 McGuire was at last enshrined in the National Aviation Hall of Fame, Wright-Paterson Field, Dayton, Ohio.

A marker will soon be placed on the spot where McGuire crashed, on Negros Occidental, P. I. The ground will be sanctified as a place where Philippine Freedom was bought by a hero's blood. (See Pg. 360)

THE LAST GREAT ACE

On January 22, 1945, a small news item appeared on the front page of the **New York Times**:

TOMMY McGUIRE LEADING ACE
KILLED IN THE PHILIPPINES

McGuire was the last of World War II's great aces remaining in combat, and he had stayed too long. The war ended in August 1945, with the dropping of the atomic bombs. The **New York Times** of August 7, 1945, carried a small headline on a front page story that almost went unnoticed among the atomic bomb stories:

JET PLANE EXPLOSION KILLS
MAJOR BONG, TOP U. S. ACE

Dick Bong died at Burbank, California, while trying to bail out of a disabled P-80 jet fighter. It happened on August 6, the day the atomic bomb was dropped. In a seven month period America's top two Aces were gone!

The nature of aerial combat has changed--gone the way of the Cavalry steed, the fort, and the cross bow--the aerial dogfight of World War I, World War II and Korea is now history. The "Top Guns" of today fly combat against each other, often with a weapon's officer flying in the back seat. Scopes and instruments have changed aerial combat from a one-on-one battle to a committee affair. Weapons are often fired without the enemy even being seen.

The battles of the future, like so many things of today, will be run by computers. Combatants will not see each other, or smell the fumes of cordite in the cockpit as they try to outguess and outfly each other. Instead they may complain about the eyestrain of looking at the glowing phosphors of a CRT during the height of battle.

McGuire and Bong were the greatest two fighter pilots the United States will ever produce--never again will we know two like them. Their names go at the top of a small list with those of Boyington, Foss, Gabreski, Johnson, Lufbery, Luke, MacDonald, McCampbell, Meyer and Rickenbacker as the best of their times.

America was deprived of its two greatest air aces essentially in accidents. After all the combat they had survived it was a shame that neither of them had a chance to enjoy the hero's life like Rickenbacker or Lindbergh. During World War I a reporter asked Raoul Lufbery, our top ace at the time, what he planned to do after the war. He replied, "There isn't any *after the war* for a fighter pilot." He died a few months later, like McGuire, in a borrowed plane.

Bong and McGuire never got to enjoy the way of life they helped protect. If they were alive today they might complain about Rock and Roll music, but it's sad neither of them lived to hear it. Knowing these two guys, they may have liked Rock and Roll. One thing is for sure-- they would surely have defended your right to listen to it if you wanted to. They were the kind of people who could have made life interesting for the people around them.

Marilynn McGuire and Marge Bong waited those tough war years only to be left with a hollow spot in their lives. They both did what human beings do--they went on living. It's a shame, after all the pain of war, that these two young wives and their husbands never got a chance to fully enjoy each other in a peaceful world. They had earned the chance and deserved it.

Marilynn McGuire has said to me several times over the years, "Charles, I still see Tommy as a young man. We've all gotten older but he remains 23 years old to me."

Adjacent to McGuire's grave at Arlington National Cemetery is the grave of a Marine killed in the bombing at the U. S. Embassy in Beirut. It is a sad reminder that conflict continues to take many of our best young men before their time.

Richard Bong was THE ACE OF ACES!

Tommy McGuire was THE LAST GREAT ACE!

ACKOWLEDGEMENTS

Marilynn McGuire Beatty spent years helping me and I can't thank her and Bobby Beatty enough. She dug through records, excerpted letters, passed on photographs from her scrapbook, and let me have copies of all of Tommy's military records. We have spent many hours on the phone. My wife and I have enjoyed attending "McGuire events" with the Beattys over the years.

Alan Altvater encouraged me over many years to complete this project and I wish I had gotten it done before his passing. John Tilley was a special help to me and he kept after me to "get that book published."

Vera Watson Schneider, Elizabeth Tolson Green, Alfred B. Tolson, Theodore E. Tolson, Jr. and Alfred B. Watson gave me memories of Tommy McGuire and his family. Joan Mallon has been of special help with information about Tommy's father. I've tried to list the people who helped me. If I left someone's name out, it was not intentional.

Carroll R. Anderson (432nd Ftr Sq.), Col. Fred Champlin, USAF, Ret. (431st Ftr Sq.), Herbert W. Cochran (433rd Ftr Sq.), Robert M. DeHaven (49th Ftr Gp.), Bob Hall (431st Ftr Sq.), Douglas C. Hall (7th Ftr Sq.), Charles C. Halton (Class 42B), George Jeschke (431st Ftr Sq.), Col. Converse Kelly, USAF, Ret. (56th Ftr Sq.), Frank Kish (431st Ftr Sq.), Maj Gen John W. Kline, USAF, Ret. (2nd AF), George A. Lawson (Class 42B), John Loisel (475th Ftr Gp.), Pete Madison (431st Ftr Sq.), Jewell C. Maxwell (Class 42B), Maj Gen C. M. McCorkle, USAF, Ret. (54th Ftr Gp.), Col. Charles McDonald, USAF, Ret. (475th Ftr Gp.), George C. McLee Jr. (431st Ftr Sq.), Danforth Miller (475 Ftr Gp.), General Franklin A. Nichols, USAF, Ret. (431st Ftr Gp.), Joe Price (433rd Ftr Sq.), General Jay T. Robbins, USAF, Ret., Douglas Thropp (431st Ftr Sq.), John Tilley (431st Ftr Sq.), Richard Van Der Geest (431st Ftr Sq.), Edwin Weaver (431st Ftr Sq.)

Dorothea M. Albritton, Eddie Albritton, Alan Altvater, Mary Altvater, Betty Russell Atkinson, John C. Bates, Clint Brandon, Frances Brown, Betty Tripp Burton, Clarence Campbell, Mrs. Louise Campbell, Caroline Cobb, Morgan Cobb, Broward Coker, Madge Coker, Howard Crawford, Jacob Dunn, Bill Dutton, Jeff Ethell, Joy Satterwhite Eyman, Mitchell Ferguson, Amos Freeland, Johnny Freeland, Albert "Chubby" Fulton, Carol Russell Gentile, Charles Gittins, Paul Gustat, Claude Hamrick, Lamar Hancock, Norma Dutton Harriss, Ike Hart, Jr., Ruth Piety Hazelwood, Mrs. Vernon Higgins, Martha Durrance Howett, Jack Ingle, Joe Jiloty, Betsy Kish, Bob Long, Verna Vail Macbeth, Billy Martin, Calvin W. Martin, Charles D. Martin, Leldon W. Martin, Jr., Maxine S. Martin, Scott Martin, Leoma Maxwell, Verdelle Sebring

Medlin, Mrs. Sophie Mae Mitchell, Tom Mitchell, Frank Pollard, Reverend Luther Price, Dorothea B. Rainey, June Adams Rehm, Rosamond Mallory Rice, Carolyn and Hood Roberts, Holley Sheppard, Eddie Stephens III, Robert L. Stephens, Suetta Blanding Story, Campbell Tappen, Velma Miller Waldron, Naomi Warren, Malcolm Watters, Mrs. Edgar Weaver, Howard Weems, Tad Whitehurst, and Carlton Wilder.

William J. Dunn, CBS Radio News, Ret.

General Larry D. Wright, Ms. Eleanor Palidore, Historian, Col. E. M. Leete, Art Cavelo, Sgt. Robert Strobel, all of McGuire AF Base, NJ.

Sister Veronica, Medal of Honor House, Freedoms Foundation, Valley Forge, PA.

Special thanks to Katherine Cassity and Ruth Hunt of the Research Division of the United States Air Force Museum, Wright-Patterson Air Force Base, OH., who helped me with McGuire's logbook.

National Archives, Suitland, MD.

Office of Public Information, Randolph Air Force Base, TX..

Robert H. Rice, Exec. Director, Georgia Tech Alumni Association

"Boats" Newberry of PT Boats, Inc. and the crew of PT 152

I got inspiration and good advice from Joseph Sackett. A retired A-6 Intruder pilot, he authored *Gray Ghosts* and *Present in Spirit.*

Hazel Cody and La-Von Green of Rose Printing

The pictures in this book were picked for content over photographic quality. Most are 55 to 75 years-old. I don't always know the source but have tried to give credit when it is known. Many just came from someone's scrapbook. Norma Dutton Harriss furnished the one of Bill Dutton and Tommy at Hollandia. The Watson family furnished many of the old family pictures as did Marilynn McGuire Beatty. Thanks to Howard Weems and Verna Vail MacBeth for helping to name the people in the band picture on page 72.

ABOUT THE AUTHOR

Charles A. Martin was raised in Sebring, Florida, the town where Tommy McGuire lived. Born in 1929, in Rome, Georgia, he moved with his family to Sebring, a few months later, where his father, Dr. Leldon W. Martin, opened a medical practice. His mother, Maxine, raised five children and played the organ many years for St. Agnes Episcopal Church.

Martin was a teenager during World War II and 15 years old when it ended. At age 16 he took flying lessons and received his pilot's license at age 18. He graduated from Sebring High School in 1948 and took a flying tour of the South as a graduation present. He was in basic training at Lackland Air Force Base, on the first anniversary of the United States Air Force becoming a separate branch of the service. He was also on active duty during the Korean War.

In 1953, Martin survived a plane crash at Stiengel Field, Gainesville, Florida, in which he brought a Stenson Stationwagon down without injury, after the engine had failed on take-off. The plane was badly damaged. Lee Baguley of Sebring, and Curtis Pitts, a world famous builder of acrobatic aircraft, happened to be witnesses to the crash.

Martin graduated from the University of Florida and was employed by Eastman Kodak as a Technical Sales Representative. He worked in the Kodak Pavilion at the New York World's Fair in 1964 and for 13 years was Kodak's representative to Triangle Publications, printer of TV Guide and Seventeen Magazine, and later Arcata Graphics, printer of Reader's Digest, Time Magazine and other publications in Buffalo.

Martin knew McGuire, nine years his senior, and tried to follow his career during the war but news was spotty. He read everything he could find about America's number two Air Ace but information was sparse. After spending a few days at McGuire Air Force Base and later reading Martin Caidin's *Forked-Tailed Devil*, the story of the P-38 Fighter Plane, he decided to write about McGuire. Twenty years were spent researching and writing and trying to get the book published. In November, 1998, Martin self-published this book.

Martin married Antoinette Dean from Jackson Heights, New York, in 1957 and they have three children. They have lived in Houston and Beaumont, Texas; Charlotte, North Carolina; Columbia, South Carolina; Flushing, New York; Rochester, New York; Jacksonville, Florida; Mt. Laurel, New Jersey; East Amherst, New York; and Fruit Cove, Florida.

Charles writes and teaches photography and Antoinette (Teaky) writes for a local newspaper. They both volunteer at the World Golf Hall of Fame Museum, St. Johns, Florida.

THE LAST PAGE

During March of 1944, when there was rain and not much flying, Tommy McGuire sat down and wrote a small text book for new fighter pilots coming into the 475th Fighter Group. It explained the tactics, formations and philosophy of the fighter pilots who had been in action against the enemy. The book was published and distributed by the Fifth Fighter Command. I know several people who had the booklet issued to them and were surprised to find out they knew the author.

On the last page of the booklet McGuire put a poem. I haven't been able to find out if McGuire wrote this or if it came from some other source. McGuire was a reader and this may well have been something he had committed to memory. If you know the source of this, I wish you would let me know.

> If of thy work thou would'st complain,
> The chance to speak, eschew it;
> Thou huntest now the biggest game
> And hast no cause to rue it;
> Thy weapon makes the surest kill,
> Thou findest sport and prove thy skill,
> And thou art paid to do it!

Charles A Martin
LastGAce@AOL.com